Colin Wilson was born in Leicester in 1931. He left school at sixteen and spent several years working in a wool warehouse, a laboratory, a plastics factory and a coffee bar before *The Outsider* was published in 1956 to outstanding critical acclaim. Since then he has written many books on philosophy, the occult, crime and sexual deviance plus a number of successful novels. His work includes *The Mind Parasites, New Pathways in Psychology* and *The Occult*. Mr Wilson is well known as a lecturer and a radio and television personality. He lives in Cornwall.

Dr Christopher Evans was a psychologist, computer scientist and a world authority on micro-processors and the future of computing. His books *The Mighty Micro* and the *Landscapes of the Night – How and Why We Dream* were international bestsellers. He died in 1979.

Also available:
The Giant Book of Crime Stories
The Giant Book of Horror Stories

THE GIANT BOOK OF
— THE —
UNKNOWN

**Edited by Colin Wilson
with
Dr Christopher Evans**

MAGPIE BOOKS
LONDON

Magpie Books
11 Shepherd House
5 Shepherd Street
London W1Y 7LD

This edition first published by Magpie Books in 1991.

Previously published by Robinson Publishing as *The Book of Great Mysteries* in 1986.

Selection copyright © Robinson Publishing.

Selected from the *Great Mysteries* series. First published in the UK by Aldus Books 1975-79.

Cover illustration courtesy The Image Bank.
Illustrations courtesy The Fortean Picture Library.

A copy of the British Library Cataloguing in Publication Data is available from the British Library.

ISBN 1 85487 118 8

Printed and bound in Great Britain by The Guernsey Press Co. Ltd., Guernsey, Channel Islands.

CONTENTS

PART 4

PART 5

INDEX

Part 1

1. Legends of Fire and Flood

The earth was at peace. A mild climate enveloped the planet and man had responded well to the beneficence of nature. He had learned to cultivate and harvest his crops. He had domesticated animals to help make his life easier. Various civilizations were beginning to blossom. Then a terrible and all-encompassing catastrophe shook the earth.

The sky lit up with a strange celestial display. Those who saw in this a portent of disaster fled for shelter. Those who watched and waited perished as the sky grew dark and a fearful rain fell upon the earth. In places the rain was red like blood. In others it was like gravel or hailstones. And it brought down fire from the sky, too. Nothing escaped this global holocaust. Men and animals were engulfed. Forests were crushed. Even those who reached the caves were not safe. Darkness gripped the earth and tremendous quakes convulsed the planet. Mountains were thrown up to the heavens and continents were sucked beneath the seas as the stricken earth rolled and tilted. Hurricane winds lashed the planet's wretched surface and tidal waves swept across vast stretches of land. Fearful explosions shook the world as molten lava spewed out from the broken crust. A terrible heat hung over the planet and in places even the sea boiled.

Some, miraculously, lived through this horrific turmoil. After many long days of darkness the mantle of gloom was lifted from the earth and the survivors slowly began rebuilding their lives. A catastrophe of such proportions would account for the sinking of a huge continent such as Atlantis—but did such an event ever take place?

If it did, we might expect to find evidence of it in the myths, legends, and folklore of the people who survived. It is a remark-

1

able fact that almost all races have a tradition, handed down through countless generations, of a catastrophe that nearly ended the world. Not only are these legends similar in essence, they are also frequently similar in detail, to such an extent that it is tempting to assume they all share a common origin: a terrifying event of global proportions.

The Babylonian *Epic of Gilgamesh*, which is around 4000 years old and records traditions of an even earlier age, tells of a dark cloud that rushed at the earth, leaving the land shriveled by the heat of the flames: "Desolation . . . stretched to heaven; all that was bright was turned into darkness. . . . Nor could a brother distinguish his brother. . . . Six days . . . the hurricane, deluge, and tempest continued sweeping the land . . . and all human life back to its clay was returned."

From ancient Hindu legend comes an account of the appearance in the sky of "a being shaped like a boar, white and exceedingly small; this being, in the space of an hour, grew to the size of an elephant of the largest size, and remained in the air." After some time the "boar" suddenly uttered "a sound like the loudest thunder, and the echo reverberated and shook all the quarters of the universe." This object then became a "dreadful spectacle," and "descended from the region of the air, and plunged head-foremost into the water. The whole body of water was convulsed by the motion, and began to rise in waves, while the guardian spirit of the sea, being terrified, began to tremble for his domain and cry for mercy."

Hesiod, a Greek poet of the 8th century B.C., writes of a legend involving the earth and the heavens. The story centers around a fiery, serpentlike creature, an aerial monster mightier than men and gods alike, that wreaks terrible havoc upon the earth: "Harshly then he thundered, and heavily and terribly the earth reechoed around; and the broad heaven above, and the sea and streams of ocean, and the abyss of earth. But beneath his immortal feet vast Olympus trembled, as the king uprose and earth groaned beneath. And the heat from both caught the dark-colored sea, both of the thunder and the lightning, and fire from the monster, the heat arising from the thunderstorm, winds, and burning lightning. And all earth, and heaven, and sea were boiling. . . ."

From Iceland we have further evidence of a global catastrophe

in the *Poetic Edda*, a collection of ancient Scandinavian legendary
poems of unknown antiquity:

"Mountains dash together,
Heroes go the way to Hel,
and heaven is rent in twain. . . .
The sun grows dark,
The earth sinks into the sea,
The bright stars from heaven vanish;
Fire rages,
Heat blazes,
And high flames play
'Gainst heaven itself."

The legends of the Cashinaua, the aborigines of western
Brazil, tell of the time when "The lightnings flashed and the
thunders roared terribly and all were afraid. Then the heaven
burst and the fragments fell down and killed everything and
everybody. Heaven and earth changed places. Nothing that had
life was left upon the earth."

In North America, the Choctaw Indians of Oklahoma have a
tradition about the time when "The earth was plunged in darkness for a long time." A bright light eventually appeared in the
north, "but it was mountain-high waves, rapidly coming nearer."

The Samoan aborigines of the South Pacific have a legend that
says: "Then arose smell . . . the smell became smoke, which
again became clouds. . . . The sea too arose, and in a stupendous
catastrophe of nature the land sank into the sea. . . . The new
earth (the Samoan islands) arose out of the womb of the last
earth."

The Bible, too, contains numerous passages that refer to
terrible conflagrations. Psalms 18:7-15 is one example: "Then
the earth shook and trembled; the foundations also of the hills
moved and were shaken. . . . The Lord also thundered in the
heavens, and the Highest gave his voice; hail stones and coals of
fire. . . . Then the channels of waters were seen, and the foundations of the world were discovered. . . ."

These are but a few of the vast number of legends dealing with
great cosmic events and cataclysmic destruction on the face of
the earth. The ancient records of Egypt, India, and China, the
mythology of Greece and Rome, the legends of the Mayas and
the Aztecs, the biblical accounts, and those of Norway, Finland,

3

Persia, and Babylon, all tell the same story. So, too, do the people of widely separated countries, such as the Celts of Britain and the Maoris of New Zealand.

What on earth, or in heaven, could have caused such seemingly worldwide catastrophe? The accounts quoted above are taken from two masterly works on the subject, both of which offer the same explanation. One is Ignatius Donnelly's *Ragnarok: The Age of Fire and Gravel*, published in 1883, whose title is drawn from the legend of *Ragnarok* (wrongly translated as "the darkness of the gods" and "the rain of dust") contained in the Scandinavian *Poetic Edda*. The other is *Worlds in Collision*, which appeared in 1950, and is the most famous of several books by Immanuel Velikovsky, a Russo-Israeli physician whose theories have made him as controversial a character as Donnelly before him. Both men suggest that a comet which came into close proximity with the earth caused the terrible events remembered by the ancient peoples of the world. They agree on many points of evidence, such as the myths and legends, and the sinking of Atlantis features in both works. But they take different stands in their search for scientific proof of their theories.

Donnelly's Theory

Donnelly devotes a large part of his book to a discussion of the drift, or *till*—a vast deposit of sand, gravel, and clay that lies above the stratified rocks of the earth's surface. The origin of the till puzzled many geologists, and Donnelly's explanation was that it had rained down from the heavens as the earth passed through a comet's tail. He argued that the comet's tail would have been moving at close to the speed of light when the earth passed through it, so only half the planet would have been covered by the till, and he sought to produce evidence to confirm his theory.

Immanuel Velikovsky

Velikovsky, though agreeing that a close earth-comet encounter lay behind the ancient catastrophe legends, has no use for the till theory—which was a foundation stone of Donnelly's treatise—and he observes: "Donnelly . . . tried in his book *Ragnarok* to explain the presence of till and gravel on the rock substratum in America and Europe by hypothesizing an en-

4

counter with a comet, which rained till on the terrestrial hemisphere facing it at that moment. . . . His assumption that there is till only in one half of the earth is arbitrary and wrong."

Neither Donnelly nor Velikovsky was the first to argue that a comet had caused havoc on this planet. The English scientist William Whiston, who succeeded Sir Isaac Newton at Cambridge, wrote a book in 1696, *New Theory of the Earth*, which attempted to prove that a comet caused the biblical Flood. There was also a belief, at the time of Aristotle, in the 4th century B.C., that a comet had joined the solar system as a planet.

But Velikovsky has pieced together a far more startling picture of cosmic activity. It began, he believes, when a planetary collision caused Jupiter to eject a comet, which went into an eccentric orbit. This brought it close to the earth in about 1500 B.C., causing global catastrophes. The comet returned 52 years later and did further damage to the earth. Its approaches even caused the planet to stop and then rotate in the opposite direction, changing the position of the poles and altering the earth's orbit. The hydrocarbon gases of the comet's tail showered down on the earth in a rain of gravel and fire that formed the petroleum deposits we now use to power our automobiles and airplanes.

The comet, having left much of its tail behind, then had a close encounter with Mars, causing that planet to leave its orbit and, in turn, to come dangerously close to the earth in the 8th and 7th centuries B.C. Meanwhile the comet joined the solar system as a planet—the one we now call Venus.

When this theory was first published, in 1950, it caused a sensation. Since then Velikovsky has become something of a cult figure, particularly among young people, though the scientific community has largely dismissed his ideas as nonsense.

L. Sprague de Camp probably expresses the opinion of most orthodox scientists and scholars in his succinct and damning appraisal of Velikovsky's "mad" theory. He writes in *Lost Continents*: "Despite the impressive build-up . . . Velikovsky neither establishes a case nor accounts for the success of the Copernicus-Newton-Einstein picture of the cosmos which he undertook to supersede. Some of his mythological references are wrong (for instance he uses the Brasseur 'translation' of the *Troano Codex*); the rest merely demonstrate once again that the corpus of recorded myth is so vast that you can find mythological allusions to back up any cosmological speculation you please. The Babylonians left clear records of observations of Venus 5000 years ago, behaving just as it does now. . . . Moreover, the theory is ridiculous from the point of view of physics and mechanics. Comets are not planets and do not evolve into planets; instead they are loose aggregations of meteors with total masses less than a millionth that of the earth. Such a mass—about that of an ordinary mountain—could perhaps devastate several counties or a small state if struck, but could not appreciably affect the earth's orbit, rotation, inclination, or other components of movement. . . . And the gas of which the comet's tail is composed is so attenuated that if the tail of a good-sized comet were compressed to the density of iron, I could put the whole thing in my briefcase!"

So that disposes of Velikovsky—or does it? Seven years after his book was published, man made his first tentative steps into space. Since then earthlings have landed on the moon, and space vehicles have probed our nearest planetary neighbors. So far, these explorations appear to have confirmed some of Velikovsky's predictions about our planetary system. He had stated that, because Venus is a newcomer to the system, it is still giving off heat. This was thought to be nonsense at the time, and the consensus of astronomical opinion was that the surface temperature of Venus was around 65°F. Radio astronomy and the arrival of space vehicles in the vicinity of the planet have proved Velikovsky right. Mariner II, when it passed Venus in December 1962, detected a temperature of over 800°F, and subsequent investigations have revealed a temperature of approximately 990°F.

The results of the Mariner probe—the first to provide reliable information about the planet—showed that, just as Velikovsky had maintained, Venus is enclosed in an envelope of hydrocarbon gases and dust. It was also revealed that Venus rotated retrogradely, a sign that either it had been disturbed or it had evolved in a different way from other planets. A Russian probe that soft-landed on the planet in October 1975 was able to relay information for 53 minutes before the extremely high pressure of the atmosphere caused it to stop transmitting. But it was enough for the Russian scientists to declare that Venus is a young planet, and still "alive."

6

Interviewed about these findings by a British newspaper, Velikovsky commented that they confirmed his theory. His book contained many other predictions about Mars, Jupiter, the earth, and the moon. "And about 30 of them have since been proved right," he claimed. If subsequent probes confirm other details of his theory, it would not be the first time that science has had to change its thinking about the history of the earth and its partners in the solar system.

The Destruction of Atlantis

Velikovsky weaves the destruction of Atlantis into his theory by suggesting that the continent sank as a result of the first approach of the Venus comet, though in order to make this idea fit his scheme he has to alter Plato's dating of the Atlantis catastrophe. There is one zero too many in Plato's date, says Velikovsky. Atlantis sank not 9000 years before Solon's trip to Egypt, but 900 years before Solon—in about 1500 B.C.

The idea that a comet destroyed Atlantis was not a new one. It had previously been put forward in 1785 by the Italian scholar Gian Rinaldo Carli—although he dated the catastrophe at 4000 B.C.—and was taken up again in the 1920s by a German writer called Karl George Zschaetzch, whose main aim was to prove the racial superiority of the Aryans by providing them with a pedigree that went all the way back to Atlantis.

Another theory to account for the Atlantis catastrophe came from Hanns Hörbiger, an Austrian inventor and engineer. Hörbiger maintained that the universe is filled with "cosmic building stuff," consisting of hot metallic stars and "cosmic ice." The collision between a hot star and a block of cosmic ice generates a tremendous explosion, throwing pieces of star material and ice particles into space. These bodies spiral inward toward the sun, causing another explosion, which covers the nearest planets with a thick coating of ice. Hörbiger believed the Milky Way to consist of ice particles, and maintained that Venus and Mercury were sheathed in ice, as was the moon. According to Hörbiger's theory, the earth had possessed several moons before the present one. Each of these moons caused violent earthquakes and floods on the earth at the time of its capture by our planet, and finally shattered, showering its fragments onto the earth's surface. These events gave rise to the catastrophe

7

myths, and it was the capture of our present moon that caused both Atlantis and Lemuria to sink. Hörbiger predicted that the eventual breakup and fall of our present moon would probably wipe out life on earth.

Hörbiger's theory, published in 1913, attracted millions of followers, and made him as much of a cult figure as Velikovsky is today. But whereas space exploration and our increased knowledge of the universe have disproved most of Hörbiger's assertions, many of Velikovsky's ideas are still living up to the expectations of his followers, who foresee them becoming the accepted scientific thinking of a future era. Unless and until that day comes, however, we need to examine the catastrophe legends and the theories of lost continents in the light of current scientific belief. The picture then becomes far less promising.

The Orthodox Approach

Orthodox scientists dismiss the idea of a global catastrophe of the kind described by Velikovsky and others. How, then, do they explain the legends? The answer is that, universal though the disaster legends may seem, they are descriptions of separate events that occurred at different times and were fairly localized. They concern tremendous earthquakes, great volcanic eruptions, massive flooding of river valleys, and inundation of areas below sea level. These events, spanning many centuries and not linked in any way, gave rise to the legends, which were doubtless exaggerated as they were handed down from one generation to the next.

Take Noah's flood, for example. According to the Bible, this great deluge drowned every living thing on earth—apart from the few survivors in the ark. It is now considered likely that this story was based on a real flood that submerged something like 40,000 square miles of the Euphrates Valley some time between 5400 and 4200 B.C. China and the lowlands of Bengal have seen similar great floods, and these, too, could have given rise to deluge legends. Many geologists believe that the Mediterranean was once a fertile valley below sea level, which was flooded long ago by the Atlantic in one terrible rush. The flooding of the former Zuider Zee (now Ijssel Lake) in the Netherlands is a more recent example of this kind of catastrophe. A storm in 1282 broke the natural dykes that protected this area of sub-sea-level land, and let in the North Sea, which submerged it in a single day.

In this century alone there have been a number of earthquakes that have taken in excess of 100,000 lives, and there are records of even more disastrous quakes in the past. The Chinese earthquake of 1556 is said to have killed 830,000 people. It would be surprising if similar quakes in ancient times did *not* give rise to catastrophe legends. To those living in the affected areas it must certainly have seemed as if the whole world were coming to an end.

An earthquake beneath the sea may cause a tidal wave. In mid-ocean the gentle slopes of a tidal wave may go undetected, but as the wave approaches and meets the shore it surges up into a massive, sometimes skyscraper-high, wall of water. In 1737, a 210-foot tidal wave was recorded in Kamchatka (now part of the eastern Soviet Union), and many others have been reported between 50 and 100 feet tall. Volcanic eruptions, in addition to wreaking their own havoc, may also set up tidal waves. The Krakatoa eruption of 1883 caused a huge wave that drowned 36,380 people living on the shores of the nearby Indonesian islands.

So, our history is rich in natural disasters that have taken a tremendous toll of human life—as they still do—and that may well have given rise to the legends. But could any of these pestilences account for the sinking of a great continent such as Atlantis? Most scientists think it extremely unlikely. An earthquake might have destroyed part of the island continent, or caused landslides around its shores, but the total area devastated by even a violent earthquake is relatively limited, and a quake that would have destroyed a huge landmass is unheard-of. Had Atlantis been an island with a very low profile it might have been at least partly submerged by flooding, but Plato describes Atlantis as a mountainous country. A tidal wave might have washed over Atlantis, but it would not have washed it away. And a volcanic eruption could have blown part of the continent into the ocean, but if Atlantis had been anywhere near the size claimed by Plato much would still be towering above the sea. In the scientists' view even a whole series of massive earthquakes, volcanic eruptions, and flooding would take many thousands of years to sink an island of anything approaching continental size— and a low, flat island at that.

9

A Geological Explanation

The only other possibility would seem to be that the earth's crust is capable of opening up and swallowing areas of land. Small islands have been submerged in living memory, and others have suddenly appeared. Could the same forces have been responsible for wiping Atlantis from the face of our planet? To answer this question we need to look at present opinion on the way the world has developed, and at the processes by which continents take shape.

According to current geological theory, the earth is encased in a crust of rock that becomes hotter and hotter as we go down toward the center of the planet. Some 50 to 100 miles beneath the surface the rock has become white-hot. From that point down the earth consists of a hot, glasslike substance called *magma*, which surrounds the nickel-iron core of the earth, a sphere about 4000 miles in diameter. The cool exterior rocks consist in general of two types: dense, heavy, magnesium-bearing rocks, called *sima*, which form most of the ocean floors, and light, aluminum-bearing rocks, called *sial*, which form most of the land areas. Geologists see the continents as beds of sial "floating" on a crust of sima. The continental blocks descend deeply into the sima, showing a comparatively small amount above the surface, just as icebergs do in water.

Over a century ago, it became apparent to some geologists that the face of our globe has not always been as it now appears. The evidence for this assumption was the same that led many biologists of the time to consider the possibility of a lost continent: namely, the existence of fossils of similar fauna and flora on continents thousands of miles apart.

Geologists who accepted fossil evidence of ancient land connections between the continents put forward the idea of a former gigantic landmass, which they called Gondwanaland, comprising present-day South America, Africa, India, Australia, and Antarctica. A second landmass, consisting of North America and Europe, was also suggested and given the name Laurasia. However, the proponents of this theory were unable to offer any convincing evidence as to how these two supercontinents might have broken up, and their idea attracted little support among fellow scientists.

Nevertheless, in the early years of the 20th century, a number of scientists began thinking along similar lines, and in 1915 the German astronomer, geophysicist, and meteorologist Alfred Wegener published the modern theory of continental drift. Wegener argued that if the continents float like icebergs on the sima crust, why should they not also drift like icebergs across the face of the earth? He suggested that all the modern continents were once joined in a single giant landmass. They have since drifted apart, and the drift is continuing; millions of years from now, the face of our planet will look very different from the way it does today.

Wegener's theory has rocked the geological establishment, and its revolutionary effect on the geological sciences has been compared to the effect of Darwin's theory of evolution on the biological sciences a century ago. But for several decades after its publication the majority of scientists continued to reject the idea of continental drift, mainly because they found it hard to envisage forces strong enough to move the continents around. (After all, even the smallest continent, Australia, weighs around 500 million million million kilograms.) In due course, however, a plausible explanation—involving convection currents driven by radioactive heat from within the earth—was put forward to account for the continental movements, and a mass of impressive evidence began piling up in support of Wegener's theory, so that most scientists now accept the reality of continental drift.

In the late 1960s computers were used to show how the continental jigsaw pieces might fit together to form the original gigantic landmass. This was not an easy task, because the shape of the continents has altered over the ages. Some minor parts of the jigsaw are missing, some have been added, and the true edges of the continents generally lie far below sea level and have not yet been plotted in detail. Nevertheless, the computer pictures showed an extremely good fit between South America and the western coast of Africa, and between Antarctica, Australia, and India. The fit of these last three continents against south and eastern Africa was less satisfactory, and some adjustment was needed to improve the fit across the North Atlantic, linking Britain and the rest of Europe with North America.

In their book *Continental Drift*, leading British geophysicist D. P. Tarling and his technical journalist wife M. P. Tarling write: "By studying the size and composition of particles in old sedimentary rocks it is possible to work out the direction and type of land from which they were derived. In Britain, we find that the source of many Caledonian Mountain sediments was a very extensive landmass which must have lain to the north and west where there is now the deep Atlantic Ocean. In North America, the sources of many Appalachian rocks lay to the south and east. To explain this before the acceptance of continental drift, geologists supposed that a continent, 'Atlantis,' must have occupied the present position of the Atlantic. This continent was thought to have sunk beneath the Atlantic waves. [But] there can be no question of the existence of a sunken continent in the Atlantic. By reconstructing the jigsaw we not only fit together the Caledonian Mountain chain, but also explain the sources of the sediments which formed it."

Most scientists agree that as we push the continents back to their original places, we effectively squeeze Atlantis off the map. So, could Atlantis have been North America, which, having drifted away, was thought to have been submerged in the Atlantic? No. The continents are moving apart at the rate of between one and six inches a year—hardly enough to give rise to Plato's account of the submergence of Atlantis in a day and a night. What is more, the original landmass is thought to have broken up before the Mesozoic era, some 200 million years ago, and the continents probably reached approximately their present positions by the beginning of the Cenozoic era, around 70 million years ago—long before man appeared on the face of the earth.

Could Atlantis have been in the Pacific, where Mu was said to have sunk, or in the Indian Ocean, where the early Lemuria enthusiasts placed yet another lost continent? Our present knowledge of the earth seems to rule out these possibilities, too. Bearing in mind the geologists' belief that the ocean floors are mostly formed of sima and the landmasses of sial, a sunken continent should be easy to detect because its rocks would be different from surrounding rocks in the deep ocean. However, geological investigation has so far revealed that the greatest areas of deep sima are in the Central Pacific, the southern Indian Ocean, and the Arctic Ocean, making these the least likely sites on earth for a vanished continent.

Not surprisingly, believers in Atlantis hotly contest the findings of modern science that seek to dismiss the existence of the lost continent. In considering the theory of continental drift they point to gaps and seeming misfits in the linking of continents across the Atlantic that might still leave room for Atlantis. Nor are they impressed by the failure of oceanographers to find evidence of a sunken civilization beneath the Atlantic. In his book *The Mystery of Atlantis*, Charles Berlitz points out that even the underwater cities of the Mediterranean have been discovered only comparatively recently and in relatively shallow water. How much more difficult, then, to discover the ruins of Atlantis beneath the far larger Atlantic, where they would be smothered by sedimentation and mud accumulated over thousands of years.

If a once-derided theory such as continental drift can eventually earn the backing of the respectable scientific community, the Atlantists argue, might not other theories, now regarded as nonsensical, one day gain the same acceptance? Perhaps man existed long before the scientists' estimates. Perhaps there was some extraordinary global catastrophe of a nature quite outside the bounds of cautious scientific conjecture. Perhaps Atlantis did exist after all.

2. Secrets of the Standing Stones

One summer evening in 1934, after a hard day's sailing up the west coast of Scotland, an Oxford University professor took his boat into Loch Roag on the Isle of Lewis to find an anchorage for the night. A full moon was rising over the hills, and silhouetted against it was a most impressive sight: the tall standing stones of Callanish, the ancient monument that has been called the Scottish equivalent of Stonehenge.

Professor Alexander Thom

Professor Alexander Thom went ashore, and, standing in the middle of the mysterious stone circle, he noticed that according to the pole star the structure was aligned due north-south. This observation fascinated him, for he knew that in the days when the stone circle was constructed there was no pole star because its constellation hadn't reached its present position. He wondered whether the alignment was a chance occurrence or had been deliberately planned. If it was deliberate it would probably be found at other megalithic sites. Thom decided to check whether it was, and thus began 30 years of painstaking study, involving survey work at no fewer than 450 sites in remote spots in the British Isles, which led to the publication in 1967 of his book *Megalithic Sites in Britain*, and in 1971 of *Megalithic Lunar Observations*. It also led to a revolution in thinking about European prehistory. It had previously been assumed that barbarians had inhabited Western Europe in prehistoric times, when civilization had first arisen in the Middle East. Thom's findings demanded a radical change of this view. "I'm an engineer," he wrote, and indeed his professorship was in engineering. "I'm certain these people were too—and proud of it."

By "these people" Thom meant the megalith builders. The word *megalith* comes from two Greek words meaning simply "large stone," and its adjective is used for a variety of structures from single standing stones known as *menhirs*, to structures in which three standing stones support an immense capstone, known as *dolmens* or *cromlechs*, and to piles of rough stones burying a tomb or serving as a memorial or landmark, known as *cairns*, and of course stone circles. Professor Glyn Daniel of Cambridge has estimated that there must be between 40,000 and 50,000 megalithic tombs or temples in Western Europe. The question of who built them has given rise to at least as much speculation and controversy as any other question in archaeology.

The phenomenon is not exclusive to Western Europe, but it is peculiarly concentrated there, particularly in the form of menhirs and stone circles. The practice of building tombs of stone—and dolmens are thought to have been tombs—is a natural development from cave burial. As such it might be expected to occur spontaneously in different parts of the world. But the erection of single standing stones, or avenues or circles of them, is a practice that at first consideration appears rather pointless. As the French archaeologist Professor P. R. Giot wrote of the standing stones: "Whether isolated or in groups, they remain enshrouded in mystery. This is no doubt why their study has, unjustifiably, been comparatively neglected. . . . With the very limited evidence at his disposal, the interpretation of single menhirs is one of the archaeologist's nightmares."

The mystery is deepened when we think of the labor involved. All other archaeological evidence bears witness to the fact that the inhabitants of Western Europe at the time when the megaliths were erected were neolithic farmers living in small communities who possessed only the most primitive tools and technology. Professor Richard Atkinson, the Englishman who excavated around Stonehenge, estimated that the transport of the 81 sarsen stones from Avebury, some 15 miles away, would have taken 1500 men working continuously for 5.5 years. And the construction of nearby Silbury Hill (which is not a megalith but is of the same period) he reckoned would have taken 18 million man-hours. In the 1830s a capstone from a megalithic tomb near Saumur in France was moved to serve as a bridge. It took 18 pairs of oxen and enormous rollers, each consisting of four oak

15

tree trunks lashed together, to shift it. The great stone known as the Grand Menhir Brisé in Brittany, which now lies broken on the ground, weighed about 380 tons and stood 60 feet high. In the famous nearby avenues of menhirs at Carnac there are no fewer than 3000 great stones. The labor involved in erecting them, and the thousands of other stones and stone structures in Brittany and the British Isles, was prodigious. The idea that they were erected by giants or magicians long prevailed, and a form of it has even been seriously proposed by a present-day British writer on the subject, John Michell. But if we do not allow ourselves flights of fancy about supernatural engineering we must assume that the megaliths were erected by manpower. The question of why such prodigious manpower was put to such a purpose then becomes one of the most intriguing puzzles that enigmatic relics of the ancient world pose for modern man.

Avebury and Stonehenge

John Aubrey, the celebrated 17th-century English antiquarian and diarist, was out hunting with some friends just after Christmas, 1648 when they came to the village of Avebury. There Aubrey experienced a revelation. He realized that he was standing in the middle of an immense prehistoric temple. Where others saw, and for centuries had seen, only a lot of old stones and a few mounds, Aubrey saw evidence of a grand design. The design stands out quite clearly on a modern aerial photograph, even though today there are far fewer stones at Avebury than there were in Aubrey's day, thanks to the efforts of such men as the 18th-century farmer known as "Stone-Killer Robinson." He devised a means of breaking them up by toppling them into fiery pits and administering a dash of cold water and a hammer blow.

The Avebury circle is so large that the medieval village has grown up within it. It was its size that had hidden it from view and made its component stones seem a mere random assembly. Stonehenge, however, could not be ignored. Standing on the open Salisbury Plain, its great stones clustered in an obviously man-made design, it invited speculation about the men who had built it. The 12th-century English historian Geoffrey of Monmouth had written that it was built about A.D. 470 as a memorial to 460 ancient British chieftains massacred by Hengist the Saxon. His view prevailed, for lack of a more authoritative one, until the 17th century, when British royalty began to take an interest in Stonehenge. King James I of England visited it, and had his architect Inigo Jones make drawings showing its original construction. Jones expressed the opinion that it had been built by the Romans in the first or second century A.D. in honor of the god Coelus, and that it could not possibly have been built by the "savage and barbarous" early Britons. They, he said, would have been quite incapable of achieving such "stately structures, or such remarkable works as Stonehenge." John Aubrey was less scornful of the early Britons, or of their priests, the Druids. When asked by King Charles II to survey the site and write an account of it, he stated that its history went back beyond Saxon and Roman times. Referring to both Avebury and Stonehenge, he wrote that since the Druids were "the most eminent order of priests among the Britons, it is most likely that these monuments were the temples of the priests of the most eminent order, the Druids, and it is strongly to be presumed that they are as ancient as those days."

Aubrey's view was taken up and elaborated in the next century by Dr. William Stukeley, whose book, *Stonehenge, a Temple restored to the British Druids*, was extremely influential. It inspired so much other fanciful literature about Druids and their practices that the popular view has prevailed down to our day that Stonehenge was erected by Druids for purposes of ritual sacrifice and sun worship. The discovery that it might have been used to predict eclipses has been, as it were, added to this view by proposing that the possession of such an expertise would have enabled the Druidic priesthood to manipulate ignorant people by demonstrating apparant magical powers over the heavenly bodies. We know about the historical existence of Druids from references in the writings of Julius Caesar. Possibly Stonehenge and other monuments throughout Britain were used by them, but they certainly did not erect the megaliths, and Stonehenge was built much earlier than 460 B.C., as Stukeley had conjectured

The Science of Archaeology

Archaeology as a scientific study could not make much progress until the late 19th century. Then the mind of Western man gradually became emancipated from the Biblical version of prehistory as it had been interpreted by Archbishop Ussher of

Armagh, Ireland, whose calculation that Man had been created on October 23, 404 B.C. had been adopted as dogma by the Church. When the findings of geology, and of fossil remains testifying to human life on earth thousands of years ago, combined with evolution theory to overthrow this dogma, the way was open for a scientific study of prehistory. The most obvious area for the pursuit of this study was the Near and Middle East, for there relics were conspicuous, varied, and well preserved. Moreover there were traditions and written records to guide archaeological field work and to help interpret its findings. Western Europe, by comparison, was unspectacular and unpromising. Its enigmatic clusters of rough stones, its great mounds and chambered tombs, could not be related to contemporary historical or literary records, and their existence was not obviously inconsistent with the idea that the people who built them were superstitious barbarians. The Swedish archaeologist Oscar Montelius expressed the prevailing view when he wrote in 1908: "At a time when the people of Europe were, so to speak, without any civilization whatsoever, the Orient and particularly the Euphrates region and the Nile were already in enjoyment of a flourishing culture."

This view led to the idea known as the theory of *diffusionism*. This suggested that civilization had first arisen in Mesopotamia and Egypt about 3000 B.C. and that aspects of it had gradually spread westward. Archaeological findings appeared to support this view. For example, it was possible to trace the spread of the practice of burial in chambered tombs from the Aegean via Malta, Spain, Portugal and France, to Britain and Scandinavia. And as the British archaeologist Sir Mortimer Wheeler wrote in 1925: "The general analogy between the *mastabas* (of Egypt) and many types of chambered tomb is too close to be altogether accidental." Evidence of the achievements distinctive of high civilizations, such as sculpture, fine metalwork, and sophisticated decorative art and design, was not to be found among the relics of Western European prehistory.

Radiocarbon Dating

The conclusion that "megalithic culture" was derived from but greatly inferior to the high civilizations of Mesopotamia, Egypt, and the Aegean was a natural one to make. It is only quite recently that it has been proved to be untenable and the diffusionist theory in its simple form has now been discredited.

The discovery in 1949, by the American chemist Willard Libby, of a means of dating prehistoric relics by measuring the amount of radioactive carbon-14 they contain, signaled a revolution in archaeology. At first the radiocarbon dating technique seemed to confirm established ideas, and the few anomalies it threw up could be ignored. Some archaeologists were skeptical of its reliability. They pointed out for instance that although we know that the building of the Great Pyramid was begun about 2600 B.C., the radiocarbon technique of dating yielded the result 2200 B.C. It was not until 1967 that the reliability of the technique was established beyond dispute. Then not only was the error in dating the Great Pyramid explained but at the same time prevailing ideas about the relative antiquity of Near, Middle Eastern, and Atlantic European artifacts were confounded.

In California there grows a tree known as the bristlecone pine. Some of these trees are 5000 years old, and as they grow one ring on their trunks each year their age can be precisely known. In 1967 Professor Hans Suess conceived the idea of taking tree-ring samples and comparing their known calendrical ages with the ages yielded by radiocarbon dating. If the latter technique were accurate, the ages should of course correspond. It turned out that they didn't correspond, but that the discrepancy between the two dates was a factor that varied predictably, becoming larger the further back in time. This meant that the old radiocarbon dates were wrong, and that, in order to correct them, dates of around 1000 B.C. had to be pushed back by 200 years and at about 3000 B.C. by nearly 1000 years. This meant that, when the original radiocarbon data for the Great Pyramid was corrected, the new date coincided with the known historical date. But when megalithic sites were radiocarbon dated they proved to be considerably older than the eastern civilizations that they were supposed to be derived from. Megalithic chambered tombs turned out to date from 4500–4000 B.C., long before the building of the Egyptian *mastabas* and of the round tombs found around the Aegean. And the first construction at Stonehenge itself was found to be at least contemporary with, and probably earlier than, the Great Pyramid of Cheops. The signs were that an indigenous culture had evolved independently in Western Europe in prehistoric times.

The year 1967 was an exciting year for students of European prehistory. In addition to the evidence of the unsuspected antiquity of megalithic artifacts afforded by the new dating estimates there came evidence of their unimagined mathematical and geometrical properties. For that year Professor Thom published his *Megalithic Sites in Britain*.

Thom's 'Megalithic Yard'

For years following his first insight at Callanish, Thom, assisted at first by his sons and later by his grandsons, had carried surveying equipment to remote megalithic sites and taken careful measurements. As he completed an increasing number of surveys, it became clear that the sites had been chosen and the stones located by men who had a knowledge of astronomy as well as of geometry and mathematics. They had also possessed sophisticated techniques and equipment. "Some sites," he wrote, "for example Avebury, were set out with an accuracy approaching 1 in 1000. Only an experienced surveyor with good equipment is likely to attain this sort of accuracy. The differences in tension applied to an ordinary measuring tape by different individuals can produce variations in length of this amount or even more."

Thom's main discovery was the "megalithic yard," the unit of measurement used by the prehistoric builders. This unit, the equivalent of 2.72 feet, together with another unit that was precisely 2.5 times the megalithic yard and which he called the "megalithic rod," Thom found to be a constant feature of the dimensions of all the stone circles he surveyed. The radii and circumferences of the structures, as well as the distances between individual stones, were found to be always multiples of the megalithic yard. Thom's surveys revealed that a majority of the structures were not exact circles. Some were egg-shaped, some elliptical, some flattened on one side, and some elongated. But whatever its shape the circumference and radius of each stone "circle" was measurable in whole numbers of megalithic yards. And always the accuracy was uncanny. It was inconceivable that this accuracy was due to chance. Thom made his discovery when surveying sites in Scotland, which being more remote are generally more intact than those further south. But as his studies progressed he found that all megalithic sites from Brittany, France to the Orkneys, the islands off northern Scotland, were all laid out according to a consistent principle of measurement. He concluded that there must have been a prehistoric culture on the European coast of the Atlantic Ocean of considerable sophistication and with some kind of central administration. For if the measuring instruments used in the construction of the megaliths were not officially standardized and issued, but were obtained by each local community copying from its neighbor's, there would certainly be a greater degree of localized error and variation than was in fact found.

When Thom first announced his findings, most archaeologists were skeptical and some were positively hostile. His findings were of course irreconcilable with the picture of Neolithic man and his culture in northwest Europe that had emerged from decades of orthodox archaeological research. But *Megalithic Sites in Britain* was such a scholarly and exhaustive study, so unsensational in its presentation and impeccable in its mathematics, that its findings could not be dismissed as nonsense. An independent mathematician, Professor David Kendall of the Statistical Laboratory at the University of Cambridge, subjected Thom's figures to a series of tests using a computer. Kendall reached the conclusion that there was no more than a one percent chance that the dimensions of the stone circles could have been achieved without the common unit of the megalithic yard. Thom was vindicated and historians had to start revising their ideas.

The revision demanded by the new evidence was not a minor one. One fact that had to be taken into account in it was that the megalith builders had understood the principle of Euclidean geometry 2000 years *before* Euclid, who lived in about 300 B.C. Within the stone "circles" Thom discovered geometrical figures formed by key features which were measured in whole numbers of megalithic yards. Of all possible triangles there are a limited number with sides measurable in whole numbers. We call them Pythagorean triangles, but the megalith builders had apparently had them all worked out long before Pythagoras. At Avebury, for instance, Thom found that "the basis of the design is a 3,4,5 triangle set out in units of exactly 25 MY (megalithic yards) so that all the resulting shapes come out in multiples of 5 or 10."

21

At Woodhenge, another site on Salisbury Plain, there are five concentric circles with perimeters measuring exactly 40, 60, 80, 140, and 160 MY, and with internal dimensions based on the Pythagorean triangle 12, 35, 37. At Stonehenge there is an outer ring known as the Aubrey Holes (after John Aubrey, who first drew attention to them), and the holes numbered 56, 7, and 28 define the points of a perfect Pythagorean right-angled triangle with sides of 40, 96, and 104 MY, as does every other corresponding set. Thom found comparable symmetries between features in all the megalithic sites he surveyed, and concluded that the megalith builders had been experienced and clever geometers and mathematicians. It appeared that they had varied the shapes of their stone "circles" by way of experimenting with different geometrical figures, and setting and solving for themselves a number of geometrical problems.

It was surely inconceivable, though, that the tremendous physical effort involved in erecting the megaliths should have been invested in mere intellectual exercises, or even in laying down demonstrations of, or "teaching machines" for, mathematical and geometrical principles for the benefit of future generations. Clearly, there must be more to them than that. And of course there was. There was the knowledge of astronomy that their siting and construction testified to.

Megaliths and Astronomy

It was the Englishman William Stukeley in the 18th century who first observed that Stonehenge is aligned to the midsummer sunrise. In 1901 Sir Norman Lockyer, director of the Solar Physics Laboratory at South Kensington, London, published a book showing that Stonehenge and many other similar monuments were aligned on many of the stars as well as on the sun. Then in the 1920s Admiral Boyd Summerville surveyed 90 sites and announced that "In every instance . . . orientation of one kind or another has been found." So when Thom began his work he had guidelines and precedents for considering the megaliths as devices for calendrical calculation and astronomical observation. It was well known that by taking sight-lines from particular marked positions in stone circles to natural or man-made features of the landscape precise observations could be made, for instance of the sun at the solstices and equinoxes. These annual pheno-

Callanish stone circle on the Isle of Lewis. It was here that Professor
Alexander Thom first came to the conclusion that the men who
constructed the stone circles had advanced knowledge of astronomy,
mathematics and geometry. *(Secrets of the Standing Stones)*

Standing stone at Avebury, Wiltshire. According to Thom, the site was
set out with an accuracy approaching 1 in 1000.
(Secrets of the Standing Stones)

Early historians thought that the ancient Britons were too "savage and barbarous" to have built Stonehenge, but research in the 1960s revealed that the monument was used to predict lunar eclipses. *(Secrets of the Standing Stones)*

mena perhaps require a little explanation. The *solstice* occurs twice a year in northwest Europe, once in summer when the sun reaches its maximum distance from the equator on about June 21, and once when it reaches the tropic of Capricorn to begin its journey back again around December 21. The *equinox* also occurs twice a year, when the sun crosses the equator, making the night equal in length to the day. These equinoxes occur about March 21 and September 23 of each year. But the full extent of the megalith builders' astronomical knowledge was not known, and it astonished Thom himself when he found unequivocal evidence of it.

The cycle of the sun's positions throughout the year is simple and constant, but the moon is quite a different matter. In fact its cyclic pattern cannot even be understood without taking into account a period of 18.6 years. Over this period it first rises and sets in extreme northerly and southerly positions. Then it moves inward from these extreme positions for a period of 9.3 years and outwards toward them again for a second 9.3-year period. Astronomers call the extreme positions reached by the moon every 9.3 years its major and minor "standstills." For a few days on either side of these standstills it is possible to observe a small perturbation of the moon's orbit, generally known as the moon's "wobble," which is caused by the gravitational attraction of the sun. It was thought that this phenomenon had first been observed at the end of the 16th century of our era, but Thom discovered clear evidence that the megalith builders had known about it. Evidence that they possessed this knowledge lay not only in their great observational exactitude and subtlety, but also their ability to predict eclipses. For it is when the moon's perturbation is at its greatest that eclipses occur.

The size and location of the fallen Grand Menhir Brisé near Carnac in Brittany, France had always been a mystery. Thom's survey of the region revealed that its purpose had been to pinpoint to within a fraction of a degree the moon's major and minor standstills and the exact amount of its perturbation. The megalith served as a foresight marker for the points of rising and setting of the moon at the extremes of its 18.6-year cycle. The eight different points that an observer would occupy in order to use the megalith in this way, one of which was as far as ten miles away from it, were predicted by Thom. At four of these sites prehistoric markers in the form of mounds or stones were found.

The power to predict is the main criterion that science demands a hypothesis should satisfy. Thom's predictions in this case and several others greatly enhanced the credibility of his astonishing disclosures. For instance, at Kintraw in Argylle, Scotland there is a single tall standing stone in a field. Thom predicted that this stone would align with a point on the horizon between two mountain peaks where the sun would have set at the mid-winter solstice, and he indicated a point on a steep slope at a distance from the stone which would have been the observation point from which this alignment was obtained. Excavations were carried out at the point he indicated. The archaeologists were astonished to find an artificial platform of rubble with two mas-sive boulders situated at one end where the observation point would have been. With such evidence, the astronomical theory of the function of the megaliths became virtually irrefutable.

Thom was not alone. There were other distinguished profes-sors canvassing the astronomical theory in the 1960s. Gerald Hawkins, professor of astronomy at Boston University, Massa-chusetts, studied Stonehenge with the help of a computer. Hawkins came up with evidence that alignments of distinctive features of the Stonehenge complex pointed to all major astrono-mical events. He also observed that the number 56 is almost exactly three times the 18.6 years of the moon's cycle, and showed how the 56 so-called "Aubrey Holes" at Stonehenge could be used to predict eclipses. England's most famous astronomer, Professor Sir Fred Hoyle, supported Hawkins' theories. He re-stated the basic and most fundamental problem posed by the megaliths as a whole when he wrote that the construction of Stonehenge demanded "a level of intellectual attainment orders of magnitude higher than the standard to be expected from a community of primitive farmers."

Who were the Megalith Builders?

So we still come back to the original mystery, the original question: who were the megalith builders? The archaeological evidence shows that without doubt the standing stones of north-west Europe were erected at a time when the lands were inhabited by uncivilized Stone Age farmers. The properties which we can now see that the megalithic structures possess must have been beyónd the comprehension of such people, and therefore we have to assume that there existed in their midst an intellectual elite, or priesthood, which coordinated its efforts over centuries. Their object was to achieve the knowledge and establish the traditions that it did, and to do so it commanded the services of a substantial labor force. Such an elite, supported by tribute and taxes paid by the farming communities that made up the population, is known to have existed in other parts of the world, such as among the Maya people of Central America. In a recent book on the megalith builders Dr. Euan MacKie of the University of Glasgow, Scotland has argued that we may in fact have archaeological evidence of the existence of an intellectual elite in Western Europe in Neolithic times which has hitherto been otherwise and wrongly interpreted.

In the winter of 1850 a tremendous storm lashed the Orkney Isles. On the western coast of the largest island it washed away some sand dunes to reveal the stone foundations of an ancient building. Later excavation of this site showed that it was a complex of buildings, some of which appeared to have been built for individual occupation and others for communal use. There were signs that a disaster had occurred there at the time when it was inhabited, and which had resulted in its abandonment. Some pottery found on the site was flat-based and decorated with deep grooves and abstract reliefs, unlike anything found anywhere else, and archaeologists long assumed that Skara Brae, as the site was called, was an isolated Neolithic farmers' village. A similar settlement, with the same type of pottery, was found on another Orkney island, Rousay, in the 1930s, and in the same decade Grooved Ware pottery, as it became known, was found at Clacton in Essex, which exploded the myth that it was a unique Orkneyan artifact. More Grooved Ware was found when Woodhenge on Salisbury Plain was excavated in the 1960s and other sites in southern England have since yielded more examples, particularly the site known as Durrington Walls, also on Salisbury Plain. Radiocarbon dating showed that the settlements at Durrington Walls and at Skara Brae had flourished at the same time, and the similarity of their artifacts suggested that Skara Brae had been something more than an isolated farming settlement. An ingenious study of the food refuse—in the form of animal bones—of the settlement at Durrington Walls, and a

25

comparison of it with the refuse from another Neolithic site, the nearby Windmill Hill causewayed camp, has shown that the Durrington Walls inhabitants enjoyed a different diet from that of the ordinary members of a Neolithic community, an interesting discovery which strongly suggests that they were members of an elite class.

At Stenness, near Skara Brae, there is a stone circle, and at Quanterness, also nearby, a chambered cairn has been found. Dr. MacKie has suggested that the three sites are related, and that his theory explains another mystery posed by megalithic remains. This is the question of who was buried in the great chambered tombs. It used to be assumed that these were the burial places of whole Neolithic communities. But as radiocarbon dating has shown that burials in particular places were spread over very long periods of time, the probability is that the few hundred occupants of these tombs found throughout the British Isles were a very select group. Therefore it seems likely that they were, in fact, members of a kind of intellectual theocracy, a class of priest-architect-designer-astronomers who were the megalith builders themselves.

3. Ley Lines

In the early 1920s a 65-year-old English merchant and amateur archeologist, Alfred Watkins, was out riding in the hills in his native Herefordshire. He pulled up in order to view the familiar landscape, and suddenly saw it as he had never seen it before, criss-crossed by straight lines that intersected at churches and at points marked by ancient stones. It was a visionary experience and, as often happens with sudden revelations, it determined the course of the rest of his life's work. He was convinced that he had seen in a flash the landscape of ancient Britain, a landscape covered with a vast network of straight tracks, many of them aligned either with the sun or with the path of a star. He called this network the "ley system."

Working on a special ordnance survey map, Watkins confirmed his vision. He found that straight lines extending many miles could be drawn to pass directly through churches, ancient sites, and man-made landmarks. It seems that for some reason not yet understood by us, but possibly for trade, straight roads were planned long before the Romans. However, because many of these tracks pass through difficult countryside with no attempt to skirt lakes, bogs, or mountains, one is tempted to think there is a deeper significance to them than a system of trade routes. The routes are marked by man-made landmarks such as cairns built on mountain slopes or notches cut in ridges, and various ancient sites.

Watkins was ridiculed for his theory because the prevailing version of ancient history at that time was that prehistoric Britons were little more than painted savages. But he stuck to his view and amassed a great deal of evidence which he published in 1925 in *The Old Straight Track*. Gradually other antiquarians became convinced, and began to investigate too.

One of these was Guy Underwood, another amateur archaeologist who learned dowsing, or water divining, in order to carry out his investigations. His research with his divining rod took him to old churches and ancient sites of traditional sanctity all over the country. He found that at the center of every circle of stones, and at a key point in every church he examined, there was an underground source of energy. A number of water lines converged in a radiating pattern to this spot. He called the spot a "blind spring." But he also found two other underground lines of force, not necessarily connected with the water line, which responded to the divining rod. One of these lines, which he called an "aquastat," seemed in some way to govern the layout of religious monuments and determine the positioning of stones, ditches, or buildings. The other, which he called a "track line," seemed to govern the route of roads and tracks. Underwood called all these subterranean lines of force "geodetic" lines. He believed that the main use early man had made of them was to mark out and divide the surface of the Earth. His research led him to the conclusion that both prehistoric and medieval builders had placed sacred sites and aligned the buildings they erected on them in observance of geodetic laws. In other words, they knew of the existence of lines of force running through the earth and, in some way, they had attempted to harness them for beneficial ends. Incidentally, Underwood found that Watkins' surface leys were often paralleled beneath the surface of the earth by a line of force.

In his book *The Pattern of the Past*, published in 1969, Underwood writes ". . . the three geodetic lines, the water line, the aquastat, and the track line appear to have much in common : they appear to be generated within the Earth; to involve wave motion; to have great penetrative power; to form a network on the face of the Earth; to affect the germination and manner of growth of certain trees and plants; to be perceived and used by animals; to affect opposite sides of the animal body, and to form spiral patterns." From these observations he goes on to say that they seem to be controlled by mathematical laws that involve the number 3 in their construction and the number 7 in their spiral patterns. These two numbers have been accorded arcane meaning from the earliest times. Underwood sees these geodetic

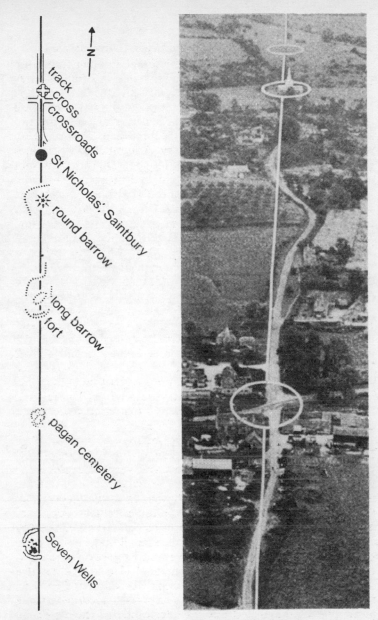

track
cross
crossroads
St Nicholas, Saintbury
round barrow
long barrow
fort
pagan cemetery
Seven Wells

Map and aerial view of Saintbury ley, Gloucestershire. The ley line runs for 3½ miles NNW to SSE in the Cotswolds. The belief that Britain's landscape was covered with a vast network of straight tracks or lines was first put forward in the 1920s. *(Ley Lines)*

lines as manifestations of an Earth Force, an idea which was central to many ancient religions. Traces of this belief can still be found throughout the world today.

When the bustling, expansionist, industrialized civilization of Western Europe tried to carry its influence into China about a century ago, its pioneers suffered a great deal of frustration and exasperation. For example, a proposal to cut a railway tunnel through a hill would be met by a polite refusal from the Chinese authorities. Their explanation would be that that particular range of hills was a terrestrial dragon, and that to cut through its tail was forbidden. Proposed sites for factories were firmly rejected for reasons that seemed to Europeans equally superstitious and nonsensical. They had not understood that in China there was an ancient and important belief in lines of force, known as "dragon current," running all over the surface of the Earth. Before any building was erected, or any tree planted, an expert known as a geomancer had to be consulted as to how the current would be affected. The Chinese were amazed on their side that the technologically advanced Europeans had no conception of this venerable science.

As everything else in Chinese philosophy, the dragon current was divided into yin and yang. The yin, or female current, was supposed to flow along gentle undulating countryside, and the yang, or male force, through steep high peaks. The most favorable position was felt to be where the two currents of yin and yang met. This was therefore often selected by a geomancer as a site for a tomb because the Chinese believed that the influences surrounding their dead ancestors played a decisive role in the future of their family.

Geomancers interpreted the earth in terms of the sky, rather like the principle of "as above, so below" that recurs so many times in ancient philosophy and magic. Mountains were thought of as stars, and large rivers as the Milky Way. Each main dragon current had small tributaries or veins, and every small vein had its own astrological interpretation. Different parts of the Earth were thought to come under the influence of the different planets then known—Jupiter, Mars, Venus, Mercury, and Saturn. These planets in turn had correspondences with colors, materials, landscape characteristics, animals, parts of the body, and so on. Between the planets and the various correspondences was a complex system of harmony and discord. As John Michell writes in *The View over Atlantis:* ". . . Venus can go with Saturn but not with Mars. Thus a high rounded hill will harmonize with one with a flat top but not with a sharp mountain peak. The two could not therefore stand together. Where nature had placed two hills in discord, Chinese geomancers had the shape of one altered. The top of the peak would be cut off or the rounded hill sharpened with an earthwork or flattened into a high plateau. In this way the paths of the various influences across the country were visibly defined, the very bones of the landscape altered to reflect the celestial symmetry."

On the Nazca plains of Peru a remarkable network of straight lines, together with various figures of men, animals, and symbols, has been etched. The paths and figures were created by removing stones and pebbles to expose the dark earth beneath. It was first discovered by pilots flying over the region. One of the many interpretations is that they are sun paths, so arranged that a person moving along a certain path at the solstice or equinox would see the sun rising or setting on the horizon, straight ahead.

In the course of her travels in Tibet, Alexandra David-Neel saw several "lung-gom-pas runners." These men travel for days across the country without stopping, maintaining an extraordinary speed and proceeding by leaps so that they seem to rebound from the earth each time their feet touch it. They always pursue exactly straight tracks, even when these lead over mountains. Alexandra David-Neel supposed that the runners' strength must be the result of prolonged physical and spiritual training. No doubt this was a part of it, but the fact that they pursued straight tracks even when these led over difficult terrain suggests, in the light of what we now know, that they might have possessed the secret of harnessing the earth force. Really advanced lung-gom-pas, it is said, could glide through the air without ever touching the ground with their feet.

Magical Flight

In other words they could fly. There are many legends of feats of magical flight performed by the ancient Britons. Bladud, an ancient magician said to fly using stones, crashed where St. Paul's Cathedral now stands in London. But another

British magician, Abiris, is said to have flown all the way to Greece without mishap. Fairy tales? Perhaps. But John Michell has a theory about magical flight. He believes that flying on a stone or other conveyance was made possible by using the magnetic force of the leys, which harnessed celestial energy. Many of the mysterious buildings of antiquity, he believes—notably Stonehenge and the Pyramids—were constructed in order to effect this fusion of terrestrial and celestial forces. This is why the cabalistic number for fusion, 1746, is to be found in their proportions. Furthermore, the energies thus generated could be employed for numerous other purposes, especially the construction of the huge monuments that survive today.

Some would say that to speculate so wildly is irresponsible. But the mysteries remain. There is no doubt that the impressive achievements of our technological civilization have been bought at a price and have resulted in a loss of coordination between human beings and their environment. Both are in jeopardy today. Perhaps we should no longer dismiss the magical and psychic sciences of our remote forebears as nonsense and superstition. In the present plight of the world, perhaps we could do with a little magic—which might just be another name for a long-lost science.

4. King Arthur: Man or Myth?

"He drew his sword Caliburn, called upon the name of the Blessed Virgin, and rushed forward at full speed into the thickest ranks of the enemy. Every man whom he struck, calling upon God as he did so, he killed at a single blow. He did not slacken his onslaught until he had dispatched four hundred and seventy men with his sword Caliburn. When the Britons saw this, they poured after him in close formation dealing death on every side. . . ."

King Arthur's defeat of Saxon invaders in southwest England is full of a superhuman heroism typical of the book it comes from: Geoffrey of Monmouth's *History of the Kings of Britain*. It was this 12th-century mixture of fantasy and fact that gave us the Arthurian legend as we know it today.

Behind the legend stands the dim figure of a 5th-century British warrior who may have led Romanized, Christian, Celtic peoples in a last great stand against barbarian Anglo-Saxon invaders. From Denmark and Germany wave upon wave of these militant migrants had invaded England after Roman rule collapsed there in about A.D. 400. In the hands of historians, poets, and romancers, Arthur grew from a little-known war leader to a great national hero whose exploits shone forth from an otherwise obscure, gloomy corner of British history. Arthur's deeds inspired pride in their nation's remote but glorious past among future generations of British readers—including the English, against whose Anglo-Saxon ancestors Arthur had traditionally fought. The man and his legend still hold a strange fascination.

But did he ever live? Do the tales woven around him enshrine a man or a myth? Recent studies of old texts and sites linked with the Arthurian legend lead some scholars to answer "yes" to both questions; others remain skeptical. To explore the question of

Arthur's identity, let us first see something of how the tales told about him took shape.

The Earliest Evidence

The oldest-known written evidence of Arthur consists of scanty references in early medieval copies by monks of much older manuscripts, most of them handed down by word of mouth. Three manuscripts are especially important. The first is a copy of a mid-6th-century Latin work by a monk named Gildas—a tedious and largely inaccurate writer who mentions a British defeat of the Saxons at the siege of Mount Badon. Gildas credits no individual leader with this victory, which apparently halted for a while the Saxon advance across England. The second source, the 10th-century *Welsh Annals*, firmly links Arthur's name with the Battle of Badon. They refer, too, to "the strife of Camlann in which Arthur and Medraut (Modred) perished." Such annals were based on yearly entries kept by monks in the Dark Ages to help them reckon the dates of Church feast days. They are often reliable guides to actual people and events. But because their starting points were often arbitrary, putting accurate dates to the events they describe is sometimes difficult.

The third early source is a *History of the Britons* compiled in the early 800s in North Wales by Nennius, a cleric translating already ancient Welsh tales into Latin. Nennius calls Arthur the Britons' *dux bellorum* (commander-in-chief), not king, at Mount Badon. Nennius goes on to list 11 more battles in which Arthur fought, based it seems on an old Welsh poem. Much of his account appears authentic, but Nennius also describes "marvels," including Arthur's son's grave which apparently altered in length each time Nennius measured it. Already, it seems, we are crossing the border from fact to fantasy.

By the time Nennius wrote his *History*, Welsh legends had firmly enshrined Arthur as a Celtic hero overcoming giants, witches, and monsters. Written in the 10th century, the poem *The Spoils of Annwn* features Arthur's overseas quest to the land of the dead for a magic cauldron—the prototype, perhaps, for the Holy Grail, a vessel that figures in later Arthurian legend. Celtic tales, too, told of heroes like Gwalchmai and Llenlleawc, patterns for the Arthurian knights Gawain and Lancelot.

Arthur's wife Guinevere first appeared in Celtic form, as Gwenhwyfar. But what is lacking is any real proof that such characters did indeed exist.

By 1100 Arthurian tales told in Wales had also reached France and beyond. In Italy, a doorway at Modena Cathedral actually featured a sculpture showing Guinevere rescued by Arthur, Gawain, and Kay.

Medieval Accounts

It was in the 12th century that Arthur's adventures began to assume their familiar literary shape. In 1125 an English chronicler named William of Malmesbury called for an authentic account of the man then hailed as Britain's national hero. He hoped that an authenticated biography and the discovery of Arthur's unknown burial place would discredit such fantasies as the legend that Arthur would one day return. Written about 1135, Geoffrey of Monmouth's lively *History of the Kings of Britain* claimed to be just such a factual account. However, the book was a stew concocted from old Celtic legends and histories and spiced by the writer's own vivid imagination.

Geoffrey tells how Merlin the magician helped the British king Uther Pendragon seduce Igerna, the wife of the Duke of Cornwall. From this union Arthur was born at Tintagel Castle. Crowned king at the age of 15, Arthur subdued much of Europe with his knights and his sword Caliburn (also called Excalibur). He set up court at Caerleon in Wales. At Camblam Arthur killed his rebellious son Modred, the fruit of an incestuous liaison, but was himself mortally wounded and taken to the Isle of Avalon to be tended. Brave, generous, and chivalrous, and with a mysterious beginning and ending, Geoffrey's Arthur emerged as a world figure, appealing hugely to the medieval love of chivalry, adventure, and mystery.

Subsequent writers embellished the story. In 1155 Robert Wace's French translation of Geoffrey's history anticipates the wounded Arthur's return from Avalon, and mentions for the first time the now famous Round Table. Less than half a century later Layamon's English version of Wace explained the table as a device to stop precedence quarrels among Arthur's knights. It also had Arthur shipped to Avalon by Morgan, a fairy queen. The tale that the boy Arthur won Britain's crown by drawing a sword from a stone emerged in the early 1200s, in Robert de Borron's *Merlin*.

Meanwhile other legends inspired the late 12th-century French romancer Chrétien de Troyes to write long poems about the amours and wondrous adventures—including the quest for the Holy Grail—of the chivalrous knights of Arthur's court at Camelot. Chrétien demoted Arthur himself to an impotent figurehead, whose wife was seduced by Lancelot.

Arthurian stories snowballed during the Middle Ages. They found their richest expression in Sir Thomas Malory's 15th-century English *Morte d'Arthur* (Death of Arthur). This work sets its last poignant scene in Glastonbury, Somerset, renowned as the Arthurian Avalon long before Malory wrote.

Plainly, much of the matter in most of these Arthurian stories is fiction—so much in fact that some people believe that historians simply invented Arthur to plug a gap in Britain's national history. But at least Arthurian legend was based on old Celtic tales of remembered events: some lost, others garbled during the centuries of retelling before men wrote them down.

Some scholars seeking to sift fact from folklore believe old documents do prove that Arthur lived. But skeptics find many of their arguments tortuous and unconvincing. For instance, whole theories have been underpinned by a medieval scribe's supposed misspelling of a single word.

At least, the Arthurians maintain, we have the names of actual places linked with Arthur's name. Several stand out: Tintagel, where he was apparently born; Camelot and Caerleon, where he held court; Glastonbury, where he died. Then there are the 13 battle sites listed in Nennius and the Welsh annals.

These sites, Arthurian scholars supposed, might hold archaeological clues helping to prove that the hero had once truly lived, reigned, and fought.

Tintagel

In some cases the first difficulty was finding a site to fit its place name. Tintagel at least posed no such problem. Geoffrey of Monmouth, who first linked Tintagel with Arthur, described a castle standing high on a coast and surrounded by sea except for a rocky isthmus joining its rock to the mainland. This description exactly fits a particular headland in North Cornwall. The headland formed part of the manor of Bossinney, listed in 1086 in *Domesday Book*. *Domesday Book* mentioned no headland castle, but archaeological studies begun in the 1800s revealed traces of ancient fortification, as well as later works. You can still see the huge bank that once commanded the landward approaches to the headland. A deep ditch fronts the bank and a palisade once crowned it. To reach the headland, people had to thread their way along a narrow passage between the ditch end and a steep-sided rock. On the peninsula itself there are traces of a great stone hall and a small chapel comprising simply nave and chancel. There were also no doubt smaller, wooden buildings which have long since disappeared. Disappointingly, however, it turned out that this stronghold was built at least 600 years' later than Arthurian times. Carved stonework discovered there in the 1800s suggests a date of about 1150 for the complex. That makes it the undoubted remains of a castle built by Henry I's illegitimate son Reginald soon after 1141 when Henry created him Earl of Cornwall. Significantly, Earl Reginald's half-brother Earl Robert of Gloucester was Geoffrey of Monmouth's patron. Almost certainly, then, Geoffrey located Arthur's birth at Tintagel to flatter the royal family whose patronage he valued. It is true Geoffrey first wrote his account of Arthur before the medieval castle had been built, but that version of his history has disappeared. Geoffrey probably produced the surviving version in about 1145, adding Tintagel as a topical—and tactful—afterthought.

If Tintagel was indeed first fortified as late as the 1140s, then it hardly seems likely that Arthur could have been born there. But evidence that there were stone buildings on the site as early as the 400s supports the claims of the Arthurians. Excavations in the early 1930s unearthed not only medieval ruins, but traces of no less than eight earlier monastic structures, all protected by the same bank and ditch that the medieval builders later reinforced. Among the ruins, the archaeologists found what they believed were the remains of monks' cells, a sacristy, a guest house, a library, and a dining hall. Proof of the monastery's date—and of its affluence—lies in numerous fragments of imported pottery found on the site. These include Samian ware of Roman times, some with crosses stamped inside the base indicating a Christian use; big Mediterranean-type jars for holding wine and olive oil; and mortars used for mashing food, probably French in origin.

The presence of such imported pottery strongly suggests that the monastery at Tintagel flourished in the late 400s and early 500s. A Celtic settlement therefore stood upon Tintagel at about the year of Arthur's reputed birth. Moreover, this was no ordinary settlement, but probably the largest complex of its kind anywhere in Celtic Britain. Even the skeptics must find these facts remarkable. In spite of the lack of trustworthy written proof, many people may still feel that Arthur and Tintagel must have been connected, though scarcely in the way that Geoffrey described: few mothers give birth in a monastery.

Where was Camelot?

Locating the place where Arthur is reputed to have been born proved a good deal easier than the next task—that is, establishing just where the shadowy monarch held court. Where was that world-famous Camelot? Caerleon, Winchester, and London have all been named by medieval writers. Caerleon does indeed contain impressive ruins, but they were Roman, and the so-called "Round Table" there is in fact what remains of a Roman amphitheater. Winchester Castle contains a massive circular table of ancient oak. Could this be the vital clue? Unfortunately, radiocarbon dating carried out in the 1970s demonstrated that the timber was after all of medieval date. The explanation is that from the 13th century growing interest in Arthuriana resulted in numerous courtly entertainments called Round Tables, where men and women imitated the feasts, dances, and jousting that they imagined had enlivened Arthur's court. In 1348, for example, England's Edward III instigated the Order of the Garter partly to revive the traditions of Arthurian knighthood. Later still, England's Tudor kings claimed Arthur as an ancestor (they were after all partly Welsh, which was something) and indeed a painted Tudor rose appears in the center of Winchester's Round Table.

Camelot's claim to be the seat of Arthur's rule is not made easier by the fact that there is no town or city in England or Wales of that name. Chrétien de Troyes was vague about its setting. Malory—evidently influenced by the Table there—equated Camelot with Winchester. Other writers claimed that Camelot could still be seen in Wales—a reference, some think, to Caerleon's (or maybe Caerwent's) ancient Roman walls.

37

South Cadbury Castle

In 1542 an antiquarian named John Leland suggested another possibility. He wrote: "At South Cadbury stands Camallate, sometime a famous town or castle. The people can tell nothing there but that they have heard say that Arthur much resorted to Camallate." No one can be certain why Leland placed Camelot at South Cadbury in Somerset, in southwest England. It may have been, as he wrote, that the local people simply believed that it had been there. Perhaps a combination of local place-names and geographical features influenced him. He certainly corrupted the "Camel" of two local villages called Queen Camel and West Camel into "Camallate." He may well have been impressed with nearby Cadbury Hill, a steep-sided limestone peak some 500 feet high which dominates the surrounding country-side. Crowning the hill is South Cadbury Castle. No castle stood here in Leland's time, for the banks and ditches, now largely wooded, that ring the hill are the remains of an Iron Age fort built on the summit before the Romans came to Britain in 55 B.C.

In Leland's time, it seems, a good deal of largely unrecorded legend was gathering about the hill. Later written tradition locates Arthur's palace on the level summit; forges a subterranean link between two hillside wells; and holds that the hill is hollow and that Arthur and his knights lay asleep inside, to emerge in time of national need.

Whatever Cadbury Hill's Arthurian connections might have been, its Iron Age fort alone suggested this to be a site worth investigation. Accordingly, for one reason or another, archaeologists have been burrowing in the hill on and off since the late 19th century.

In 1890, South Cadbury's rector reported opening a hut-dwelling on the summit and discovering a flagstone that—contrary to workers' expectations—did not lead to King Arthur's cave. Twenty-three years later a somewhat sketchy but better documented dig revealed pottery attributed to late Celtic times. But justification for large-scale excavation emerged only in the 1950s when plowing turned up surface finds including scraps of Tintagel-type pottery and a piece of glass from Dark Age France. It was not much. But it was enough to convince Ralegh Radford, a leading British archaeologist, that South Cadbury Castle had indeed been Camelot. Moreover in 1955 an aerial photographic

Glastonbury Tor rising above the fields of the North Somerset plain. In Arthurian times the hill was a peninsula flanked by shallow sea and marsh. It has often been identified with Avalon, where the wounded Arthur was traditionally carried to die. (*King Arthur: Man or Myth?*)

In 1542 an antiquarian named John Leland wrote: "At South Cadbury stands Camallate, sometime a famous town or castle." An archaeological excavation from 1965-70 on the summit of South Cadbury Hill in Somerset (pictured here) revealed a wealthy Dark Ages settlement and a substantial fort which may well have been Arthur's Camelot. (*King Arthur: Man or Myth?*)

The monks of Glastonbury Abbey claimed to have found the bones of Arthur and Guinevere buried near the Abbey Church's Lady Chapel in 1191. The remains were moved to a black marble tomb at the spot illustrated above, but the tomb was destroyed and the bones lost during the Dissolution of the Monasteries. (*King Arthur: Man or Myth?*)

survey revealed dark patches on the pale, cultivated summit—crop-marks betraying extensive areas of ancient soil disturbance. Interest in a major excavation now gained momentum.

In 1965 leading archaeologists and Arthurian scholars formed the Camelot Research Committee which found enough money to finance a trial dig in 1966, under Leslie Alcock, an authority on the archaeology of Dark Age Britain. What followed proved so fruitful that the project ran on to 1970.

The first problem was deciding where to work. The 18-acre summit was too big to excavate entirely. The team thus set out to find those areas most likely to reward investigation. Surveyors drew up a contour plan, and the archaeologists used a banjo-shaped metal detector to criss-cross the hilltop in a search for buried metal objects. At the same time, local variations in the soil's electrical conductivity showed up the sites of old, filled-in post-holes where upright building supports had once stood.

The first season's digging hinted at a long but remote history of habitation. Neolithic, Bronze Age, and Iron Age peoples had all left their mark upon the hill. More importantly for the Camelot Research Committee, so had Celtic peoples of Arthurian times. The personal possessions found seemed unexciting: a small misshapen iron knife and fragments of Tintagel-type pottery. Significantly, though, these fragments came from each of the three trial sites. This suggested extensive Dark Age occupation by a relatively wealthy group. But what most excited some archaeologists were the remains of a Dark Age defensive wall and other structures uncovered during the five seasons' work.

Trenches cut across the inner defensive rampart revealed seven phases of building and rebuilding between pre-Roman and medieval times. One rampart in particular produced the kind of evidence that enabled scholars to say with certainty that it had been a barrier erected in Arthurian times by Celts, presumably against the Saxons. It survived as a rather low narrow mound of rubble, but in places it was plain that the outer surface had been faced by stones, with gaps once filled by posts—supports for a timber breastwork built above the rubble mound. Moreover alignments of the stones inside the core revealed that the walls had consisted of a timber framework held in place by rubble heaped up on the beams. Presumably defenders would have stood, protected by the breastwork, on a wooden platform placed above the stonework. The fort's Celtic builders had evidently lacked the Romans' skill in dressing stones and bonding them with mortar. Instead, they plundered dressed stones from nearby Roman ruins, and in particular a temple standing on a hill. They then built their drystone wall somewhat in the fashion of the pre-Roman Britons. Unsophisticated, maybe, but impressive none-theless, for their defense extended some 1200 yards, surrounding the entire surface of the hilltop. Leslie Alcock felt that the sheer size of the area enclosed implied that South Cadbury had acted as a base for an army large by late Celtic British standards—possibly created from the independent Celtic kingdoms' small fighting forces, gathered at this strategically important site to halt the Saxons' attacks on southwestern Britain.

Tell-tale soil stains derived from rotted timbers reinforce this picture of military strength by helping archaeologists to visualize the impressive gate tower that commanded the southwest entrance to the fort. We must imagine here a narrow wooden passage led into the wall, closed by two pairs of doors and capped by a protected lookout platform raised above the general level of the rampart.

Late on in the excavations another exciting find appeared. Pits and post-holes confusingly covered the summit center—burrow-ings spread out over several centuries. From this confusion close study extracted a pattern made up of rows of post-holes. In Arthurian times these holes had evidently held posts supporting a timber hall over 60 feet long and half as wide, with a screen near one end separating one-third from the rest. Wooden posts had apparently helped to support a thatched roof laid on a wooden framework. In this primitive hall the camp's com-mander-in-chief had almost certainly held counsel and issued commands. Arthur himself, perhaps?

This barnlike building is a far cry from the splendid palaces in which writers describe Arthur holding court. But the real Camelot—if it ever existed—may well have been more like a "Wild West" frontier fort than a sophisticated city.

Glastonbury and Avalon

Twelve miles northwest from Cadbury Hill the steep-sided mass of Glastonbury Tor rises above the fields of the north

Somerset plain. In Arthurian times the hill was a peninsula flanked by shallow sea and marsh. Antique lettering on some modern maps identifies Glastonbury Tor as the Isle of Avalon, where the mortally wounded Arthur was traditionally carried. Here, too, the legend states that he died and his body was buried low down on the hill's western flank. Reports of Arthur's links with Glastonbury date from about 1150, when Caradoc of Llancarfan wrote a *Life of St. Gildas.* Caradoc describes how the Abbot of Glastonbury helped Arthur rescue Guinevere from King Melwas, her abductor. But people seem to have connected Glastonbury with Avalon in the 1190s. By then, the monks of Glastonbury Abbey claimed to have found the bones of Arthur and Guinevere buried near the abbey church's Lady Chapel. Gerald of Wales, who visited the abbey soon afterward, claimed that he saw the bones. He also mentioned a golden lock of hair that turned to powder when seized from the grave.

Thirty years later, Ralph of Coggeshall described the exhumation. But the least fanciful account—based largely on oral tradition—appeared a century later. This was by Adam of Domerham, a Glastonbury monk. On two important points accounts agreed: a lead cross had marked the grave, and the grave had been sited between two ancient pyramids. Otherwise the versions differed tantalizingly. A "hollowed oak" had held the bodies, claimed Gerald; Ralph referred to a sarcophagus. Ralph wrote that the Latin text upon the cross had read: "Here lies the famous King Arthur, in the Isle of Avalon buried." Gerald phrased the inscription differently and included a mention of Guinevere.

To honor their famous find the monks installed them in a superbly carved double tomb within the abbey church. Adam of Domerham's account tells what happened next. At Easter 1278, King Edward I watched while the tomb was opened and the bones removed. Arthur's were "of great size" and Guinevere's "of marvellous beauty." Edward ceremonially laid the bones in caskets, minus the skulls which were removed for public veneration. The tomb containing the caskets was then resited before the high altar.

During the Reformation, religious zealots smashed the tomb, and no one knows what happened to the bones. Researchers came across the tomb's foundations in 1931 in the ruined abbey. Traces of the original burial persisted, too. John Leland saw what was claimed to be the cross after 1540. An engraving of it features in William Camden's *Britannia* early in the 1600s. The cross apparently survived at Wells until the 18th century and then simply vanished.

However, in 1962 archaeologists discovered what could have been the very grave from which the medieval monks had lifted Arthur's bones. Digging into the old cemetery south of the site of Glastonbury's Lady Chapel they found traces of a broad pit that may have held the base of a massive cross. Some three yards south of this lay fragments of an ancient mausoleum. Cross and mausoleum were probably the "pyramids" already mentioned. Writing early in the 12th century, William of Malmesbury had implied that both were really crosses, built up in several stages.

Between the two, archaeologists found a large hole had been dug and filled in about 1190. Proof of that date were distinctive stone chips lying in the hole—waste struck from masonry by the chisels of masons constructing the nearby Lady Chapel in the 1180s.

Here, then was Arthur's grave. Or was it? Skeptics claim that the 12th-century monks had forged both grave and antique lettering upon the cross. They had the motive: they badly needed cash to make good fire damage done in 1184. By claiming to hold Arthur's bones they would attract pilgrims—and donations—to Glastonbury.

However, supporters of the monks' account claim that the cross, although post-Arthurian, really did predate the medieval exhumation. They argue that St. Dunstan, then Abbot of Glastonbury, could have had it made about 945 when he removed old grave markers in the course of building up the level of the cemetery. From Arthur's burial, so this theory goes, St. Dunstan took away a stone slab bearing a simple 6th-century inscription and replaced it with the cross—a more elaborate memorial in keeping with Arthur's growing reputation. Disappointingly, no Arthurian period pottery turned up at Glastonbury Abbey. But a dig on the top of nearby Glastonbury Tor bared scraps of amphoras, old hearths, and other proofs of Dark Age settlement. Who the settlers were, however, remains a mystery.

Arthur's Battles
So far we have looked at the evidence for Arthur's supposed

birthplace, his capital, and the place where he was buried. The other sites associated with his name are chiefly battlefields. Dark Age battles were generally fought at strategically important river crossings. Those linked with Arthur's name suggest he campaigned all over Britain. Of the 13 battles named in early works, 12 are victories from the old Welsh list reported in Nennius' *History of the Britons*; the 13th and last is the final "Camlann" cited in the *Welsh Annals*. Unfortunately Nennius does not say who Arthur conquered and it is hard to find the sites described. His first battle took place at the mouth of the River Glein. There were two English rivers called Glen but there were doubtless more before the Anglo-Saxons changed their names. So we have no idea where Arthur fought his first battle.

Nennius sites the next four battles on the River Dubglas in a district named as Linnuis. Some scholars suggest that Linnuis was one of two Roman sites called Lindum. The more likely of the two would place the battle in a Scottish valley called Glen Douglas near Loch Lomond. There, Arthur could have fought against the Scottish kingdom of Dalriada though four times seems improbable. Another explanation is that Linnuis is a scribe's misspelling of *lininuis*, a word supposedly derived from *Lindinienses*, the name of a tribal group living near two "Dubglas" rivers that cross the north Dorset Downs of southern England. Leslie Alcock argues that this would be a likely area for Arthur to engage Saxons advancing from the east.

The 6th, 8th, and 10th battles named by Nennius fit no known place names. But the 7th was "the battle of the Caledonian Forest" (the "wood of Celidon"). This must mean a battle fought in Scotland, which the Romans called "Caledonia." Just where it happened and who Arthur fought there we cannot say.

The 9th battle occurred in the "city of the legion" which scholars identify as either Chester or Caerleon. Arthur reputedly won his 10th victory at Agned. Geoffrey of Monmouth equates Agned with Edinburgh. The hill there called Arthur's Seat does hold traces of a Dark Age fort. But some old manuscripts name the battle site as Breguoin or Breguein—names that set the scholars scurrying off to places in England.

The last two battles were the crucial ones for Arthur. Mount Badon seems to have represented Arthur's greatest triumph. Here, he felled 960 men, single-handed, in one day, Nennius declares, in true heroic mein. The *Welsh Annals* imply that the whole battle lasted three days and nights, during which Arthur "carried the cross of our Lord Jesus Christ on his shoulders." Gildas calls the struggle a siege. Moreover, he makes it plain that Badon was a British, Christian victory against the invading Saxon heathens. The date of Badon is debatable—A.D. 490 or 518 appear the likeliest contenders. The place is also uncertain. It could have been one of the five Badburys (named from an Old English word for Badda's fort—Badda being possibly some legendary Saxon hero). Bath in Avon (or rather, a nearby hill) is another possibility because "Badon" would have been pronounced "Bathon" in the old British tongue.

This brings us to the last struggle—the "Camlann" of the *Welsh Annals* and Geoffrey of Monmouth's "Camlam." It was this evidently civil strife (variously dated 510 and 539) in which Arthur was killed and which apparently left the British kingdoms divided against their common Anglo-Saxon foes. The names of the Cornish River Camel and Somerset Cam have helped to make each popular as the likely battle site. Slaughterbridge near Camelford in Cornwall does have an old memorial stone called "Arthur's tomb." But place-name experts identify Camlann with Camboglanna, a Roman fort in northwest England and a likely site for civil war between two British armies.

The uncertainty surrounding Arthur's battle sites has led some scholars to dismiss the whole list as legendary. Others think that Arthur's name became attached to battles fought by several warriors. Others declare that he was a purely northern figure, and that all southern so-called Arthurian sites are spurious. Evidence for this theory comes largely from a sentence in Aneurin's 6th-century *Y Gododdin*. Describing the mighty warrior Gwawrddur, Aneurin wrote: "He glutted black ravens on the wall of the fort, though he was not Arthur." In other words, in battle Gwawrddur was as valiant as Arthur, slaughtering enough enemies to gorge the birds that feed on carrion. Traditionalists claim this shows that the Arthur of Tintagel and Camelot was already venerated as a national hero by the 9th century when *Y Gododdin* was probably first written down.

This chapter has merely nibbled at the mystery surrounding King Arthur. What underlying truths, if any, have we managed to expose? Certainly not the Arthur of medieval chivalry and splendor. Arthur was more probably commander-in-chief of a British force that briefly stemmed the westward-flowing Anglo-Saxon flood. He may possibly have been an obscure Scottish chieftain's son. One fact is certain: the only datable evidence for Arthur lies in archaeology and old manuscripts. The first provides no mention of his name. The second is scanty, ambiguous, and unreliable.

5. The Enigma of Caspar Hauser

On Whitmonday in the year 1828 Georg Weichmann, a shoemaker of Nuremberg, Germany, noticed an oddly dressed youth of about 16 wandering aimlessly in the square near his home. The youth, a total stranger, looked like he might be drunk by the way he moved so uncertainly. Weichmann approached him.

The youngster handed Weichmann a letter addressed to the captain of the 6th Cavalry Regiment, then stationed in the Bavarian city. The shoemaker took the time to find out where the captain was housed, led the boy there, and left him after ringing the bell.

When the door was opened by a servant, the youth handed over his letter and said in a broken dialect, "I want to be a soldier like my father was." The captain was away, but his wife ordered food and drink to be brought to the young stranger, who looked worn out and could walk only with difficulty. He rejected what was offered, but when plain black bread and water were put before him, ate as though he were starved. When asked who he was and where he came from, he seemed not to understand what was being said to him. To all queries he either repeated, "I want to be a soldier like my father was," or grunted a few disconnected words such as "horse," "home," "my father"—all of which he seemed to have learned by heart. He frequently pointed to his feet and wept, as though in pain.

When the captain returned, he could get no further with the boy. The envelope addressed to him turned out to have two letters within, both of which added to the mystery rather than clearing it. The introductory letter said that the writer, who did not identify himself, had had the child left with him on October 7, 1812, and had never let him go out of the house. It added: "If his parents had lived, he might have been well educated; for if you show him anything, he can do it right off." The second letter, written to give the impression that it was from the youth's mother to the writer of the first letter, was dated 1812, 16 years before. It said that the youngster's name was Caspar, and it asked that he be taken to Nuremberg at the age of 17 because his dead father had belonged to the 6th Cavalry Regiment. Since the 6th Cavalry had been stationed in Nuremberg for only a short time, the letter could hardly have been written so long before. Both letters were believed to be forgeries.

The captain decided that the matter was one for civil authorities, and turned the youth over to the police. At the police station the same situation occurred. The youth made no sensible answers to questions, seeming to have no comprehension of what was going on around him. Sometimes he repeated his few stock of words or pointed, weeping, to his feet. When a kindly soldier gave him a small coin he was delighted and called out, "horse, horse," making signs that he wanted to hang the bright object around a horse's neck. His manner was that of a three-year-old child, but no one could decide whether he was a born idiot or someone who had lost his wits. A few even suspected that he might be an imposter. When provided with paper, pen, and ink he immediately wrote the name Caspar Hauser in a firm legible hand. He could write nothing else, and no more information could be obtained from him since his replies were irrelevant. He ignored threats of punishment, showing neither fear nor defiance. Finally he was taken to a nearby prison for vagabonds and suspicious persons; there he fell asleep instantly on a hard straw bed.

Apart from the two letters, Caspar's only possessions were some pious tracts and the clothes he stood up in—worn shoes, a red leather hat lined with yellow silk, a black silk kerchief around his throat, and a gray suit that looked as if it had been made from the cast-offs of a gentleman. In his pocket he had a white handkerchief with a red border and the initials C.H. worked in red.

When Caspar wept his face became ugly, like the puckered face of a crying baby, but when he smiled his face lit up so attractively that people said it was the face of an innocent child. The soles of his feet were as soft as a baby's, as though he had never before worn shoes and never walked. In fact, he moved like a child learning how to walk, often losing his balance and falling.

47

The jailer became deeply interested in Caspar and put him in a room in his own apartment where he could watch him unobserved through a secret opening in the door. After careful observation the jailer decided that his charge was neither an idiot nor a madman nor an imposter. In his opinion Caspar was a child in experience and behavior—if not in age—and he believed some great mystery lay beneath this unnatural state.

One day a friendly soldier gave Caspar a white wooden toy horse, which utterly delighted him. When other toy horses were given to him, he was content to play with them all day. He offered each one a tiny portion of his bread and water, and apologized to them if he knocked them over. When he fell off a rocking horse one day and hurt his finger on the floor, he complained that the horse had bitten him. Such behavior is characteristic of the very young.

At first all communication with the strange boy called Caspar Hauser had to be carried on by signs, except for the few words he knew and kept repeating. But under the jailer's careful guidance he began to learn rapidly, showing an eagerness to acquire knowledge on all subjects. About six weeks after his arrival in Nuremberg, the Burgomaster drew out of him a halting account of his previous life.

For as long as he could remember, Caspar said, he had been kept in a cell about six-feet long, four-feet wide, and five-feet high. This tiny room had two shutters that were kept permanently closed. His feet were bare, and he sat and slept on a mat of straw. His food consisted of black bread and water which was placed in his cell while he was asleep. Sometimes the water had a bitter taste and he fell asleep directly after drinking it, when he woke again his clothes had been changed and his nails trimmed. He had two wooden horses and a wooden dog to play with. A man looked after him, but Caspar had never seen his face. Shortly before his departure from the cell this man showed him how to write the words "Caspar Hauser." His impressions of the journey to Nuremberg were confused, as well they might be. On coming into the open air for the first time he fainted, and walking in shoes was a torture to him.

The Burgomaster appealed to anyone who had known Caspar Hauser to come forward, but no one did. The city of Nuremberg then adopted him and entrusted him to a Professor Daumer with

A contemporary engraving of Caspar Hauser, a strange youth of about 16 who was found aimlessly wandering the streets of Nuremburg, Germany in 1828. Unable to speak more than a few words, he had been imprisoned for as long as he could remember in a tiny cell. Thought to be the missing prince of Baden by some, and an imposter by others, he was murdered by an unknown assailant in 1833. (*The Enigma of Caspar Hauser*)

whose family Caspar went to live. His good nature and open-heartedness impressed everyone, and one observer described him as "a being such as we may imagine in Paradise before the Fall."

The appearance of this mysterious youth from out of nowhere created great excitement throughout Europe. Rumors abounded. Some said that Caspar had been kept in isolation to hide his noble birth. This idea gained more and more credence—and accusing fingers pointed finally at the Grand Duke of Baden.

The Grand Duke of Baden

The ruling family of Baden was renowned for the extravagance and immorality of its princes and the violence that ended so many of their lives. Karlsruhe, the capital of Baden, had been founded in the early 18th century by the Margrave Charles William who kept a harem of 160 beautiful girls. He was succeeded in 1738 by his grandson Charles Frederick who ruled for 73 years. Three sons were born to Charles Frederick by his first wife, and after her death in 1783 the 60-year-old Margrave married a 19-year-old lady-in-waiting at the court. Unknown to him, she was already the mistress of his third son Ludwig. On the day of her marriage she was created Baroness and later Countess Hochberg, but because she was not of royal birth, her children stood little chance of succeeding her elderly husband. Within six years she gave birth to four boys and a girl—popularly believed to be Ludwig's children.

The margrave's eldest son Charles Ludwig died in 1801 after his carriage overturned, although no one else was injured. It was said that the prince had received a blow on his head. Even at the time the death was considered suspicious, and in later years it was regarded as the first unholy fruit of an alliance between Ludwig and the Countess to ensure the succession of their children.

In 1806 Napoleon created the aged margrave a grand duke and arranged a marriage between his stepdaughter, Stephanie de Beauharnais, and the Grand Duke's 20-year-old grandson and heir, Charles. This was a setback for the conspirators, but they met it by encouraging Charles to ignore his young wife by a life of dissipation. For four years he lived apart from her, but then her beauty and intelligence won through and he settled down to married life. In 1811 she bore a daughter, and in that same year the aged Grand Duke died and young Charles became the new ruler. In 1812 Stephanie bore a son. Was this baby switched with another to do him out of his succession? Did he appear 16 years later as Caspar Hauser?

Those who believed that Caspar was the Grand Duke's rightful heir said he had been smuggled out of the palace like this. The Countess Hochberg took a recently born and sickly baby from one of her peasants. She then dressed herself up as "the White Lady," a ghost traditionally said to make its appearance just before a death in the royal family, and concealed the ailing baby under her veil. Making her way to the newborn prince's bedchamber along secret passages which had a secret door in a tapestry, she could give a ghostly impression of appearing and disappearing. A lackey who caught sight of her fell to the ground in a faint. A watchman saw her vanish through the wall.

The royal baby's two nurses had been drugged, it was said, and the wet nurse was allowed out of the palace for the night. The substitution was easily and swiftly made, and the infant prince removed to a castle outside the city. When the wet nurse returned to the nursery she was refused entry on the grounds that the baby was very ill. She tried to get to Grand Duchess Stephanie but was told that she also was ill and too weak to be disturbed. When the wet nurse finally managed to reach the Grand Duchess she found the royal mother frantic with anxiety because she too was being denied sight of the child. Later that night the Grand Duchess was told that her baby was dead, having been in the care of Margrave Ludwig's physician. She never saw his dead body, nor did the wet nurse. The body was examined by doctors who had never seen the baby alive. The verdict of death was cerebral meningitis, which could mean that the skull had been opened in an effort at treatment. At all events, the body was unrecognizable when the Grand Duke saw it. This substitution theory requires a large number of confederates, especially among the palace servants, but it need not be rejected on that count.

In 1815 the Grand Duke, who was only 29, was struck by a lingering illness that he came to believe was caused by the steady administration of poison. The following year a second son was born. For a year he was closely guarded by trusted attendants, but a week after his first birthday he developed a fever. The Grand Duchess' physician did not want Margrave Ludwig's physician to attend the child, as had been the case with the first boy, but he was overruled. The child died the next day. Grand Duke Charles followed him to the grave a year later and Margrave Ludwig at last took power. One of his first acts was to recognize the Hochberg children as his heirs. Ludwig was still ruling when Caspar Hauser turned up in Nuremberg.

By then, in 1828, the Countess was dead and Grand Duke Ludwig had become a prey to morbid melancholy. Ludwig's chief aide was a certain Major Hennenhofer, who had been instrumental in the successful plot to abduct the royal heir in 1812. He is said to have wanted the stolen prince killed at the beginning, but was overruled by the Countess who felt that the survival of the prince was her only hold over Ludwig to prevent him from marrying and producing other children that would supplant hers. If Caspar were the prince, he was still a threat to Ludwig, so why was he allowed to go free? The substitution theorists say that the plotters thought he would disappear into the Bavarian army. Since that plan had miscarried, and Caspar was protected by the city of Nuremberg, Hennenhofer reverted to his original plan of assassination. In October 1829 Caspar was discovered unconscious from a stab wound in the cellar of Professor Daumer's house. On recovering, he said he had been attacked by a man wearing a black mask. Caspar's critics, who say he was never anything but a cunning imposter, say he must have stabbed himself in order to regain the limelight. Whatever the truth, he was removed from the Daumer household to the care of a Nuremberg businessman. At this point in the mystery, Philip, 4th Earl Stanhope, enters.

Lord Stanhope

Lord Stanhope belonged to an English family noted for its eccentricity and wild behavior. Was it only a whim that made him interested in the case? Whatever it was that drew him, he made several visits to Baden. He called on both the Grand Duke and Hennenhofer and ingratiated himself with Grand Duchess Stephanie, who was greatly agitated on learning that her firstborn son might still be alive. From this time on, the erratic English noble was never without funds, though he had previously been chronically short of money.

In May 1831 Stanhope arrived in Nuremberg and proceeded

to charm himself into Caspar's affections. He showered him with clothes and money, walked arm in arm with him through the streets, and soon began talking of his wish to adopt him. This proposal met with opposition, but Stanhope overcame it all. In November he took Caspar from Nuremberg to Ansbach, a town 20 miles closer to Baden, lodged him with a Protestant pastor named Meyer, and employed Police Lieutenant Hickel to act as his bodyguard. An unhappy period in Caspar's life began.

Meyer was short-tempered and suspicious of Caspar; Hickel actually believed he was an imposter. In spite of escaping outright cruelty because of the wide interest in him, Caspar underwent petty persecution at his guardians' hands. Fortunately for the youth, he formed many friendships in Ansbach, and was eventually apprenticed to a bookbinder. As for Stanhope, no sooner had he inveigled the youth away from Nuremberg than he ceased to spend much time with him. After a while he declared that Caspar was an imposter and left Ansbach. Soon his letters stopped and Caspar was left completely in the care of Meyer and Hickel, whom he came to mistrust. In September 1833 he made a return visit to Nuremberg, where he renewed contacts with old friends and was introduced to the King of Bavaria. The King's mother, Queen Caroline, was an aunt of the heir said to have died in 1812, having been a princess of Baden. She recognized a family likeness in Caspar and became a firm believer that he must be her nephew.

A few weeks after this royal recognition Stanhope wrote that he was returning to Ansbach. On his way he visited Baden, apparently leaving at the end of November in the company of Hennenhofer.

On December 11, 1833 the 21-year-old Caspar Hauser returned from a walk in the park with a mortal wound in his side. He told Meyer that a man had asked him his name and, after hearing it, had stabbed him in the ribs. Meyer refused to believe Caspar and charged the young man with having once again inflicted a self-injury to gain attention. Doctors were summoned, but the police were not informed. Three days later it was clear that Caspar was dying. Calm and conscious to the last, he resisted all efforts by Meyer to get him to confess that he was an imposter, and he maintained to the end that the story of the attack on him was true.

Who killed him is unknown. Queen Caroline of Bavaria accused Lord Stanhope to his face of the murder, though no record exists to show that he arrived in Ansbach until after Caspar's death. Whether Caspar Hauser was in truth the missing prince of Baden was never decided and probably never will be. There seems no reason to doubt that for many years of his life before arriving in Nuremberg he was kept closely confined in the manner he described. But all the evidence relating to the ducal family of Baden is largely circumstantial, if persuasive, and is unlikely to be proved.

On his tombstone in Ansbach cemetery are carved the following words: "Here lies Caspar Hauser, Enigma." He remains an enigma to this day.

6. Mysteries of the Sea

The captain of the English brig *Dei Gratia* was the first to see the strange two-masted ship sailing an erratic course, with only the jib and the foretopmast staysail set. Though the vessel was on a starboard tack, the jib was set to port—a sure sign to a sailor that a ship was out of control, the crew either injured or dead. Captain Edward Morehouse decided to close in, but the sea was running high after recent squalls and two hours passed before he was near enough to read the name. It was the *Mary Celeste*.

The Tale of the *Mary Celeste*

Captain Morehouse knew the vessel well. He also knew Captain Benjamin Spooner Briggs, the man in command. Only a month ago their two ships had been loading cargo at neighboring piers in the East River in New York. The *Mary Celeste* had set sail for the Italian port of Genoa on November 5, 1872; 10 days later the *Dei Gratia* had followed across the Atlantic, bound for Gibraltar. Now Morehouse had caught up, only to find the ship drifting halfway between the Azores and the coast of Portugal. No one was at the wheel, no one on deck.

Morehouse sent Oliver Deveau, his first mate, to see what was amiss. Deveau was a large man of great physical strength, described as "absolutely fearless." He and two seamen rowed over to investigate the mystery. The ship seemed deserted. The first thing Deveau did on boarding her was to sound the pumps. He found that one of the pumps had been drawn to let the sounding rod down, so he used the other pump, leaving the first on the deck as he found it. There was a great deal of water between decks, probably as a result of recent storms, two sails that had been set had blown away, and the lower foretopsails were hang-

ing by the corners. In spite of these problems, however, Deveau
established that the *Mary Celeste* was in no danger of sinking.

Deveau and the second mate, John Wright, searched the
vessel; they found no one aboard, alive or dead. They did find
that the binnacle had been stoved in, destroying the compass,
that two of the hatches were off, and that one cask of crude
alcohol in the hold had sprung its lid. Otherwise the cargo
seemed in good order and the ship's wheel, which had not been
lashed, was undamaged. It looked as though the *Mary Celeste*
had carried a yawl on deck, lashed to the main hatch. Two fenders
were in position on the hatch, showing that a yawl could have
been there, and two sets of rails had been removed apparently
in order to launch it.

In the cabin Deveau and Wright discovered that the six starboard windows had been nailed up with planks, but there was
no way of telling if they had been so fastened before the voyage
or during it. The port windows were shut but still let in some
light. Much water had entered the cabin through the open door
and through the skylight that was also open. The clock had been
ruined by the water and much of the bedding and clothing was
wet. Because the linen and clothes were difficult to dry out,
Deveau concluded that they had been made wet by sea water.
He later testified:

"The bed was as it had been left after being slept in—not
made . . . I judged there had been a woman aboard. I saw female
clothing . . . I noticed an impression in the bed, as of a child
having laid there. There seemed to be everything left behind as
if left in a great hurry, but everything in its place. There were
boxes of clothing. There were also work bags with needles,
threads, buttons, books, and a case of instruments, a writing
desk. A harmonium or melodeon was in the cabin."

In those days it was not uncommon for a captain's wife to
accompany him on a voyage, and Sarah Briggs had in fact done
so. The couple had also brought their two-year-old daughter
Sophia Matilda. They had left their other child, seven-year-old
Arthur, with his grandparents in Marion, Massachusetts, to
continue his schooling.

Almost as many legends have attached themselves to the *Mary
Celeste* as there were barnacles on its hold. One of these is that a
half-eaten meal was discovered on the cabin table, and that

breakfast was still cooking in the galley. Deveau's sworn statement shows otherwise. Though the rack for stopping dishes from sliding off the table was in position, he reported, there were no eatables in the cabin, nor was any cooked food found in the galley. Pots and kettles had been washed up and stowed away. An open bottle of medicine was found, which suggested that whoever had taken it had left in too much of a hurry to put the cork back into the bottle. From the meager evidence, it was presumed that the ship had been abandoned some time in mid-morning—late enough for breakfast to have been cleared away, but not before Mrs. Briggs had made the bed. This presumption was partly based on the fact that no New England woman of Sarah Briggs' background would have allowed the beds to remain unmade till late in the morning, even at sea.

Less water had entered the seamen's quarters than the cabin. The seamen's chests were dry, and there were no traces of rust on the razors left behind. The crew had evidently gone in a great hurry, leaving behind as they did not only the contents of their chests—everything of value they possessed—but also their oil-skin boots and even their pipes, articles no sailor would abandon unless in a state of panic.

Looking for some explanation, Deveau studied the logbook in the mate's cabin. The last entry was dated November 24, and it gave the ship's position as 100 miles southwest of San Miguel Island in the Azores. There was some later information jotted on the log slate, found in the captain's cabin. It showed that the next day, November 25, at 8 a.m. the ship passed Santa Maria Island. Eleven days had passed since that final entry had been made. In that time the ship had continued for another 500 miles, apparently on course. For some undetermined period of that time, however, it had been unmanned. The date of the last entry on the log slate does not necessarily mean that the *Mary Celeste* was abandoned on the 25th. In small ships the log is not regarded as very important, and is seldom written up every day. For example, in the 18 days that the *Mary Celeste* had been at sea before sighting the Azores, only seven entries had been made in the log. There was no way of telling exactly when Captain Briggs took his wife, child, and crew of seven onto the yawl—if he actually did so. Neither was there any indication why they had left a sound and seaworthy vessel in an apparent hurry.

To some, the story of the *Mary Celeste* could be seen as a warning that the name of a ship should never be changed. Long John Silver of Stevenson's "Treasure Island" said: "I never knowed any luck as came of changing of a ship's name. Now what a ship was christened, so let her stay, I says." When the future *Mary Celeste* was built on Spencer's Island, Nova Scotia, in 1861, it was christened the *Amazon*. From the start the vessel was an unlucky-one. The first captain died 48 hours after the *Amazon* was registered. On the maiden voyage, it ran into a fishing weir off the coast of Maine and damaged the hull. While being repaired, fire broke out amidships. In the Straits of Dover, it collided with another brig, which sank. By that time the ship had had three captains. Under the fourth, the *Amazon* ran aground on Cape Breton Island and was wrecked. It was salvaged, however, and then passed quickly through two or perhaps three other owners, one of whom renamed it the *Mary Celeste*. As such the vessel was bought by James H. Winchester, founder of an eminent shipping firm that still bears his name in New York. On discovering dry rot in the timbers, he rebuilt the bottom with a copper lining. He also extended the deck cabin and generally put the ship in excellent condition. The *Mary Celeste* had exchanged the red ensign of the British merchant navy for the stars and stripes.

Early in September 1872 the newly named vessel was tied up at Pier 44 in New York's East River being loaded with about 1700 red oak casks of commercial alcohol. In one of her last letters to relatives, Sarah Briggs described her reaction to this cargo, saying that she thought she had gone slightly daft with the "amount of thumping and bumping, of shaking and tossings to and fro of the cargo." She also mentioned "screechings and growlings," which could have been caused by sweating casks of a volatile liquid such as crude alcohol.

At a nearby pier the *Dei Gratia* was taking on a cargo of petroleum, and the two captains, Briggs and Morehouse, dined together the night before the *Mary Celeste* sailed. The curious coincidence that it was the *Dei Gratia* which later found the *Mary Celeste* abandoned was to sow suspicion in the minds of the members of the Board of Inquiry trying to decide what had happened.

Captain Briggs was master of the vessel and part owner,

having purchased a few shares of the ship from Winchester. He was an experienced seaman of 37, robust, correct, and temperate. Having been brought up among New England puritans, he never allowed liquor aboard a vessel under his command.

In after years several grizzled sailors claimed to be survivors of the *Mary Celeste*, but the names of the crew of seven are all known. The first mate was Albert Richardson, who was married to Winchester's niece. Andrew Gilling, the second mate, and Edward Head, the steward-cook, were the other Americans of the crew. The four seamen were all German: Volkert and Boz Lorensen, brothers from Schleswig-Holstein; Arian Martens, and Gottlief Goodschaad (or Gondschatt). In one of her letters to her mother-in-law Sarah Briggs said that she was not sure how smart the crew would prove to be, but Captain Briggs was satisfied they were reliable.

When Deveau and White had completed their examination of the drifting ship, they returned to the *Dei Gratia* to report to Captain Morehouse. In spite of his friendship with Briggs, Morehouse apparently did not go aboard the *Mary Celeste* for a personal look. Either he or Deveau proposed taking the abandoned ship into Gibraltar to claim salvage. Deveau returned to the *Mary Celeste* later that afternoon with two seamen, taking their ship's small boat, a barometer, sextant, compass, watch, and some food prepared by their steward. In two days the *Mary Celeste* was ready to sail and the two ships set out, remaining in sight of each other till they reached the Straits of Gibraltar. At that point a storm separated them. The *Dei Gratia* reached Gibraltar on the evening of December 12, and the *Mary Celeste* arrived the following morning. Then, unexpectedly, the arguments began.

The Suspicious Proctor Flood
A claim for salvaging an abandoned ship on the high seas generally presents no problem because in the vast majority of cases the crewless vessel is dismasted, waterlogged, or otherwise in bad shape. But the case of the *Mary Celeste* was different. F. Solly Flood, the British Admiralty Proctor in Gibraltar, said in his report to London: "The account which they [the salvors] gave of the soundness and good condition of the derelict was so extraordinary that I found it necessary to apply for a survey."

The surveyors reported that the hull of the *Mary Celeste* was perfectly sound, and that the ship was not leaking and had not been in a collision. However, they remarked on two curious grooves which seemed to have been cut with a sharp instrument on each side of the bows, several feet back from the prow and a foot or two above the waterline. There was no damage within the ship, no trace of an explosion, no suggestion of a fire. The *Mary Celeste* was said to be in better shape than many of the small ships that did the Atlantic run. How could the captain, mate, and crew of the *Dei Gratia* swear that they had come upon this seaworthy and amply provisioned vessel drifting in mid-ocean? The British authorities in Gibraltar found such testimony hard to believe. In their view, it was far more likely to be a case of collusion between the crews of the two ships to claim the salvage money, the cargo alone being worth $30,000. Flood suspected even worse. He believed the case to be one of mutiny, piracy, and multiple murder. Described as a fussy and pompous man, Flood's good qualities were the counterpart of such faults: he was a painstaking investigator and he was dedicated to the rule of law. He was not going to let criminals, if so they proved, get away with their crimes.

Flood suggested that the groove on the bows had been deliberately made to look as if the vessel had struck rocks. Horatio J. Sprague, the United States Consul in Gibraltar, hotly disputed this interpretation, and when the *USS Plymouth* put in at Gibraltar, he asked the captain to give his opinion of the grooves. Captain Schufeldt thought that the grooves were "splinters made in the bending of the planks which were afterward forced off by action of the sea without hurting the ship."

Meantime, Flood had found brown stains, which might have been blood, on the deck. More such stains were also found on the blade of an ornate Italian sword under the captain's berth. Deveau was closely questioned about these, but denied he had cleaned or scraped the decks to remove other similar stains. He maintained that his attention was fully occupied in running the ship, and he refused to accept that there was anything remarkable about the sword. It is a measure of the mistrust in which he and his companions were held that when samples of the brown stains were analyzed, the *Dei Gratia* crew was charged with the cost of analysis. Flood not only declined to reveal the report of the analysis, but also refused to give Sprague a copy. Even more surprising, he withheld the report from his own government! Could he have been hiding the fact that the results indicated no blood? Not until 1887, fourteen years later, was Sprague able to obtain a copy of the results of the analysis.

Flood also discovered irregularities in the log Deveau had kept while on board the *Mary Celeste*. At Captain Morehouse's instructions, he had written it up after arriving at Gibraltar. One entry stated that Morehouse had come on board the *Mary Celeste*, but Deveau insisted that he had made an error and that Captain Morehouse did not step foot on the ship till it had arrived in Gibraltar. Even more suspicious, in Flood's opinion, was the way the ship had continued on course for 11 days after November 25. He took this as an indication that the *Dei Gratia* crew must have boarded the *Mary Celeste* much earlier than they said they had.

Fortunately for the *Dei Gratia* crew, the members of the Board of Inquiry were experienced naval men. They knew that logs were not always kept without fail, and they could appreciate that Deveau, with only two men to help him sail the ship, had enough work on his hands without wanting to bother with paperwork. Unlike F. Solly Flood, they did not find anything untoward in the grooves on the bow or in the stains on the deck, and once all the available facts had been presented to them, they were quick to clear Morehouse and his men of any suspicion. In contrast, they spent a long time trying to work out what could have happened to Captain Briggs and his crew. When Winchester came over to Gibraltar from the United States in hopes of speeding the inquiry, he found himself subjected to such close questioning about his ship, the crew, the captain, the history, and himself that finally he got angered.

"I'm a Yankee with some English blood," he cried out, "but if I knew where it was, I'd open a vein and let the damned stuff out!"

The Court Baffled

When the court eventually handed down its judgment in March 1873, it confessed itself unable to decide why the *Mary Celeste* had been abandoned. This was the first time in its history it had failed to come to a conclusion. It awarded to the *Dei*

Gratia a sum equivalent to about one-fifth of the combined value of the *Mary Celeste* and its cargo. The *Mary Celeste* was returned to Winchester, and under a new captain and a new crew, sailed to Genoa. There the cargo was unloaded—three-and-a-half months late, but otherwise intact. Winchester sold the ship as soon as it returned to New York, but its reputation as an unlucky vessel kept seamen from signing on as crew. The *Mary Celeste* changed hands rapidly, bringing little profit to any of its short-term owners.

In 1884 the ship was acquired by a disreputable captain named Gilman C. Parker, who deliberately ran it onto a reef in the West Indies for the sake of the insurance. Even this desperate measure brought no profit. The insurance companies became suspicious, asked awkward questions of the crew, and brought Captain Parker and his associates in the scheme to trial. Because the penalty for destroying a ship on the high seas was death by hanging, the jury, mindful of the ship's unlucky history, was reluctant to convict. The defendants were freed on a technicality, but within eight months Parker was dead, one of his associates went mad, and another committed suicide. Their association with the *Mary Celeste* brought them nothing but grief.

As to what really happened to the *Mary Celeste* on that morning in late November 1872, somewhere between the Azores and Portugal, there have been many guesses. Surprisingly, interest in the subject was slow to develop, and for 11 years the mystery remained relatively unknown outside the seafaring community. Then an impecunious young doctor with an ambition to become an author wrote a story based on the affair. Entitled "J. Habakuk Jephson's Statement," the story appeared in *The Cornhill Magazine* in January 1884 with the ship's name changed to the *Marie Celeste*. In the story, the ship had been taken over as part of what would now be called a Black Power plot. According to the author's version of events, the lifeboat was still on board when the vessel was found.

When the identity of the writer became known, he was launched on the road to fame. The author was Arthur Conan Doyle, and his fictionalization of the *Mary Celeste* mystery started a flood of books and articles on the subject. Since then, so many books and articles have been devoted to the riddle that the Atlantic Mutual Insurance Company in New York has an entire room kept as a *Mary Celeste* Museum. One writer imagined that the *Mary Celeste* was attacked by a kraken or giant squid that picked off the crew one by one, sliding its tentacles through the portholes until it had consumed the last morsel of human flesh. Charles Fort suggested that the crew had been snatched away by a "selective force" which left the ship untouched. One of the more original theories had it that the crew built a platform under the bow in order to watch a swimming race around the ship between the captain and the mate. This explained the strange grooves. The platform collapsed and all were drowned. This explained the disappearance of everyone aboard. UFOs have also been held responsible.

Logical Explanations

What are some more logical ideas about the mystery?

One fact to be taken into account is that everyone left the ship in obvious great haste. Mrs. Briggs left her child's clothing behind, the seamen abandoned their pipes and oilskin boots. Clearly they left in panic, perhaps in deadly fear of something they believed was about to happen. They almost certainly left in the yawl, and they appear to have done so under the guidance of someone responsible—the captain or the first mate—because the chronometer, the sextant, and the ship's papers were not found on board and must therefore have been taken along.

There are three credible theories as to what caused the abandonment of the *Mary Celeste*.

The first was believed to be the likely explanation by Captain Morehouse and Captain James Briggs, brother of the mystery vessel's captain. Knowing that on the morning of the 25th the wind had dropped after a night of violent storm, they thought the ship may have been becalmed in the Azores and found itself drifting toward the dangerous rocks off Santa Maria Island. Everyone on board took to the yawl for safety, staying near the ship. But suddenly a wind got up and took the ship away, and though the men in the boat rowed frantically, the *Mary Celeste* drew farther from them. In the gales that again blew up in the afternoon, a single wave would have swamped the little boat.

Against this theory is the widely accepted surmise that the *Mary Celeste* kept to a steady course for several days after the 25th. This makes it more probable that the abandonment took place on a later date.

The second theory with a logical basis was proposed by Deveau and would explain why the pump plunger was found lying on the deck. He pointed out that the ship had been through heavy storms, and some of the water between decks had found its way into the holds. This may have given the impression that the ship was leaking, so the pump plunger was drawn and the pump sounded—by someone who misread the depth. He at once spread the alarm that the ship was on the point of going down. Panic followed.

This would be neither the first nor the last time a crew had panicked on grounds that later proved unjustified. For example, when Captain Cook's famous *Endeavour* was in difficulties off the East Australian coast, the ship's carpenter was sent to sound the well. He mistook the reading and, in the ensuing hysteria, the crew would have abandoned the ship had Cook not been able to restore calm. In 1919 the schooner *Marion G. Douglas*, which carried a cargo of timber, was abandoned by the crew off the coast of Newfoundland. They had believed their ship to be sinking—but a moment's thought would have reassured them that a ship with a cargo of timber was unlikely to go down. It went on to sail across the Atlantic without them.

The flaw in Deveau's theory is that it means there was a sudden loss of nerve on the part of the captain, and this conflicts with what is known of Briggs' character. Some supporters of this theory have gotten around that point by arguing that Briggs could not exert his leadership because he suffered a heart attack during the panic.

The last of the three most likely theories was the one put forward by Winchester, and it focuses on the nature of the cargo. Captain Briggs had never before carried crude alcohol, and possibly did not know how it would react on the voyage. The change in temperature from wintry New York to the warmer climes around the Azores would cause the casks to leak and sweat. Then the stormy weather, severely buffeting them, would create vapor, and the pressure that built up could have been enough to blow out the forward hatch cover. The sweating would have been accompanied by rumbling noises that must certainly have sounded ominous to men who did not know the natural explanation for such sounds. Captain Briggs may have ordered the hatches opened to let some vapor escape, and what looked like smoke emerged. One of the casks had been opened, which indicates that it had been inspected. If there had been a naked light in the vicinity, there could well have been a small explosion—too small to leave a trace but enough to start a panic.

In the wake of this threat, the captain's anxiety will have been increased by the presence of his wife and small daughter. Thinking primarily of their safety, he may have ordered everyone into the yawl until they saw whether or not the ship would blow up. There was no explosion—but a great gust of wind filled the sails, the towline connecting the small boat to the ship snapped, and the *Mary Celeste* inexorably sailed away from them. Their little boat could not withstand the waves and winds of the ocean and finally capsized, drowning all of them.

Other Deserted Ships

Was this what happened? No one knows for certain—and probably no one will ever know.

The *Mary Celeste* is the most famous drifter of the sea, but it is only one of many others. Some have the added macabre touch of still being crewed—by corpses. In September 1894, for instance, the British brig *Abbey S. Hart* was found drifting in the Indian Ocean. A boarding party found three seamen dead in their bunks and a fourth man, apparently the captain, delirious or mad. He died an hour later without having uttered one understandable word. The ship had sailed from Java a week previously, and it was assumed that some deadly fever had struck the crew down. It is known that in the days of long voyages under sail, tropical diseases could decimate a crew trapped together far from land.

Other killers at sea are less easy to explain than disease. The Dutch freighter *Ourang Medan* was overwhelmed by an unknown tragedy in February 1948 while steaming through the Straits of Malacca bound for Indonesia. SOS signals from the ship were heard by other vessels in the vicinity, and they hurried to its assistance. The distress calls continued meanwhile, until there came an alarming message: "All officers including captain dead, lying in chartroom and on bridge . . . Probably whole crew dead." This was followed by a series of dots and dashes that made no sense and then the words, "I die." After this—silence.

When the *Ourang Medan* was located, it was drifting with the current but a thin ribbon of smoke still issued from the funnel. The captain was found dead on the bridge. Throughout the ship —in the wheelhouse, chartroom, and on the decks—lay the lifeless bodies of the unfortunate crew. The body of the radio operator was found slumped in a chair, his fingers against the transmitter key. Even the ship's dog was found with his lips drawn back in a rictus of death. "Their frozen faces were upturned to the sun," stated the report in the Proceedings of the Merchant Marine Council, "the mouths were gaping open and the eyes staring."

No wounds were discovered on the bodies, and the vessel seemed undamaged. The boarding parties were uncertain what to do next when suddenly flames surged out of the hold and spread rapidly. Everyone hastily returned to their own vessels. Within a short time the boilers of the *Ourang Medan* exploded and the ship sank. Could the crew have been overcome by carbon monoxide or some other poisonous fumes generated within the hold or in the boilers? If so, it is hard to see how that could have killed everyone, even those who were in the open air.

In *Invisible Horizons*, a book of sea tales, Vincent Gaddis cites an even more grisly example of a floating morgue. In the summer of 1913 the British ship *Johnson* caught sight of a sailing vessel drifting off the coast of Chile. As they drew near they could see that the masts and sails were covered with green mold. On the prow, faded with the passing of many years, could still be seen the name *Marlborough*. The timbers of the deck had decayed so greatly that they crumbled as the boarding party picked a way across them. A skeleton was discovered beneath the helm, six more were found on the bridge, and 13 others elsewhere in the ship.

It was later learned that the *Marlborough* had left Littleton, New Zealand, 23 years before in January 1890 with a cargo of wool and frozen mutton. There were also several passengers aboard, including one woman. Nothing had been heard of the ship since it had been sighted on the regular course passing through the Straits of Magellan 23 years before. What had happened? Where had the ship been to remain undiscovered for nearly a quarter of a century? Could it have been trapped in an ice ocean like the schooner *Jenny* and others?

The unfortunate *Jenny* was discovered by the whaling schooner *Hope* south of Drake Strait in the Antarctic on September 22, 1860. The towering wall of ice parted abruptly and the *Jenny* emerged, the hull battered and encrusted with ice, snow upon the decks, the rigging fallen, the sails in icy shreds. The cold had preserved the corpses of the crew perfectly, in natural attitudes. The captain's body was seated in a chair, a pen in his hand and leaning backward. Examination of the log revealed that the *Jenny* had been imprisoned in the ice for 37 years. The last entry, signed by the captain, read: "May 4, 1823. No food for 71 days. I am the only one left alive."

The *Octavius* and the Northwest Passage

The ice of the Arctic Ocean on the other side of the world proved too much for the *Octavius* in 1762. This vessel left England in 1761 bound for China. On the return journey the captain is thought to have decided to look for the elusive Northwest Passage rather than to sail all the way around South America. But they got no further than the north coast of Alaska when the ice trapped them. Thirteen years later the whaleship *Herald* caught sight of the *Octavius* drifting into open water between icebergs. The crew of the *Herald* sensed at once that this was a ship of the dead, and they only reluctantly obeyed their captain's order to lower the longboat in preparation for boarding. Captain Warren led the party.

On the ice-coated deck of the *Octavius* there was no sign of life. Captain Warren made his way to the forecastle, and after kicking away the snow, opened the door. He was met by a heavy musky odor. Stepping inside he saw that every bed, 28 in all, was occupied by a dead seaman, perfectly preserved by the freezing air. The men were heavily wrapped with blankets and clothing, but the Arctic cold had proved too great for them.

In the captain's cabin a dank and mustier smell greeted them. A thin green mold had spread over the dead captain's face although his body was otherwise well preserved. He lay slumped at a table, his hands spread out and a pen beside them. Captain Warren handed the logbook to one of his sailors and stepped into the next cabin. There he found the body of a woman in the bunk covered with blankets. Gaddis writes: "Unlike the captain, her flesh and features were unmarked and lifelike. Her head was

66

resting on her elbow and it appeared as if she had been watching some activity when she died. Following the line of her vision, Captain Warren saw the body of a man cross-legged on the floor and slouched over. In one hand he held a flint and in the other a piece of steel. In front of him was a heap of wood shavings. Apparently he had been attempting to start a fire when death had claimed him. Beside the man was a heavy sailor's jacket. When the captain picked it up, he found the body of a small boy underneath."

Captain Warren's men got panicky and insisted that he let them return to their ship. Back on the *Herald* the captain settled down to read the log, only to find that the sailor entrusted with its care had dropped the center pages into the sea while hastening into the longboat. The surviving front pages gave details of the ship's company and recorded the successful start of the voyage to China. The account of the following 14 months was missing, and the only remaining page was the final one. Dated November 11, 1762 it read: "We have now been enclosed in the ice 17 days, and our approximate position is Longitude 160W, Latitude 75N. The fire went out yesterday, and our master has been trying to rekindle it again but without success. He has handed the steel and flint to the mate. The master's son died this morning and his wife says she no longer feels the terrible cold. The rest of us seem to have no relief from the agony."

The most outstanding feature of the discovery of the *Octavius* is that it occurred in Greenland waters, at the eastern end of the Northwest Passage, even though the ship had been locked in the ice when north of Alaska, at the western end. Only one explanation was possible. The ship must have found the Northwest Passage on its own. Season by season it had crept eastward, frozen up each winter and drifting on again during the short summer thaw, until at last it reached the North Atlantic. Ironically, the *Octavius* was the first ship to navigate the Northwest Passage—but the crew and the captain never knew it.

Another ship that went it alone in the Arctic is the *SS Baychimo*. Owned by the Hudson's Bay Company, the *Baychimo* is a trim, steel-clad cargo steamer, considered the finest possible craft for battling the pack ice and the floes. The ship joined the far northern fleet in 1921 and made nine annual visits to the bleak Arctic coasts of Canada, buying furs from the trading posts along the Beaufort Sea and the McClintock Channel. No other vessel had managed to make the perilous trip more than two years in succession.

The *S.S.Baychimo* — 30 Years Adrift

On July 6, 1931 the *Baychimo* left Vancouver, Canada, with a crew of 36 under the command of Captain John Cornwall. Passing through the Bering Straits, the ship entered the Northwest Passage. The captain spent hundreds of thousands of dollars buying furs along the Victoria Island coast. On the return journey the ship was caught in early winter pack ice during a howling blizzard, and was unable to move. With the vessel in danger of being crushed, Captain Cornwall and his crew established a camp on safer ice closer to shore, and prepared to wait there till the spring. A three-day storm early in November brought a rise in temperature, enabling the men to emerge for a look around. They found that the *Baychimo* had snapped its moorings and disappeared.

Captain Cornwall led his men to the safety of Point Barrow, 50 miles away, where they learned that Eskimos had sighted the missing ship 45 miles southwest of its former position. The crew and a party of Eskimos managed to reach the ship, and after 15 days of difficult work, removed the bulk of the valuable cargo. Before they could finish, however, the *Baychimo* had vanished again.

The following spring the ship was observed 300 miles further east near Herschel Island. A young trapper and explorer, Leslie Melvin, found the *Baychimo* while on a journey by dog team. He boarded the drifter and reported that it was in excellent condition.

Since then the *SS Baychimo* has been sighted frequently. A party of Eskimos boarded the ship in 1933, but were trapped by a sudden storm and drifted for 10 days before they could make their way to shore on a raft of ice. In June 1934 Isobel Hutchinson, a Scottish botanist, sighted it and went aboard. Year after year reports of sightings have come in from whalers, prospectors, Eskimos, travelers. In November 1939 an attempt to tow the ship into port had to be abandoned in bad weather. Still it survives. After a period of no reports on the *Baychimo*, a party of Eskimos saw it in March 1956, moving north in the Beaufort

68

Sea. In March 1962 fishermen found the still apparently sea-worthy ship in the same area. The *Baychimo* seems to have disappeared since then, but may yet turn up again. There is no parallel in modern times for a ship to sail the seas without a crew for so long a time. For over 30 years the *Baychimo* has survived the ice in one of the cruellest seas of the world.

7. The Turin Shroud

Throughout the Middle Ages religious relics allegedly associated with Jesus, the Virgin Mary, or the Apostles were revered by pious but gullible men and women throughout Christendom and exploited by such unscrupulous rogues as the Pardoner in the *Canterbury Tales* by the 14th-century English poet Geoffrey Chaucer. Among these relics there were several shrouds that were claimed by their devotees or owners to be the original burial cloth in which Jesus' body had lain in Joseph of Arimathea's tomb after being taken down from the cross. But unique among these shrouds was the one in the possession of the Dukes of Savoy (later, Kings of Italy), for it had upon it faint shadowy stains merging into one another which, from a distance, took on the outlines of a human figure lying with hands crossed. The stains were held to be the imprints of Jesus' physical body miraculously preserved on the Savior's burial cloth. The legend surrounding the shroud states that it was taken from Jerusalem to Constantinople, where it was seen in 1204. In 1353 Robert de Charny built an abbey for it at Chambery. Then in 1578 it was taken to Italy so that the aged Archbishop of Milan should be spared the journey across the Alps to see it. It has remained there ever since safely stored in a silver casket in the Cathedral of Turin. It is still unique, for it is the only alleged religious relic that, instead of having been proved bogus by scientific investigation has on the contrary convinced many scientists that it must be genuine.

The question whether the "Holy Shroud of Turin" is an authentic artifact directly associated with the historical Jesus is one of the most intriguing of all religious mysteries; the more so because the full mystery has only emerged in the present

70

century.

Secondo Pia's Discovery

It was in 1898 that a Turin photographer named Secondo Pia was commissioned by King Humbert I of Italy, the "guardian" of the Shroud, to take the first-ever photographs of the holy burial cloth. When he developed his photographic plates, Pia was astonished and at first thought that he must have made some mistake, for on his negative plate he saw not a reversed image of the brown stains but a picture of a bearded face wearing an expression of great serenity and nobility. Whereas the face visible on the Shroud was rather blurred and the features were ill-defined, the one on the plate was perfectly clear. When he recovered from his initial astonishment, the photographer realized what must have happened. As the picture on his negative plate was a positive, he must have photographed a negative. Incredibly, the shadowy markings on the cloth were the opposite way round in terms of light and shade, like a photographic negative. Others were to puzzle over the problem of how this could be and propose various explanations, but it seemed to Secondo Pia when he looked at his first negative plate that he had witnessed a miracle. It was as if the Holy Shroud had been waiting 19 centuries for man's discovery of the art of photography to unlock its secret.

When Secondo Pia's discovery was announced and his photographs were made available for study, there were naturally people who suggested that a clever fake must have been perpetrated. More photographs were taken with the same results, which exonerated Pia, but it was now suggested that the shroud had been faked by a Medieval artist who had painted the markings on it. But when this possibility was examined the mystery deepened. Microscopic examination showed that there were no deposits of paint on the fabric, every individual thread was distinctly visible, those that were stained were stained right through, and there were no outlines or shadings such as would be found on work done by human hand. Furthermore, not only was it technically impossible for an artist to have faked the image on the Shroud, but also nobody in the Middle Ages, when of course the principles of photography were unknown, could have conceived or executed the idea of reversing the light and shade and so imprinting a negative image on the Shroud.

71

The testimony of medical men also ruled out the possibility of Medieval forgery. In those days knowledge of anatomy was rudimentary and nothing was known of the circulation of the blood, but the markings on the Shroud are exact in anatomical detail and proportion and the authenticity of marks made by blood flowing from the wounds is confirmed by forensic medicine, which has shown those marks to be consistent with the known behavior of shed blood. Forensic examination has, moreover, confirmed the gospel accounts of the execution of Jesus. The dark stains on the Shroud that come up white on the photograph clearly show wounds on the left wrist (the right one is covered by the left hand), on the soles of the feet, on the right breast, on the brow and all over the back, which respectively bear out the story that Jesus was crucified, pierced by a Roman soldier's lance, crowned with a crown of thorns, and scourged. Medical men have also noted that the expanded rib cage and the drawn-in hollow below it indicate that the man of the Shroud died while hanging by the arms.

A Macabre Experiment

In the many paintings of the crucifixion, Christ is shown nailed to the cross through the palms of his hands, but the wound markings on the Shroud suggest that the nails penetrated the wrists. A French doctor, Pierre Barbet, conducted what must have been the most macabre scientific experiment ever when he crucified the body of a deceased patient with nails through the palms of the hands, only to find that the nails tore through the hands as soon as the cross was raised. At a second attempt Dr. Barbet hammered the nails through the wrists and found that the bony structure there could support the weight of the body. And he noticed another thing: that when a nail penetrated the wrist the thumb bent inward into the palm. The absence of thumbs from the hands of the man of the Shroud had until then been an unexplained puzzle for the students of the relic.

Scientists have also tried to explain how the negative image might have become imprinted on the Shroud. John's gospel states that Joseph and Nicodemus bound Jesus' body into the Shroud with a mixture of powdered myrhh and aloes. These spices, it has been suggested by Dr. Paul Vignon, a professor of biology, could act like the sensitized plate of a film in a camera, and a chemical reaction upon them produced by ammonia vapors rising from the body could account for the photographic effect on the linen. An alternative theory, which is supported by Dr. Barbet, is that the cloth is stained with a component of aloes known as aloentine which was produced by moisture given off by the body. Both theories have been put to the test with a degree of success sufficient to establish the point that markings like those on the Shroud could have been caused by a chemical action upon the spices with which the Shroud and Jesus' body were liberally covered (according to John, Nicodemus brought about "a hundred pounds' weight" for the purpose) before being put in the tomb. Another theory that has been proposed but which cannot be tested experimentally is that the image on the Shroud was produced by chemical action at the moment of Jesus' resurrection, caused by a radiation of energies particular to that unique event.

As science becomes more sophisticated and more tests are devised in the hope of finally authenticating the Shroud or proving it a fake, the relic continues to baffle those who hope to discredit it. At a conference on the Shroud held in the United States in March, 1977, some recent developments were reported. Physicists from the Jet Propulsion Laboratory in Pasadena, California, used the computer techniques employed to enhance or magnify photographs sent back from Mars on a photograph of the Shroud, and they made two significant discoveries. First, the lack of what they call "linear directionality" in the shading of the image indicates that it was not painted on the fabric; and second, the enhancement technique enabled them to produce a three-dimensional version of the images on the Shroud, and it was found that the intensity of the image varied according to the distance the sheet would have been from the body at each point.

Pollen Analysis

Textile experts long ago confirmed that the linen of the Shroud is identical in material and weave pattern to many fabrics from the eastern Mediterranean that have been reliably dated from the 1st to the 3rd centuries. Now a Swiss professor named Max Frei has come up with more evidence that supports the tradition that the Shroud was taken from Jerusalem to Constantinople and then brought to Europe at the time of the

Crusades. Frei is a pollen analysis expert. Pollen, which does not deteriorate with time, indicates where things have been, and Frei has discovered that some of the pollen on the Shroud is identical with that from 2000-year-old sediments from Lake Galilee, and that other pollen traces show that the Shroud moved through Palestine, Asia Minor, and Savoy.

Up to now the custodians of the Shroud have refused to sacrifice a portion of it for a carbon dating test, which could determine its age to within 100 years. But recently a Chicago microanalyst, Dr. Walter McCrone, has improved carbon dating technique so that now only half a square inch, instead of two square feet, of the material need be destroyed for the test. Even so, it is doubtful whether even this small amount will be made available for the test. If it is, and if the Shroud is proved to be 2000 years old, then the very least that could be said for it is that its association with the Jesus of the gospels and of the Christian faith will not have been disproved. Yet the mystery of the Shroud will remain, as will the mystery of its supposed one-time occupant, the most loved and revered as well as most enigmatic and elusive of historical figures.

Part 2

Part 2

8. Curious Rain

We use the phrase "raining cats and dogs" to describe a downpour. But rains of many kinds of living creatures have actually been reported from earliest times and all over the world. On May 28, 1881 during a thunderstorm on the outskirts of Worcester, England, tons of periwinkles and small hermit crabs fell on Cromer Gardens Road and the surrounding fields. They came down out of the sky in a broad band extending for about a mile. When news of this amazing fall reached the center of Worcester, a town 40 miles from the sea, many people hurried to Cromer Gardens Road carrying pots, pans, bags, and even trunks. One garden alone yielded two sacks of periwinkles; 10 sacks of them altogether were taken back to the markets of Worcester for sale.

Showers of fish, frogs, and many other animals are rare but have long been known of. Like comets and shooting stars, they were frequently interpreted as omens of calamity. Such an attitude is understandable. People need an ordered environment if they are to feel at home in the world, and fish falling from the sky is a clear sign of disorder. In the 18th and 19th centuries many rationalists overreacted to what they took to be the superstitions of earlier ages, and denied altogether the possibility of such marvels. So the case of the Worcester periwinkles was explained as the result of a fish dealer who abandoned his stock on the road before the storm. Two people were found who reported that they had seen the periwinkles on the ground before they came down from the sky. It is hard to understand why a fish dealer would want to get rid of his winkles when, as was pointed out, they would sell at a high price in Worcester that day. This unseen merchant, then, introduces a solution as unlikely as the idea that periwinkles and small crabs somehow managed to get into the air and later fell out of it.

About 20 years earlier, on February 16, 1861, a weird shower had been reported from Singapore. An earthquake had been followed by three days of incessant rain, in the course of which great numbers of fish were found in the puddles of streets throughout the city. Local residents reported that the fish had fallen from the sky. One writer of an account in *La Science pour Tous* stated that he himself did not see any of the fish falling—adding that the deluge of rain was so heavy that sometimes he could not see more than three yards ahead of him. But he specifically mentioned that some of the fish had been found in his courtyard, which was surrounded by high walls. The explanation generally accepted, however, was that overflowing streams had left the fish on the land after the waters receded.

Occasionally there is some truth in the explanation that objects said to have fallen from the sky were on the ground all the time. Showers of frogs and toads have been reported many times, frequently in Italy in both ancient and modern times. Arguments regularly broke out as to whether the animals had originated on the earth or in the clouds. Some witnesses reported that they had seen the frogs fall. Other witnesses said that they had seen them only close to the walls of houses, which could mean that they had slipped down from the gutters of the roofs. A German naturalist writing in 1874 observed that frogs said to have been rained down but not seen to fall were seldom dead, lamed, or bruised because, he implied, they had been on the ground all the time. "The appearance of the frogs after a rain is easily accounted for by the circumstance that during a long-continued drought they remain in a state of torpor in holes and coverts, and all that the rain does is the enlivening of them, giving them new spirits, and calling them forth to enjoy the element they delight to live in."

Thomas Cooper, a popular 19th-century lecturer on Christianity, witnessed the phenomenon of raining frogs during his boyhood in Lincolnshire, England. "I am as sure of what I relate as I am of my own existence," he declared. He said that the frogs were alive and jumping, and that they "fell on the pavement at our feet, and came tumbling down the spouts from the tiles of the houses into the water tubs." It is interesting that in most of the reports of frog showers, the size of the frogs is always very small.

There seems no reason to doubt that showers of frogs occur

from time to time—which is not to deny that at other times the frogs simply emerge from holes in the ground when the first raindrops enliven them. It seems hasty to conclude either that frogs seen after a rainstorm have always fallen from the skies, or that frogs seen after a rainstorm were always on the ground beforehand. The evidence seems to show that sometimes frogs fall from above and sometimes they don't.

Hurricanes and Whirlwinds

The scientifically accepted explanation for a frog rain is that they have been carried in the air, sometimes for great distances, from a pool or stream where they were sucked up by sudden strong winds. Charles Hay Fort, the cataloger of phenomena who was rejected by science in his day, regarded this as unlikely. But Fort was also guilty of error, and not above altering the evidence when it suited his argument. In *The Book of the Damned* he wrote: "After one of the greatest hurricanes in the history of Ireland, some fish were found as far as 15 yards from the edge of the lake." In these words he implied that an unprecedented hurricane is required to move a fish a few yards, because he wanted to cast doubt on the likelihood of the wind moving any object a matter of miles—for instance, periwinkles 40 miles from the mouth of the nearest river to Worcester, or the enormous number of eels that fell in Coalburg, Alabama, on May 29, 1892.

The power of the wind is enormous. On August 19, 1845 a whirlwind in France uprooted 180 large trees in a few seconds in Houlme, and destroyed three mills in Monville, dropping planks from the factory buildings half an hour later on the outskirts of Dieppe 20 miles (32 kilometers) away. Though it takes a whirlwind to transport planks, a far less violent wind can bear away small frogs, periwinkles, and eels.

So many eels fell in Coalburg that farmers came into town with carts and took them away to use as fertilizer for their fields. Eels also fell in Hendon in the northeast of England on August 24, 1918. Hundreds of them covered a small area about 60 by 30 yards. Hendon is a coastal town, but the eels were probably carried in the air for some time and from another part of the coast because, according to witnesses, "the eels were all dead, and indeed stiff and hard, when picked up, immediately after the occurrence."

79

Fish that fall in showers generally are dead. Lunged creatures are frequently alive, making it difficult to say how long they have been in the air. Live lizards fell on the streets of Montreal, Canada, on December 28, 1857. Snails fell in such quantities in Redruth, England, on July 8, 1886, that people were able to gather them up in hatfuls. A yellow cloud appeared over Paderborn, Germany, on August 9, 1892, and a torrent of rain from it brought hundreds of mussels. More recently, on September 28, 1953 a shower of toads fell on Orlando, Florida, in the middle of the afternoon.

A Shower of Live Fish

An uncommon shower of live fish descended on Mountain Ash, Wales, on February 11, 1859. The vicar of the neighboring town of Aberdare interviewed John Lewis, an employee of the sawmill in Mountain Ash. Said Lewis: "I was getting out a piece of timber for the purpose of setting it for the saw, when I was startled by something falling all over me—down my neck, on my head, and on my back. On putting my hand down my neck I was surprised to find they were little fish. By this time I saw the whole ground covered with them. I took off my hat, the brim of which was full of them. They were jumping all about. They covered the ground in a long strip of about 80 yards by 12, as we measured afterward." These fish fell in two showers, with an interval of about 10 minutes, each shower lasting about two minutes. Some people, thinking they might be sea fish, placed them in salt water, whereupon they instantly died. Those that were placed in fresh water thrived well, and were later identified as sticklebacks.

Showers of living objects fall over a relatively small area, but other kinds of unnatural rain can sometimes cover an entire country. Yellow rain has been reported from all parts of the world, and because of the Christian link-up between brimstone and hell, the yellow has been popularly identified as sulfur and regarded as a warning from on high. Although yellow rain does not look different while it is falling, the ground is afterward found to be covered with a fine yellow dust. This dust burns easily, encouraging the belief that it is sulfur, but in the majority of cases the accepted explanation is that the yellow is pollen from trees. A forest of hazelnut trees coming into flower in April, or beeches in May or June, or pine trees from midsummer onward, can produce a vast amount of fine pollen—and a strong wind following a spell of tranquil weather can bear away enormous quantities, which may subsequently fall down with rain.

Sometimes a yellow substance falls in the absence of rain. On February 27, 1877 in Peckloh, Germany, a golden-yellow fall was found to contain four different kinds of organisms. Their shapes resembled microscopic arrows, coffee beans, horns, and disks, and none was identified as pollen.

Another unnatural shower often reported is black rain. The blame for this has usually been placed fairly on smoke belching from factory chimneys in an industrial area somewhere along the path of the wind. But on August 14, 1888 there was a heavy downpour of black rain on the Cape of Good Hope, a part of South Africa then remote from any large concentration of industry. Could the blackness have come from a forest fire? This was the explanation given to account for the celebrated Canadian black rain 69 years before the Cape Hope incident, when it had been said that the rainclouds had been stained by the dense smoke of forest fires south of the Ohio River. In the case of the Cape of Good Hope, however, the direction of the prevailing wind makes it unlikely that fires in the forest region could have been the cause. Nor would smoke have produced a rain so black as to be described as "a shower of ink."

What was not realized in the past was how enormous a quantity of material the wind can carry, and how vast the distances it can carry the burden. Concentrations of dust in major storms have been estimated to reach as much as 200,000 tons per square mile of land surface. In February 1903 large areas of Western Europe were covered by a dark sand blown from the Sahara Desert. It varied widely in color, different reports describing it as reddish, yellowish, gray, and the color of chocolate. In one place it was described as "sticky to the touch and slightly iridescent." A quantity amounting to about 10 million tons is calculated to have fallen on England alone. A similar fall occurred in the south of England and Wales on June 30, 1968, when storms broke after the hottest day for 11 years. The following morning a fine sandy dust was found coating parked cars, greenhouses, windows, and washing. The dust was yellow, pink, or bright red, and analysis established that it had originated in the Sahara.

Red rain—popularly mistaken for showers of blood—has in

the past understandably spread more alarm than rain of any other color. Homer tells of showers of blood that fell upon the Greek heroes at ancient Troy as an omen of their approaching death in battle. References to similar showers in Roman times mention the terror they caused among the populace. St. Gregory of Tours, the 6th-century historian of the Franks, recorded that in A.D. 582 in the Paris region "real blood rained from a cloud, falling on the clothes of many people, and so staining them with gore that they stripped them off in horror."

A long list of unnatural rainfalls was compiled by the French astronomer and writer Camille Flammarion, who died in 1925. He was fascinated with anything to do with the heavens, and in the chapter entitled "Prodigies" in his book *The Atmosphere*, he listed over 40 references to "showers of blood" before 1800 and a further 21 that had been reported in the 19th century. The reports cover a wide area, from Brussels to Baghdad, from Hungary to Lisbon. When the reaction of the populace is given it is invariably one of panic. Supernatural signs were sometimes reported as accompanying the showers. During a red rain that fell on France and Germany in March 1181 a luminous cross was observed in the skies. Frequently the showers were said to be the warning of death; when showers of blood persisted intermittently for three days and nights in Brescia, Italy, they were followed by the death of Pope Adrian II on the fourth day.

One of the first to attempt to find a cause for these fearful showers was a Mr. de Peiresc. When numerous red spots had been discovered on the walls and stones on the outskirts of Aix-en-Provence in July 1608, the local priests attributed them to the influence of the Devil. Mr. de Peiresc examined the spots carefully and concluded that they were not of blood—the Devil's or otherwise—but the secretions of a butterfly. He pointed out that the species now known as the Large Tortoiseshell, which has a red secretion, had been seen in unusually large numbers that month. Moreover, red spots were absent from the center of the town, where the butterflies had not made an appearance, and had been found on the higher parts of the buildings, about the level to which they flew. However, the citizens of Aix preferred to believe that the Devil was the culprit.

In general, the cause of rains of blood is, like that of yellow rain, dust originating in a desert region. Signor Sementini, professor of chemistry at Naples, was ahead of his time when in 1813 he accurately identified as dust the red shower that fell on Gerace, Italy, on March 14 of that year. He also recorded a vivid impression of the event. "The wind had been westerly for two days," he wrote, "when at 2 p.m. it suddenly became calm, the atmosphere grew cloudy, and the darkness gradually became so great as to render it necessary to light candles. The citizens, alarmed by the obscurity, rushed in a crowd to the cathedral to pray. The sky assumed the color of red-hot iron, thunder and lightning continued for a considerable length of time, and the sea was heard to roar, although six miles from the city. Large drops of rain then began to fall, which were of a blood-red color."

The rain deposited a yellow powder and had a slight earthy taste. Sementini analyzed it and concluded that it was a terrestrial dust of some kind, but could not guess where it came from. It is now difficult to establish if it had blown from the Sahara since one account states that the wind was westerly while another gives it as easterly. Such a basic error, made at a time when accurate observations were being attempted, throws serious doubts on earlier reports, made when natural phenomena were unquestioningly regarded as direct communications from God, and reported in that light.

Crosses from Heaven

In this category must be included showers of crosses. In France in the year 764 crosses were said to have appeared on men's clothes during a shower of blood. In 1094 crosses are reported to have fallen from heaven, alighting on the garments of priests. In 1501 crosses rained down in Germany and Belgium during the week before Easter, and left marks on clothes, skin, and bread.

In the annals of unusual rains, "the Miracle of Remiremont" holds a unique position. On the afternoon of May 26, 1907 the Abbé Gueniot was snug in his library as a hailstorm battered down outside. Suddenly his housekeeper called to him to come see the extraordinary hailstones. She told him that images of Our Lady of the Treasures were printed on them. The Abbé later described the event like this:

"In order to satisfy her, I glanced carelessly at the hailstones, which she held in her hand. But, since I did not want to see anything, and moreover could not do so without my spectacles, I turned to go back to my book. She urged, 'I beg of you to put on your glasses.' I did so, and saw very distinctly on the front of the hailstones, which were slightly convex in the center, although the edges were somewhat worn, the bust of a woman, with a robe that was turned up at the bottom, like a priest's robe. I should, perhaps, describe it more exactly by saying that it was like the Virgin of the Hermits. The outline of the images was slightly hollow, as if they had been formed with a punch, but were very boldly drawn. Mlle. André asked me to notice certain details of the costume, but I refused to look at it any longer. I was ashamed of my credulity, feeling sure that the Blessed Virgin would hardly concern herself with instantaneous photographs on hailstones.''

Nonetheless, the Abbé picked up three of the hailstones to weigh them and found they weighed between six and seven ounces. One was perfectly round and had a seam all around it, as though it had been cast in a mold. Later he collected the signatures of 50 people who had seen the extraordinary hailstones.

There seems little doubt that the hail that fell on Remiremont that afternoon bore strange markings. The Secretary of the French Academy wondered whether lightning might have struck a medal of the Virgin and reproduced the image on the hailstones. Other reports state that the print was found on the inside of the hailstones after they had been split. The key to the mystery probably lies there. When hailstones are formed, they are frequently tossed up and down between layers of cold and less cold air, in the process accumulating several layers of ice that show as rings on a cross-section of the individual hailstone. The circumstances of hail formation at Remiremont may have been such as to allow an irregular layering of ice that was then seen to resemble the appearance of the Virgin. It is worth mentioning that a few days before the storm, the local government had forbidden a religious procession through the town and this had created a high degree of agitated excitement among the devout—an atmosphere conducive to the occurrence of a miracle.

Showers of a liquid looking like milk have been reported at various times in Italy. In one such rain, coins and copper pots exposed to the downfall became silvered, and kept this appearance for three days. This suggests that the rain contained mercury, although it is hard to imagine the circumstances under which this would be possible.

Showers of fish, frogs, eels, lizards and many other creatures have been recorded throughout history. This woodcut of a fall of fish is from Olaus Magnus's *Historia de Gentibus Septentrionalibus*, dated 1555. (*Curious Rain*)

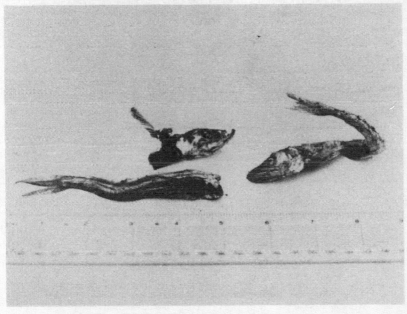

Fish recovered from a shower of fish in East Ham, London in May 1984. (*Curious Rain*)

Charles Hay Fort, the intellectual rebel and recluse who died in New York in 1932 at the age of 57. Fort collected data on thousands of mysterious events which he published in several books, including *The Book of the Damned, Lo!* and *Wild Talents*. He was particularly interested in stories of objects falling from the skies. (*Curious Rain*)

In the Silesian province of what is now Poland, at a time of great shortage of wheat, a violent storm broke over the country-side—and afterward the ground was covered with small round seeds. The country folk at first believed their prayers had been answered and that the skies had rained millet. Unfortunately, the seeds proved to be from a local species of the herb speedwell. In 1804, however, a real wheatfall took place in parts of Andalucia in southern Spain. What happened was that a hurricane removed the grain from a threshing floor in Tutua on the Moroccan coast, carried it across the Straits of Gibraltar, and dropped it on the amazed and grateful Spanish peasants.

The Theories of Charles Hay Fort

Fort gives his own eccentric possibilities for these phenomena:
"Debris from interplanetary disasters.
"Aerial battles.
"Food-supplies from cargoes of super-vessels, wrecked in interplanetary traffic."
In the spring of 1695 dwellers in the Irish counties of Limerick and Tipperary experienced showers of a greasy substance having a "very stinking smell." This grease, which the local people called "butter," fell in lumps an inch in diameter, and was soft, clammy, and dark yellow in color. The Bishop of Cloyne called it "stinking dew." Fort says, "We'll not especially wonder whether these butter-like or oily substances were food or fuel . . ." and goes on to suggest that they fell from "a super-construction, plying back and forth from Jupiter and Mars and Venus."
Fort's achievement in tracking down many thousands of strange happenings—and urging people to think about them— is undermined by the weird theories he put forward to account for them. It is as though he were still a little boy deliberately pasting wrong labels on cans, as he used to do in rebellion when working in his father's store. In his rebellion against autocratic science, did he sometimes deliberately apply a wrong label? In any case, his view of the universe was something like a store out of which he pulled a variety of goods.
For example, sometimes he imagined that a circle of ice surrounded the earth, that fragments break off and fall to the earth as hail, and that we see the stars through the resulting gaps. Other times he felt that the earth is ringed with a gelatinous substance,

and that globs of this jelly also fall down. He talks of a "super-geographical pond" above the earth—his Super-Sargasso Sea.

Fort may not have believed all these fanciful theories—or at least not all of them at the same time—but the space probes of the 1960s and 70s have exposed them as nonsense. Nowadays it is difficult to read any of Fort's books without finding a foolish and disproved theory on every page, including the gelatin ring.

But can there be a fall of jelly? In Massachussetts on the night of August 13, 1819 a bright light was seen moving above Amherst, and a sound was heard that was described as being as loud as an explosion. Next morning, in the front yard of a professor, was found a substance "unlike anything before observed by anyone who saw it. It was a bowl-shaped object, about eight inches in diameter, and one inch thick. Bright, buff-colored, and having upon it a fine nap. Upon removing this covering, a buff-colored pulpy substance of the consistency of soft soap was found, of an offensive, suffocating smell. A few minutes of exposure to the air changed the buff color to a livid color resembling venous blood. It absorbed moisture quickly from the air and liquefied."

No explanation of this strange object was put forward at the time, but a few years later a similar one was found near the same place. It was shown to Professor Edward Hitchcock, who pronounced it to be a gelatinous fungus. He said similar fungi might spring up within the next 24 hours, and sure enough two others had done so before nightfall.

Nostoc and Manna

The moving light and the loud sound remain unexplained, but the fungus was probably of the kind called nostoc. Natural appearances of nostoc in unusual places presumably gave rise to the reports of more jellylike falls in several other parts of the United States over the years. Lumps of jelly looking like coagulated white of egg have been found in Rahway, New Jersey. A mass like boiled starch was reported from West Point, New York. The flakes of a substance that looked like thin slices of beef floated down from a clear sky at Olympian Springs, Kentucky. This was a thick shower, but fell only on a narrow strip of land about 100 yards long and about 50 yards wide.

Nostoc—a word first coined by the 16th-century German physician and alchemist Paracelsus—is usually considered, like frogs, to have been on the ground all the time when said to have fallen from the sky. But there is no reason why it should not occasionally, again like frogs, be borne in the air by winds and fall to the ground when the wind drops. A primitive alga, nostoc is thought to be one of the world's oldest organisms. In dry periods the common form of nostoc can shrivel into paper-thin strands, swelling up again after rain or in the presence of moisture. Practically invisible when dry, the fungus colonies can take in water and enlarge quickly to the size of a grapefruit. These sudden appearances have often given rise to the idea that they dropped from the sky.

Some varieties of nostoc are eaten by South American Indians, and one of its species may have been the substance called manna in the Bible. Manna, which provided food for the Israelites during their wanderings in the Sinai desert, cannot now be identified with any certainty. The sweet globules produced by the lichen *Lecanora esculenta* are thought to be one of the most likely sources, although this lichen is not now found in Sinai. Another possibility is the secretions of an insect that sucks the sap of the tamarisk, small drops of which fall to the ground as sticky honeydew. At the beginning of Chapter 16 of Exodus, Moses tells the Israelites that the Lord will rain bread from heaven, but the belief that the manna would come from above is linked to the old and widespread idea that dew falls from the sky. "In the morning the dew lay round about the host. And when the dew that lay was gone up, behold, upon the face of the wilderness, there lay a small round thing, as small as the hoar frost on the ground."

It is now known that dew is not a precipitation like rain, but is formed on the ground as a deposit of water vapor. But the idea that dew drops from the sky is persistent. Schoolchildren in France in the early years of this century were still being taught that it dropped. At an earlier period pearls were thought to be congealed dew. It was said that oysters rose to the surface of the sea during the night and caught the falling dewdrops, which in time hardened into pearls.

Extraterrestrial Phenomena

Although Charles Fort is mistaken in most of his theories, he is not entirely wrong in suggesting that certain mysterious happenings are extraterrestrial: meteorites, for example. Their seemingly supernatural origin has frequently led to them becoming objects of worship. One that fell in Arabia about the time of Muhammad is still preserved in Mecca, built into a corner of the sacred shrine known as the Kaaba; every pilgrim must kiss it in the course of his visit to the city. The Roman Emperor Heliogabalus had a black meteorite carried in solemn procession through streets strewn with gold dust. Even when not worshipped, the fallen meteorite was long regarded as a miraculous object. The oldest authenticated meteorite in a museum is the one that fell on the Swiss town of Ensisheim in 1492. The local church records give a good contemporary account of the event.

"On the 16th November 1492 a singular miracle happened: for between 11 and 12 in the forenoon, with a loud crash of thunder and a prolonged noise heard afar off, there fell in the town of Ensisheim a stone weighing 260 pounds. It was seen by a child to strike the ground in a field near the canton called Gisgaud, where it made a hole more than five feet deep. It was taken to the church as being a miraculous object. The noise was heard so distinctly at Lucerne, Villing, and many other places that in each of them it was thought that some houses had fallen. King Maximilian, who was then at Ensisheim, had the stone carried to the castle: after breaking off two pieces, one for the Duke Sigismund of Austria and the other for himself, he forbade further damage, and ordered the stone to be suspended in the parish church."

Not all visiting objects that arrive from beyond the earth come as stones. The strange dry fogs that at long intervals blanket wide parts of the globe may occur when the earth passes through the vast clouds of dust that are believed to occur in the depths of space. The dry fog that in A.D. 526 covered the Eastern Roman Empire with a reddish haze may have been caused in this manner. So also with the blue fog that hung over much of the northern hemisphere for most of the summer of 1783. It began at Copenhagen on May 24, and by June had extended to Germany, France, and England. Eventually it spread eastward as far as Syria and westward over a large part of North America. It showed no trace of humidity and was unaffected by rain or wind. The pale blue haze was sometimes so dense that visibility was reduced to half a mile, and the sun only became visible when it stood 12° above the horizon. The fog had a strong, disagreeable odor, and caused severe catarrh in humans and animals as long as it lasted. Another strange feature of the blue fog was the peculiar phosphoric gleam that accompanied it, and made reading possible at night, even small print. The same gleam came with a haze in 1831, when the sun appeared tinged with green.

Many people thought such an extraordinary event must mean the approaching end of the world. Sir Arthur Conan Doyle may have had such fears in mind when he wrote *The Poison Belt*, a story in which the earth passes into a cloud of interstellar gas, bringing death and widespread fire in its inexorable progress across the globe.

Whether or not meteoric dust brings about the end of civilization, it seems certain that meteorites helped to get it going. Of the three main types of meteorite, one is almost entirely composed of pure iron, a crucial metal in the development of civilization. Iron occurring naturally on earth is invariably combined with other elements and gives no indication of its special properties. But meteoric iron found by primitive mankind was literally "a pure gift from heaven," needing no more attention than softening by fire and hammering to a convenient shape. The Eskimos have long used meteoric iron for spears, axe heads, and knives. Fragments of such iron have been found in the burial mounds of the prehistoric Hopewell Indians of North America.

Even Fort's theory of an extraterrestrial source for life on earth has received support from the recent chemical analysis of meteorites. In 1969 the British chemists J. Brooks and G. Shaw examined the meteorite that had fallen at Murray, Kentucky, in 1950 and discovered that it contained sporopollenin, a highly complex biological substance that forms the outer coating of pollen grains. In another meteorite the quantity of sporopollenin was found to be four percent of the total weight.

When an enormous fireball swept over the countryside of Victoria, Australia, on September 28, 1969, it exploded near the town of Murchison and showered the area with fragments. Examples sent to the NASA Research Center in Ames, California, revealed large quantities of five of the 20 amino acids found in living cells. The presence of these chemicals is considered to be essential before life can originate on a planet. Experiments have shown that they could have been generated by the action of lightning on the gases that composed our earth's primitive atmosphere—ammonia, methane, water vapor, and hydrogen. But an extraterrestrial origin for life on earth cannot be ruled out.

9. Fires from Nowhere

In the summer of 1921 the Reverend John Henry Lehn, then a young man of 24, had a strange experience during an electrical storm. He saw a ball of lightning enter his bathroom, roll around his feet, and jump up into the wash basin before it soundlessly disappeared.

"It was about the size of a grapefruit and yellow in color, similar in hue to sodium flame, though it did not dazzle my eyes," he later wrote of this odd event. "It made no sound at any time."

The ball lightning had somehow managed to get through the wire screen of the open window without losing its form and without damaging the screen in any discernable way. But that was not all that was surprising about its behavior. It also melted the steel chain holding the rubber stopper of the drain, leaving it in two parts. The whole mysterious episode lasted only several seconds, and the young man was left guessing where the bright ball had gone. He thought it must have disappeared "down the drain."

A few weeks later during another electrical storm, almost exactly the same thing happened in the same bathroom. The lightning globe entered through the window without melting the screen and circled Lehn's feet as before. Then it again melted a chain holding a rubber drain stopper—this time the one in the bathtub!

Is the phenomenon called ball lightning explainable as a natural happening? Scientists do not even agree that these floating balls of fire are lightning at all in the strict sense of the word. Although ball lightning is always reported as luminous, it is variously described as to size and color—from a few inches to several feet in diameter, and from a dull white to a fiery red. Sometimes the lightning balls disappear with a loud bang, suddenly, and sometimes they merely fade away in silence. Ball lightning does not act like lightning, in fact. It moves more slowly, lasts much longer, and disregards conductors. It does not seem to harm humans, even when it vanishes with a blast. Most curious of all, it seems to display an independent will. For as John Henry Lehn remarked with good humor, "maybe the second sphere wanted a chain of its own to melt in two—at any rate, that's what it did."

A Will of its Own?

Other reports appear to support the theory, formulated by Vincent Gaddis in his book *Mysterious Fires and Lights* (1967), that ball lightning has a definite will of its own, and that it is benevolent toward humans. Gaddis cites several examples of what he calls "socially minded lightning balls" from the collection of incidents recorded by the French astronomer Camille Flammarion. In one of these, a fiery globe actually pushed open the door in order to get into the house it invaded. Another time, a ball of light stopped at the top of a tree, went down it slowly from branch to branch, and moved carefully across a farmyard. When it arrived at the door of the stable, one of two children standing there kicked it. The ball lightning exploded with a deafening noise, but left the children unhurt. Not so the animals inside the barn. Several of them were killed.

Flammarion recounts another instance in which animals suffered death from contact with a lightning ball that did no injury to people. It happened in a village in southwest France. A burning sphere came down the chimney of a farmhouse and, passing through a room with a woman and three children in it, entered the adjoining kitchen. During its progress through the kitchen, it nearly touched the feet of a young farmer, who was not harmed. The ball lightning ended up in a small stable that was part of the house. There, as though it was its intent, it touched a pig as it vanished—and left the animal dead.

No cases have been reported of people being killed by ball lightning. But there is another fiery phenomenon that seems to be malevolent toward human beings. This is the fireball. Unlike ball lightning, fireballs are not connected with electrical storms.

They fall suddenly, move quickly, and cause intense heat in their vicinity. Something of the power possessed by these strange objects can be seen from the experience of Richard Vogt of Eagle Bend, Minnesota. Driving home on the night of May 10, 1961 he saw what looked like "a ball of fog, about three feet in diameter and slightly elongated." It was heading for his car at about a 45-degree angle, and came so rapidly that he could not hope to avoid it. Indeed, he did not. The bright ball struck his car just in front of the windshield, exploding as it did. At this, the car became so hot that Vogt had to jump out as quickly as he could. When he touched the windshield, which had been cracked by the impact, he could not leave his fingers on it for more than a second. Asked to give an opinion on the incident, scientists from the University of Minnesota could not offer much help. They were as baffled as anyone that the object fell out of a perfectly clear sky.

The sky was also clear on May 29, 1938 when a fiery object dropped to earth and burned nine men in a town in England. They described the mysterious menace as "a ball of fire." When the barn on a Massachusetts farm was burned down on April 29, 1965, more than one witness said that they saw a sphere that looked like a "flaming basketball" fall near the barn just before the outbreak of the fire. The local fire chief said that he did not think the fire could have started from a natural cause.

Perhaps the strangest and least understood of all kinds of burning from a seemingly unnatural cause is that in which the human body is consumed by a heat so great as to turn bones to ash. Some cases of death by burning have been so baffling that the only answer seems to be an impossible one: spontaneous human combustion. How else to explain a body burned to ashes when nothing—or very little—around it has been in any way touched by flames?

The classic case supporting the idea of spontaneous human combustion is that of Mary Hardy Reeser, who died on July 1, 1951 under circumstances that have never been explained. When found in her apartment, almost nothing remained of the 170-pound woman—only her liver still attached to a piece of backbone, her skull, her ankle and foot encased in a black satin slipper, and a little heap of ashes. These gruesome remains lay inside a blackened circle about four feet in diameter, which also contained a few coiled seat springs. Nothing outside the four-foot circle had been burned. No flames had been seen to alarm her landlady or neighbors. The landlady had suspected nothing when she went to deliver a telegram to the widow at eight o'clock in the morning. Having found the doorknob too hot to handle, however, she had sought help in getting into the apartment and, with the two workmen who came to her aid, had made the appalling discovery. She remembered that she had looked in on her tenant about nine o'clock the night before and had seen her seated in her armchair, ready for bed but smoking a last cigarette.

Could the cigarette have ignited Mary Reeser's rayon night-gown and burned her and the chair? No fire started in this way could possibly have consumed flesh and bone so completely. In crematories, for example, a temperature of 2500°F or more, sustained for three or four hours, is required to cremate a body; sometimes pulverization is still necessary to reduce the bones to a powder. After long and intensive investigations, no one could come up with a reasonable solution—not firemen, not detectives, not outside experts, including a leading pathologist specializing in deaths by fire. A year after Mary Reeser's death, the detective on the case admitted, "Our investigation has turned up nothing that could be singled out as proving, beyond a doubt, what actually happened." The police chief agreed, saying, "As far as logical explanations go, this is one of those things that just couldn't have happened, but it did."

Is it possible that spontaneous combustion is the logical explanation, little as people want to believe it? Spontaneous combustion is fully accepted as a natural occurrence in the vegetable and the mineral kingdoms. Haystacks and ricks of corn have frequently been consumed by the heat generated during the fermentation produced from moisture within them. Barns, paper mills, stores of explosives, all have gone up in flames from the same causes. In certain circumstances a mass of powdered charcoal will heat up as it absorbs air and spontaneously ignite. Bird droppings can produce the same effect; it has even been suggested that some church fires have been caused by the spontaneous ignition of bird droppings accumulated over the centuries on the roof.

The surface of the earth can also burn, usually because of the presence beneath the topsoil of oil-bearing shale or coal. The so-called Burning Cliff near Weymouth, England periodically burns for days, and in past centuries did so for years. Around the English village of Bradley, a thick bed of coal lying eight feet below the surface began burning in the 1750s, and continued to do so for at least 60 years.

Spontaneous Human Combustion

Though doctors and scientists accepted these forms of spontaneous combustion, however, they remained largely blind to any evidence that the same phenomenon could occur in humans. Dr. Alfred Swaine Taylor, author of the influential *Principles and Practice of Medical Jurisprudence*, wrote in 1873: "The hypothesis of such a mode of destruction of the human body is not only unsupported by any credible facts, but is wholly inconsistent with all that science has revealed." Ignoring the possibility that science had not by 1873 revealed all the facts of the universe, he went on to say, "In the instances reported which are worthy of any credit, a candle, a fire, or some other ignited body has been at hand, and the accidental kindling of the clothes of the deceased was highly probable."

It is interesting to follow in successive editions of Taylor's great work a modification of this denunciatory attitude. The editor of the 8th (1928) edition, while still "absolutely rejecting any doctrine of spontaneous combustion," thereupon adds, "it must be admitted, on the other hand, that there are cases recorded by credible authorities which require some explanation to account for the unusual amount of destruction (burning) which has been produced in a human body by what are at first sight very inadequate means."

Doctors of an earlier century found no difficulty in accepting the fact of death by spontaneous combustion, although in nearly all the cases they considered the deaths to be the result of too much drinking. Thomas Bartholin, a 17th-century Danish medical writer, described the case of a poor woman of Paris who "used to drink spirit of wine [brandy] plentifully for the space of three years, so as to take nothing else. Her body contracted such a combustible disposition, that one night, when she lay down on a straw couch, she was all burned to ashes except her skull and the extremities of her fingers."

A celebrated murder case in 18th-century France brought about a more scientific study of spontaneous human combustion in Europe. The lawyer in the case got his client acquitted by producing evidence to support the idea of spontaneous combustion of the victim rather than murder. The fact that the dead woman was an habitual drunkard led to a connection being made between deaths by unexplained burning and alcohol. In 1763 a book dealing with "the spontaneous burnings of the human body" was published in France. Medical writers in the Netherlands, Germany, and elsewhere followed with their studies. One book of 1832 cited a case of 100 years before in Italy. It had happened in Cesena in 1731 when the 62-year-old Countess Cornelia Bandi died under mysterious circumstances. What was left of her body was found about four feet from her bed—her legs, her half-burned head, and a pile of ashes. No other signs of fire were present.

The authorities laid the cause of death to "internal combustion"—and gossip added that the Countess often washed her body with "camphorated spirit of wine" when "she felt herself indisposed." So alcohol makes its appearance again, if in a discreet way. It would not do to suggest that a countess went to bed drunk, but alcohol had to be introduced in some manner. Doctors began to warn their drinking patients to steer clear of flames—and no doubt similarly warned them against cooling themselves with camphorated spirit of wine.

It was not hard to find examples of those who had disregarded such warnings. In 1744 a woman in Ipswich, England, who "had drunk plentifully of gin," was found burning like a log near the grate—but there was no fire going. A few years later a woman "much addicted to drinking" was found dead in similar circumstances in Coventry, England. John Anderson of Nairn, Scotland, a carter known for his indulgence in whisky, was found "smoldering" and dying by the roadside outside his hometown.

Deaths like this were ammunition for the rising Temperance Movement. The abstainers warned of the horror of dying from an inner, self-started fire. It was said that water could not extinguish these particular flames; that they burned from within and destroyed nothing but the drunken victim; even that the smoke which issued from the bodies was unlike other smoke, depositing an oily, sticky soot on whatever it touched.

It was also as the consequence of—and sometimes the punishment for—drunkenness that spontaneous human combustion entered the novels of the 19th century. The best known incident of spontaneous combustion in the fiction of the period occurs in Charles Dickens' *Bleak House*, in which the old miser Krook meets this repulsive death. The build-up to the discovery is vivid with horrifying details—the smell like burning chops in the air outside the room, the soot that smears "like black fat," the "thick yellow liquor" that drips from the corner of a window sill to lie in a "nauseous pool." Once inside Krook's room: "There is a very little fire left in the grate, but there is a smoldering suffocating vapor in the room, and a dark greasy coating on the walls and ceiling." And so to the discovery between the chairs: "Is it the cinder of a small charred and broken log of wood sprinkled with white ashes . . .?" It is not. It is all that remains of old Krook—a man "continually in liquor."

Dickens received many letters from readers who found this death incredible, and who took him to task for "giving currency to a vulgar error." But Dickens was not merely a sensationalist. He had attended an inquest on just such a case when he was a cub reporter 20 years before, and he had followed later developments in the subject.

The Medical Controversy

Searching for a pattern in human deaths by mysterious burning, Michael Harrison in his book *Fire from Heaven* considers the possibility that the better educated are spared from seemingly malicious attacks by fire. He cites the case of James Hamilton, who was a professor of mathematics at the University of Nashville, Tennessee. In January 1835 Hamilton was standing outside his house when he felt a stabbing pain in his left leg—"a steady pain like a hornet sting, accompanied by a sensation of heat."

When he looked down, he saw a bright flame, several inches long, "about the size of a dime in diameter, and somewhat flattened at the tip." It was shooting out from his trousered leg. He tried to beat it out with his hands but this had no effect. He did not give way to panic, however. Although what he was seeing was clearly impossible, he accepted that it was taking place. Possibly without consciously recalling the fact, he knew that

97

combustion requires oxygen. He cupped his hands around the flame, cutting off the supply of oxygen, and the flame went out.

Hamilton's quick-wittedness saved him from a fiery attack, and perhaps even death. But how can some people's apparently natural immunity to fire be explained? The well-known Bible story in which Shadrach, Meshach, and Abednego walk around in a fiery furnace without getting a single mark on them or their clothes depends on a divine agency for protection. What about the many recorded cases of mystics and shamans who walk unscathed across red-hot beds of coal or lava? How can certain people control fire so that it does not burn them?

In Paris in the 18th century, two young women demonstrated remarkable ability to submit themselves to what would be torture by fire for others. Gabrielle Moler and Marie Sonet were *convulsionnaires*, the name given to those who claimed miraculous cures after experiencing convulsions at the tomb of a highly esteemed local deacon known for his kindness and humility. Gabrielle Molet astounded onlookers by thrusting her face into a blazing fire and withdrawing it unburned. She would also leave her feet in the fire until her shoes and socks were burned away—and come out without a burn on her flesh. Marie Sonet went even further. She exposed her whole body except her head and feet to a raging fire by lying over it supported on stools at each end. Wrapped only in a sheet, she remained rigid over the flames for hours.

The 19th-century medium Daniel Dunglas Home also exhibited feats of daring with fire. While in a trance or semi-trance, he could handle scorching hot coals as though he had asbestos gloves on. Once he was reported to have picked up a glass lampshade, touching a match against it. The glass was hot enough to ignite the match. Home then put the shade between his lips, which showed no ill effects from the intense heat. This medium, who was never caught in fraud throughout his exceptional career, also had the added quality of being able to transfer his own immunity to fire to other people and to objects. For example, it was said that he could hand searingly hot coals to someone else without that person feeling any pain or burning. He also put such coals against handkerchiefs or clothing without so much as singeing the cloth.

It is an accepted fact that an increase in body temperature is

The only remains of Dr John Irving Bentley, who died on 5 December 1966 in northern Pennsylvania, U.S.A., a victim of spontaneous human combustion. (*Fires from Nowhere*)

one of the physical changes sometimes associated with trances and other unusual states. The most celebrated 20th-century case is that of Padre Pio, a saintly Capuchin friar who lived in the southern Italian town of Foggia and was known for performing miracle cures. His normal body temperature was slightly below normal, but during one of the ecstatic states he experienced, it would soar beyond the reach of an ordinary clinical thermometer to the extraordinary figure of 118.4°F. During his trancelike states, it was observed that Padre Pio seemed to glow. This phenomenon is frequently mentioned in the lives of saints and other holy figures. Saint Philip Neri, Saint Ignatius Loyola, and Saint Francis de Sales are among the many who are said to have been seen surrounded by a bright light when preaching or saying mass. When Moses came down from Mount Sinai "the skin of his face shone," and in the presence of other people he had to wear a veil. In Christian religious art God and Christ are represented as being surrounded by a shining nimbus or glory. The golden haloes shown encircling the heads of saints are stylized expressions of this same glow. Travelers who have climbed to the summits of mountains in stormy weather have sometimes observed sparks shooting from their clothes and hair. Their heads can even be surrounded by an electric aureole very like that of a medieval saint, and it is possible that some people can unconsciously produce a similar effect at ordinary altitudes.

Is there, then, such a thing as a human firefly? Take the case of Anna Monaro, whose strange glowing hit headlines all over the world in May 1934. An asthma patient in the hospital at Pirano, Italy, Mrs. Monaro emitted a blue glow from her breasts as she slept. This emanation lasted for several seconds at a time, occurred several times a night, and continued for a period of weeks. Many doctors and psychiatrists observed the phenomenon. None could explain it.

Can some of the mysterious fires and lights be connected with the poltergeist phenomenon? There are many well-attested and recent reports of poltergeist activity involving fire, including self-destructive attacks as well as assaults on others. Harrison in *Fire from Heaven* also sees in this an unconscious suicide bid—and most cases of spontaneous combustion as an unconscious suicide bid that succeeded. He theorizes that in a trancelike state, or when half-sleeping, intoxicated, or in some other manner "outside themselves," the victims were able to call forth fires or flameless heat because they were possessed of an unconscious wish to die. Can the mind influence matter so much?

10. Monsters of the Deep

In 1938 a strange fish was picked up in the nets of a South African trawler. It turned out to be a coelacanth, a fish that had been in existence about 300 million years ago, and was believed by scientists to have been extinct for about 70 million years. The coelacanth had no special protective features, so its survival all these millions of years was particularly remarkable. If the lowly coelacanth had such powers to survive, why not other ancient marine species? Might there be a few survivors somewhere in the depths of the ocean? The sea is vast and incredibly deep. Ships travel over only a small portion of the surface, and trawlers normally sink their nets to a depth of about 60 feet. Until recently scientists believed that fish could not survive at great depths, but a research vessel has now brought up a fish from a depth of over 26,000 feet. Although the ocean at that level is totally black, that fish still retained two small eyes—evidence that it had once lived far closer to the surface. We know that marine creatures are amazingly adaptable. Salmon leap rapids. A variety of lung fish can live out of water for four years. It is not impossible that certain prehistoric sea monsters have adapted to living in the ocean deeps.

At one time, perhaps as long as 200 million years ago, the sea was filled with giant monsters. There were massive sharks far larger than any we know today, enormous crabs, sea serpents of fantastic lengths, and huge lung fish, skates, and rays. Many of these creatures developed body armor and protective devices such as stings to insure their survival. In 1930 Dr. Anton Brun caught the six-foot-long larva of an eel at a depth of only 1000 feet. On the assumption that it would mature to 18 times its length—although some eels reach 30 times their larval size—

this eel would grow to a mammoth 110 feet. Perhaps there are still larger species existing at still greater depths.

But whether they exist or not, sea monsters have long been a part of mariners' tales. Among the many stories is one that took place in the late 18th century when a Danish sailing ship had been becalmed off the coast of West Africa. Her captain, Jean-Magnus Dens, decided to put the time to good use and ordered the crew to scrape and clean the outside of the boat. To do this the men worked from planks on the ship's side. Suddenly, without warning, a giant sea monster emerged. Wrapping two of its enormous arms around two of the men, it dragged them into the sea. A third arm went around another sailor, but, as he clung desperately to the rigging, his shipmates freed him by hacking off the monster's arm. Despite repeated attempts to harpoon the monster, it sank out of sight into the water. The bodies of the first two victims were never recovered, and the third sailor died that same night. The captain later described the part of the arm that had been hacked off. He said it was very thick at one end and tapered to a sharp point at the other. It was about 25 feet long and covered with large suckers. Judging from the size of the cut-off portion, the captain estimated that the whole arm must have been between 35 and 40 feet in length.

Pierre Denys de Montfort

This is a typical seaman's story of a monstrous sea creature—exaggerated, fantastical, but fascinating. Such stories were often believed in earlier times. However, even in the late 18th century, Captain Dens could find few to credit his. The big exception was the young French naturalist Pierre Denys de Montfort, who was determined to prove to the skeptical scientific world that octopuses of colossal size existed. Choosing to believe that Dens' monster was a huge octopus, he included Dens' account in his unfinished six-volume work *The Natural History of Molluscs*. These books were published in Paris between 1802 and 1805, and, unfortunately for Denys de Montfort's reputation, he included a mixture of science and imagination in which fact was hard to distinguish from fiction. The Frenchman's one scientific supporter was the German naturalist Lorenz Oken, who, for all his renown, was slightly suspect because he also believed there were more and stranger things beneath the surface of the sea than had ever been seen above it. Despite great ridicule and criticism, Denys de Montfort continued to compile reports of "the sightings of monsters and serpents of the sea by mariners whose sincerity I do not and will not doubt."

True to his word, he followed every lead to find his giant octopus. Sometime in the 1790s he journeyed to the northern port of Dunkirk, where a group of American whale fishers were living and working. He wanted to interview the seamen and hear at first hand of the experiences that few people apart from himself would credit. For example, here is a report he repeated: "One of these captains, named Ben Johnson, told me that he had harpooned a male whale, which, besides its very prominent penis placed under the belly, seemed to have another one coming out of its mouth. This surprised him greatly, and also the sailors, and when they had made the whale fast to the ship, he had them put a hook through this long round mass of flesh which they hauled in with several running nooses . . . They could hardly believe their eyes when they saw that this fleshy mass, cut off at both ends and as thick as a mast at the widest point, was the arm of an enormous octopus, the closed suckers of which were larger than a hat; the lower end seemed newly cut off. the upper one . . . was also cut off and scarred and surmounted by a sort of extension as thick and long as a man's arm. This huge octopus's limb, exactly measured with a fishing line, was found to be 35 feet long, and the suckers were arranged in two rows, as in the common octopus. What then must have been the length of arm which had been cut off at its upper extremity where it was no less than six inches in diameter?" It seemed to Denys de Montfort that at least 10 feet had been sliced off the upper end, and a further 10 to 25 feet off the lower —making a total length of some 80 feet.

During his stay in Dunkirk, he found that the whale fishers were eager to speak of their encounters with monsters. He gave an account of what was told by an American captain named Reynolds. "One day," Denys de Montfort recorded, "he and his men saw floating on the surface of the water a long fleshy body, red and slate colored, which they took to be a sea serpent, and which frightened the sailors who rowed the whaleboats." However one sailor noticed that the supposed snake had no head and was motionless, so they found the courage to haul it aboard. They then discovered from the suckers that it was an octopus or squid arm—one that measured 45 feet in length and $2\frac{1}{2}$ feet in diameter.

The Monster of St Thomas's Chapel

The arm, which would have been a convincing piece of evidence, was nowhere to be found by the time Denys de Montfort heard about it. Although disappointed at not seeing it, the naturalist's hopes rose when he heard of an extraordinary painting of a sea monster on view further along the coast in St. Malo. He hurried to go to St. Thomas' chapel where the picture, given in thanksgiving for their survival by a ship's crew, was hanging. Before inspecting it, however, he quizzed several of the port's fishermen about its story. They related how a local sailing ship had run into trouble off the West African coast, and how her crew had been set upon by a "monster straight from Hell." As Denys de Montfort told it from the accounts he heard:

"The ship had just taken in her cargo of slaves, ivory, and gold dust, and the men were heaving up anchor, when suddenly a monstrous cuttlefish appeared on top of the water and slung its arms about two of the masts. The tips of the arms reached to the mastheads, and the weight of the cuttle dragged the ship over, so that she lay on her beam-ends and was near to being capsized. The crew seized axes and knives, and cut away at the arms of the monster; but, despairing of escape, called upon their patron saint, St. Thomas, to help them. Their prayers seemed to give them renewed courage, for they persevered, and finally succeeded in cutting off the arms, when the animal sank and the vessel was righted. Now, when the ship returned to St. Malo the crew, grateful for their deliverance from so hideous a danger, marched in procession to the chapel of their patron saint, where they offered a solemn thanksgiving, and afterwards had a painting made representing the conflict with the cuttle, and which was hung in the chapel."

On hearing this story, Denys de Montfort rushed into the chapel as eagerly as the seamen themselves had done, and gazed up at the fantastic and fearsome scene that the painting depicted. The monster, whose arms were wound around the tops of the three masts, was as gigantic and hideous as the naturalist could have yearned for, and he was grateful for the boost it gave to his theories. He took the painting to be an exact description of a real event, which his obsessional belief in monstrous octopuses made entirely plausible to him. He had a copy of the painting made by an artist who had not seen the original, and who therefore made it seem even more fantastic. On publication of the copy, critics called it an even bigger fake than his books. He was branded "the most outrageous charlatan Paris has known," and no one accepted his challenge to travel the 200 miles to St. Malo to see the original for themselves. The picture was later taken from the chapel and either hidden or destroyed. Denys de Montfort sank into disrepute and obscurity. He wrote a phrase book and a book on bee-keeping, and, on their failure, became a pedlar of sea shells. Having fallen into deep poverty, he was found dead in a gutter in 1820 or 1821. His reputation as an eccentric overshadowed his fine early work on mollusc shells, and it was too soon forgotten that he had created 25 new genera still in use today.

For some decades after, no naturalists were prepared to risk their career by writing about marine monsters, whether or not they thought some of the tales might have a basis in fact. A more recent author views the whole subject in more perspective, however, and writes: "The sea serpent—or at any rate his cousin, the sea monster . . . is at least as ancient, and therefore as respectable, as the fairies, and a good deal older than the modern ghost." Tales of the Norwegian monkfish, for instance, go back to medieval times. The first one was caught off the coast after a great tempest. It "had a man's face, rude and ungraceful with a bald, shining head; on the shoulders something resembling a monk's cowl; and long winglets instead of arms. The extremity of the body ended in a tail." According to the historian who described it, the peculiar-looking monkfish was given to the King of Poland who took pity on it and had it placed back in the sea.

The Kraken

In 1680 a frightful kraken, which is a legendary giant sea monster, swam too close to the shore of Norway, became jammed in a cleft of rock, and remained there until it died. The stench from the kraken polluted the entire neighborhood, and it was months before the local people could go within miles of the rotting carcass. More than 50 years later, in 1734, another kraken was observed by the celebrated Danish missionary Hans Egede—this time near Greenland. He recorded the experience in his diary stating: "The monster was of so huge a size that, coming out of the water, its head reached as high as a main-mast; its body was as bulky as the ship, and three or four times as long. It had a long pointed snout, and spouted like a whale-fish; it had great broad paws; the body seemed covered with shellwork, and the skin was very ragged and uneven. The under part of its body was shaped like an enormous huge serpent, and when it dived again under the water, it plunged backward into the sea, and so raised its tail aloft, which seemed a whole ship's length distant from the bulkiest part of its body."

Another 18th-century writer on the kraken was the Nor-wegian Bishop of Bergen, Erik Pontoppidan. He wrote a book about the natural history of Norway in 1752, and, although he did not see a sea monster himself, he believed the scores of fishermen who told him that they had. He described the kraken as it was described to him. "Its back or upper part, which seems to be about an English mile-and-a-half in circumference, looks at first like a number of small islands surrounded with some-thing that floats and fluctuates like seaweed . . . at last several bright points or horns appear, which grow thicker and thicker the higher they rise above the water. . . . After the monster has been on the surface for a short time it begins slowly to sink again, and then the danger is as great as before, because the motion of his sinking causes such a swell in the sea and such an eddy or whirlpool, that it draws everything down with it . . ."

In 1765, the same year that Bishop Pontoppidan's book appeared in English translation, *The Gentleman's Magazine* in London stated that "the people of Stockholm report that a great dragon, named Necker, infests the neighboring lake, and seizes and devours such boys as go into the water to wash." This did not stop the Bishop of Avranches from swimming there on a sunny summer day, although the onlookers "were greatly surprised when they saw him return from imminent danger."

With some three-fifths of the earth's surface covered with

106

Descriptions of long, serpent-like creatures are common in accounts of sea monsters throughout history. Illustrated above is a woodcut from the 16th century of the Great Norwegian sea serpent. *(Monsters of the Deep)*

The sea serpent seen by Captain Peter M'Quhae and other crew from the Daedalus between the Cape of Good Hope and St. Helena on 6 August 1848. *(Monsters of the Deep)*

Sea monster photographed by Robert Le Serrec at Stonehaven Bay,
Hook Island, Australia on 12 December 1964. (*Monsters of the Deep*)

water, it is hardly surprising that stories of sea monsters arose. Sightings were reported in many parts of the world, including North America after it was settled by Europeans. The coast of New England soon became a popular place for serpent encounters, and between 1815 and 1823, hardly a summer went by without someone meeting up with a sea monster. In June 1815 a strange animal was observed moving rapidly south through Gloucester Bay. Its body, about 100 feet long, seemed to have a string of 30 or 40 humps, each the size of a barrel. It had a head shaped like a horse, and was dark brown in color. Two years later it was again seen in the bay, and the *Gloucester Telegraph* reported: "On the 14th of August the sea serpent was approached by a boat within 30 feet, and on raising its head above water was greeted by a volley from the gun of an experienced sportsman. The creature turned directly toward the boat, as if meditating an attack, but sank down. . . ."

The following year, the same or a similar creature was observed in Nahant. One of the clearest accounts was given by Samuel Cabot of Boston. Mr. Cabot was standing on the crowded Nahant beach when he noticed that a number of boats were speedily making for the shore. "My attention," he wrote, "was suddenly arrested by an object emerging from the water at the distance of about 100 or 150 yards, which gave to my mind at the first glance, the idea of a horse's head. It was elevated about two feet from the water, and he depressed it gradually to within six or eight inches as he moved along. His bunches appeared to me not altogether uniform in size. I felt persuaded by this examination that he could not be less than 80 feet long." The horse-like monster reappeared again the next summer, and it was watched by dozens of vacationers. "I had with me an excellent telescope," declared one knowledgeable witness, "and . . . saw appear, at a short distance from the shore, an animal whose body formed a series of blackish curves, of which I counted 13 . . . This at least I can affirm . . . that it was neither a whale, nor a cachalot [sperm whale], nor any strong souffleur [dolphin], nor any other enormous cetacean [water mammal]. None of these gigantic animals has such an undulating back."

Within a short while the creature had shown itself to the crew of the sloop *Concord*. The captain and the mate made a deposition of what they had seen before a local Justice of the

Peace as soon as they reached shore. In his sworn statement the mate said in part: "His head was about as long as a horse's and was a proper snake's head—there was a degree of flatness, with a slight hollow on the top of his head—his eyes were prominent, and stood out considerably from the surface . . ." The same animal was later seen and identified by Reverend Cheever Finch, who said he spent a half-hour watching its "smooth rapid progress back and forth."

Ogopogo

Many lakes are immensely deep, and could provide suitable habitats for large monsters. In fact, the next North American area to be infiltrated by sea serpents was British Columbia, where deep-water lakes are spaced between the Rockies and the Pacific. It was while taking a team of horses across Lake Okanagan in 1854 that an Indian halfbreed claimed to have been "seized by a giant hand which tried to pull me down into the water." He managed to struggle out of the grip, but the horses in his charge were not so lucky. The monster—which apparently had several long and powerful arms—got a hold on the animals and pulled them under the surface; all of them drowned. The sea serpent was known as Naitaka to the Indians and Ogopogo to the settlers. It was seen regularly from then on, and a pioneer named John McDougal later recounted an experience similar to the halfbreed's. Again the man escaped with his life, and again the horses were the victims. By the 1920s the "thing in the lake" was internationally famous, and a London music hall ditty immortalized it with the words: "His mother was an earwig / His father was a whale / A little bit of head / And hardly any tail / And Ogopogo was his name."

From Canada the story of the serpents moved south to the Mormon settlement of Salt Lake City. In July 1860 the newspaper there, *The Desert News*, offered new testimony about the monster of Bear Lake. Up to that time, the Shoshone Indians of Utah had been the principal witnesses of the "beast of the storm spirits," and they were seldom taken seriously. The newspaper story, however, recounted the experience of a respected local resident who had been going along the east shore of the lake. "About half-way," wrote a reporter, "he saw something in the lake which . . . he thought to be a drowned person . . . he rode to the beach and the waves were running pretty high. . . . In a few minutes . . . some kind of an animal that he had never seen before . . . raised out of the water. He did not see the body, only the head and what he supposed to be part of the neck. It had ears or bunches on the side of its head nearly as big as a pint cup. The waves at times would dash over its head, when it would throw water from its mouth or nose. It did not drift landward, but appeared stationary, with the exception of turning its head." The next day, July 28, the creature was seen by a man and three women—but this time it was in motion and "swam much faster than a horse could run on land."

Reports of the Bear Lake serpent continued for several decades, but were temporarily eclipsed in 1941 with the advent of Slimey Slim, the serpent that inhabited Lake Payette in Idaho. During July and August that summer more than 30 people—most of them boaters on the lake's seven miles of water—saw the monster. For a while, they kept quiet about it. Then Thomas L. Rogers, City Auditor of Boise, Idaho, decided to speak up. He told a reporter: "The serpent was about 50 feet long and going five miles an hour with a sort of undulating movement. . . . His head, which resembles that of a snub-nosed crocodile, was eight inches above the water. I'd say he was about 35 feet long on consideration."

With the publication of this story the lake was inundated with camera-wielding tourists hoping for a glimpse of Slimey Slim. After an article about him appeared in *Time* magazine, the monster seemed to turn shy, and little more was heard or seen of him. With Slim's disappearance, attention returned to Ogopogo, who, having been seen by a captain in the Canadian Fishery Patrol, had been described as being like "a telegraph pole with a sheep's head." An American visitor to Canada was struck "dumb with horror" on catching sight of the monster. On July 2, 1949, Ogopogo was seen by the Watson family of Montreal together with a Mr. Kray. Newsmen reported of their experience: "What the party saw was a long sinuous body, 30 feet in length, consisting of about five undulations, apparently separated from each other by about a two-foot space . . . . The length of each of the undulations . . . would have been about five feet. There appeared to be a forked tail, of which only one-half came above the water."

Three summers later Ogopogo presented himself to a woman visitor from Vancouver, swimming within a few hundred feet of her. "I am a stranger here," she said shortly afterward. "I did not even know such things existed. But I saw it so plainly. A head like a cow or horse that reared right out of the water. It was a wonderful sight. The coils glistened like two huge wheels. . . . There were ragged edges (along its back) like a saw. It was so beautiful with the sun shining on it. It was all so clear, so extraordinary. It came up three times, then submerged and disappeared."

Reports of the sea serpent mounted until 1964, when Ogopogo apparently went into retirement. However, one of the most graphic accounts of the creature was featured in *The Vernon Advertiser* of July 20, 1959. The writer, R. H. Millar, was the newspaper's owner-publisher, and the sighting of "this fabulous sea serpent" was clearly the highlight of his journalistic life. "Returning from a cruise down Okanagan Lake, traveling at 10 miles an hour, I noticed, about 250 feet in our wake, what appeared to be the serpent," he recorded. "On picking up the field glasses, my thought was verified. It was Ogopogo, and it was traveling a great deal faster than we were. I would judge around 15 to 17 miles an hour. The head was about nine inches above the water. The head is definitely snakelike with a blunt nose. . . . Our excitement was short-lived. We watched for about three minutes, as Ogie did not appear to like the boat coming on him broadside; [he] very gracefully reduced the five humps which were so plainly visible, lowered his head, and gradually submerged. At no time was the tail visible. The family's version of the color is very dark greenish. . . . This sea serpent glides gracefully in a smooth motion . . . . This would lead one to believe that in between the humps it possibly has some type of fin which it works . . . to control direction."

Other North American Lake Monsters

The publicity given to Ogopogo brought eye-witness versions of serpents in other North American lakes, including Flathead Lake in Montana; Lake Walker, Nevada; Lake Folsom, California; and Lake Champlain, Vermont. From Monterey in Southern California came reports of the so-called "monster of San Clemente," who was also known as the Old Man of

110

Monterey. Further north, on Vancouver Island, a serpent nick-named "Caddy" made a rival bid for the headlines. The most sober and authentic sounding account of Caddy goes back to 1950, when he was seen by Judge James Thomas Brown, then one of Saskatchewan's leading members of the judiciary. He was spending a winter holiday on the island when he, his wife, and daughter spotted Caddy some 150 yards from shore.

"His head [was] like a snake's [and] came out of the water four or five feet straight up," stated the judge. "Six or seven feet from the head, one of his big coils showed clearly. The coil itself was six or seven feet long, fully a foot thick, perfectly round and dark in color. . . . It seemed to look at us for a moment and then dived. It must have been swimming very fast, for when it came up again it was about 300 yards away . . . I got three good looks at him. On one occasion he came up almost right in front of us. There was no question about the serpent—it was quite a sight. I'd think the creature was 35 to 40 feet long. It was like a monstrous snake. It certainly wasn't any of those sea animals we know, like a porpoise, sea-lion and so on. I've seen them and know what they look like."

Monsters of the lakes and seas continued to make appearances in the present century. Passengers and crews of the *Dunbar Castle* in 1930, and again of the *Santa Clara* in 1947, sighted such monsters in the Atlantic. It must have been an added thrill for the passengers as they spotted the serpents swimming nearby. In the summer of 1966, while rowing across the Atlantic in their boat *English Rose III*, Captain John Ridgway and Sergeant Chay Blyth were nearly rammed by one of the marine monsters. It was shortly before midnight on July 25, and Blyth was asleep. Captain Ridgway, who was rowing, was suddenly "shocked to full wakefulness' by a strange swishing noise to starboard.

"I looked out into the water," he recounts in their book *A Fighting Chance*, "and suddenly saw the writhing, twisting shape of a great creature. It was outlined by the phosphorescence in the sea as if a string of neon lights were hanging from it. It was an enormous size, some 35 or more feet long, and it came toward me quite fast. I must have watched it for some 10 seconds. It headed straight at me and disappeared right beneath me. I stopped rowing. I was frozen with terror . . . I

111

forced myself to turn my head to look over the port side. I saw nothing, but after a brief pause I heard a most tremendous splash. I thought this might be the head of the monster crashing into the sea after coming up for a brief look at us. I did not see the surfacing—just heard it. I am not an imaginative man, and I searched for a rational explanation for this incredible occurrence in the night as I picked up the oars and started rowing again . . . I reluctantly had to believe that there was only one thing it could have been—a sea serpent."

As far back as 1820 the English naturalist Sir Joseph Banks, who had sailed around the world with Captain Cook, had given scientific credence and his "full faith" to "the existence of our Serpent of the Sea." He was followed in this a few years later by the botanist and director of Kew Gardens, Sir William J. Hooker, who said of the sea serpent that, "It can now no longer be considered in association with hydras and mermaids, for there has been nothing said with regard to it inconsistent with reason. It may at least be assumed as a sober fact in Natural History . . ."

Explorers of the Depths

Since that time, much has been learned about life underneath the ocean and about the ocean bed itself. In 1865 a Frenchman descended to a depth of 245 feet. Within a hundred years that record was smashed by Dr. Jacques Piccard and Lieutenant D. Walsh of the U.S. Navy. On January 23, 1960, these two men took the bathyscaphe *Trieste* down to a depth of 35,802 feet at Mariana Trench in the Pacific. This is the world's deepest trench and, measured from top to bottom, is higher than Mount Everest. They described the bottom as a "waste of snuff-colored ooze." Being able to go so far into the ocean's depths has increased the chances of an encounter with a deep-sea monster that may date from prehistoric days.

Explorers such as Piccard and the world-famous Captain Jacques Cousteau have seen species of fish that were previously unknown to or unseen by man. Swimming through the deep troughs, trenches, and ridges that make the ocean bed a kind of underwater mountain area are millions of hitherto unclassified creatures. "I was astounded by what I saw in the shingle at Le Mourillon," writes Cousteau of one of his expeditions,

112

". . . rocks covered with green, brown, and silver forests of algae, and fishes unknown to me, swimming in crystal clear water. . . . I was in a jungle never seen by those who floated on the opaque roof." In 1969 the world's largest research submarine—the electrically powered *Ben Franklin* designed by Jacques Piccard—drifted to a depth of 600 feet below the Gulf Stream. Its six-man crew surfaced with numerous reports of sightings made through one or another of the craft's 29 viewing ports, including the observation of the tiny purple colored hatchet fish.

From these and other expeditions it is obvious that man is determined to explore and chart the world beneath the sea. Scientists state that before long some 98 percent of the ocean floor will have been explored, and that such exploration could mean the discovery of any monster or monsters which have been living in the ocean ridges. The U.S. Navy is developing a Deep Submergence Search Vehicle, which will be prepared if it encounters more dangerous inhabitants than the prawns, starfish, and copepods already found to be living in the low-level oozes. Underwater television, sonar sensing equipment, and electronic flash lamps and floodlights will compensate for the lack of light.

Men like Cousteau have pioneered in building underwater houses and villages—such as the U.S. Navy's *Sealab* machines—in which aquanauts can live beneath the oceans for periods of up to 30 days. In Switzerland today there is a special tourist submarine that takes visitors beneath the surface of a lake for a view of the wonders down below. From that it is just another large step to underwater cruise liners which are being planned to take tourists under the waters of the ocean.

In recent years giant sharks whose heads measure some four feet from eye to eye have been photographed on the sea bed. This suggests that even bigger fish—the traditional monsters—are waiting to be found. In their places of so-called eternal darkness, the oceans go down six miles or more—and it is there that the kraken survivors or descendants may lurk. Not long ago a giant pink squid was captured off the coast of Peru. Its 35-foot-long tentacles and its eyes of a foot in diameter caused a sensation. Scientists suggest that the pink squid is nothing compared to the creatures that have yet to be caught. To back up their argument, they point to certain pieces of squid that have been taken from the stomach of whales. Projecting the size of the whole squid from the pieces, they say it would be more than 100 feet in length.

It does not seem too fanciful to imagine that one day in the future a nuclear powered submarine, such as the U.S. Navy's *Nautilus*, could be drifting silently beneath the ice cap at the North Pole when it was suddenly attacked by an underwater monster in defense of its home or family. A similar fate could happen to one of the proposed deep-sea cruise liners. No one knows who would emerge the victor, or how many lives might be lost. But one thing is certain. It would make the most sensational sea monster news in centuries—and this time the accounts could not be put down to the imagination or exaggeration of sailors.

11. The Loch Ness Monster

The African python, which is capable of swallowing a goat, has been seen swimming in the Indian Ocean, sometimes traveling from island to island in search of food. Attempts by large snakes such as this to board passing ships in search of a resting place have naturally given rise to tales of sea monsters. Bits of floating timber or shipwreck may account for other monster stories. But it is possible that some accounts of sea monsters are genuine. They are disbelieved mainly because the creatures seen have not yet been identified by scientists, or are thought to be long extinct.

About 80 to 90 million years ago giant reptiles roamed the earth and scoured the oceans in search of food. For survival they depended on brute strength, adaptation to changing environments, and hiding from any danger they could not cope with. For many millions of years the seas were dominated by the fish-eating *plesiosaurus* with its barrel-shaped body and serpentine neck, and the sharklike *ichthyosaurus*, or fish lizard. Gradually these animals were displaced by the aggressive 40-foot-long sea lizard, the *mosasaurus*. We know that giant land animals began to disappear from the earth, but we do not know what happened to species of animals that were equally at home in the water. Could they have used their skills of adaptation and hiding to penetrate the depths of oceans and lakes and find a way to survive? It is not entirely impossible. After all, huge sea animals really did exist. They are not a figment of our imagination as some skeptics seem to imply. Let us explore the possibilities that may defy the skeptics.

Many of the Scottish lakes, or lochs as they are known in Scotland, are extremely deep. One of the deepest ones, Loch Ness, has become almost legendary because of its associations with repeated sightings of a monster. A dramatic and recent sighting took place in July 1933. Mr. and Mrs. George Spicer were driving home to London along the south bank of Loch Ness when they saw a strange creature emerging from the bracken. It appeared to have a long undulating neck little thicker than an elephant's trunk, a tiny head, a thick ponderous body, and four feet or flappers. Carrying what seemed to be a young animal in its mouth, it lurched across the road, lumbered into the undergrowth, and disappeared with a splash into the lake. The whole startling incident lasted only a few seconds, but it left an indelible impression on the couple. Mr. Spicer later described the creature to a newspaper reporter as a "loathsome sight." He said it looked like "a huge snail with a long neck."

Despite the scorn heaped on Mr. Spicer by the leading scientists and zoologists of the day, there were many who believed his story of the 25-to-30-foot-long monster. Indeed, Spicer was not the only nor the first person to have seen—or claimed to have seen—the beast from the deep. Ever since the early 1880s there had been regular sightings of "Nessie," as the Scottish lake monster affectionately became known. Unaccountably, Nessie was popularly regarded as being female. At various times she was seen by a stonemason, a group of schoolchildren, and a forester working for the Duke of Portland. Further appearances were noted in 1912, 1927, and 1930, and descriptions of her personality and activities appeared in newspapers from Glasgow to Atlanta. However, it was not until the summer of 1933—the same summer that the Spicers reported their experience—that Nessie became an international pet. In that year, a new road was built on the north shore of the beast's lake home between Fort William and Inverness. According to local inhabitants, Nessie was roused from her sleep hundreds of feet beneath the surface of the lake by the noise of the drilling, the vibrations from the explosions, and the boulders that every now and then crashed down the banks. Annoyed at having her slumber disturbed, she broke water, clambered ashore, and proceeded to roam through the surrounding bracken feasting on any young animals she could get her teeth into.

It was around this period that an Automobile Association patrolman also spotted the sea serpent. He too described it as "a thing with a number of humps above the water line. . . . It

116

had a small head and very long slender neck." Shortly after this a third person—local resident Hugh Gray—actually took a photograph of Nessie, and it was reproduced in newspapers and magazines throughout the world. This photograph, like many that were subsequently taken, was not well-defined. Doubters dismissed the object in the picture as a floating tree trunk or log. For those who accepted this theory, the explanation for the Loch Ness phenomenon was clear: some careless road construction workers had thrown a large piece of wood into the loch. Other disbelievers in the monster's existence preferred to think that someone was trying to pull the public's leg.

In order to seek the truth, journalists from all parts of the globe descended on the area—feature writers and photographers from New York, Rio de Janeiro, and Tokyo among them. They were joined in their watch for the monster by a troop of Boy Scouts. When an old lady disappeared from her home nearby, some said that she had become Nessie's latest victim, and declared that the beast was an agent of the devil. Others asserted that she wouldn't attack a human, and was timid and unaggressive by nature. However, both camps agreed that the monster could change shape at will, that she could rise and sink in the loch vertically, and that her body was iridescent, which made her color vary with the light. To support their view that Nessie was alive, well, and dwelling in the lake, her fans produced statistical and historical evidence.

Nessie in History and Folklore

First of all they pointed out that Loch Ness—the largest mass of fresh water in Great Britain—was $22\frac{1}{2}$ miles long and 734 feet deep in the middle. This meant it could easily be the watery home of any huge monster, serpent, or "thing from the deep." They then delved back to the year 565 when a sighting of Niseag—to give Nessie her Gaelic name—was noted by the Irish Saint Columba. For two years previously, Saint Columba had been working to convert the heathen Picts, Scots, and Northumbrians to Christianity from his new monastery on the island of Iona, off the west coast of Scotland. His mission took him throughout the north of the country. When he came to Loch Ness he found some of the local people burying a neighbor who had been badly mauled by the lake monster while out swimming, and who afterward died of his wounds. The corpse had been brought to land by

117

boatmen armed with grappling hooks, but this did not deter one of the missionary's followers from swimming across the narrows at the head of the loch in order to bring over a small boat moored on the other side. Clad only in his loin cloth, the man was making good headway when he was suddenly confronted by a "very odd looking beastie, something like a huge frog, only it was not a frog."

After surfacing and gulping in some air, the monster proceeded to make an open-mouthed attack on the swimmer. She bore down on the defenseless man, and would undoubtedly have swallowed him alive had it not been for the intervention of Columba. Used to dealing with the "irreligious savages," he thought nothing of addressing a monster equally in need of God. With head raised and arms outstretched he commanded: "Go thou no further nor touch the man. Go back at once!" Then, according to an 8th-century biography of the saint, "on hearing this word . . . the monster was terrified and fled away again more quickly than if it had been dragged on by ropes, though it approached Lugne [the swimmer] as he swam so closely that between man and monster there was no more than the length of one punt pole." This feat was hailed by the potential converts as a manifestation of holy power, and the saint—who was noted everywhere for his "cheerfulness and virtue"—recruited scores of new believers.

From then on the Loch Ness monster became as much a part of Scottish lore as the teachings of Columba himself. At the beginning of the 19th century, children were warned against playing on the banks of the lake because it was rumored that Nessie was once again restless and about to pounce. Even such a level-headed, no-nonsense person as the novelist Sir Walter Scott perpetuated monster stories. On November 23, 1827, he wrote in his journal: "Clanronald told us . . . that a set of his kinsmen—believing that the fabulous 'water-cow' inhabited a small lake near his house—resolved to drag the monster into day. With this in view, they bivouacked by the side of the lake in which they placed, by way of nightbait, two small anchors such as belong to boats, each baited with the carcass of a dog, slain for the purpose. They expected the water-cow would gorge on the bait and were prepared to drag her ashore the next morning when, to their confusion, the baits were found untouched."

Perhaps the lake monster cleverly avoided the trap. In any case she seems to show herself only when she wants to, often unexpectedly. A few decades later, in 1880, a diver named Duncan McDonald came across the beast while attempting to salvage a boat wrecked on Loch Ness. "I was underwater about my work," he said, "when all of a sudden the monster swam by me as cool and calm as you please. She paid no heed to me, but I got a glance at one of her eyes as she went by. It was small, gray and baleful. I would not have liked to have displeased or angered her in any way!" By then the major feeling about Nessie was that although ugly of face and bad-tempered when aroused, she did not go out of her way to trouble or frighten people.

Another 19th-century account of the Loch Ness monster gives an entirely different view of the lake inhabitant. It said: "A noted demon once inhabited Loch Ness and was a source of terror to the neighborhood. Like other kelpies [water-spirits in the shape of a horse] he was in the habit of browsing along the roadside, all bridled and saddled, as if waiting for someone to mount him. When any unwary traveler did so, the kelpie took to his heels, and presently plunged into deep water with his victim on his back." The teller of this tale mustered up few believers, perhaps because of the great disparity between his description and the more generally accepted ones.

The Coming of the Hunters

Coming up to the 1930s period when Nessie was at the peak of her popularity, hotelier John Mackay sighted the lake serpent on May 22, 1933. He said that he saw the lake animal make the water "froth and foam" as she reared her ludicrously small head in the air. Although Mackay beat the Spicers by two months in his encounter with Nessie, it was George Spicer's story that was most listened to and believed in nonprofessional quarters.

Before the year 1933 was out Loch Ness and its celebrated inhabitant had become one of the principal tourist attractions of Great Britain. Holiday makers by the thousands got into their cars and headed north to park along the shores of the lake and gaze out over the water. Between 1933 and 1974, some 3000 people attested to having spotted Nessie as she surfaced, dived, or swam tranquilly along. Claims were also made that the monster made a sound—a cry of "anger and anguish" when nearly run down by a car. Waiting for Nessie rivaled watching flagpole squatters and marathon dancers, which were big vogues of the mid-30s. Hundreds of sun-dazzled or fog-smeared photographs—with an indistinct blur in them—were offered as Nessie at play. The eager Nessie-hunters were given short shrift by E. G. Boulenger, Director of the Aquarium in the London Zoo. He wrote in October 1933 that:

"The case of the Loch Ness monster is worthy of our consideration if only because it presents a striking example of mass hallucination . . . For countless centuries a wealth of weird and eerie legend has centered around this great inland waterway . . . Any person with the slightest knowledge of human nature should therefore find no difficulty in understanding how an animal, once said to have been seen by a few persons, should shortly after have revealed itself to many more."

Another reason for so many sightings was suggested by the more cynical, who pointed to the rewards being offered for the capture of Nessie alive. The money prizes included one for $500 from the New York Zoo, £20,000 from the Bertram Mills circus, and a mammoth £1 million from the makers of Black and White Whisky. The whisky firm stipulated that the monster, if taken, had to be declared genuine by officials of the British Museum. Debate on Nessie even reached the British House of Commons, and, on November 12, 1933, a member of Parliament called for an official investigation to settle the "monster matter" for once and all. The Government spokesman who replied stated that such an endeavor was "more properly a matter for the private enterprise of scientists aided by the zeal of the press and photographers."

It was on the same day of the government debate that Mr. Hugh Gray took the famous picture mentioned before. It was published first of all in the Scottish *Daily Record*, and then reproduced throughout the world. That was all the confirmation Nessie's admirers needed. According to Gray, he was walking along the loch shore near Foyers, camera in hand, when, from his vantage point on a 30-foot-high cliff, he saw the quiet water beneath him "explode into commotion." A huge form reared in front of him and a long neck stretched out. During the few seconds that the monster was on the surface, Mr. Gray took five hasty shots of her. Due to the spray that was thrown up, the "object of considerable dimensions" was not clearly discerned. Later, four of the five negatives proved to be blank. The good negative was shown to technical experts of the Kodak camera company, who testified that it had not been tampered with in any way—and once again only the professional zoologists remained dissatisfied. Mr. J. R. Norman of the British Museum stated that "the possibilities leveled down to the object being a bottlenose whale, one of the larger species of shark, or just mere wreckage." Professor Graham Kerr of Glasgow University considered the photograph to be "unconvincing as a representation of a living creature."

A local bailiff, Alexander Campbell, held stage center in June 1934 when he told his Nessie tale. According to him, he had been out fishing in a row boat with two friends when a "dark gray, rocklike hump" rose from the water, stayed there for a moment, and then submerged without causing more than a few ripples. (Campbell was persistent if not consistent. In 1958 he said that Nessie had again appeared before him, but this time she created a "small tidal wave" that sent him toppling into the lake.)

In 1934, too, came the first of the numerous books about the celebrated Loch Ness monster. It listed 47 sightings complete with drawings and photographs. In January a newsreel film said to be of Nessie was shown in London to a private audience. The camera caught her about 100 yards away as she swam past. Of this event *The Times* on January 4 said: "The most clearly evident movements are those of the tail or flukes. This appendage is naturally darker than the body. The photographers describe the general color of the creature as gray, that of the tail as black. Indeterminate movements of the water beside the monster as it swims suggests the action of something in the nature of fins or paddles." Unfortunately, this film disappeared before any study of its authenticity was made.

Three months later Nessie reached the attention of royalty when the Duke of York—who became King George VI—addressed the London Inverness Association, and told members:

"Its [Nessie's] fame has reached every part of the earth. It has entered the nurseries of this country. The other day, I was in the nursery, and my younger daughter, Margaret Rose [now Princess Margaret], aged three, was looking at a fairy-story picture book. She came across a picture of a dragon, and described it to her mother: 'Oh, look Mummy, what a darling little Loch Ness monster!' "

The Surgeon's Photograph

The Abbot of the Monastery in Fort Augustus, at the foot of the loch, added his opinion to the controversy with his announcement that, "the monster is a true amphibian, capable of living either on land or in water, with four rudimentary legs or paddles, an extraordinarily flexible neck, broad shoulders and a strong, broad, flat tail, capable of violently churning the waters around it." Then, in April 1934, came the famous "surgeon's picture" taken by a London surgeon named Kenneth Wilson. He had a telephoto lens on his camera for his hobby of photographing trains. While driving south from a vacation in northern Scotland, he stopped the car at 7:30 a.m. and got out to stretch his legs. He was on a slope 200 feet above the surface of Loch Ness when he suddenly saw the water begin to swirl, and spotted "the head of some strange animal rising." He ran back to the car, returned with the three-quarter plate camera, and rapidly took four pictures. Two of them turned out to be duds, but one showed the monster's long, arched neck, and the last plate revealed its out-of-proportion small head about to submerge. The picture of the head and neck appeared in the London *Daily Mail*. As so often in the past, the public showed interest, but the authorities remained skeptical.

How can a creature of Nessie's size hide out so well in a lake, even one as large as Loch Ness? Part of the answer is that this lake is the receptacle of peat particles from 45 mountain streams and five rivers. Little is visible below a depth of six feet, and underwater exploration by lung divers is stymied by the dense, impenetrable murk. For the most part, Nessie has been seen as a series of humps when she came up from the depths for air. This proved the case with the investigation backed by the insurance tycoon Sir Edward Mountain, who kept an intense five-week watch on the loch in the summer of 1934. Of the 17 monster sightings reported, 11 of them were of humps. This was also true when a Glendoe sawmill worker saw Nessie at 9 a.m. that same summer. He reported a series of 12 humps "each a foot out of water." He said in an article in the *Scotsman* of July 6, 1934: "The day was so clear that I could distinguish drops of water as they fell when the monster shook itself. It reached Glendoe Pier and stretched its neck out of the water where a stream enters the loch.

Four photographs of the Loch Ness Monster.
(*Top left*) The first known photograph was taken by local resident Hugh Gray on 12 November 1933 from the top of 30-foot-high cliff on the loch shore near Foyers.
(*Top right*) The famous "Surgeon's Picture", taken by R.K. Wilson on 19 April 1934 at about 7.30 a.m.
(*Botton left*) A picture taken by Anthony Shiels on 21 May 1977, from Urquhart Castle.
(*Bottom right*) The work of an anonymous holiday cyclist who stopped to take a picture of the view in mid-September 1983 near Achnahannet. (*The Loch Ness Monster*)

Possible photograph of "Morag", the monster of Loch Morar, taken by Miss M. Lindsay, on 31 January 1977. Thirty miles to the west of Loch Ness, Loch Morar became famous in the early 1970s as the home of a monster similar to "Nessie". (*The Loch Ness Monster*)

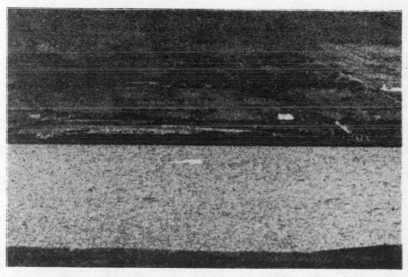

The "Moby Dick" monster photographed in Lough Keel, Achill Island, Co. Mayo, Ireland in early September 1983 and seen by four witnesses. (*The Loch Ness Monster*)

It did not actually come ashore, but seemed to be hunting about the edge, and I cannot see how it could move as it did without using flippers or feet."

The start of World War II in 1939 put an end to speculation about lake serpents for a time, and it wasn't until the early 1950s that Nessie made news again. Then came the usual spate of sightings and photographs. An account of one of the sightings appeared in *Harper's Magazine* in 1957. The witness, Mr. David Slorach, told how he had been driving to Inverness for a business appointment on the morning of February 4, 1954. On looking to his right to admire the view of Loch Ness, he saw something unusual in the water. Its shape reminded him of a "comic ornament popular at one time—a china cat with a long neck. The thing ahead of me looked exactly like the neck and head part. One black floppy 'ear' fell over where the eye might be, and four black streaks ran down the 'neck' . . . The object [was] traveling through the water at great speed, throwing up a huge wave behind. I slowed to around 35 miles per hour, but the object raced ahead and was soon out of sight behind a clump of trees."

The BBC Investigates

Inspired by the renewed interest in Nessie, the BBC sent a television team equipped with a sonic depth-finder to the loch in an attempt to prove or disprove the legend. Obligingly, a "mysterious object" came into range, was recorded some 12 feet below the surface, and was followed to a depth of 60 feet before it lost the depth finder. Experts of the British Museum and the Zoological Society of London were asked their opinions, but they scoffed at the idea of an unfamiliar beast. Instead they spoke of sturgeons, fin whales, sperm whales, and that old standby, the tree trunk. One man was not convinced by the scoffing professionals, however. This was the author and journalist F. W. Holiday. As he put it, his "consuming interest in the problem of the Loch Ness Orm or monster began in 1933 when I was 12 years old." One morning 29 years later, in August 1962, he settled himself on a hillside near Foyers, and, with his binoculars, waited for the monster to make an appearance. He described what happened in his book *The Great Orm of Loch Ness*:

"A dozen or so yards into the loch, opposite the leat [a water channel] an object made a sudden appearance. It was black and glistening and rounded, and it projected about three feet above the surface. Instantly it plunged under again, violently, and produced an enormous upsurge of water. A huge circular wave raced toward me as if from a diving hippopotamus . . . Just below the surface, I then made out a shape. It was thick in the middle and tapered toward the extremities. It was a sort of blackish-gray in color . . . When a chance puff of wind touched the surface, it disappeared in a maze of ripples; but when the water stilled, it was always there. Its size—judging from the width of the leat—was between 40 and 45 feet long."

Holiday also recorded that a film taken at the loch in 1960 was later shown to specialists at the Ministry of Defence's Joint Air Reconnaissance Intelligence Center. After carefully studying and analyzing the images—which showed the customary humped object moving through the water—the experts decided that something, if not Nessie, existed in the deep. They came to the conclusion that the subject of the film "probably is an animate object." However, Nessie came the nearest to getting a certificate of authenticity in 1963 when on the evening of February 2 Grampian and Border Television, an independent British station, transmitted a program about her. The program was presented as a panel discussion, and one of the participants was David James, a Highland laird and a Member of Parliament at the time. He had a few months before kept a two-week, round-the-clock watch on the shores of the loch. Mr. James, founder of The Loch Ness Phenomena Investigation Bureau, told viewers that his watch had been successful. He said:

"On October 19 [1962], in the middle of the afternoon, we had seven people at Temple Pier, and suddenly everyone was alerted by widespread activity among the salmon. After a few minutes the salmon started panicking—porpoising out in the middle of the loch—and immediately we were aware that there was an object following the salmon which was seen by practically everyone there for three or four minutes." On hearing that—and after sifting through years of recorded evidence—the panel announced that: "We find that there is some unidentified animate object in Loch Ness which, if it be mammal, reptile, fish, or mollusc of any known order, is of such a size as to be worthy of careful scientific examination and identification. If it is not of a known order, it represents a challenge which is only capable of being answered by controlled investigation on carefully scientific principles."

Six years after this television program, in August 1968, a team from the Department of Electronic Engineering of Birmingham University mounted a sonar system on one of the piers on the loch. The scan was directed at the southeast corner, and, according to author Holiday, the scientists achieved "dramatic success." The cathode display screen was photographed every 10 seconds by a movie camera, but for some days, nothing of interest was seen. Then, at 4:30 on the afternoon of August 28, there occurred a remarkable 13-minute sequence. "A large object rose rapidly from the floor of the loch at a range of .8 kilometer, its speed of ascent being about 100 feet a minute," Holiday wrote. "It was rising obliquely away from the sonar source at a velocity of about 6.5 knots, and was soon 1 kilometer away. Its upward movement had now slowed to about 60 feet a minute. This object then changed direction to move toward the pier at about 9 knots, keeping constant depth. Finally, it plunged to the bottom at about 100 feet a minute before rising again at .6 kilometer range, when it apparently moved out of the sonar beam and was lost to record. Meanwhile, a second large object had been detected at .5 kilometer from the pier which finally dived at the astonishing velocity of 450 feet a minute. Both objects remained many feet below the surface."

One of the leaders of the team, Dr. H. Braithwaite, later wrote a magazine article on the sonar experiment in which he stated that, "the high rate of ascent and descent makes it seem very unlikely [that the objects were shoals of fish], and fishery biologists we have consulted cannot suggest what fish they might be. It is a temptation to suppose they must be the fabulous Loch Ness monsters, now observed for the first time in their underwater activities."

There the matter rested and there—admired or maligned, sought-after or ignored—lies Nessie. Among the latest to try to explain her away is Dr. Roy Mackal of the Biochemistry Department of the University of Chicago. On visiting Loch Ness in 1966, he suggested that the monster was most likely some kind of "giant sea slug." Four years later another American, Dr. Robert Rines of the Massachusetts Academy of Applied Science, took a Klein side-scan sonar to the banks of the loch. In the deeper water he detected several large moving objects, and said afterward in a radio interview: "We wouldn't have been here if we didn't have the suspicion that there is something very large in this loch. My own view now, after having personal interviews with, I think, highly reliable people, is that there is an amazing scientific discovery awaiting the world here in Loch Ness."

The Monster of Loch Morar

However, Loch Ness is far from being the only fresh-water lake with a quota of monsters. Loch Morar, some 30 miles to the west and completely separated from Loch Ness, has its own Great Worm. At the beginning of 1970 a scientific team headed by the British biologist Dr. Neill Bass began a survey of the site. The team's efforts were rewarded on the afternoon of July 14 when Dr. Bass and two colleagues went for a walk on the north shore of the loch. It started to rain and, while his companions sheltered under some nearby trees, Bass gazed out over the rain-flecked water. Then, just as the weather improved and a breeze came up, the surface was broken by a "black, smooth-looking hump-shaped object." It was some 300 yards away, and by the time his fellow scientists had joined him, the creature had submerged vertically. Thirty seconds later, however, there was another disturbance in the water. It was followed by what the survey's final report called "a spreading circular wake or ripple which radiated across the waves to about 50 yards diameter." For a while Bass thought the object might have been a giant eel, but then realized that the movement was uncharacteristic of such a fish. In the end the report declared it to be "an animate object of a species with which he [Bass] was not familiar in this type of habitat."

The following month a zoology student, Alan Butterworth, also spotted the monster through binoculars while keeping watch on Loch Morar. The water was calm, and visibility was good. The watcher observed a "dark-colored hump," dome-shaped and similar to a rocky islet. The object was about $1\frac{1}{2}$ miles away. Butterworth left to get his camera, and when he returned with it the Great Worm had disappeared. So the most important goal—to obtain authentic film of the monster—was not fulfilled.

Not to be outdone by Scotland, countries from France to Australia to Argentina have claimed that their inland lakes contain their own mysterious and outsized monsters. Ireland, whose legends of lake monsters go back to ancient times, easily heads the list.

Another region with a long tradition of lake monster stories is Scandinavia. It was while visiting Scandinavia and Iceland in 1860 that the English clergyman and author Reverend Sabine Baring-Gould heard of the Skrimsl, a "half-fabulous" monster said to inhabit some of the Icelandic lakes. Although he didn't see any of the beasts himself, he spoke to educated and respectable lawyers and farmers who told of one particular Skrimsl. It was almost 50 feet long and apparently looked much like the more famous Nessie. "I should have been inclined to set the whole story down as a myth," wrote Baring-Gould, "were it not for the fact that the accounts of all the witnesses tallied with remarkable minuteness, and the monster is said to have been seen not in one portion of the lake (the Lagarflot) only, but at different points."

The clergyman also learned of a similar creature in Norway—a slimy, gray-brown animal that terrified the people living around Lake Suldal. Its head was said to be as big as a rowboat. The story was told of a man who, crossing the lake in a small craft, was set upon by the monster and seized by the arm. The attacker let go only when the victim recited the Lord's Prayer. But the man's arm was mangled and useless thereafter.

In Sweden itself Lake Storsjö has long been associated with monsters, and a turn-of-the-century zoologist, Dr. Peter Olsson, spent several years analyzing and sifting through 22 reports containing numerous sightings. The Lake Storsjö monster, or leviathan, was said to be white-maned and reddish in color, more like an enormous seahorse than anything else. It was first spotted in 1839 by some farmers, and reports of it continued well into the 20th century. The creature differed from its fellows by virtue of its speed, which was estimated at a rapid 45 m.p.h. Olsson regarded it as "the fastest and most fascinating of all lake dwellers," a view which was shared by the *New York Times* in 1946. Under the heading, "Normalcy?," an article in the paper stated that, after the insanity of World War II, things were getting back into their old familiar and comforting routine because monsters were being seen again.

Shortly afterward a Stockholm newspaper reported that a group of three people had seen the Lake Storsjö monster when the lake's "calm shining surface was broken by a giant snakelike object with three prickly dark humps. It swam at a good parallel to the shore, on which the waves caused by the object were breaking." More sightings were reported in 1965. This inspired the local tourist board to use a color picture of the monster in its brochures, and to boast that the beast was Sweden's answer to the Loch Ness monster.

Sightings in the Irish Lakes

Ireland is Scotland's nearest rival in the "creature in the lake" stakes, however. There are innumerable reports, accounts, and twice-told tales about such beings. In recent times the stories have proved as vivid and interesting as ever. For example, there is the one of three Dublin priests. On the evening of May 18, 1960, Fathers Daniel Murray, Matthew Burke, and Richard Quigly went trout fishing off Lake Ree—called Lough Ree in Ireland—on the River Shannon. They were exceedingly pleased with the warmth, the calmness of the water, and the way the fish were biting. All at once the tranquility was shattered by the approach of a large flat-headed animal they couldn't identify. It was about 100 yards from where they sat. When it swam up the lake toward them, the startled priests jumped to their feet. "Do you see what I see," one of them cried out, and the other two nodded their heads in amazement. "It went down under the water," stated one of the priests later, "and came up again in the form of a loop. The length from the end of the coil to the head was six feet. There were about 18 inches of head and neck over the water. The head and neck were narrow in comparison to the thickness of a good-sized salmon. It was getting its propulsion from underneath the water, and we did not see all of it."

Lough Ree, where this sighting took place, is one of many small lakes in Ireland, whose west coast is dotted with them. Each lake it seems has its own particular inhabitant. It was this fact which in the 1960s inspired Captain Lionel Leslie, an explorer and cousin of Sir Winston Churchill, to mount his own investigation of the monsters. In October 1965 he went to Lough Fadda in Galway, and exploded a small charge of gelignite against a rock. He hoped that this would bring a *Peiste*, or lake monster, to the surface. Sure enough, a few seconds later a large black object appeared some 50 yards from the shore. Dismissing

128

the possibility of it being a piece of wood or debris, Captain Leslie later told a reporter from *The Irish Independent*, "I am satisfied beyond any doubt that there is a monster in Lough Fadda." A subsequent netting operation failed to capture the creature. Captain Leslie tried again in 1969. In the company of author F. W. Holiday, he plumbed the depths of Loughs Shanakeever, Auna, and Nahooin, but came up with nothing. Television cameras were on hand to record the hoped-for event, but all they were able to film was Captain Leslie, his disheartened band of monster hunters, and the constant rain.

Such experiences—even though they make ready fodder for newspapers and TV—tend to lessen scientific belief in the existence of lake creatures. John Wilson, warden of the bird sanctuary operated by the Royal Society for the Protection of Birds in Lancashire, England, is another skeptic. Writing in the Society's journal in the summer of 1974, he says that Nessie, and presumably those like her, could well be a group of otters at play. "Four or five otters swimming in line with heads, bodies, and tails continually appearing and disappearing combine to look like a prehistoric monster," he states.

For the steady line of Nessie-spotters since George Spicer hit the headlines in 1933, the Loch Ness monster is very much a reality. For the disbelievers, explanations like Dr. Mackal's sea slug or Mr. Wilson's otters are perfectly logical and satisfactory. What is the real truth? No one knows yet!

12. The Walking Dead

"The eyes were the worst. It was not my imagination. They were in truth like the eyes of a dead man, not blind, but staring, unfocused, unseeing. The whole face, for that matter, was bad enough. It was vacant, as if there was nothing behind it. It seemed not only expressionless, but incapable of expression. I had seen so much previously in Haiti that was outside ordinary normal experience that for the flash of a second I had a sickening, almost panicky lapse in which I thought, or rather felt, 'Great God, maybe this stuff is really true . . .' "

This was how William Seabrook described his encounter with one of the most horrifying creatures ever to step from the realms of the supernatural. For Seabrook was face-to-face with a zombie—a walking corpse. And in that moment he was prepared to believe all he had heard about zombies since he first arrived on the island of Haiti.

The zombie's fate is even worse than that of the vampire or the werewolf. The vampire returns to his loved ones. He may be recognized and lain to rest. The werewolf may be wounded and regain human form. But the zombie is a mindless automaton, doomed to live out a twilight existence of brutish toil. A zombie can move, eat, hear, even speak, but he has no memory of his past or knowledge of his present condition. He may pass by his own home·or gaze into the eyes of his loved ones without a glimmer of recognition.

Neither ghost nor person, the zombie is said to be trapped, possibly forever, in that "misty zone that divides life from death." For while the vampire is the living dead, the zombie is merely the walking dead—a body without soul or mind raised from the grave and given a semblance of life through sorcery. He is the creature of the sorcerer, who uses him as a slave or hires him out—usually to work on the land.

The Fate of Marie

Haiti is the home of the zombie, and the island abounds with stories of people who have died, been buried and reappeared as a walking corpse sometimes years later. One of the most famous cases, first recorded by American writer Zora Hurston in 1938, is still recounted in Haiti today. It concerns Marie, a lovely young society girl who died in 1909. Five years after her death, Marie was seen by some former school friends at the window of a house in Haiti's capital Port-au-Prince. The owner of the house refused to allow anyone to investigate, and Marie's father was reluctant to push the matter. Later, however, the house was searched, but by then the owner had disappeared and there was no trace of the girl. Meanwhile the news had spread all over Port-au-Prince, and to satisfy public opinion Marie's grave was opened. Inside was a skeleton too long for the coffin. Neatly folded alongside the skeleton were the clothes in which Marie had been buried.

People say that Marie had been dug up and used as a zombie until the sorcerer who had held her captive died, and his widow turned her over to a Catholic priest. After her schoolmates had seen her, it was said that her family smuggled her out of Haiti, dressed as a nun, and sent her to a convent in France. There she was later visited by her brother.

It is a sad aspect of most zombie stories, however, that no one generally comes to zombies' aid. Family and friends may never learn of the zombie's plight, or if they do, they are much too frightened to intervene. One mother told Zora Hurston about her son who had died and been buried. After the funeral friends stayed overnight with the grieving woman and her daughter. During the night the boy's sister awoke to the sound of chanting and of blows in the street outside. Then she clearly heard her brother's voice. Her screams awoke the rest of the house, and everyone looked out of the windows. Outside a grim procession was wending its way along the street, and in its midst was the boy they had buried that very day. As he stumbled sightlessly by, they all heard his anguished cry. "But such is the terror inspired by these ghouls," wrote Zora Hurston, "that no one, not even the mother or sister, dared to go out and attempt a rescue." The procession shuffled out of sight. The boy's sister subsequently went insane.

Why are the Haitians so terrified of zombies? What might happen to relatives who try to free their dead loved one? Do zombies even exist? To answer all these questions we need to look at Haiti's past, and in particular at the beliefs and practices of Haiti's voodoo religion.

Origins of Voodoo

Voodoo is a unique combination of African, Roman Catholic, and even some American Indian beliefs plus traditional occult practices from Europe. Its deepest roots are in Africa, and voodoo began with the arrival in Haiti of large numbers of African slaves. This terrible traffic in human life, started when Haiti belonged to Spain in the 16th century, gathered momentum in the late 17th century when the island passed into French hands. Haiti was France's wealthiest colony—and depended on slave labor to stay that way. European traders on the west coast of Africa, already supplying millions of slaves to the plantations of the New World, were only too ready to meet France's growing demands. On the rare occasions when the French authorities needed to justify this trade, they did so on the grounds that slavery was the best means of converting the heathen African to Christianity. Many slaves did become members of the Catholic Church, but they adapted the doctrines of Christianity to their own temperaments and needs, and blended Christian rites with their own religious rituals—a combination that was to persevere down the centuries. Even today many Haitians practice both voodoo and Catholicism, despite the disapproval of the Church.

Slaves were brought to Haiti from every part of Western Africa, but the majority came from areas dominated by the Yoruba-speaking peoples. These groups had a strong belief in possession by the gods. Torn from their homeland and their families, transported under appalling conditions to a strange land, the slaves nevertheless carried with them their traditions, their belief in magic and witchcraft, and the memory of the gods and ancestors they had worshiped in the forests of Africa. In Haiti these were to form the basis of voodoo. The new

132

religion became a solace and a rallying force for a suffering and uprooted people, and it was swiftly banned by the French authorities. Driven underground, voodoo grew stronger and more sinister.

Slavery was big business. The thousands who died during or after their journey were continually replaced. By the 1750s, 30,000 slaves were being landed in Haiti every year. As one generation of slaves succeeded another, a terrible yearning set in, and nostalgia for the past fed the flames of rebellion. The first attempt for independence in Haiti took place in 1757. Macandal was the leader of this rebellion of fanatical fugitives, but he was captured by the French and burned to death. Several revolts followed, forcing the proclamation of Haitian independence in 1804. With the retreat of the French colonists who were the upholders of the Christian faith, the voodoo religion became firmly established.

Voodoo is a formalized religion with its own gods and forms of worship. But it also has its sinister side—the voodoo of black magic, sorcery, and superstition, of monsters, murder, and raising the dead. Blood is an essential part of some ceremonies, usually involving the sacrifice of such animals as pigs, hens, and cockerels.

Voodoo ceremonies take place in *tonnelles*. These may be either simple rough huts with mud floors or an elaborate building, but they always contain a covered area for ritual dance. It is during the dance that worshipers undergo the central experience of voodoo worship—possession by the gods. The dancing, chanting, and throbbing of drums are said to generate an atmosphere in which god and worshiper may become one, and at the height of the dance the worshipers enter a state of trance a sort of collective delirium—which ends in collapse.

A dancer may be possessed by any one of a huge number of gods and spirits, many of whom are still known by their African names. During possession the dancer is believed to *become* the god or spirit, adopting not only the god's personality but his or her physical appearance, gestures, and behavior. Thus a dancer possessed by the ancient spirit Papa Legba—guardian of the gateway to the other world and god of crossroads, whose symbol is a crutch—becomes apparently old and lame. Others, recognizing the spirit, run forward with sticks and crutches to help him. A sea god will row with invisible oars. A flirtatious female god will make a possessed man or woman assume mincing, flaunting gestures. A traditional goddess from Dahomey called *Agassa*—a royal union of panther and woman—continues to exert her power in Haiti, causing possessed dancers to stiffen their fingers into claws. Evil spirits might throw a dancer into convulsions. Possession can last for several hours and be so absolute that the possessed walk on burning coals or hold their hands in boiling water without flinching, just as the members of some African tribes used to cut off their own fingers in a state of trance.

A British visitor to Haiti, Patrick Leigh Fermor, gives this interpretation of how possession—or the supposed incarnation of the gods in their worshipers—takes place. In his book *The Traveller's Tree*, written in 1950, he notes, "Every Haitian . . . from his earliest childhood, is spiritually geared for the event of incarnation; and he knows that the moment of miracle occurs in the dark *tonnelle* where the air is afloat with mysteries, and where the drums are already violently reacting on his nerves and brain . . . and so, when he has been brought by the drums, the dance, and the divine presence to a state of hysteria and physical collapse, a dormant self-hypnosis, finding no opposition, leaps to the surface of his brain and takes control."

Certainly it has been established by electrical recordings of the human brain that it is particularly sensitive to rhythmic stimulation. The *hungan*, or voodoo priest, may therefore increase suggestibility by altering the pitch and pace of the ceremonial rhythms. Hungans are also known to use magical powders and herbs as aids to possession, and it is said that even a substance as ordinary as pepper may be enough to bring on possession in the feverish atmosphere of a voodoo ceremony.

Gros-bon-ange and Ti-bon-ange

Whatever the trigger that induces possession, voodoo worshipers believe that the god cannot take over their body unless their soul is first displaced. The soul is believed to consist of two spirits: the *gros-bon-ange* (big good angel) and the *ti-bon-ange* (little good angel). The ti-bon-ange is what we might call a person's conscience. The gros-bon-ange is his essential soul—everything that makes him what he is.

Without the gros-bon-ange, the ti-bon-ange and the body lose
contact. It is the gros-bon-ange that is displaced during possession, so that a person is no longer himself but the god who has
taken over his body. Normally possession ends spontaneously,
and the worshiper's gros-bon-ange is automatically restored to
him. But sometimes the return to oneself will only happen with
the hungan's help. Great care is also taken after a person's death
to provide his disembodied soul with an alternative dwelling
place. The soul, which first spends some time at the bottom of
a river, is recalled by the hungan during a special ceremony, and
placed in a sacred jar—a substitute for the physical body. It then
becomes an ancestral spirit who will advise and protect his
family.

This idea of the soul lies at the heart of many voodoo superstitions, including the belief in zombies. For a soul that has been
displaced for the ceremony of possession may fall into evil hands.
Having one's soulless body possessed by a god is devoutly to be
wished, but it also opens up the possibility of a body being taken
over by the evil machinations of the sorcerer.

The voodoo sorcerer, or *bokor*, is a terrifying character who
communes with the dead and practices all the darkest arts on
behalf of himself and his clients. Sometimes hungan and sorcerer
are one and the same person, for it is said that a priest must be
well acquainted with the techniques of sorcery if he is to combat
them successfully. A hungan might fight a curse with white magic
one day, and cast a spell with black magic the next. Hungans can
invoke good spirits, or evil ones like the *Zandor* who turn
people into snakes or vampire bats. Voodooists maintain,
however, that the true hungan will have nothing to do with
sorcery, and there certainly are bokor who are not voodoo
priests. The bokor inspire criminal societies, worship the devil
and gather in cemeteries to practice the sinister cult of the dead.

Such sorcerers make powders out of cemetery earth and dead
men's bones to "send the dead" against an enemy. Spreading the
powder outside the victim's door or across some path he often
takes is enough to paralyze or kill him, unless another hungan
works some counter-magic in time. Another dreaded custom is
the dressing of a corpse in the clothes of an intended victim and
concealing it in some secret place to rot away while the living
person goes mad searching for it. As students of Haitian belief

have pointed out, if the victim knows what is happening and believes in the force of the magic, it can easily have fatal results.

Haitians tell spine-chilling tales of corpses being dragged from the grave to serve the cruel will of the sorcerer. In his book *The Magic Island*, written in 1936, William Seabrook records this story of a young wife, Camille, and her husband Matthieu Toussel. On their first wedding anniversary Toussel took his wife to a feast soon after midnight. He insisted that Camille wear her bridal dress and she, being afraid of him, obeyed. As the couple entered a candlelit room laid for a banquet, Camille saw that there were four other guests, all in evening clothes. But none of them turned to greet her. Toussel excused their behavior, promising that after dinner all four men would drink and dance with her. His voice was odd and strained. Camille could see the fingers of one guest clutched, motionless, around a tilted, spilling wineglass. Seizing a candle she looked into his face—and realized she was sharing a banquet with four propped-up corpses.

The panic-stricken girl ran for her life, but she never recovered from her nightmare experience. Friends who returned to the scene later the same day found everything laid out exactly as she had described—but no trace of the silent guests nor of Toussel, who is said to have fled the island.

Legend or fact? The machinations of a sorcerer husband or the imaginings of an unbalanced wife? The Haitians who told Seabrook this story believed it was true. They knew other stories like it. Haitian children are raised on tales of black magic, bogies, and sorcerers' spells. Their mothers warn them never to play with their shadows, and tell them that the bokor or the *tonton macoute*—traveling voodoo magician—will get them if they don't behave—a threat that could have proved only too true under Haiti's dictator Dr. Francois Duvalier, whose strong private army was dubbed the *tontons macoute*.

It is this atmosphere of fear and superstition that has bred belief in the zombie. From cemetery cults and disinterred bodies it is but a short step to the idea of a corpse brought back to half-life by black magic—and some would say this was Toussel's intention for his dinner guests. Of all the supernatural horrors that sorcery may reserve for the unwary, becoming a zombie is the most dreaded fate of all, and a threat that even the most sophisticated may find hard to shrug off. Alfred Metraux, author of *Voodoo in Haiti*, made a study of zombies in the late 1950s. He says, "At Port-au-Prince there are few, even among the educated, who do not give some credence to these macabre stories."

One of the macabre stories that Metraux recorded concerns a young girl who rejected the advances of a powerful hungan. He stalked off, muttering threats about her future. Sure enough, the girl grew ill and died. For some reason, she was buried in a coffin too short for her, and her neck had to be bent to fit her in. While this was going on, a candle near the coffin was overturned, burning the girl's foot. Years later, people claimed to have seen the girl, apparently alive and clearly recognizable by her stoop and the burn on her foot. It was said that the jealous hungan had made her into a zombie, and kept her as a servant in his house until so much attention was drawn to the case that he was obliged to set her free.

This hungan was motivated by revenge—a common reason for the creation of zombies. Other times, zombies are made simply to provide cheap and uncomplaining labor when any suitable corpse will do. More rarely, they are the carefully chosen victims of a pact with the forces of evil, who demand payment in human souls for services rendered. For while Christians talk of selling one's soul to the devil, a voodoo follower sells the souls of others. In return for power, wealth, or some other favor, he must pledge the souls of those nearest and dearest to him. Each year the horrible sacrifice must be repeated until there are no more relatives or beloved friends left to give, and the person must then give himself. He too surrenders his soul. Then his body, like theirs, becomes a zombie.

Such pacts are made with the help of the bokor, and only he can create zombies. After dark he saddles a horse and rides, backward, to the victim's house. Placing his lips against a slit in the door he sucks out the person's soul, and traps it in a corked bottle. Shortly afterward the victim falls ill and dies. At midnight on the day of burial, the bokor goes with his assistants to the grave, opens it, and calls the victim's name. Because the bokor holds his soul, the dead person has to lift his head in answer. As he does so, the bokor passes the bottle containing the soul under the corpse's nose for a single brief instant. The dead person is then reanimated. Dragging him from the tomb, the bokor chains his wrists and beats him about the head to revive him further. Then he carefully closes the tomb, so no one will notice it has been disturbed.

Led by the bokor and his associates, the victim is first taken past his own house. This is said to insure that he will never again recognize his home and try to return there. He is then taken to the bokor's house or a voodoo temple, and given a secret drug. Some say this is an extract of poisonous plants like datura (jimson weed) or belladonna (deadly nightshade), which were sometimes used by the slaves of colonial days to kill their masters. Others maintain that the potion is made of drops that fall from a corpse's nose.

There are other methods of ensnaring a person's soul. A jar containing herbs and magical objects may be placed beneath a dying man's pillow to draw off the soul, or the soul of an insect or small animal may be substituted for the human soul. In neither case does the victim realize what is happening. It is even possible to take the soul from a person already dead. Whatever the method used, the soul plays the same part in the ritual at the tomb, and after the giving of the magic drug, all is complete. The victim has become a zombie—a hideous, mesmerized, walking corpse, ready to do the sorcerer's will.

Elaborate precautions are taken to prevent the sorcerer from raising the dead and creating a zombie. A family that can afford it may bury its dead beneath solid masonry. Others will make sure that the grave is dug in their own back yard or close to a busy road with plenty of passers-by. Since only a fresh or well-preserved corpse will serve the bokor's purpose, relatives may keep a continuous watch at the tomb until the body has decomposed. Sometimes the corpse is killed again, being shot through the head, injected with poison, or strangled. Occasionally it is buried with a dagger in its hand to defend itself. Often the body is placed face downward in the grave with its mouth full of earth, or its lips are sewn together so that it cannot speak to answer when the sorcerer calls its name.

Once people become zombies they can never escape from their deathly trance unless they taste salt (frequently a symbol of white magic). They then become aware of their fate and, knowing they are dead, will return to the grave forever.

In his book *The Invisibles*, British anthropologist Francis Huxley tells a story he heard from a Catholic priest of a zombie who wandered back to his own village in 1959. He was taken to the police station, but the police were too frightened to do anything and simply left him outside in the street. After several hours someone plucked up the courage to give the zombie a drink of salt water, and he then stammered his name. Later his aunt, who lived nearby, identified him. According to her, he had died and been buried four years before.

A priest was called and, after he arrived, the zombie revealed the name of the sorcerer for whom he and a band of other zombies had been forced to labor. The police, thoroughly scared now, sent a message to the sorcerer offering him his zombie back. However, two days later the zombie was found, well and truly dead this time—presumably killed by the sorcerer because of his damaging revelations. The sorcerer was eventually arrested, but his wife and the other zombies were never traced.

There is a strong element of doubt in many zombie tales. Evidence is often missing or incomplete. Other stories are less easy to dismiss. Catholic priests and Protestant clergymen report having seen people die, conducted their burial service, shut the coffin lid, and watched the grave closed—only to see that person days or weeks later not dead but staring, inarticulate, and apparently insane.

Felicia Felix-Mentor

Zora Hurston notes that such creatures were occasionally brought to a missionary by a bokor who had been converted—or by a sorcerer's widow who wished to be rid of them. She herself was one of the few visitors to Haiti to see, touch, and actually photograph a zombie. The zombie was Felicia Felix-Mentor, who had died of a sudden illness in 1907. In 1936 she was found wandering naked on the road near her brother's farm. Both her brother and her husband identified her as the woman they had buried 29 years before. She was in such a wretched condition that she was taken to the hospital, and it was there, a few weeks later, that Zora Hurston saw her. "The sight was dreadful," she wrote later. "That blank face with the dead eyes. The eyelids were white all around the eyes as if they had been burned with acid. There was nothing that you could say to her

139

or get from her except by looking at her, and the sight of this wreckage was too much to endure for long."

So zombies or zombielike creatures do exist. But are they really walking corpses? Is it possible for a dead body to be given the semblance of life? Montague Summers, an authority on witchcraft and black magic, once wrote: "That necromancy can seemingly endow a dead body with life, speech, and action is not to be disputed, but the spell is invariably of short continuance and the operation, from the confession of sorcerers, is considered to be one of the most difficult and most dangerous in all witchcraft, a feat only to be accomplished by wizards who are foulest and deepest in infernal crime."

A spell of "short continuance" would hardly explain the reappearance after 29 years of Felicia Felix-Mentor. A far more likely explanation is that so-called zombies have never been dead at all. Some people have suggested that zombies are simply the doubles of persons who have died. If so, why do such doubles always have the characteristic zombie appearance and gait? Zombies are known for their expressionless and often downcast eyes, their blank faces, and shambling walk. They appear not to hear when spoken to, and their own speech, uttered in a nasal twang, is almost always incoherent. Often it consists only of grunts or guttural noises deep in the throat.

These are often the hallmarks of the mentally defective, and it seems probable that many alleged zombies are in fact morons concealed by their family and deliberately made out to be dead until they are seen again, perhaps many years later. Alfred Metraux was introduced to a zombie only to find a "wretched lunatic." On the next day this zombie was identified as a mentally deficient girl who had escaped from her home, where her parents normally kept her locked up.

Students of Haiti have pointed out that the harsh treatment meted out to zombies is no worse than the treatment of the mentally sick, who are commonly beaten to cow them into compliance. Once he had recovered from his initial shock at the sight of those "staring, unfocused, unseeing eyes," William Seabrook too concluded that the zombies he had seen were "nothing but poor ordinary demented human beings, idiots, forced to toil in the fields," rather than half-alive corpses.

What, then, of the reliable witnesses who have testified to the

140

burial of some so-called zombies? Were they lying? Not all zombies started out as morons. What about the person friends remember as a sane, intelligent individual, who suddenly reappears as a vacant, gibbering wreck of his former self? This has to be a different kind of case.

Article 246

The answer comes from a surprising source—Article 246 of the old Haitian Criminal Code. "Also to be termed intention to kill," it states, "is the use of substances whereby a person is not killed but reduced to a state of lethargy, more or less prolonged, and this without regard to the manner in which the substances were used or what was their later result. If following the state of lethargy the person is buried, then the attempt will be termed murder."

From this it can be inferred that a zombie may really be a person buried and mourned by his family, and dragged from the grave by the bokor as the legend says. But he has been buried alive after being drugged into a deathlike trance from which he may never recover.

A prominent Haitian doctor interviewed by William Seabrook was convinced that at least some reported zombies were victims of this kind of treatment. Doctors with whom Zora Hurston discussed the case of Felicia Felix-Mentor agreed. "We discussed at length the theories of how zombies come to be," she writes. "It was concluded that it is not a case of awakening the dead, but a semblance of death induced by some drug—some secret probably brought from Africa and handed down from generation to generation . . . It is evident that it destroys that part of the brain which governs speech and will power. The victims can move and act but cannot formulate thought. The two doctors expressed their desire to gain this secret, but they realized the impossibility of doing so. These secret societies are secret. They will die before they will tell."

The idea, if not the making, of the zombie almost certainly originated in Africa, where legendary tales are still told of sorcerers who can raise the dead. The true zombie, however, is unique to Haiti. While cynics would say that so-called zombies must be lunatics or people temporarily in a state of trance, there are undoubtedly cases that can only be explained on a deeper and more sinister level. Today voodoo is often exploited as a tourist attraction, and spectacular displays of black magic may be mounted for the entertainment of foreigners and natives alike. Francis Huxley tells, for instance, of a magistrate who saw a hungan take a body from the grave and apparently reanimate it. Inside the grave the magistrate found a tube leading out to the air. The "corpse" was really the hungan's accomplice, and had been able to breathe in comfort while awaiting his resurrection.

Haitians know about hoaxes like this. Yet many of them still believe in zombies, and have a deep-rooted fear of joining their ranks. For while zombies may not be raised from the grave, they may well be people reduced by drugs to a state that is scarcely distinguishable from death. Who would say which fate is the worse? In either case, the zombie is truly one of the walking dead.

13. Man into Beast

In the year 1598, in a remote patch of forest in Western France, an
archer and a group of armed countrymen came across the naked
body of a boy. The corpse had been horribly mutilated and torn.
The limbs, still warm and palpitating, were drenched with
blood. As the Frenchmen approached the body, they caught
sight of what appeared to be two wolves running off between the
trees. The men gave chase, but to their amazement, they found
they had caught, not a wolf, but what proved to be a man—tall,
gaunt, clothed in rags, and with matted, verminous hair and
beard. To their horror they noticed that his hands were still
stained with fresh blood, and his claw-like nails clotted with
human flesh. The man, it turned out, was a wandering beggar
named Jacques Roulet, and he was brought to trial at the town
of Angers in August, 1598. And if the discovery of Roulet was a
shock to the people of Angers, the trial proceedings were
shattering.

Roulet confessed to the court: "I was a wolf."

"Do your hands and feet become paws?"

"Yes, they do."

"Does your head become like that of a wolf?"

"I do not know how my head was at the time; I used my
teeth."

In reaching their verdict the court had to decide whether
Roulet was a werewolf, as he claimed, or a lycanthrope, which is
related but different. A werewolf or werwolf is a living person
who has the power to change into a wolf. The word comes from
Old English *wer*, meaning man, and wolf. A *lycanthrope* is someone suffering from a mental illness that makes him believe he is
transformed into a wolf. This word comes from the Greek for

wolfman. In either case, Roulet could have faced execution. But the court showed a compassion rare for its time. Judging Roulet to be mentally sick—and therefore a lycanthrope—they sentenced him to a madhouse for only two years.

A true werewolf was generally believed to undergo an almost complete transformation into a wolf, unlike the werewolf of Hollywood movies who remains basically human in appearance. Much controversy arose in the past over people who were said to disguise the fact that they were wolves by wearing their fur on the inside. It was claimed that such people looked ordinary enough, but that their skin was inside out. When they were torn apart—as hundreds of innocent people were at various times in past centuries—the hair, or wolf fur, could be seen on the other side of the skin.

The werewolf and the vampire have much in common. In fact it was often assumed that a werewolf would become a vampire after death unless special precautions, such as exorcism, were taken. Anyone who ate the flesh of a sheep killed by a wolf was liable to become a werewolf. A person who ate a wolf's brains or drank water from his footprints was certain to become one. In some places, eating certain large and sweet smelling flowers or drinking from a stream where a wolfpack had drunk was a sure way to turn into a wolf.

Anybody with small pointed ears, prominent teeth, strong curved fingernails, bushy eyebrows that met over the nose, a third finger as long as the second on each hand, or even a lot of hair—especially on the hands and feet—was immediately suspect. However, if you are tempted to take a closer look at your friends next time you see them, remember that the eyes of a werewolf always remain human.

Like the belief in vampires, these beliefs stemmed from peoples' ignorant fear of anyone who was different. In some traditions it was easy to become a werewolf by accident. In others, you had to be especially evil to merit such a fate. Some tales suggest that a bestial person would return after death as a wolf. Ghostly werewolves, however, are extremely rare in folklore, which is where the werewolf differs most from the vampire. The vampire is akin to the ghost. The werewolf is very much a living person, and more akin to the witch in that he or she may actively seek to become a werewolf. This can be done by entering into a pact with a demon known as the Wolf Spirit or with the Devil himself.

Werewolf Rituals

Surprising though it may seem, many people actually wanted to become werewolves and, in addition to the magical methods already mentioned, went through elaborate rituals in the hope of doing so. The right moment for such a change was at midnight by the light of a full moon. The would-be werewolf drew a magic circle and built a fire over which he placed a cauldron containing a potion of herbs and drugs. Then he smeared his body with an ointment made from the fat of a newly killed cat, mixed with ingredients like aniseed and opium. Around his waist he bound a belt made of wolf's skin. Kneeling inside the circle as the magic potion simmered, he chanted an incantation that went something like this:

"Hail, hail, hail, Great Wolf Spirit, hail!
A boon I ask thee, mighty shade. Within this circle I have
   made,
Make me a werewolf strong and bold,
The terror alike of young and old.
Grant me a figure tall and spare;
The speed of the elk, the claws of the bear;
The poison of snakes, the wit of the fox;
The stealth of the wolf, the strength of the ox;
The jaws of the tiger, the teeth of the shark;
The eyes of a cat that sees in the dark."

Such a powerful plea might sound irresistible. To the skeptical mind, however, it is significant that the simmering potion included large amounts of poppy seed, and the salve contained opium. This suggests that the initiate may have been in a drugged condition. The incantation concluded with the cry:

"Make me a werewolf! make me a man eater!
Make me a werewolf! make me a woman eater!
Make me a werewolf! Make me a child eater!
I pine for blood! human blood!
Give it to me! Give it to me tonight!
Great Wolf Spirit! give it to me, and
Heart, body, and soul, I am yours."

If the ritual had been correctly carried out, the aspirant would then begin to change into a wolf. Tall and phantomlike, his figure would glow in the darkness until it assumed the "form of a tall thin monstrosity, half human and half animal, gray and nude, with very long legs and arms, and the feet and claws of a wolf." Once fully transformed, he would indulge in the werewolf's traditional nighttime activities of hunting, killing, and eating. The commonest reason for wishing to become a wolf was said to be a desire for revenge.

The man or woman who has achieved the power of metamorphosis will change into a wolf at sunset every night until death, reassuming human shape at dawn. Some folk tales say that the werewolf must roll in the dirt or the morning dew in order to change back into a human; others that the transformation occurs automatically at daybreak. A werewolf that is wounded or killed immediately becomes human again. Usually the creature can be caught or destroyed like an ordinary wolf, but the most effective way of killing a werewolf is to shoot it with a silver bullet. The corpse must then be burned rather than buried.

To most people all this sounds like a welter of primitive superstition, and it is significant that reports of werewolves decreased as cities spread into the countryside. Such tales have always been commonest in remote regions where the wolf was the foremost beast of prey. Today, when the wolf has all but disappeared from the United States and many European countries, it may be hard for us to imagine the terror this animal inspired in our ancestors. In northern countries especially, the wolf was a deadly enemy, hated and feared for its ferocious attacks on flocks and people alike. But the wolf also seemed eerie, moving mainly by night, ghostly gray and silent, almost invisible except for the slanting eyes that glowed red by firelight and yellow-green by moonlight. Add to this its spine-chilling howl—said to be an omen of death— and it is not surprising that the wolf came to be regarded as an evil, almost supernatural monster. Wherever there were wolves there were also reports of werewolves, whom people feared with a panic verging on hysteria.

Nevertheless there are eminent authorities on werewolves who do not regard the idea of a human turning into a wolf as superstitious fantasy, and who take reports of werewolves seriously. Sabine Baring-Gould, author in 1865 of the *Book of Were-wolves, Being an Account of a Terrible Superstition*, maintained that because the legend was so persistent "everywhere and in all ages, it must rest upon foundation of fact." He claimed that "Half the world believes, or believed in werewolves."

Writing in this century, Elliott O'Donnell agrees, and declares that there is no conclusive evidence that the people who claimed to be werewolves were shams. It was a characteristic of trials for lycanthropy that the accused seemed eager to confess. He suggests that many of the accused had been victimized and confessed under torture, which is doubtless true. But even if they were shams, O'Donnell thought this "would in nowise preclude the existence of the werewolf." He becomes less convincing, however, when he asserts that werewolves were created by "malevolent forces, the originators of all evil."

Early Documentation

As with vampirism, reports of werewolves have been documented all over the world since ancient times. As early as the 5th century B.C. Herodotus, who is known as the "father of history," wrote: "Each Neurian changes himself once a year into the form of a wolf and he continues in that form for several days, after which he resumes his former shape." In the 2nd century A.D. a Roman doctor observed that "lycanthropia is a species of melancholy which can be cured at the time of the attack by opening a vein and abstracting blood."

Petronius, the 1st-century Roman satirist, tells a werewolf story with a universal theme. It concerns a servant who accompanied a soldier on a night's journey out of town, and was aghast to see him strip off his clothes by the roadside and change into a wolf. With a howl the creature leaped into the woods and disappeared from view. When the servant reached his destination, he was told that a wolf had just broken into the farm, and had savaged the cattle before being driven away by a man who had thrust a pike into the animal's neck. Hurrying home at daybreak, the servant came to the place where the soldier's clothes had been, but he found only a pool of blood. Back home, the soldier lay wounded with a doctor dressing his neck.

This epitomizes a constant theme of the werewolf legend: the wolf is wounded in a fight and a human being is later discovered suffering from the same wound. A story from the Middle Ages tells of a Russian noblewoman who doubted that anyone could change into an animal. One of her servants volunteered to prove her wrong. He changed into a wolf and raced across the fields, chased by his mistress' dogs which cornered him and damaged one of his eyes. When the servant returned to his mistress in human form he was blind in one eye.

Another famous case took place in the Auvergne region of central France in 1558. A hunter out in the forest met a neighboring nobleman who asked him to bring him back some game if the hunt was successful. The hunter was later attacked by a savage wolf, but was able to drive it away after slashing off one of its paws. He put the paw in his pouch as a memento, and set off for home. On the way he stopped at the nobleman's chateau and told him of his adventure. Reaching in his pouch for the wolf's paw, he was amazed to find a delicate female hand in its place. The nobleman was even more astonished as he recognized the gold ring on one of the fingers. Dashing upstairs he found his wife bandaging the bleeding stump of her wrist. She confessed to being a werewolf, and was burned at the stake.

Just as the vampire has its traditional home in Eastern Europe, the forests of France seem to have been the natural home of the werewolf. Reports of werewolves, called *loups-garoux* in French, reached epidemic proportions in the 16th century. As many as 30,000 cases were listed between 1520 and 1630.

One of the most famous werewolves in history is a stooping, bushy-browed hermit called Gilles Garnier. On September 13, 1573, authorities in the French town of Dôle gave permission for a werewolf hunt after several local children had been found killed and partially eaten. The permission read: "And since he has attacked and done injury in the country to some horsemen, who kept him off only with great difficulty and danger to their persons, the said court, desiring to prevent any greater danger, has permitted and does permit, those who are dwelling in the said places, notwithstanding all edicts concerning the chase, to assemble with pikes, halberds, and sticks, to chase and pursue the said werewolf in every place where they may find or seize him; to tie and to kill, without incurring any pains or penalties." Clearly the peasants were convinced that a werewolf was to blame before they had even started the hunt. It is extraordinary that in all such reports there is never any suggestion that the victims might have been seized by a real wolf.

Two months later a group of villagers heard the screams of a child and the baying of a wolf. Hurrying to the spot—expecting to find a werewolf—they discovered a small girl, badly mauled, and thought they recognized Garnier in the wolf that raced away. When a 10-year-old boy disappeared six days later, they raided the hut of "the hermit of St. Bonnet," as Garnier was known, and arrested both him and his wife.

Garnier made two immediate confessions. One concerned a 12-year-old boy killed in a pear orchard the previous August. Garnier had been about to eat the boy's flesh when he was interrupted by some men. They testified that Garnier was in the form of a man, not a wolf. On October 6, in a vineyard near Dôle, Garnier had attacked a 10-year-old girl, this time in the guise of a wolf. He killed her with his teeth and claws, stripped her, and ate her, enjoying the meal so much that he brought some of the flesh back for his wife's supper. On the evidence of this confession, Garnier was burned alive on January 18, 1574.

Grenier's Confessions

Thirty years later the similarly named Jean Grenier, a handsome 14-year-old shepherd boy, confessed to a series of crimes in the Bordeaux area of southwest France. For what his confession is worth, he admitted to having eaten more than 50 children. Sometimes, he said, he lay in wait in the woodlands until dusk fell and his transformation into a wolf took place. Then he watched for victims from a thicket beside a favorite pool. Once he surprised two girls, bathing naked; one escaped, but he devoured the other. When he was provoked by extreme hunger, he said, he hurled himself fearlessly into a crowd until he was driven off.

Grenier confessed with suspicious eagerness, reciting his crimes with such relish that he even caused laughter in the crowded courtroom when he talked of pursuing an old woman only to find her flesh "as tough as leather." He also complained about a child in this way: "When I lifted it out of its crib, and when I got ready for my first bite, it shrieked so loud it almost deafened me." There had been killings in the area, and three girls testified against Grenier, so his detailed confession was believed. However, Grenier accused other people of being werewolves too, and the judge found the evidence so appalling that he sent Grenier to a higher court for further investigation of the strange case.

The houses of the people named by Grenier were searched,

and although nothing was found, Grenier's father and a neighbor were arrested. Monsieur Grenier impressed the higher court judge with testimony that his son was a well-known idiot who boasted that he had slept with every woman in the village. Nevertheless, Grenier continued to confess with such conviction that his father and the neighbor were reexamined. Under torture they admitted that they had sought young girls "to play with, but not to eat."

Grenier was sentenced to be burned, but the case had caused such a stir that it was eventually reviewed by the high court of justice in Bordeaux. Judge de Lancre recorded this testimony by the youth: "When I was 10 or 11 years old, my neighbor del Thillaire introduced me, in the depths of the forest, to the Maître de la Fôret [Lord of the Forest], a black man, who signed me with his nail, and then gave me and del Thillaire a salve and a wolf skin. From that time I have run about the country as a wolf." Grenier maintained that he went hunting for children at the command of this Lord of the Forest, changing his shape with the help of the salve and the wolf skin after hiding his clothes in the thicket.

Like the beggar Roulet before him, this self-confessed werewolf was treated with a rare degree of understanding. The high court called in two doctors who decided that the boy was suffering from "the malady called lycanthropy, which deceives men's eyes into imagining such things," although they added that the illness was the result of possession by an evil spirit. Judge de Lancre gave an intelligent summing up, which must apply to many similar contemporary cases of alleged werewolves: "The court takes into account the young age and the imbecility of this boy, who is so stupid and idiotic that children of seven and eight years old normally show more intelligence, who has been ill fed in every respect and who is so dwarfed that he is not as tall as a 10 year old. . . Here is a young lad abandoned and driven out by his father, who has a cruel stepmother instead of a real mother, who wanders over the fields, without a counselor and without anyone to take an interest in him, begging his bread, who has never had any religious training, whose real nature was corrupted by evil promptings, need, and despair, and whom the devil made his prey."

The boy's life was spared, and he was sent to a monastery

which the judge visited several years later. He found that Grenier's mind was completely blank, unable to comprehend the simplest things, yet the young man still maintained he was a werewolf and that he would eat more children if he could. Also, he wanted "to look at wolves." Grenier died in 1610 as a "good Christian," but it is not altogether surprising that anyone in the region with the name of Garnier or Grenier was regarded with suspicion for a long time afterward.

The Werewolves of St Claude

The case of a whole family of werewolves was recorded in western France in 1598. Two sisters, their brother, and his son were known as the Werewolves of St. Claude. One of the girls, Peronette, was plainly suffering from lycanthropic hysteria, and ran about on all fours. She attacked two children who were picking fruit in an orchard, and when the four-year-old boy tried to defend his sister, she seized a knife and gashed him in the throat. Before he died he testified that this wolf had human hands instead of paws, and the enraged peasants tore Peronette to pieces before she could be brought to trial. Her sister was then accused of also being a lycanthrope who had the additional evil gift of producing hail. She was said to sleep with the devil who came to her in the shape of a goat. Their brother Pierre confessed that he turned himself into a wolf, and that the three would chase people or animals around the country "according to the guidance of their appetite" until they were exhausted. His son testified that he covered himself with a magic salve to turn into a wolf, and that he had gone hunting with his two aunts and had killed some goats.

The judge visited the wretched family in jail. "I have seen those I have named go on all fours in a room just as they did when they were in the fields," he said, "but they said it was impossible for them to turn themselves into wolves, since they had no more ointment, and they had lost the power of doing so, by being imprisoned. I have further noted that they were all scratched on the face and hands and legs; and that Pierre Gandillon was so much disfigured in this way that he bore hardly any resemblance to a man, and struck with horror those who looked at him." This last sentence is revealing. If Pierre had been disfigured since birth, he may well have desired the company and guise of animals. The

151

verdict was not merciful this time, however, for the entire family was burned to death.

The most notorious German werewolf was Peter Stubb or Stump, who was tried in Cologne in 1589. An historian has written of his trial: "It is interesting to note the ease with which otherwise intelligent persons rationalized the impossible and made negative evidence into positive proof." This is another poignant case of a man destroyed by his own confessions—forced from him under torture—and who was prejudged before his trial began. Stubb claimed he had a magic belt that transformed him into "a greedy devouring wolf, strong and mighty, with eyes great and large, which in the night sparkled like brands of fire, a mouth great and wide, with most sharp and cruel teeth, a huge body, and mighty paws."

The accusers searched the valley where Stubb said he had left this belt, but found nothing. However, this did not prevent the magistrates from believing Stubb's confession. On the contrary, they declared "it may be supposed that the belt has gone to the devil from whence it came." Their revenge was terrible. Stubb was condemned to have "his body laid on a wheel, and with red hot burning pincers in ten several places to have the flesh pulled from the bones; after that, his legs and arms to be broken with a wooden ax or hatchet; afterward to have his head struck off from his body; then to have his carcass burned to ashes."

In surprising contrast to these horrifying real-life stories there are reports of protective werewolves, which sound about as unlikely as "benign vampires." In Portugal there was said to be a type of werewolf that never attacked anyone and fled if approached, whimpering pitifully—a cowardly werewolf if ever there was one. Sometimes a person who had become a werewolf by accident would welcome the wound that transformed him back into permanent human shape again. A case recorded in Britain in 1214 tells of a carpenter who fought off a wolf, severing its paw. The animal instantly turned into a man who, though crippled, expressed his gratitude.

Protective Werewolves

France is the favorite locale for protective werewolves as well as savage ones. One French tale concerns an abbot who

152

drank too much at a country fair and was so overcome with
the wine and sun on his journey home that he fell off his horse.
He hit his head on a stone and bled so profusely that the
scent attracted a pack of wildcats that lived in the forèst. As
the wildcats moved in, a werewolf bounded to the abbot's
rescue—and even escorted the tipsy, bleeding monk back to
his monastery. There the wolf was welcomed and its wounds
were treated. At dawn, however, it resumed human shape—
that of a stern Church dignitary who reprimanded the abbot
most severely for his conduct, and stripped him of his privileges.
A moralistic, if protective, werewolf.

Another story concerns the captain of a schooner employed
in attacks on the Huguenots—French Protestants—fighting
against Catholic persecution in the 16th and 17th centuries.
After one such raid the captain's ship foundered in the wide
waters of the Rhone estuary, and he would have drowned if
someone had not come to his rescue and dragged him ashore.
Reaching out his hand in thanks, the captain was dismayed
to find himself grasping a huge hairy paw. Convinced that this
must be the devil, who had saved him as a reward for his
atrocities against the Huguenots, the captain fell on his knees
and asked for the forgiveness of God. The wolf waited grimly,
then lifted the sailor up and took him to a house on the outskirts of a village. Once inside, the captain saw the werewolf's
face clearly in the light of a lantern, and fell headlong to the
floor in an effort to escape. Again, the wolf lifted him gently,
and then gave him food before leaving him in a locked room.
The captain ran to the window, but it was barred. Then he
noticed the horribly mutilated body of a woman lying in a
corner of the room, and he feared that the same fate was
intended for him. But the next morning the werewolf returned
in human shape. He was a Huguenot minister, and he revealed
that the woman was his wife, cruelly murdered by the captain's
crew when they ransacked the village the day before. He
himself had been forced aboard the captain's ship in order to
be tortured and drowned.

"Well," said the minister, "I am a werewolf; I was bewitched
some years ago by the woman Grenier [again that name] who
lives in the forest at the back of our village. As soon as it was
dark I metamorphosed; then the ship ran ashore, and everyone

leaped overboard. I saw you drowning. I saved you . . . you who had been instrumental in murdering my wife and ruining my home! Why? I do not know! Had I preferred for you a less pleasant death than drowning, I could have taken you ashore and killed you. Yet, I did not, because it is not in my nature to destroy anything." Needless to say, the captain was so moved by this act of mercy that he became a devoted friend of the Huguenots until the day of his death.

It is a romantic tale, and this may be one reason for the appeal of the werewolf legend. There may even be a fragment of fact behind the tales of protective werewolves. Modern studies indicate that the wolf is not necessarily the voracious monster it is traditionally made out to be. Rescues of a human being by an animal are not unknown, and there may have been isolated cases in the past in which a wolf was responsible for saving a man's life. Nevertheless, it is the image of the wolf as a cruel and ferocious beast that prevails. Kindly werewolves are rare, and the werewolves of legend are almost always bent on the vicious killing and devouring of their victims.

The concept of a man or woman turning into a wolf is no more outrageous than that of a corpse emerging from the coffin at night to drink human blood. Yet it is somehow even harder to believe in werewolves than in vampires. This may be partly because the werewolf fits so neatly into folklore. The monstrous wolfman made the ideal character for a good horror tale to tell around the fire in remote regions, where there was little to talk about apart from the wild animals of the forest and perhaps the even wilder characters in the village. Werewolves were alleged to be especially partial to small boys and girls, so they would serve as a natural threat for the peasants to their children. "Don't go out in the woods tonight or the werewolf will gobble you up," they might say, just as London Cockneys warned their children not to roam the streets of the East End after the murders of 1888 "or Jack the Ripper will get you."

But the belief in werewolves has deeper roots. The met-amorphosis of men into animals is part of primeval legend, a power attributed to the gods and heroes of mythology. The Scandinavian god Odin turned into an eagle; Jupiter, the Roman god, became a bull; Actaeon was changed into a stag by the Greek goddess Artemis. There are counterparts of the werewolf in almost all parts of the world, varying according to climate: were-tigers in India; were-leopards, were-hyenas, and even were-crocodiles in Africa; and were-bears in Russia, which also had its fair share of werewolves. In his book on werewolves, Elliott O'Donnell quotes eyewitness accounts of an Indian youth who changed into a tiger, and of two Javanese children who turned into jaguars. Significantly, were-animals are always creatures that inspire fear; you never hear of a were-tortoise.

The Berserkers

The *berserkers*—ancient Norse warriors who fought with murderous frenzy—exploited the fearsome reputation of wild animals by wearing bearskins in battle. These gangs of Nordic fighters would work themselves into a state of diabolical madness as they hurled themselves into the attack, howling like animals and foaming at the mouth. Our word *berserk*, meaning violently enraged, comes from the *bear sark*—bearskin—the berserkers wore. Just as the word lives on, so the memory of these barbaric warriors may have contributed to the werewolf legend. To the peaceful villagers whose community was attacked one day by fur-clad berserkers and another by a pack of howling wolves, there can have seemed little enough difference between the two. Both might have seemed like men dressed as animals—or like men completely transformed into raging beasts.

Others trace the werewolf legend back further still to the time when prehistoric man began to don animal disguise for the hunt, and to invoke the spirit of a powerful animal in the hope of inheriting that animal's strength. In his book *Man Into Wolf* Dr. Robert Eisler, a British writer with a profound knowledge of ancient history and legend, develops a fascinating theory of the origins of the werewolf idea. Eisler's explanation starts with the idea that man was once a peaceful vegetarian, but was driven to seek new food by changing conditions—such as the arrival of an Ice Age. He was forced to eat meat, to cover himself with animal skins, to hunt, and to imitate the behavior of ferocious wild animals in his struggle to survive. Gradually man himself acquired the same blood lust, probably even turning to cannibalism in times of extreme food shortage. This traumatic upheaval left its scars that lingered on in man's unconscious, says Eisler, giving rise among other things to the werewolf legend.

There are also more straightforward explanations. Furs were worn in winter as a protection against cold, and a fur-clad figure might easily be mistaken for an animal. Werewolves might have been children who had been lost or abandoned in the forest, raised by a pack of wolves, and therefore practicing all the skills of the wild animal. But Eisler's theory is still the most attractive. Writing about the concept of *metempsychosis*— the passing of a soul from one body to another after death— Baring-Gould refers' to "the yearnings and gropings of the soul after the source whence its own consciousness was derived, counting its dreams and hallucinations as gleams of memory, recording acts which had taken place in a former state of existence."

To some extent this echo exists in us all. The counterpart of the female vamp is the male wolf—a man who pushes his attentions on women—and he is still with us today, complete with wolf whistle. The werewolf is a monster of the unconscious, "the beast within" that may still emerge in our dream life. American psychoanalyst Dr. Nandor Fodor has recorded a number of dreams reported by patients in which the werewolf theme figures prominently, complete with all the brutal details of transformation, savage attack, and killing.

At its fiercest extreme, however, this primeval instinct is seen most clearly in the secret societies of the Leopard Men in West Africa, who continue to disguise themselves as leopards up to the present day. Although it is most unlikely that man can change into wolf, it is certain that man frequently imitates the wildest of animals, even to assuming their skins.

A true werewolf is believed to undergo an almost complete transformation from man into wolf. A lycanthrope, illustrated here, is a man suffering from a mental illness which makes him believe he is a wolf. This condition may account for the werewolf epidemic in 16th-century France, when 30,000 cases were reported between 1520 and 1630. *(Man Into Beast)*

Highgate Cemetery, London, where more than 100 vampire hunters converged in the early 1970s after David Farrant, president of the British Occult Society, stated that a seven-foot high vampire had been seen there. (*The Legend of the Vampire*)

14. The Legend of the Vampire

One night in January 1973 John Pye, a young British police officer, was called to investigate a death. Within an hour what had seemed like a routine mission turned into one of the strangest cases any policeman can have encountered. Police Constable Pye found the dead man's room plunged in darkness. The man had apparently been so terrified of electricity that there were no light bulbs in his room. But gradually the beam from the policeman's flashlight revealed an extraordinary scene. P.C. Pyle was looking at a fortress prepared against an attack by vampires. Salt was scattered around the room and sprinkled over the blankets. A bag of salt rested by the dead man's face, and another was laid between his legs. The man had mixed salt with his urine in various containers. Outside on the window ledge he had placed an inverted bowl that covered a mixture of human excreta and garlic.

The dead man was Demetrious Myiciura, a Polish immigrant who had left his country for Britain 25 years earlier. He had worked as a potter in Stoke-on-Trent in the heart of England's pottery district. That is where he met his bizarre death. It would certainly be hard to imagine a place more remote from the traditionally vampire-haunted forests of Transylvania in Romania. Stoke-on-Trent is an industrial town, set in a landscape mutilated by factory chimneys and slag heaps. Opposite the station is a large old-fashioned hotel in front of which is a statue of the town's most famous citizen—Josiah Wedgwood, who made pottery a major industry. There is the usual imposing town hall. Otherwise the streets of little houses are uniformly black and narrow. It is all the more surprising, therefore, to come across the line of large old-fashioned dwellings where Myiciura had made his home. The houses look gloomy and somehow eerie. They are called, simply, "The Villas," and it was at number 3 that Myiciura met his death.

The body was duly removed for examination. At the inquest the pathologist reported that Myiciura had choked to death on a pickled onion. The coroner thought this unusual, but commented that it was not unknown for people "to bolt their food and die." Meanwhile the young policeman could not forget what he had seen. He had gone to the Public Library and read the *Natural History of the Vampire* by Anthony Masters. His suspicions were confirmed: salt and garlic are traditional vampire repellants, and the mixture on Myiciura's window ledge was intended to attract the vampires who would then be poisoned by the garlic. When told of this, the coroner ordered a reexamination of the alleged pickled onion. It was found to be a clove of garlic. As a final desperate measure to ward off the vampires, this wretched man had slept with a clove of garlic in his mouth, and the garlic had choked him to death. So in a roundabout way, the vampires did get him in the end.

What, then, are these vampires that literally scared Myiciura to death? Vampires are corpses, neither dead nor alive, that rise from the grave at night and suck the blood of the living. They gradually drain the blood of their victims, who must then become vampires in turn. The legendary home of the vampire is in Eastern Europe, notably Romania. It was there, in the province of Transylvania, that British author **Bram Stoker** set his famous story of Dracula. His Count Dracula, with arched nostrils, blood-red lips, and long sharp teeth, has come to typify our image of a vampire. But like the legendary vampires, Dracula could readily change into an animal such as a wolf or a bat. A vampire might even become a vapor to filter around the window frames in search of his or her chosen victim. When their gruesome feast of blood is over, the vampires crawl back into their coffin, where they can easily be recognized by the excellent state of preservation of their body. No matter how long vampires have been buried, it is said, they look as if they were still alive. Garlic, salt, or a crucifix may drive them off, but the only way to destroy them is to plunge a stake through their heart—at which time they give a horrible death shriek. They may need to be beheaded and burned as well.

A primitive superstition? Perhaps. Nevertheless, Myiciura believed it. He was convinced that vampires exist—and not just in the faraway forests of Transylvania. Demitrious Myiciura believed that he was being threatened by vampires in a British city in the 1970s.

"This man genuinely believed," remarked the coroner afterward. He denied that Myiciura was mad, although "obsessed perhaps." The Pole, who was born in 1904, had lost everything in World War II. His farm had been taken over by the Germans, and his wife and family had been killed. He arrived in England after the war with nothing.

"I've been a lawyer for a long time," said the coroner, "dealing with courtroom cases of all kinds. I've seen all sorts of depravity, all sorts of nonsense, but I can visualize what was behind this man. A lot of evil had happened to him. All right, he thought, I'll cling to evil, and he happened to believe in vampires. I am convinced, even after this inquest, that this man genuinely was afraid of vampires and was not trying to kill himself."

Vampires of New York

Even in New York, surely a most unlikely hunting ground for vampires, there have recently been two strange cases reported by writer Jeffrey Blyth. A girl calling herself Lillith told two psychic researchers that she met a young man in a cemetery who tried to kiss her. It is not clear what she was doing in the cemetery in the first place, but instead of consenting to the kiss she plunged her teeth into the man's neck with such a surge of strength that she drew blood. "I never considered myself a Dracula," she said, "but rather a very evil person who liked the taste of blood." The second vampire was a young man named Carl Johnson who crept into his sister's bedroom while she slept, gently pricked her leg, and sucked her blood. This gave him a thirst, he said, and he could feel himself gaining in strength as he drained his victim.

Such cases indicate that far from being a legend of the past, vampirism exists today, if only in people's minds. Indeed, there has been an amazing revival of interest in vampires on both sides of the Atlantic. There is a Dracula Society in London and another in California. Modern British writers have studied the vampire, and professors in the United States and Canada have published learned books and papers on the subject. Countless movies are still made about Dracula and vampires—and so are studies of the movies. In Britain, a national poll revealed that the actor Denholm Elliot was the most "dreamt of" person in the country after he had portrayed Count Dracula on television. It has also been discovered recently that mental patients tend to identify themselves with Count Dracula as much as with Napoleon.

The latest to climb on the bandwagon are the travel agencies. Pan American blazed the trail when they offered a "Package Tour with a Toothy Grin" in 1972, and the first British Airways "Dracula Tour" set out for Romania in 1974. Now the Romanians themselves have awakened to the extraordinary tourist potential that lies on their own Transylvanian doorstep. They are planning to cash in on this horror counterpart of Disneyland by selling Count Dracula on the souvenir stalls and by opening The Castle Dracula Hotel in 1977. The hotel will be in the Borgo Pass made famous in the Stoker story of Dracula, and taped wolves will howl at prearranged spots as the tourists drive to their destination through the mists at nightfall.

For the most part this modern preoccupation with vampires is little more than a harmless fantasy. But there are elements, such as the recent desecration of graveyards in Britain, that are disturbing. The graveyard activity reached an unpleasant climax with the so-called vampire hunters of Highgate Cemetery in London. Highgate Cemetery was once a place of splendor. It was designed by the best 19th-century British architects and landscape gardeners, and has graceful avenues of trees for the bereaved families to stroll through. It has deteriorated, however, and is so thickly overgrown that the atmosphere is sinister even on a bright sunlit morning. Reports of black magic are all too believable, and the work of vandals is only too evident.

The case of the vampire hunters was again brought to public notice in 1974 with a second trial of David Farrant, president of the British Occult Society, who was described as a "High Priest" in court. News stories were limited because of the bizarre details of the case, but headline writers went as far as they could with lines like "Capers among the Catacombs" and "High Priest Lectures Judge on Witchcraft." When told of girls dancing naked at witchcraft ceremonies, the judge commented with dry legal wit that they must have found it extremely chilly in October.

Here is what happened. After Farrant stated in a television interview of 1970 that a seven-foot vampire had been seen in Highgate Cemetery, 100 vampire hunters converged on the place. Farrant was brought to trial. The startled jury learned that iron stakes had been driven through mutilated corpses after their tombs had been smashed in. (The bodies were later returned to their graves as discreetly as possible to spare the feelings of relatives.) Photographs of a naked girl in a mausoleum were found in Farrant's home, and a police inspector reported that a witness he visited "had salt around the windows of the room, salt around the doorway, and a large wooden cross under his pillow." It was also revealed that voodoo dolls with pins through their chests had been sent to the police by Farrant.

Farrant was charged with damaging a memorial to the dead, entering catacombs in consecrated ground, and interfering with and offering indignity to the remains of a body "to the great scandal and disgrace of religion, decency, and morality." Admitting that he frequently held occult ceremonies in Highgate Cemetery, he denied all the charges and conducted his own defense, claiming that a Satanic sect and vandals had been responsible for the damage. He was found guilty on two of five charges, and sentenced to jail for almost five years.

Exorcism as a Defence

It is tempting, and probably correct, to dismiss such cases as a form of unhealthy aberration. Yet not far from Highgate Cemetery lives a man who takes reports of vampirism seriously. The Reverend Christopher Neil-Smith is a leading British exorcist and writer on exorcism. He can cite several examples of people who have come to him for help in connection with vampirism. "The one that particularly strikes me is that of a woman who showed me the marks on her wrists which appeared at night, where blood had definitely been taken. And there was no apparent reason why this should have occurred. They were marks almost like those of an animal. Something like scratching." He denies that this might have been done by the woman herself. She came to him when she felt her blood was being sucked away, and after he performed an exorcism the marks disappeared.

Another person who came from South America "had a

similar phenomenon, as if an animal had sucked away his blood and attacked him at night." Again, the Reverend Neil-Smith could find no obvious explanation. There was a third case of a man who, after his brother had died, had the strange feeling that his lifeblood was being slowly sucked away from him. "There seems to be evidence this was so," says Neil-Smith. "He was a perfectly normal person before, but after the brother's death he felt his life was being sucked away from him as if the spirit of his brother was feeding on him. When the exorcism was performed he felt a release and new life, as if new blood ran in his veins." Neil-Smith rules out the possibility of a simple psychological explanation for this, such as a feeling of guilt by the survivor toward his brother. "There was no disharmony between them. In fact he wasn't clear for some time that it [the vampire] *was* his brother."

The clergyman describes a vampire as "half animal, half human," and firmly refutes the suggestion that such things are "all in the mind." "I think that's a very naive interpretation," he says. "All the evidence points to the contrary." Concluding that there is such a thing as vampirism, he identifies this strange belief as a persistent form of devil worship.

Many people will say that Neil-Smith is easily taken in. Most will dismiss reports of vampirism in the modern world as so much nonsense. And yet, as Hamlet tells Horatio in Shakespeare's play, "There are more things in heaven and earth, Than are dreamt of in your philosophy." But do these undreamed of things include vampires? On the face of it, how can anyone believe that corpses can rise from their coffins at night to suck the blood of the living, make new vampires of their victims, and return to the grave before daybreak? Skeptical minds find this incredible. Some even say it is the silliest superstition of all.

Yet people have believed in vampires all over the world since the earliest recorded times. Legends reach back many centuries before Christ to ancient Assyria and Babylonia—and always vampirism includes the drinking of blood, the life-giving fluid.

Aztecs poured blood into the mouths of their idols. In India, rajahs drank blood from severed heads. In China, the family would guard a corpse the night before burial lest a dog or cat jump over the body and transform it into a vampire. This belief is echoed in a book called *Antidote Against Atheism* written in the

17th century by Dr. Henry Moore. He tells the story of Johannes Cuntius of Silesia in central Europe, whose dead body was scratched by a black cat before the funeral. Sure enough, Cuntius was later reported to have reappeared, and to have drunk blood. When his body was duly dug up again, it was said to be in the typical well-preserved vampire condition.

The ancient Greeks, and the Romans after them, believed in a type of female vampire called a *lamia* who seduced men in order to suck their blood. Later the Greeks had another word for the vampire: *vrukalakos*, a creature who was able to revive the dead and whose victims would then feast on the living. Anyone—male or female—with red hair, a birthmark, or even blue eyes was suspected of being a vampire. Blue eyes are rare in Greece. But those born on Christmas Day, a seventh son, a person with a hare lip, or anyone in the slightest bit unusual were also suspect, so many people would easily fit the description of vampires.

Vampires were so rife on the Greek island of Santorini, now called Thera, that Greeks would say "send a vampire to Santorini" just as we talk of "taking coals to Newcastle." In 1717 a distinguished French botanist, Joseph de Tournefort, stated that throughout "the whole Archipelago there is no Orthodox Greek who does not firmly believe that the devil is able to reenergize and revitalize dead bodies."

Closer to home and as recently as 1874, a man in Rhode Island dug up his daughter and burned her heart because he believed she was draining the lifeblood from the rest of his family.

The Vampire's True Home
The true home of the vampire, however, lies in Eastern Europe, and the vampire legend as we know it today grew up in Romania and Hungary around the start of the 16th century. The word itself comes from a Slavonic term, and did not exist in English until the 1730s. At that time, reports of vampires were numerous in Eastern Europe. These accounts were picked up by travelers whose writings about them spread the vampire story all over Europe. Fiction then made the vampire famous. In the 19th century best-selling horror writers seized on the vampire tale. Even great poets like Byron, Goethe, and Baudelaire tried their hand with the vampire theme. It was British author Bram Stoker, however, who finally took the many jumbled strands of the

vampire legend and wove them into the classic *Dracula*, published in 1897. His mixture of fact and fiction has dominated our conception of a vampire ever since.

Stoker never went to Transylvania which is now a province of Romania, and where his story opens. But his research into museum records and guidebooks on the area was extremely thorough, and *Dracula* contains a great deal of authentic Slavonic folklore. The choice of Transylvania as Dracula's homeland was an apt one. The swirling mists, the peasants in colorful national costume, and the wooden crucifixes beside the Borgo Pass that Stoker described in his book are all still there. In this part of Europe, vampirism was a part of life—and death. As the Reverend Montague Summers, a leading historian of vampirism, wrote, ". . . in Romania we find gathered together around the Vampire almost all the beliefs and superstitions that prevail throughout the whole of Eastern Europe."

We tend to think of the vampire as pale, gaunt, and emaciated. This is misleading, for after a feast of blood the creature would be replete, red-lipped, and rosy-hued. In some ways this image of the vampire as something sleek with blood is even more horrifying. But, deathlike or robust, do such beings exist? Many early authorities were tempted to think so, including the French monk Dom Augustin Calmet. He was the author of one of the earliest learned studies of vampires, published in 1746. Calmet strived to maintain an open mind, but he wrote: "We are told that dead men . . . return from their tombs, are heard to speak, walk about, injure both men and animals whose blood they drain . . . making them sick and finally causing their death. Nor can the men deliver themselves unless they dig the corpses up and drive a sharp stake through these bodies, cut off their heads, tear out the hearts, or else burn the bodies to ashes. It seems impossible not to subscribe to the prevailing belief that these apparitions do actually come forth from their graves."

Other eminent writers had no doubts about the existence of vampires. Jean-Jacques Rousseau, the famous French philosopher of the 18th century, declared, "If ever there was in the world a warranted and proven history, it is that of vampires. Nothing is lacking: official reports, testimonials of persons of standing, of surgeons, of clergymen, of judges; the judicial evidence is all-embracing."

164

In our own time Colin Wilson, author of *The Occult* (1971), agrees. He says: "There *must* have been a reason that these vampire stories suddenly caught the imagination of Europe. Obviously *something* happened and it seems unlikely that it was pure imagination." He, too, refers to the documentation: "Examples of vampirism are so well authenticated that it would be absurd to try to maintain a strictly rationalist position."

An Epidemic of Vampirism

There is a surprising weight of evidence in support of the vampire legend, much of it collected and endorsed by army surgeons. In the Yugoslavian village of Meduegna near Belgrade, for example, a group of doctors investigated an epidemic of vampirism. On January 7, 1732 Johannes Flickinger, Isaac Seidel, Johann Baumgartner, and a lieutenant colonel and sub-lieutenant from the capital of Belgrade signed the medical report. They testified to an examination of 14 corpses. Only two—a mother and baby—were found to be in a normal state of decomposition. All the others were "unmistakably in the vampire condition."

There were so many such reports of vampirism in the mid-18th century that it was said by one surgeon to have "spread like a pestilence through Slavia and Walachia . . . causing numerous deaths and disturbing all the land with fear of the mysterious visitors against which no one felt himself secure."

A classic case history of the time concerned a Hungarian soldier who was billeted on a farm near the Austro-Hungarian frontier. He was eating with the farmer and his family one evening when they were joined by an old man. The soldier noticed that the family seemed extremely frightened of the man, who simply touched the farmer on the shoulder and then left. Next morning the soldier learned that the farmer was dead. Apparently the old man was the host's father, and had been dead for 10 years. When he visited and touched his son, he both announced and caused that son's death.

The soldier told the story to other men in his regiment, and the old man was soon labeled a vampire. For although he had not taken blood from his son, his coming showed him to be a member of the living dead, and he had certainly brought about his son's death. The affair was beginning to spread alarm among the soldiers, so it was investigated by the infantry commander, some other officers, and a surgeon. The farmer's family was questioned under oath. testimony was taken from villagers, and eventually the old man's grave was opened. His body looked like that of a man who had died recently—not 10 years earlier—and "his blood was like that of a living man." The commander of the regiment ordered that the vampire's head be cut off, and the body was laid to rest again.

During their inquiry the officers were told of another vampire who returned at 10-year intervals to suck the blood of members of his family. It is a notable feature of vampire stories that the vampire's relatives or lovers are usually the first to suffer attack. One case in a remote village in Yugoslavia concerned a particularly pernicious vampire who killed three of his nieces and a brother within a fortnight. He was interrupted just as he was starting to suck the blood of his fifth victim—another beautiful young niece—and he escaped.

A deputation, whose members' credentials seem impeccable, was sent from Belgrade to investigate. The party consisted of civil and military officials and a public prosecutor. They went to the vampire's grave as dusk fell, accompanied by the villagers. The man had been buried three years before, but when the investigators opened his grave they found his body intact with hair, fingernails, teeth, and eyes all in good condition. His heart was still beating, unbelievable as that seems. When the investigators thrust an iron stake through the corpse's heart a white fluid mixed with blood burst out. They then cut off the head with an ax. Only when the body was finally reburied in quicklime did the young niece who would have been the vampire's fifth victim begin to recover.

Usually in such cases a terrible smell was reported around the corpse, but that is hardly surprising. One body was described graphically as "puffed and bloated like some great leech about to burst," and when the customary stake was plunged into the breast of another, "a quantity of fresh scarlet blood issued, and from the nose and mouth as well; more issued from that part of his body which decency forbids me to name." There was another poignant case when tears sprang from the vampire's eyes as he gave his last scream of anguish.

One of the chief reasons for people's acute fear of vampires is

166

their alleged power to infect victims with their own insatiable lust for blood. According to some traditions, only people who die from loss of blood after repeated vampire attacks will become vampires themselves. Other vampire tales maintain that one or two attacks are enough, and that any victim of a vampire will come back as a new vampire after his or her natural death. The vampire is said to hypnotize its victims while it feeds so that the person remembers nothing of the gruesome experience, but simply complains of disturbed sleep and a strange lack of energy. Thus the vampire can safely return night after night to the same victim if it wishes until that victim grows progressively more anemic and dies. Sometimes there are tell-tale puncture wounds on the victims' neck. In that case, if they believe in vampires, they may well suspect their plight.

Arnold Paole

An example of how one vampire creates another was reported to the Imperial Council of War in Vienna in the 1730s. It involved a Hungarian soldier, Arnold Paole. He had been killed when a cart fell on top of him, but he was said to have returned from the dead 30 days later and claimed four victims who eventually died "in the manner traditionally ascribed to vampires"—presumably from the typical weakness attributed to loss of blood. Friends remembered Paole saying that he had been attacked by a vampire himself during military service on the Turko-Serbian border. But he thought he had cured himself of any possible infection by the traditional remedy of eating earth from the vampire's grave, and rubbing himself with its blood. This had obviously failed, however, for when Paole's body was exhumed, it "showed all the marks of an arch vampire. His body was flushed; his hair, nails, and beard had grown, and his veins were full of liquid blood which splashed all over the winding sheet." The local Governor ordered the inevitable stake to be thrust through the heart, and the vampire uttered the familiar shriek. Then the body was burned. The same procedure was also applied to the four recent victims in case they became active.

All these precautions apparently proved futile. Five years later there was a further outbreak of vampirism in the same area, and 17 people died. One woman claimed that her son, who had died nine weeks earlier, had attempted to strangle her while she slept;

she died three days afterward. The governor demanded another inquiry, and it was learned that Arnold Paole had attacked animals as well as humans during his reappearance as a vampire. Parts of the flesh of these animals had been eaten and, in due course, had caused the new epidemic. This time all the new infected vampires were exhumed, staked, decapitated, and burned. For good measure their ashes were thrown into the river. This seemed to be effective at last, and the terror was over.

Local bishops frequently sought the advice of the Pope on the vampire problem, but they received little help. The Church maintained, with some justification, that such phenomena were delusions. However, at one point the Vatican issued the cautious advice that suspect bodies should be exhumed and burned. Dom Calmet is one of the few authorities who quelled his occasional doubts and managed to remain objective. He showed a rare compassion for the vampires, especially if they were really innocent victims of superstition: "They were killed by decapitation, perforation, or burning, and this has been a great wrong; for the allegation that they returned to haunt and destroy the living has never been sufficiently proved to authorize such inhumanity, or to permit innocent beings to be dishonored . . . as a result of wild and unproved accusations. For the stories told of these apparitions, and all the distress caused by these supposed vampires, are totally without solid proof." Ever open-minded, however, he eventually came to the conclusion that, "This is a mysterious and difficult matter and I leave bolder and more proficient minds to resolve it."

Dom Calmet rightly uses the word "mysterious," and this element of mystery may be one simple reason for the lasting fascination of the vampire legend.

From Outcast to Vampire?

There are other vampire stories, however, which are far from entertaining and which stem from genuine fear. It was part of the vampire legend that people who were outcasts of society in life would remain outcasts after death, and might return as vampires. This compares to the Western European folklore that an evildoer—or the victim of evil—is often fated to return after death as a ghost. The Church may have found it useful not to discourage this belief that served as a warning to the guilty. In Eastern

Europe around 1645, it was stated that people who had led a "wicked and debauched life" or had been "excommunicated by their bishop" were likely to be condemned to the fate of the vampire, forever searching for the peace that was denied to them. The same threat applied to all suicides; those buried without the proper religious sacraments; perjurers; people who died under any kind of curse; and, in Hungary, to the stillborn illegitimate children of parents who were also illegitimate. In other words, anyone who had defied the social conventions of the times might become a vampire after death.

A vampire's grave is reputed to stink, and the creature's breath is said to smell foul from its diet of blood. The appearance of a vampire is also often heralded by an appalling odor. Interestingly, an abominable smell is also a frequent element of possession by the devil even today, and features prominently in the popular book and film *The Exorcist*. A vampire story that demonstrates this aspect well was recounted by Dr. Henry Moore in 1653, and concerns a Silesian. The story goes as follows: "One evening when this theologer was sitting with his wife and children about him, exercising himself in music, according to his usual manner, a most grievous stink arose suddenly, which by degrees spread itself to every corner of the room. Hereupon he commended himself and his family to God by prayer. The smell nevertheless increased, and became above all measure pestilently noisome, insomuch that he was forced to go up to his chamber. He and his wife had not been in bed a quarter of an hour, but they find the same stink in the bedchamber; of which, while they are complaining one to another, out steps the specter from the wall, and creeping to his bedside, breathes upon him an exceedingly cold breath, of so intolerable stinking and malignant a scent, as is beyond all imagination and expression."

This smell sounds like a symbol of impending plague, and was frequently interpreted as such. As early as 1196 the historian William of Newburgh told of a "lecherous husband" who returned from the grave to terrify people in his home town. He said: "For the air became foul and tainted as this fetid and corrupting body wandered abroad, so that a terrible plague broke out and there was hardly a house which did not mourn its dead, and presently the town, which but a little before had been thickly populated, seemed to be well nigh deserted, for those who had survived the pestilence and these hideous attacks hastily removed themselves to other districts lest they should also perish."

Two young men, plainly braver than the rest, traced the living corpse to its grave and cut its head off with a spade so that the red blood gushed out. The body was then burned. This destruction of the corpse in the fashion of a vampire succeeded. "No sooner had that infernal monster been thus destroyed," the story goes on, "than the plague, which had so sorely ravaged the people, entirely ceased, just as if the polluted air was cleansed by the fire which burned up the hellish brute who had infected the whole atmosphere."

It is interesting to see how the infernal monster is used as a scapegoat for the plague, with the added condemnation that he was a lecherous husband, as if his behavior when he was alive was responsible for the whole calamity. It is true that epidemics of vampirism and plague did tend to go together: in 1729 it was said that any plague where, "within a few hours five or six persons fell ill in the village," would automatically be linked to vampirism. But it is not a case of the vampires causing the plague. On the contrary, periods of plague created the perfect atmosphere for a belief in vampires.

There are, therefore, several perfectly reasonable explanations for the proliferation of the vampire legend; but nevertheless the doubts remain. As the curtain fell on the first stage production of *Dracula*, the producer Hamilton Deane came out in front of the curtain to warn the audience to take care as they went home. "Remember," he cried in sepulchral tones, "There are such things!"

15. The UFO Phenomenon

High above Kentucky the plane climbed at top speed in an effort to close on an unidentified object in the sky. It had been spotted by many observers below, including the control tower operators at Godman Air Force Base. Three F-51 Mustang fighters had been diverted from a training exercise in an attempt to identify the mysterious craft. Captain Thomas Mantell, flying the leading plane, had outdistanced his wingmen when his first dramatic radio call came to the tower: "I see something above and ahead of me, and I'm still climbing." Mantell was asked to describe what he could see. "It looks metallic and is tremendous in size...." Seconds later he called, "It's above me, and I'm gaining on it. I'm going to 20,000 feet." Those were the last words he spoke. Later on that fateful day of January 7, 1948, Mantell's body was found near the remains of his disintegrated aircraft, 90 miles from Godman Base. The unknown flying object had escaped. Some people believed that Mantell and his plane had been attacked by an alien spaceship, and rumors even spread that the dead pilot's body had been burned by a mysterious ray. The United States Air Force explanation did little to soothe growing public uneasiness about flying saucers. According to the version of the story as told by the United States Air Force, the skilled veteran pilot, known to be level-headed and careful, had gone to his death chasing the planet Venus. It seemed incredible to most people that the experienced Mantell and the trained control tower observers could mistake a familiar heavenly body for an object described by some witnesses as "a huge ice cream cone topped with red."

Fifteen days after Mantell's death the USAF's official investigation of flying saucers—now more commonly referred to as UFOs or unidentified flying objects—went into operation. It

171

was code named Project Sign, and its existence indicated that the authorities were in reality concerned about the strange aerial intruders that had flown into the headlines a little over six months before the Mantell incident.

On June 24, 1947, Kenneth Arnold saw nine shining disks weaving their way in formation among the peaks of the Cascade mountains of Washington state, and first alerted the world to the possibility that planet Earth was being visited by beings from another civilization. Arnold—a private pilot, member of the Idaho Search and Rescue Mercy Flyers, and Flying Deputy for the Ada County Aerial Posse—at the time was searching for a commercial plane that had crashed in the mountains. He was after a $5000 reward for locating the lost plane. Arnold never found the wreckage, but his sighting made him world famous.

Describing the flying objects he had seen to reporters, Arnold said that they moved "like a saucer skipping across water." An inventive reporter coined the phrase "flying saucer," and it soon became a household term—even flying into the pages of the dictionary. The popular term is not used by serious investigators, however. They prefer the more exact term UFO.

Kenneth Arnold was not the first man to see strange flying objects in the sky, nor even the first to describe them as saucer-like. A Texas farmer once saw a fast moving object in the sky and said that the only way he could describe it was as a large saucer. That was on January 24, 1878! Strange aircraft were also reported throughout World War II, and were often thought to be secret weapons of the enemy. But Arnold's sighting seemed to mark a turning point in UFO activity as well as supplying the media with a neat and colorful description. Perhaps it was because people recovering from a second major global war in only 25 years were hoping that there were wiser creatures in the Universe who could help put the Earth's troubles into perspective. Perhaps it was Arnold's estimate of the flying saucers' amazing speed of an incredible 1700 miles per hour that caught the public imagination. It might even simply have been the description of the flying crafts' shape that interested and amused people.

Four days after Arnold's saucer sighting two pilots and two intelligence officers saw a bright light performing "impossible maneuvers" over Maxwell Air Force Base in Montgomery, Alabama. On the same day an Air Force jet pilot saw a formation

172

of five or six unconventional aircraft near Lake Meade, Nevada. Another formation of flying saucers was seen by the pilot and copilot of a commercial DC-3 on July 4. They watched the five objects silhouetted against the sunset for 45 minutes. Soon after this group disappeared, a second formation of four came into view. Could they have been the same nine disks Arnold had seen? Only a few days later in early July a supersecret Air Force test center in the Mojave desert of California was being treated to a whole series of aerial visitations. The first sighting was by a test pilot at Muroc, now Edwards, Air Base. He was preparing for a flight in an experimental aircraft when he saw a yellow spherical craft moving against the wind. Several other officers at the base had seen three similar UFOs ten minutes earlier. Two hours later technicians at nearby Rogers Dry Lake saw a round object of aluminum appearance. After watching it for 90 seconds they decided that the strange craft was "man-made." Later that same day, a jet pilot flying 40 miles south of Edwards saw above him a flat object that reflected light. He tried to investigate but his aircraft could not climb as high as the UFO.

In the early days of UFO reports many people believed that Arnold and others had observed a new secret aircraft or guided missile being developed by the United States military. Arnold himself believed that for a time. But following a spate of sightings from reliable and competent witnesses—many of them experienced pilots fully aware of the latest aeronautical developments—the Air Force got jittery about UFOs. Behind the scenes the USAF was exploring the possibility that they belonged to a foreign power. After all, at the end of the war the Allies had obtained complete data on the latest German aircraft and missiles that had been under development. Had the Soviet Union uncovered a new aerodynamic concept from the German data? Or had they developed their own unique form of aircraft with which to spy on the United States?

It was soon clear that the Soviet Union could not have produced an aircraft that matched the flight characteristics of the UFOs in such a short period. Even if they had been able to do so, it was extremely unlikely that the Soviets would risk exposing the secret so soon by flying over so many countries. For, ever since Arnold had reported flying saucers skimming around the snow-clad mountain peak of Mount Rainier, UFOs had made appearances over every country in the world.

Once it was apparent that no nation on earth was capable of producing the UFOs, the possibility that another civilization was watching our planet had to be faced. This idea had already been put forward by some writers. But there was an alternative. Perhaps "saucer fever" had gripped the nation, causing ordinarily cautious people—and even experienced observers—to see UFOs in everyday objects. This seemed to be the official line as report after sensational report was explained away as balloons, birds, meteorites, planets, conventional aircraft, or natural phenomena. So why did investigations under Project Sign continue, to be followed in time by Project Grudge and Project Blue Book? Because a small but significant percentage of UFOs reported remained unidentified and unexplained as natural phenomena after experts had ruled out every known possibility. Often these were the best reports in the files in terms of the eliability of witnesses or the standard of supporting evidence such as radar reports.

The military establishment worried that a foreign power could use the flying saucer craze as a cover for spying over United States territory, because the deluge of UFO reports that accumulated during the late 1940s caused an understandable public apathy about objects in the sky. Not that people were no longer concerned, but in most cases it had become physically impossible to do more than log in reports in the hope that some pattern would emerge from the data to aid ultimate identification. Yet until the origin of UFOs was known, they had to be regarded as a potential threat.

After six months of intensive saucer activity, even the most nervous citizens had to admit that if the saucers were hostile they were taking a long time to show it. Then, after the devastating news of Captain Mantell's death, public disquiet increased. At the official level, Project Sign investigators learned that same year of a pilot's duel with a flying saucer. It happened near Fargo, North Dakota on October 1, 1948. Lieutenant George F. Gorman of the North Dakota Air National Guard, was nearing the air base after a cross-country flight. When he had radioed for landing instructions, the control tower had told him that a Piper Cub was the only other aircraft in the vicinity, and Gorman could see the light aircraft below him as he made his approach.

Kenneth Arnold, a private pilot who saw nine shining disks weaving their way in formation among the peaks of the Cascade Mountains of Washington State on 24 June 1947. His sighting was the first in a deluge of UFO reports in the late 1940s and made him world-famous. The term "flying saucer" was coined by a journalist describing Arnold's experience. (*The UFO Phenomenon*)

(Top) Close-up of a UFO photographed by Paul Trent over McMinnville, Oregon in 1950. *(The UFO Phenomenon)*

(Bottom left) "I see something above and ahead of me, and I'm still climbing. It looks metallic and is tremendous in size ... It's above me, and I'm gaining on it. I'm going to 20,000 feet." The last words of Captain Thomas Mantell, pictured above, the veteran United States Air Force pilot who died pursuing an unidentified object flying in the sky above Kentucky on 7 January 1948. *(The UFO Phenomenon)*

(Bottom right) UFOs over Conisbrough, South Yorkshire, photographed on 28 March 1966. *(The UFO Phenomenon)*

Suddenly a light passed him to the right. He thought it was the tailplane light of another aircraft, and called the control tower to complain. When he was told there was nothing else in the sky except the Piper Cub he decided to pursue the light.

As he turned to intercept he could see the other aircraft clearly silhouetted against the city lights. The mysterious light, however, did not appear to be attached to a solid body. Gorman closed in at maximum speed. At 1000 yards he could see that the light was six to eight inches in diameter and blinking. When he got this close, the light became steady and the aircraft banked sharply to the left with his jet on its tail. After a series of abrupt maneuvers Gorman found himself on a collision course with the UFO. When it became clear that the light was not going to take evasive action the National Guard pilot took a dive. The saucer missed the plane's canopy with only feet to spare. The "duel of death" continued, and Gorman had to dive a second time to avoid a head-on collision. Moments later the strange light began to climb. It disappeared as a shaken Gorman returned to Fargo to file his astonishing report.

His account to the Air Technical Intelligence Center (ATIC) included these words: "I had the distinct impression that its maneuvers were controlled by thought or reason." Four other observers saw a fast moving light in Fargo at the same time, but no one witnessed the dogfight.

Ruppelt's Report

To saucer advocates, the Mantell and Gorman cases were sufficient proof that superior beings in vehicles of advanced technology were patrolling our skies. Some assumed they were hostile, or at least capable of retaliating if pursued. Others thought the Mantell incident was an accident, and that the Gorman case was no more than a playful game on the part of the spacemen. Meanwhile the Air Force maintained the line of dismissing reports publicly while investigating them with renewed intensity. Their reasoning became clearer with the publication of the late Captain Edward J. Ruppelt's book *The Report on Unidentified Flying Objects*, published in 1956. Ruppelt had been chief of the USAF's Project Blue Book, successor to Project Sign, from 1951 to 1953. Ruppelt tried to throw new light on some of the famous early accounts that had remained unsatisfactorily explained.

The Mantell case had nothing to do with the planet Venus, he admitted. Ruppelt had discovered that Venus could not have been visible at the time of the chase, though if it were it would have been in the same place in the sky as the UFO. Ruppelt offered a far more plausible explanation. Mantell died while trying to intercept a secret skyhook balloon, he said. The skyhook project, designed to collect information from the fringes of the atmosphere by balloon, was highly classified when Mantell tried to identify the UFO. Ruppelt claimed that everyone involved in the official investigation of the Mantell case was convinced that he had been after a spaceship, so no one bothered to "buck the red tape of security to get data on skyhook flights." By the time Ruppelt checked on this possibility there were no longer any records of the 1948 skyhook flights, but those involved thought that at that time they were being launched from Clinton County Air Force Base in southern Ohio. Winds records for the day in question showed that a skyhook launched from Clinton would have been visible from all the points in the area of Godman Base from which the UFO was seen. The skyhook would have climbed to 60,000 feet, and then drifted in a southerly direction. Mantell died because he did not know he was chasing a balloon, Ruppelt argued. "He had never heard of a huge 100-foot diameter balloon, let alone seen one," he explained. If a skyhook balloon had been launched from Clinton on January 7, even the staunchest believers in flying saucers would have to admit that the facts and description of the sightings tally beyond doubt. If, however, it could be proved that no skyhook balloons climbed into the jet stream over the Godman area that day, then even the saucer skeptics would have to admit that the object which took Captain Thomas Mantell to his death remains one of the most perplexing puzzles of the UFO enigma.

Ruppelt offered an equally plausible explanation for Gorman's strange duel with a flying saucer. Gorman was fighting a small lighted balloon, he said in his book. An almost identical incident had occurred over Cuba in September 1952. A Navy pilot, who spotted a large orange light to the east after making practice passes for night fighters, was told that no other aircraft were in the vicinity. He tried to intercept the flying object. At closer quarters he described it as having a green tail between five and

Close-up of a UFO photographed by George J. Stock over Passaic, New Jersey on 29 July 1952. (*The UFO Phenomenon*)

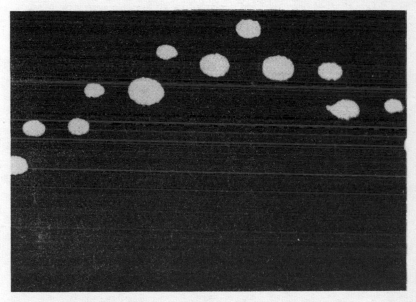

The "Lubbock Lights" photographed by Carl Hart Jr. on 30 August 1951. (*The UFO Phenemenon*)

(*Top left*) Captain Edward J. Ruppelt, chief of the United States Air Forces's Project Blue Book investigating the UFO phenomenon from 1951-53 and author of *The Report on Unidentified Flying Objects* published in 1956. (*The UFO Phenomenon*)

(*Bottom left*) UFO over Trinidad, 16 January 1958. (*The UFO Phenomenon*)

(*Right*) UFO beaming down a ray of light on to water, Pennsylvania, 1961. (*The UFO Phenomenon*)

10 times its diameter. It seemed to be climbing, changing course, and even responding to his plane's movements. After reaching 35,000 feet, the light began a rapid descent. The pilot took two runs at it on a 90-degree collision course. On both occasions the object traveled across his bow. On the third run he reported that he came so close to the light that it blanked out the airfield below him. Then it dived, and although the pilot followed, he lost the light at 1500 feet.

"In *this* incident," Ruppelt wrote, "the UFO *was* a balloon." This was proved by sending a lighted balloon up the following night and ordering the pilot to compare his experiences. "He duplicated his dogfight—illusions and all . . . Gorman fought a lighted balloon too. An analysis of the sighting by the Air Weather Service sent to ATIC in a letter dated January 24, 1949, proved it."

Did it? Major Donald E. Keyhoe, a staunch advocate of the interplanetary spaceships theory and a well-known author of UFO books, agrees that a weather balloon was released in Fargo on the night of Gorman's strange encounter. But he maintains that the Weather Bureau observer who tracked it recorded a course that took it away from the area in which the aerial duel was fought.

Even if the Mantell and Gorman cases were misidentification of different types of balloons, the fact remains that the U.S. Air Force had many more startling cases in its files about which the public knew nothing. An ATIC study of the flying saucer reports received in the year after the Kenneth Arnold sighting had culminated in an historic, top secret "estimate of the situation," which concluded that UFOs were interplanetary. Air Force Chief of Staff General Hoyt S. Vandenberg was not convinced, however, and rejected the report.

Whether people believed in them or not made no difference to the flying saucers. They continued to appear with startling regularity, often giving ground observers spectacular displays of aerial acrobats.

Conflicting Evidence

As officialdom found new explanations for the UFOs, they appeared to be proving their own theories wrong. Mantell, for example, may have died while chasing a skyhook, but it was certainly not possible to dismiss all unidentified flying objects as huge metallic-looking balloons. On one occasion near the top secret White Sands Proving Grounds in New Mexico, the crew of an aircraft was tracking a skyhook when they saw two disks fly in from just above the horizon, circle the balloon at nearly 90,000 feet, and rapidly depart. When the balloon was recovered it was ripped. Captain Ruppelt, who published this account, does not specify the date but it would have been in either 1948 or 1949. Compare it with the experience of six observers in 1951. Two of the witnesses were from General Mills, whose aeronautical division had launched and tracked every skyhook balloon prior to mid-1952. The other witnesses were from Artesia, New Mexico. The group had been watching the movements of a skyhook for about an hour when one of them noticed two specks on the horizon. He pointed them out because two aircraft were expected at Artesia airport at about that time. But the specks were not aircraft. They flew in fast in close formation, heading straight for the balloon. They circled the skyhook once and flew off in the direction from which they had come, disappearing rapidly over the horizon. As they circled the skyhook the two dull white objects tipped on edge, and the observers saw that they had a disk shape. Their estimated size was 60 feet in diameter.

People who believed that UFOs were natural phenomena, such as meteorites, were finding it difficult to convince others because eminent astronomers and scientists were among the UFO observers. For example, the man who reported a flight of six or eight greenish lights in Las Cruces, New Mexico in August 1949 was Professor Clyde W. Tombaugh, discoverer of the planet Pluto. New Mexico was being plagued by a special type of UFO known as green fireballs. Dr. Lincoln La Paz, world-famous authority on meteorites, and a team of intelligence officers made a full investigation of the sightings. Many of them saw the green fireballs—including La Paz—but no physical evidence was found to show that they were a special type of meteorite. In fact, Dr. La Paz concluded that whatever they were, they most certainly were not meteorites.

Physical evidence was what was missing from all the early UFO reports, however good. There were many excellent visual reports, but no photographs or film of sufficient quality to aid identification. There were intriguing radar reports of strange fast-moving

178

objects. But without visual corroboration that an object was where the radarscope recorded it, the report had to be dismissed as either a malfunction of the equipment or a misidentification of an echo caused by weather, birds, or other familiar objects. What the saucer buffs needed to prove their case was a sighting that combined visual and radar evidence. Gradually, such reports began to trickle through, building up to a flood, with an astonishing visitation in the skies to the Capital itself.

The spectacular began in the dying hours of July 19, 1952, when two radars picked up eight unidentified objects on their screens at Washington National Airport. Whatever the objects were, they were roaming the Washington area at speeds of between 100 and 130 miles per hour. They would suddenly accelerate to "fantastically high speeds," and leave the area. The long-range radar in Washington has a 100-mile radius, and was used for controlling all aircraft approaching the airport. The National Airport's control tower was equipped with a shorter range radar designed for handling planes in its immediate vicinity. Just east of the airport was Bolling Air Force Base, and ten miles further east was Andrews Air Force Base, which were also equipped with short-range radar. All these airfields were linked by an intercom system. All three radars picked up the same unknown targets. One object was logged at 7000 miles per hour as it streaked across the screens, and it was not long before the UFOs were over the White House and the Capitol, both prohibited flying areas. Radar experts were called in to check the equipment, though it was clear that the odds against three radarscopes developing identical faults were exceptionally high. They were found to be in good working order. Visual sightings were made as airline pilots came into the area and saw lights they could not identify. The lights were exactly where the radars were picking up UFOs. A commercial airline pilot was talking to the control tower when he saw one of the lights. "There's one—off to the right—and there it goes," he said. As he reported, the controller had been watching the long-range radar. A UFO that had shown to the airliner's right disappeared from the scope at the very moment the pilot said it had.

One of the best ground sightings that night came when the long-range radar operator at the airport informed Andrews Air Force Base tower that a UFO was just south of them, directly

179

over the Andrews radio station. When the tower operators looked out they saw a "huge fiery orange sphere" hovering in the sky at exactly that position.

Incredible as it may seem, no one thought to inform ATIC, and it was nearly daylight when a jet interceptor arrived over the area to investigate the phenomena. Its crew searched the skies, found nothing unusual, and left—but the UFOs had left the radar screens by then in any case.

A week later almost to the hour, the flying saucers were back over Washington to give a repeat performance. The same radar operators picked up several slow-moving targets at about 10:30 p.m. on July 26. The long-range radar operators began plotting them immediately. They alerted the control tower and Andrews Base, but it already had them on its screens and were plotting them. A call went out for jet interceptors. Once again there was a delay but two jets finally arrived soon after midnight. The UFOs mysteriously vanished from the screens just as the jets arrived. The pilots could see nothing during their search, and returned to base. Minutes after the jets left the Washington area the UFOs came back! The jets were called back, and this time when they reached the area, the UFOs remained. The controllers guided the pilots toward groups of targets, but each time the objects flew away at great speed before the pilots could see more than a strange light. At times it seemed that the lights were somehow monitoring the control tower conversations with the pilots, and responding before an aircraft had time to change course. On one occasion a light remained stationary as the jet pilot flew at it with full power. As he closed in the light suddenly disappeared, like a light being switched off. Both Washington sightings lasted several hours, and the second one gave some of the Air Force's top saucer experts an opportunity to rush to the airport, watch the radar screens, and listen to the pilots' accounts.

The USAF Press Conference

After growing pressure from the press and public the Air Force held a press conference—the largest and longest since World War II. It was presided over by Major General John Samford, Director of Intelligence at the Pentagon. He offered no concrete explanation, but hinted that the lights came from strong temperature inversions, during which light waves are refracted or bent. Therefore an object on the ground or the moon, sun, or stars may be reflected on a layer of inverted air. Similarly, temperature inversions could cause activity on radar screens.

However, the men controlling thousands of lives in and out of Washington National Airport had had years of experience, and were used to seeing and identifying every type of radar blip. They knew about temperature inversions, and were certain that they were not responsible for the radar UFOs whose blips came from solid objects. Besides, as Captain Ruppelt admitted much later, the temperature inversions known to exist on the nights in question were not strong enough to affect radar in the way they normally do. In fact, mild inversions existed on practically every night of June, July, and August 1952. The sensational Washington sightings therefore remain unexplained.

The 1950s progressed without any significant lull in flying saucer sightings. More good sightings were added to the bulging files, but none proved sufficiently outstanding to convince officialdom that the saucers were interplanetary. The public was easier to convince, and the ranks of the believers in UFOs grew all the time. Many asked what it would take to convince the authorities. The answer seemed to be nothing short of a mass landing on the White House lawn.

In August 1953 the Air Defense Command radar station at Ellsworth Air Force Base near Rapid City, South Dakota, picked up a "well-defined, solid and bright" target at the spot where a ground observer had reported seeing a light. Height-finding radar also recorded it at 16,000 feet. The object was almost stationary. Then it picked up speed, circled Rapid City, and returned to its original place in the sky. This maneuver was watched on radar and reported by the ground observer.

A jet hurried to the scene, and soon spotted the light. It closed in to within three miles of the object. Then the light sped off with the jet on its tail. There was a limit to how close the UFO allowed the aircraft to come before pulling away, as though its power supply was automatically linked to a device measuring the distance of its pursuer. Captain Ruppelt reported what happened next in *The Report on Unidentified Flying Objects*:

"The chase continued on north—out of sight of the lights of Rapid City and the base—into some very black night.

"When the UFO and the F-84 got about 120 miles to the north, the pilot checked his fuel; he had to come back. And when I talked to him, he said he was damn glad that he was running out of fuel because being out over some mighty desolate country alone with a UFO can cause some worry.

"Both the UFO and the F-84 had gone off the scope, but in a few minutes·the jet was back on, heading for home. Then 10 or 15 miles behind it was the UFO target also coming back."

The alert pilots of the jet interceptor squadron at the base had heard the conversation between the controller and pilot. Another jet with a veteran of World War II and Korea at the controls was standing at the ready. This pilot wanted to see a flying saucer for himself. Permission was given and he climbed into the sky, spotted the UFO, and closed in. Once again the object sped away, keeping a three-mile distance. The pilot switched on his radar-ranging gunsight which in seconds showed that there was something solid in front of him. At that point he got scared and broke off the interception. The UFO, on this occasion, did not follow him back to base. That encounter, according to Ruppelt, "is still the best UFO report in the Air Force files."

Washington National Airport was the scene of more UFO activity in July 1955 when a brilliant circular object with a tail four or five times its length flew into the airport, stopped and hovered. It oscillated before taking off at high speed, and was caught in the beam of a searchlight; but the searchlight suddenly went out. According to Brinsley le Poer Trench, a well-known British author of flying saucer books. "The UFO also caused the ceiling lights at the airport to go out, but these lit up again the moment the UFO left the airport."

When the first decade of flying saucer activity was over, the puzzle remained. There were photographs, radar reports, and thousands of sightings from experienced observers. But the experts were no nearer solving the flying saucer mystery than they were when Kenneth Arnold's sighting hit the world headlines. Then the Soviet Union launched the first man-made satellite on October 4, 1957.

Humankind was on the verge of exploring space—and sending our own UFOs to other worlds.

16. The Inhabited Universe?

President Jimmy Carter has seen a flying saucer. It happened in 1973 after he had made a late-evening speech to a Lions Club meeting in Thomaston, Georgia. As he left with a group of friends he saw the UFO, apparently hovering above a field.

"It was a very peculiar aberration, but about 20 people saw it," he told the *National Enquirer* newspaper during his presidential election campaign. "It was the darndest thing I've ever seen. It was big, it was very bright, it changed colors and it was about the size of the Moon. We watched it for 10 minutes, but none of us could figure out what it was. One thing's for sure, I'll never make fun of people who say they've seen unidentified flying objects in the sky!" Carter's 23-year-old son gave the newspaper further details about the UFO: "It had three lights—clustered together about the size of the Moon. My dad said they were changing color from red to green. It was positioned off to one side of the Moon."

It is now up to the American President, who is on record as saying "I am convinced UFO's exist because I have seen one," to take time from the burdens of his office and open the UFO files to public inspection—for millions of his countrymen believe that the American authorities know more about UFOs than they are saying.

Many other authorities adopt a secretive policy on UFOs, as can be seen from a statement made in July 1976 by another eminent UFO eye-witness, General Carlos Cavero, commanding officer of the Spanish Air Force in the Canary Islands. While spending a few days near Sabada, a village in a remote part of eastern Spain, he saw a bright UFO traveling at a speed of 22,000 miles per hour. He calculated the speed from the time it took the

183

UFO to travel the 12 miles to the next village—just two seconds. General Cavero said, after reporting his sighting to the Spanish Air Ministry in Madrid: "As an Air Force officer I hold, officially, the same opinions as the Air Ministry. But personally, I think these unidentified flying objects come from other planets."

The UFO seen by one of Spain's top serving officers, was also apparently seen by a well known local doctor, Francisco Padron, who had a close encounter with the object. "It was nearly dark," he said, "and I was driving along a lonely road. Then I saw a round sphere about 40 feet in diameter hovering above the road ahead of me. It was emitting a blueish light and was about 20 feet above the ground. As I approached, my radio cut out but my headlight kept working. I passed right underneath and saw, silhouetted inside through a type of porthole, two very tall figures dressed in bright red. Then it took off and vanished in the direction of Tenerife."

So, despite the official denials and the negative findings of investigations such as the Condon Committee, the flying saucer mystery deepens with an American president and a Spanish air force general among the eye-witnesses in the 1970s. The UFOs refuse to go away; so, again, what are they?

There are two modern mysteries to add to the already long list of mysteries for which there appears to be no official explanation. One relates to the cold wastes of Siberia and the other concerns a tribe living in sub-Saharan Africa. Either of these may in time prove to be a vital key in unlocking the secrets of UFO phenomena.

The Tunguska Incident

A giant ball of fire shot across Western China and Mongolia on the morning of June 30, 1908, and exploded with a deafening roar in the desolate marsh region of Tunguska in the heart of Siberia, 2200 miles east of Moscow. Seismographs as far away as Washington registered the event and a series of thunderclaps were heard 500 miles away. A "black rain" of debris fell over a wide area and trees were flattened over an area of 1500 square miles (whereas the Hiroshima atom bomb flattened only 18 square miles). It seemed to be a spectacular meteorite. But there is a mystery: A meteorite that could cause such devastation should have left a gigantic crater on impact, but no crater nor remains of the meteorite have been found. Because of Russia's internal problems, the Siberian explosion was not investigated for 19 years. When Leonid Kulik, a meteorite expert, led an expedition to the area in 1927 he found a charred forest with flattened trees—their roots pointing to the center of the blast. But strangely, the trees at the center were still upright. One explanation is that whatever it was that exploded did so high above Tunguska.

In 1976 the Russians announced that a new study of the mystery was to be carried out. This followed the discovery of very strange effects in the area. The Tunguska peat swamps receive their minerals only from the air and they grow at a regular rate, so it has been possible to examine the layer that formed at the time of the great explosion. Silicate particles have been found that are of a composition which not only differs from that found in ordinary meteorites, but has no equivalent in known earthly bodies. Genetic mutations have now been reported from the area and a mighty coniferous forest has blossomed in the once devasted region. The natural rate of genetic change in the region's flora has increased twelvefold, it is said, in which case some exciting discoveries could appear when the Russian expedition publishes its result.

What, then, caused the 1908 Tunguska explosion? It would be easy to dismiss it as just a supermeteorite, or a comet, or even an as-yet unknown cosmic object that strayed too close to the Earth and exploded in the atmosphere. Some scientists have suggested that it might have been an object made of antimatter that was annihilated by the Earth's matter in a fantastic explosion. Others believe it might have been a small exploding black hole. But there is one disturbing aspect of the Siberian mystery that does not fit any of these theories. From a study of eye-witness accounts of the great ball of fire, Dr Felix Ziegel of the Moscow Institute of Aviation has concluded that the object made a 375-mile arc in the air before crashing or exploding. "That is," says Dr Ziegel, "it carried out a maneuver." This has led some scientists to suggest that the Tunguska object was a spacecraft that got into difficulties and crashed or exploded. Perhaps it was the first probe sent out by beings in another solar system and the information it sent back enabled them to build new spaceships—the present-day UFOs—that were able to carry out surveillance of our planet without difficulty.

Our astronomical knowledge has taught us that while some stars are still forming in clusters of gas and dust, there are also stars that are far older than our Sun. If these stars have planetary systems, then life could have evolved to our present level many thousands of years ago. If that is so, then Earth could have been visited over regular periods by space people. They may even have made contact with early civilizations and influenced them. That is the conclusion drawn by Robert Temple, a young American with a degree in Oriental Studies and Sanskrit, after a detailed study of the Dogon people who live in Mali, in the former French Sudan in Africa.

The Sirius Mystery

The Dogon people, says Temple in his book *The Sirius Mystery*, preserve a tradition of what seems to have been an extraterrestrial contact. The Dogon's most secret traditions all concern a "star" to which they give the same name as the tiniest seed known to them. The botanical name of the seed is *Digitaria*. Temple first came across this strange fact in an account written in 1950 by two eminent anthropologists, Marcel Griaule and Germaine Dieterlen of France, who had lived with the Dogon and won their confidence. The mystery was contained in one passage: "The starting-point of creation is the star which revolves round Sirius and is actually named the '*Digitaria* star'; it is regarded by the Dogon as the smallest and heaviest of all the stars; it contains the germs of all things. Its movement on its own axis and around Sirius upholds all creation in space. We shall see that its orbit determines the calendar."

It is astonishing that a relatively primitive people should understand that stars revolve on their axis and follow orbits, but what is really incredible about the Dogon traditions is that the star to which they refer (known to astronomers as Sirius B) is totally invisible without the aid of a telescope, and was not discovered until the last century. It was only photographed in 1970 and it is so faint that even if it were not obliterated by the brilliant star Sirius it would still be invisible to the naked eye. The reason is that it is a white dwarf—the tiniest form of visible star in the Universe. At the time of its discovery in the middle of the 19th century it was unique, but a hundred or more have now been seen by astronomers and there must be many thousands more in our galaxy alone. Sirius B is a very dense star, the smallest and heaviest type (except for neutron stars, which are invisible), just as the Dogon say. According to their traditions it is made of a metal that is so heavy "that all earthly beings combined cannot lift it." That's a surprising concept but a correct one: A cubic foot of Sirius B matter would weigh 2000 tons. The Dogon also describe the elliptical orbit of the dark companion of Sirius and say that it takes 50 years to orbit the bright star, which has since been confirmed.

Sirius has always been an important star. It is the brightest in the sky and was the basis of the Egyptian calendar. So it would not be surprising for the Dogon or any other people to have myths about it. But what is uncanny is that the Dogon regard Sirius as relatively unimportant. It is described only as the focus of the elliptical orbit of the invisible *Digitaria*. What makes Temple's well-researched book so impressive is that much of the evidence supplied came from the two French anthropologists who were simply reporting the Dogon traditions without attempting to explain or understand them. It is clear that Griaule and Dieterlen had hardly any astronomical knowledge and did not realize that the Dogon traditions about the Sirius star system were incredibly accurate.

But why should a sub-Saharan tribe have sophisticated knowledge of exotic stars and their behavior? Temple offers evidence that the information the Dogon possess is more than 5000 years old and was possessed originally by the ancient Egyptians in pre-dynastic times before 3200 B.C. The Dogon, he says, are partially descended culturally and probably physically, too, from these people.

Although he attempts to give the facts without speculation, Temple admits that his findings "seem to reveal a contact in the distant past between our planet Earth and an advanced race of intelligent beings from another planetary system several light-years away in space." He puts that cultural contact at some time between 7000 and 10,000 years ago but admits that it may go back farther, and that civilization as we know it could even have been an importation from another planet in the first place.

"Nommo is the collective name for the great culture-hero and founder of civilization who came from the Sirius system to set up society on the Earth," says Temple, referring to the Dogon tradition. "The Nommos were amphibious creatures . . . more or less equivalent with the Sumerian and Babylonian tradition of Oannes [the demigod-leader of the amphibious Annedoti, creatures who brought civilization to Earth]."

If these interpretations are correct then at this very moment there is a largely ocean-covered planet in the region of Sirius just 8.6 light-years away, inhabited by creatures far in advance of us. They have visited Earth in the past and perhaps they are still keeping us under observation, possibly in conjunction with other superior beings with whom they enjoy intergalactic collaboration.

But let us for a moment put aside all the evidence of the Dogon, the Tunguska "thing" that exploded, and the thousands of unexplained UFO sightings, and look at the possibility of life elsewhere in the Universe from a different standpoint. We have to face the possibility that the Earth may be unique in supporting intelligent life. If that is so, then we have a tremendous responsibility to ensure the survival of the human race. If we are the first seed of life in the Universe then we may be destined to people other planets and spread life to other Solar Systems and even to other galaxies. But is that likely? The Universe that we observe is governed by cosmic laws that do not seem to encourage uniqueness. As astronomers discover a new cosmic object—a pulsar, a quasar, or a radio galaxy, for example—it is not long before they find others of the same type. So, since planets have formed around our Sun it seems certain that the same phenomenon will have occurred elsewhere in the Universe. It could be that every star has a planetary system, but even the nearest star is too far away for us to detect such orbiting, non-luminous bodies.

Dr R. N. Bracewell of the Radio Astronomy Institute of Stanford University has estimated that 10,000,000,000 planets in our galaxy alone could support life. Dr Melvin Calvin, of the Department of Chemistry, University of California at Berkeley, has said: "There are at least 100,000,000 planets in the visible Universe which were, or are, very much like the Earth. . . ." Life, according to these and other scientists, could be a common phenomenon throughout the Universe. But how does it form? The theory that has enjoyed support for many years suggests that while the Earth was still at a primitive stage of evolution, lightning flashes in the atmosphere would have supplied sufficient energy to break the chemical bonds of certain molecules on our planet causing a rearrangement of the atoms into amino acids and nucleotides from which living organisms are made. A similar event can be produced in a laboratory with electrical discharges.

The 'Cradles' of Life

In 1977 two astronomers suggested a new and exciting theory which, if confirmed, would seem that life is undoubtedly a widespread phenomenon. Fred Hoyle the British astronomer and Chandra Wickramasinghe, professor of applied mathematics and astronomy at University College, Cardiff, Wales, have suggested that life forms in space. Their theory is based on studies of meteorites and interstellar dust, particularly molecular clouds in which new stars are forming. They say: "We regard pre-stellar molecular clouds, such as are present in the Orion nebula, as the most natural 'cradles' of life. Processes occurring in such clouds lead to the commencement and dispersal of biological activity in the galaxy." They suggest that extremely complex molecules could be preserved in "grain clumps" that are carried through space inside meteorites and deposited on planets. At the moment, they point out, 100 tons of meteoritic material enters the Earth's atmosphere *every day*. Meteorites known as *carbonaceous chondrites* are believed to be the most primitive accumulations of solid material in the Solar System. They account for about half of all types of meteorite and are of particular interest because, say the two, "a few of the 20 biologically important amino acids have actually been identified in these meteorites."

In the past, theories that meteorites contain primitive life-forming substances have met with skepticism. Meteorites do not drop out of the sky and land at the feet of astronomers for instant study. Months or years may elapse before a meteorite is found and then it is difficult to know which substance it brought with it and which are the result of terrestrial contamination. One attempt to overcome this problem is a network of cameras arranged to photograph meteors and fireballs so that their trajectories can be established and their point of impact calculated. A European network, covering 425,000 square miles of Germany and Czechoslovakia has not made a single recovery in more than 13 years. The Canadian Research Council, Ottawa, runs a similar scheme which has been more successful. Known as the Meteorite Observation and Recovery Project (MORP), it has 16 camera stations that cover 308,000 square miles. It came into operation in 1971 and has succeeded in recovering a four pound 10 ounce meteorite that fell at Innisfree, Canada, on February 5, 1977. Once the information from the network was processed the search operation began and the meteorite was found within four hours (on February 17) just 545 yards from the predicted impact point. The recovery just 12 days after it fell greatly reduced the chances of contamination of the meteorite, a chondritic type. It was taken for study to laboratories around the world. No reports have yet been published, but it will be interesting to see whether they will lend support to the Hoyle-Wickramasinghe theory that "the transformation of inorganic matter into primitive biological systems is occurring more or less continually in the space between the stars." Another form of evidence would be the discovery of microfossils in the Innisfree meteorite. Such organized cell-like structures, microscopically similar to geological microfossils, were said to have been found by investigators in the early 1960s in carbonaceous chondrite meteorites, and though this interpretation was later disputed by other scientists, new supporting evidence has been offered that suggests that pollen-like spores *are* carried by meteorites.

Messages from Space

So we might soon know for certain if meteorites and other cosmic bodies do scatter the seeds of life throughout the Universe. But whatever the origin of life, we know it has evolved on one planet, Earth, and the same may also be true of other planetary systems. Space travel is too slow a form of communication for beings on evolved planets unless they can travel at the speed of light. What seems more likely is that they would signal to each other over vast distances. They might even be trying to communicate with newly evolved civilizations, such as our own. But it was not until 1960 that Earth scientists began the first serious attempt to listen in to messages from other beings in the Universe. The man behind the attempt was Dr Frank Drake of the National Radio Astronomy Observatory at Green Bank, West Virginia. For 150 hours Dr Drake listened to the two nearest stars most like our Sun—Tau Ceti and Epsilon Eridani—with the observatory's 87 foot radio telescope. He found no trace of radio signals on the frequency he used. The search has continued, however, with larger radio telescopes and with other astronomers, including those in the USSR. Wavelengths monitored now range from radio to the ultraviolet, and the search has broadened from the nearest stars to distant galaxies.

For the first time, says Dr Carl Sagan, Professor of Astronomy and Space Sciences at Cornell University, man has the tools to make contact with civilizations on planets of other stars. "It is an astonishing fact," he writes in his book *The Cosmic Connection: An Extraterrestrial Perspective*, "that the great 1000-ft-diameter radio telescope of the National Astronomy and Ionosphere Center, run by Cornell University in Arecibo, Puerto Rico, would be able to communicate with an identical copy of itself anywhere in the Milky Way Galaxy."

Of course, there could be millions of civilizations capable of communicating, but if they all confine themselves to *listening* for messages then the Universe would be deceptively quiet. So the Earth's astronomers decided that as well as monitoring signals from other beings they should beam out a message about our tiny planet to anyone who may be listening.

Instead of aiming signals to one spot in the sky, a better way of announcing our scientific "maturity" is to set up transmitters that will radiate signals in the plane of our galaxy so that the vast majority of stars in the Milky Way will be swept, like a "lighthouse" beam, as the Earth rotates. This seems the most likely next step in the search for intelligent life in the Universe that is now advancing on a very broad front. Although no signals have been received in the first 17 years of searching this has surprised no one. Estimates suggest that man will have to extend his search to as far as 1000 light-years, surveying perhaps 100,000 stars, before receiving the first extraterrestrial message. So far, less than 1000 individual stars have been covered in the search.

If the entire hunt for intelligent life in the Universe fails to produce any sign of other civilizations will it mean that man is alone? It would be a disappointment, naturally, but it could be that other living beings are communicating in different ways using means that we have not yet discovered. Primitive men communicated over large distances by beating messages on a drum. Some peoples on Earth still use this method of communication, unaware that they are surrounded by radio messages and unable to tune in because they do not have radio receivers. Similarly, planets that are, for example, just 10,000 years ahead of us technologically may regard radio communication as a primitive method of making contact. If so, the Universe may be teeming with intelligent dialogues transmitted on wavelengths that we have not yet monitored or that have not yet been discovered by us.

Although the quest to find someone else in the Universe is important, the distances that separate the stars and galaxies make any form of transmitted conversation unlikely. If we are going to make contact with intelligent beings the chances are that it will come about as a face-to-face confrontation. And since it seems unlikely that advanced life exists in our Solar System and we are not going to reach other stars for many generations, the best hope of interplanetary communication will be in the form of visitors arriving on Earth. That brings us back to the UFO question and the attitude that governments should be taking. It does seem odd that while America and the Soviet Union are funding the radio search for intelligent life with vast amounts of money, the possibility that extraterrestrials may be all around us seems to have been neglected apart from well-meaning but biased civilian investigations.

When the American Astronomical Society sent a questionnaire on UFOs to its 2611 members, 80 percent of the 1356 who responded said the phenomenon deserved scientific study. The results of the study, organized by Professor Peter Sturrock, a Stanford University, California, astrophysicist, were announced early in 1977. It means that at least 40 percent of the AAS total membership is in favor of a UFO investigation. What is more, 62 of the astronomers who replied claimed to have seen a UFO. Five of these witnessed unidentified objects through telescopes and a further three made sightings with binoculars. In seven cases there were even photographs of UFOs, though Professor Sturrock believes he can explain two of them in normal terms.

Not all the astronomers supported the investigation. It was regarded as unnecessary by 20 percent and some members were very outspoken in their criticism. "I object to being quizzed about this obvious nonsense," said one, while another insisted that "there is no pattern to UFO reports except that they predominantly come from unreliable observers." Professor Sturrock is a staunch supporter of a renewed investigation of UFOs and is a strong critic of the Condon Committee report, which brought the USAF's "Project Blue Book" to an end.

Meanwhile, as the UFO mystery persists here on Earth, our planet has launched its own "UFO" into interstellar space in the form of Pioneer 10. It left Earth in 1972 on a trajectory that took it across the orbit of Mars, through the asteroid belt and on to Jupiter, which deflected the path of Pioneer 10 and swung it past the orbit of Uranus and on out of our Solar System. It will continue to travel for 2,000,000 years before approaching the star Aldebaran, and for 10,000,000,000 years before entering the planetary system of another star—unless it is intercepted earlier by space travelers. If it is found, the extraterrestrial intelligences who investigate this "unidentified flying object" in space, or in their sky, should be able to discover its origin very quickly. The American space scientists placed a gold-anodized aluminum plaque on Pioneer 10 with an etching showing the Solar System in a coded form with clues which, though they would mystify most Earth people, are designed to tell a superior race exactly where the spacecraft originated. The plaque included line drawings of a naked man and woman to show the beings responsible for launching the craft.

Dr Carl Sagan was the man who conceived the message from Earth and his artist wife, Linda, drew the terrestrials on the golden greeting card. He described his special "communications" project as "very much like a shipwrecked sailor casting a bottled message into the ocean—but the ocean of space is much vaster than any ocean on Earth." Nevertheless, messages in bottles have been washed ashore in time to save shipwrecked mariners, so there is a remote chance that Pioneer 10 will meet up with intelligent beings on a distant shore. The likelihood is, however, that when that happens man will have vanished from his "island" in space.

While we wait for a reply to our space messages, however, scientists are continuing to develop instruments and space exploration techniques that will help to solve the many mysteries of the Universe, some of which have puzzled us for centuries while others have only just begun to tantalize us. One fascinating new type of object that is high on the list for investigation is the X-ray burster. These were first detected after an analysis of records from a Dutch satellite in December 1975. Then astronomers from the Massachussetts Institute of Technology (MIT) examined records from the SAS-3 satellite launched in May of that year and discovered the same bursts. These X-ray sources suddenly flare up and die down in seconds, making them difficult to detect. So far 30 such bursters have been found. Dr Walter H. G. Lewin of the MIT, explained in 1977: "There is something in nature that can produce energy greater than a million suns and can turn it on in just one second." These explosions of "mind-boggling" power are all taking place in our own galaxy. Astronomers are now hoping to find objects, such as stars, at the points where the astonishing X-ray bursts are occurring. One of the sources, MXB 1730-335, is bursting at an astonishing rate: The time between each flare up varies from about six seconds for small bursts to between five and ten minutes for massive bursts.

What are the X-ray bursters? And what about the other questions we posed such as, What are quasars? How was the Earth formed? Are there such things as black holes? Can anything go faster than light? Does life form in outer space? Can a comet become a planet? Will the Universe expand for ever? Will man ever know all the answers or will there always be new mysteries to challenge his ingenuity and understanding? The next few years may provide some surprising answers.

The mystery of unidentified flying objects is a different matter, for even if every sighting of a "flying saucer" could be proved to be no more than misidentification, hallucination, or deliberate fabrication, the next one—arriving from somewhere deep in our mysterious Universe—could be for real.

Part 3

17. Psi Powers

Few of us would flatly deny that the universe is a stranger place than the generally accepted natural laws can account for. Most of the time we choose not to think about it. When we discover that some people appear to have strange powers, powers that apparently enable them to ignore the normal physical laws that contain the rest of us, we prefer not to think about that either because we have no easy explanation. It makes life more complicated, and it is a subtle threat to our own sense of safety in a known world. When we do think about it we hunt for the trick, the deception, the proof that everything is as we would like it to be so that we can return, safely, to not thinking about it. But these wild talents tug at our sleeves, whisper in our ears. Throughout all recorded history people have been fascinated and have felt threatened by these unexplained abilities. In our recent history we have conducted complicated tests and formulated sophisticated explanations—and then a young Israeli comes along and stops clocks and bends spoons: trivial accomplishments in themselves, but how do we explain them? Then we find we have started to think about strange powers and extraordinary events.

I met the young Israeli wonder worker Uri Geller one morning in the summer of 1974 in the office of a London business tycoon. The meeting had been arranged with a view to my working on a film about Geller's life. A secretary showed me into the inner office. Uri, a good looking but seemingly quite ordinary young man, appeared to be a little nervous or preoccupied. We chatted briefly, after which the three of us went to lunch at a nearby restaurant. We sat at a table in the corner, the woman and I side by side and Uri opposite us with his back to the room. When we had ordered, he offered to try to demonstrate his powers, but said, "I don't know if it will work. Sometimes it doesn't."

We began with an experiment in *telepathy* (the transmission of thoughts by means other than the five senses). Uri handed me one of the restaurant cards on the table and, turning away from me, asked me to make a drawing on its blank side. I made a sketch of a creature I had invented some time ago to amuse my children. It took only a few seconds, as I had drawn it many times before. I glanced at Uri as I did it. He was staring out across the restaurant, and he could not have watched me without being seen to do so by the secretary beside me. When I had finished, he asked me to cover the drawing with my hand. Then he turned back to the table and took another of the cards. He asked me to concentrate hard and to try to transmit the thought of what I had sketched. A minute went by with no result. Uri shook his head. "It seems very complicated; is it a kind of amoeba?" Slowly and hesitantly he began to draw the creature's right ear—the spot where I always begin the drawing. "You've got it," I said. "Go on!" He completed the drawing quickly. I had carefully redrawn the picture in my mind as I tried to transmit it—which probably accounts for the identical starting point.

Uri then demonstrated other powers. He caused a restaurant spoon to bend by stroking it gently. He made the hands of my watch turn back two hours and the date go forward two days by stroking a coin placed over its face, explaining afterward that he derives power from metal. He had a little trouble trying to break my American Automobile Association key. Ideally, he said, the key should have more personal associations. However, he placed it against a metal radiator, and after a few seconds said, "It's starting to go." The key snapped in two.

Finally, he tried to transmit a picture to me by telepathy. I attempted to make my mind receptive, but no image came into it. Feeling rather embarrassed, I just drew the first thing that came into my head: a check mark. Uri showed me the piece of paper he was holding away from me. It contained a mirror image of the symbol I had drawn. It could be significant in this connection that Uri is left-handed.

After I left Uri Geller I immediately began to sift my impressions. Only the day before, a highly skeptical scientist had warned me to watch carefully for conjuring tricks, especially as Uri had earlier been a stage conjuror. I had to admit that most of the things he had done could have been tricks. For instance, snapping the key with his fingers, and altering the hands and date on my watch with the winder would have been well within the ability of a skillful conjuror. But how could he have faked the drawing of what I had drawn? And if that feat was due to genuine telepathic powers, the other demonstrations could also be genuine.

A couple of months after this Ted Bastin, a quantum physicist, and I appeared on a television discussion show about supernormal powers—a subject about which Ted is distinctly skeptical. When I mentioned Uri Geller, however, Ted told me he had conducted extensive tests and was convinced that Uri was genuine. A few days later Ted rang me up to announce that Uri had just performed a most spectacular feat in his laboratory. He had dematerialized half a crystal that had been sealed in a metal container. Bastin said that there was no way in which Uri could have touched the crystal.

Energy and the Subconscious

Assuming that Uri Geller possesses extraordinary powers, where do they come from? I think the answer must be from his subconscious mind. In recent years psychologists have come to the conclusion that *poltergeists* (ghosts or spirits that make noises or fling objects) originate in the subconscious minds of teenagers who have been seriously disturbed by the problems of adolescence. On the other hand, some investigators believe that poltergeists have a separate existence—that is, that they are real ghosts—but that they have to borrow energy from disturbed adolescents before they can become active. Whatever the truth of the matter, it seems probable that the subconscious mind provides the energy that causes heavy objects to rise and fly across a room or doors to open and bang shut. If this is so, it is reasonable to assume that the energy which causes spoons to bend and broken watches to tick originates in Uri Geller's highly active subconscious mind.

If these strange powers exist in some hidden depths of the mind, what are they doing there? Are they common to all of us, and are they available to anyone who knows how to use them? We may find part of the answer in an experience of John G. Bennett, the foremost living disciple of the remarkable Russian mystic Georgei Gurdjieff.

In 1923 Bennett was at Gurdjieff's Institute for the Harmonious Development of Man at the Prieuré in a suburb of Paris. For some days Bennett had been suffering from almost constant diarrhea, and each morning he felt weaker and found it harder to get up. One morning he woke up shaking with fever, and decided to stay in bed. But in the instant of making this decision, he found himself getting out of bed and dressing. It felt, he said, as if he was being "held together by a superior Will that was not my own." After a morning's work, he felt too ill to eat lunch. Nonetheless, he joined a dancing class in the afternoon. Gurdjieff's dances involved movements of great complexity, requiring tremendous concentration and physical coordination. As the exercises continued Bennett felt an immense lassitude descend on him. It became agony even to move, but he forced himself to go on. Gurdjieff introduced new exercises which were so complex that the other students began to drop out one by one. Bennett, however, felt Gurdjieff's eyes on him as if commanding him to go on, even if it killed him.

"Suddenly, I was filled with an influx of immense power. My body seemed to have turned into light. I could not feel its presence in the usual ways. There was no effort, no weariness, not even any sense of weight. . . ." When the lesson was over he decided to test the power that had entered his body. He took a spade and began to dig at a rate that would normally have exhausted him in two minutes. In spite of the summer heat, he continued digging for over an hour.

The Great Reservoir

Later Bennett went for a walk toward a nearby forest where he met Gurdjieff. Without preliminaries, Gurdjieff began to talk about energies. "There is a certain energy," he said, "that is necessary for work on oneself . . . we can call it the Higher Emotional Energy. . . . There are some people in the world, but they are very rare, who are connected to the Great Reservoir or Accumulator of this energy. . . ." Gurdjieff implied that he was one of those who can tap the Great Reservoir and permit others to borrow its energy.

Bennett continued his walk in the forest, still filled with a tremendous sense of power. He recalled that Peter Ouspensky, another Russian mystic and associate of Gurdjieff's, had once said that if we wish to prove how little control we have over our emotions, we have only to try to be astonished at will. Bennett said to himself: "I will be astonished." Instantly he felt overwhelmed with amazement. "Each tree was so uniquely itself that I felt that I could walk in the forest forever and never cease from wonderment. Then the thought of 'fear' came to me. At once I was shaking with terror. Unknown horrors were menacing me on every side. I thought of 'joy,' and I felt that my heart would burst from rapture. The word 'love' came to me, and I was pervaded with such fine shades of tenderness and compassion that I saw that I had not the remotest idea of the depth and range of love. Love was everywhere and in everything. It was infinitely adaptable to every shade of need. After a time it became too much for me; it seemed that if I plunged any more deeply into the mystery of love, I would cease to exist. I wanted to be free from this power to feel whatever I chose, and at once it left me."

What is this strange power that Gurdjieff was able to evoke in his disciples? It is not as mysterious as it sounds. We are all familiar with its commonest form, which we call "second wind."

In most energetic sports, such as long distance running, we force ourselves beyond the normal point of exhaustion. Then sometimes, quite suddenly, we feel a resurge of energy that enables us to continue for longer than usual. On rare occasions we can even force ourselves to continue until we get our third wind. The American philosopher and psychologist William James wrote about this in his essay "The Energies of Man."

"Everyone is familiar with the phenomenon of feeling more or less alive on different days. Everyone knows on any given day that there are energies slumbering in him which the incitements of that day do not call forth, but which he might display if these were greater. Most of us feel as if a sort of cloud weighed upon us, keeping us below our highest notch of clearness in discernment, sureness in reasoning, or firmness in deciding. Compared with what we ought to be, we are only half awake. Our fires are damped, our drafts are checked. We are making use of only a small part of our possible mental and physical resources."

"Stating the thing broadly, the human individual thus lives unusually far within his limits; he possesses powers of various sorts which he habitually fails to use. He energizes below his *maximum*, and he behaves below his *optimum*."

In other words, for everyday purposes human beings have certain predetermined limits. It is like the thermostat on a central heating system. When the temperature rises above a certain point it automatically switches off the heating. When our tiredness reaches a certain limit, we also switch off automatically, and allow ourselves to sink into a passive state. But if some crisis arises, we refuse to allow ourselves to remain passive. We become alert and suddenly, as our thermostat readjusts itself, we discover we have become fully alive again.

The implication seems to be that each of us contains a vast reservoir of energy. William James also asks what it is that gives a Leonardo or a Beethoven his creative energy. His answer is excitement, determination, a sense of purpose. He adds: "We live subject to arrest by degrees of fatigue which we have come only from habit to obey. Most of us may learn to push the barrier further off, and to live in perfect comfort on much higher levels of power."

This was the aim of Gurdjieff's work. He forced his students to keep pushing the barriers farther and farther back. One of his followers, Fritz Peters, has described how Gurdjieff gave him the task of mowing the lawns at the Prieuré. At first the work took Peters several days. Gradually Gurdjieff accustomed him to doing more and more in a day until finally Peters could mow all the lawns, which consisted of several acres, in one day. What Gurdjieff called his "dervish dances" were also designed to break the chain of habit. Try rubbing your stomach with one hand while patting yourself on the head with the other, or tapping the toes of one foot on the floor while rubbing the other foot back and forth like a pendulum. Most people find such movements difficult. Yet Gurdjieff trained his students to do something different with feet, arms, and head at the same time. He would also suddenly order them to break off whatever they were doing, and to freeze in some complicated attitude.

As Gurdjieff recognized, even exercises as difficult as these can become a habit. Fritz Peters tells a story which reveals that Gurdjieff himself could forget how to establish contact with his own reservoir of energy. At the end of World War II Peters, then a soldier and suffering from battle fatigue and nervous strain, called on Gurdjieff at his Paris apartment. Gurdjieff was busy and asked Peters to wait for him in another room. After a minute or two alone, Peters felt so miserable and desperate that he interrupted Gurdjieff again. Gurdjieff instantly saw the seriousness of the situation, and set his work aside. As he sat with Gurdjieff, Peters experienced a sudden trickle of power flowing into him like a spring. It slowly increased until all his tiredness had vanished. But Gurdjieff himself now looked completely exhausted. Peters had no doubt that Gurdjieff had somehow given him his own energy. A crowd of people then arrived at the house, and Gurdjieff dragged himself away to entertain them. Five minutes later he returned to the kitchen radiating vitality, and remarked to Peters that the experience had been good for both of them. In other words, the effort of revitalizing Peters had awakened Gurdjieff to a recognition that he had lost touch with his own "source of power, meaning, and purpose." He promptly reestablished contact, and recharged his own batteries.

The Robot within Us

There is nothing mystical or occult about this. We all have within us a robot, akin to the automatic pilot in an airplane, whose task is to simplify our lives by handling a series of routines. Learning to type or speak French or drive a car requires considerable effort and concentration, but once we have mastered it, our robot takes over and does it far more quickly and efficiently than we could do it consciously. The trouble is, the robot can become so efficient that it takes over most of our life. We begin to live like a robot. We automatically drink our martini, eat our dinner, watch TV. It takes a holiday or some sudden crisis to jar us out of this automatic living, to allow our real selves to take over from the robot.

There can be no doubt that Gurdjieff helped Bennett overcome his fatigue, just as he helped Peters. But at a certain point, Bennett's own inner dynamo took over and he wrested control from his robot. He was suddenly dazzled by vistas of possible feeling. For, like our bodies, our feelings are also controlled by the robot. We seldom experience new feeling. For the most part, we play the same old phonograph record over and over again—a record that, except in times of crisis, is full of bland harmonies. What Bennett had realized was that he could experience new intensities of feeling every day; that he could experience a compelling feeling for every tree and every blade of grass.

Our minds contain a vast unused library of "phonograph records." And not just our minds. The world around us is full of an infinite number of interesting things that the robot has been trained to ignore. This is perhaps the most important insight that arises from Bennett's description of his experience: ". . . I was pervaded with such shades of tenderness and compassion that *I saw that I had not the remotest idea of the depth and range of love.*" We accept the universe around us as stable and normal, just as a child who knew nothing about water might accept the surface of a pond as a glittering mirror, unaware that there are green depths below, teeming with innumerable forms of life. How many other things is this true of? How much mystery and complexity and reality is hidden from us by ignorance and habit?

Human beings live within arbitrary limits. Not only do we have an arbitrary idea of our powers and capabilities, but we also have an arbitrary idea of the complexity and interestingness of the world around us. Habit has confined human beings in a thoroughly stale universe.

A word of caution should be offered, however. Why should Bennett get tired of the power to see and feel more widely than ever before? Why does he say: "I wanted to be free from this power to feel whatever I chose . . ."? The reason is that these arbitrary limits to our powers are also safety limits. Our habits, which can become so oppressive, are also intended to protect us. Bennett could have achieved many of the same effects of power and perception by taking a psychedelic drug such as mescalin or LSD. These also destroy the robot and disconnect our habit mechanisms so that the world appears new and strange. Psychedelic drugs also release the capacity to feel whatever we choose—the thought of love can produce a tidal wave of love.

On the other hand, a negative thought produces equally

powerful results. One man who had taken LSD under medical supervision described how the thought of death produced the hallucination that peoples' faces had become grinning skulls, and the air seemed thick with the smell of earth and decaying flesh. Some people who have had bad trips have become permanently unbalanced mentally. The power of the mind can be highly dangerous, and meddling with it simply for kicks is as irresponsible as allowing a child to drive a high-powered car. Bennett realized that it would be wiser to learn to extend the range of his consciousness step by step, and to consolidate each step before moving on rather than to take a sudden leap into powers that were beyond his understanding and almost certainly beyond his ability to control.

Once we know the world is not as dull and ordinary as it may seem, we have taken a major step toward doing something about it. The real objection to habit is that it makes us lazy, paralyzing the will. Once we realize that our robot is insulating us against much that is rich and rewarding in the world around us, we can begin to organize the will to resist the power of habit.

The Projection of Energy

While we know enough about second wind to understand Bennett's experience, it is altogether more difficult to grasp how Gurdjieff could have projected energy into Bennett and Peters. What is the nature of this energy? The following may throw some light on it.

In 1919 Bernard Kajinsky, a Russian electrical engineer, was awakened in the night by a ringing sound like that of a spoon hitting glass. The next day he learned that his closest friend had died of typhus. When he called on his friend's mother, he discovered that she had been about to give him a dose of medicine at the moment he died. Kajinsky, suddenly excited, asked her to show him exactly what she had done. She took a silver spoon and dropped it into a tumbler. It made the same ringing sound that had startled him awake.

Kajinsky was a scientist with no interest in telepathy or extrasensory perception. But he had no doubt that his friend had thought of him at the moment of death, and that the sound of the spoon striking glass had somehow been conveyed to him. He thereafter made an exhaustive study of telepathy and reached the conclusion that "the human nervous system is capable of reacting to stimuli whose source is not yet known."

Kajinsky's work came to the attention of a famous Russian animal trainer, Vladimir Durov, who was convinced that his animals could read his mind. Durov began to conduct experiments in association with Vladimir Bekhterev, a distinguished neurologist. Under Bekhterev's supervision, Durov gave complicated telepathic orders to his animals. Usually the animals would carry them out. For example, Bekhterev wrote instructions on a sheet of paper and handed it to Durov. Durov looked into the eyes of his German shepherd dog Mars for several seconds without speaking. Mars went into the next room, looked on three tables and, finding what Bekhterev had asked for on the third—a telephone directory—carried it to Durov in his mouth.

Many animal lovers have noticed that their pets seem to possess some telepathic power. Edward Campbell, a British newspaper editor who studied this question, tells an interesting story about a German animal trainer, Hans Brick. Brick's favorite lion was a man eater named Habibi, and Brick's bond with the lion was a strange one. It was tacitly agreed between them that the lion—which was savage and unbroken—was entitled to kill Brick if it could find a moment when his attention lapsed. While Brick maintained his full attention the lion never attacked him. But on several occasions when his attention had wavered, an attack came instantly. Brick insisted it was his own fault. "I know the rules; so does he," he said.

During World War II Brick was interned in England for a while, and Habibi was looked after by a zoo. When Brick was released, a British film company asked him to supervise some wild animal sequences in a film using Habibi. A problem arose because the owner of the zoo wanted payment for having tended Habibi, and Brick could not afford the fee. According to Campbell, at six o'clock on Sunday morning Brick walked into the zoo, went to Habibi's cage on an upper floor, released the lion, and looped a whip loosely around his neck. Brick then made a mental pact with the animal: Habibi was not to attack him while they were making their escape from the zoo.

The animals in other cages were in an uproar as the lion walked out. Rabbits and peacocks were ranging freely about

Doc Shiels spoon bending in 1975. The ability to bend metal by stroking it, stop watches by mental effort and even dematerialize matter are examples of energy projected from the subconcious mind. This energy probably occurs in the form of waves, similar to radio waves, but possessing the power to affect objects physically. *(Psi Powers)*

the floor, but Habibi made no attempt to attack them. Brick walked to the door, Habibi following. They went down a flight of stairs and into the street. The lion walked quietly behind Brick and entered a traveling cage that he had parked in the next street. In effect, Brick had told the lion telepathically: "These are special circumstances. You want to get out; I want to get you out. No tricks·. . ." And the lion had kept to his side of the bargain.

Psi Waves

So far we have been speaking of telepathy which, most investigators agree, seems to depend on some form of waves. They are generally known as *Psi* waves (Psi is a Greek letter used in parapsychology for psychic ability or phenomenon.) At present we have no idea of the nature of such waves. We might compare Psi waves with radio waves. But radio waves can be used only to communicate, whereas when Gurdjieff used Psi power on Bonnett and Peters he seems to have been doing much more than merely communicating.

In 1940, not long before the invasion of the USSR, Joseph Stalin ordered an investigation into the powers of a psychic named Wolf Messing, who· appears to have possessed Psi powers to an extraordinary degree. Messing described these experiments in a Soviet science magazine. His first test was to walk into a bank, present the cashier with a note, and will him to hand over 100,000 rubles in cash. Two official witnesses went with Messing when he did this. They saw the cashier take packets of banknotes out of the safe and hand them over. Messing put them in a briefcase and left. Then, with the two witnesses he reentered the bank, and handed back the money and the note—which was in fact a sheet of blank paper. The clerk looked at it, suddenly realized what he had done—and collapsed with a heart attack.

The stories about Brick and Messing may make one conclude that Gurdjieff simply used his Psi powers to suggest certain feelings to Fritz Peters. But it is difficult to see why, in that case, the effort should have exhausted Gurdjieff—and even more difficult to see how Peters could have been so genuinely reinvigorated. For the moment, it may be best to acknowledge that we do not even begin to understand the possibilities of Psi, and leave it at that.

Psi powers are not as rare as we might suppose. In fact, there are a number of simple experiments that anyone can do to verify that they are more than merely autosuggestion. The simplest test requires four or five people. One of the group, the subject, stands in the center of the room with the others around him. The subject closes his eyes tightly, and the others place their fingers gently against his chest, shoulders, and back making sure not to exert pressure. The aim of the experiment is to make the subject sway in a particular direction, which the others can decide upon by movement of the eyes or a nod of the head. They concentrate hard on willing the subject to sway in the chosen direction. He usually feels a force pulling him in the chosen direction, as if he were a compass needle and someone had brought a magnet close to him. It usually takes only a few seconds, depending on the suggestibility of the subject.

The second experiment, which also takes five people, is lifting a seated person using only index fingers. It is familiar to most schoolchildren. The chosen subject sits in a chair, and the the other four attempt to lift him by placing a finger under his armpits and knees. It is, of course, impossible. Then the four place their hands, one on top of the other, on the head of the seated person. No person should have his own two hands next to each other. All concentrate hard for about 20 seconds. Then they quickly remove their hands from the head, place their index fingers under the subject's knees and armpits—and the seated person is lifted effortlessly into the air. The glib explanation of this is that the hands piled on the subject's head operate as a kind of Psi accumulator. The interesting question is why and how they do so—and at present we have no answer.

The Rotating Paper Dart

The third experiment can be performed with a sheet of paper about two inches square. Fold it from corner to corner, from top to bottom, and from side to side. By pinching the corner folds, it can now be turned into a kind of paper dart, its point at the intersection of the fold lines. Take a needle and stick it blunt end first into a cork. Balance the paper dart on the needle point so that it looks like a partly opened umbrella. Making sure that you do not breathe on it, try to will it to rotate about the needle point.

The first time I attempted this, nothing happened—which is what I expected. However, I kept the dart by my typewriter, and every now and then I tried to make it turn, cupping my hands around it. Eventually I stopped trying to make it move by sheer will power, and imagined that it was moving. Immediately, it began to rotate. I thought for a moment that this was due to the heat from my hands, so I tried stopping it. It stopped. Then I made it turn in the opposite direction. Once I had acquired the trick, I found it easy to make it rotate in either direction, even without my hands cupped around it.

The original paper model for this experiment was sent to me by Robert Leftwich, a water diviner who also claimed to be able to dispel clouds by concentrating on them. Although I later met Leftwich, I never saw him dispersing clouds. However, a well-authenticated experiment in cloud dispersal was filmed by a British television program in June 1956 on Hampstead Heath in London. This kind of Psi power is known as *telekinesis* (making objects or bodies move without visible force). Many experiments on this subject have been carried out by Soviet researchers.

It seems possible, then, that thought can exert some form of pressure quite distinct from powers of telepathic suggestion. This in turn suggests that stories of the power of blessings and curses may have a foundation in fact. If Gurdjieff could make Peters feel better, he could also, presumably, have made him feel worse. Ira Levin's novel *Rosemary's Baby* has an episode in which a black magic group wills a man to death. If thought pressure is a reality, such telekinetic homicide may be possible. Donald Omand, a Church of England clergyman who has performed many exorcisms, believes that if a group of people determinedly brood on someone they dislike, they can inflict psychic damage. Directing mental forces may be as harmful as physical assault.

Gurdjieff tells this story about a station master in a small Russian town. Early every morning as he rang the bell announcing the arrival of the mail train, the station master would also shout curses. Asked why he did this, he explained that whenever he rang the bell, people all over the town woke up and invoked curses on his head. In order to fend these off, he redirected the malevolence back against the townspeople.

By the beginning of the 20th century scientists knew a great deal about the nature of light waves. One of the things they thought they knew was that light is an imponderable, that if it consisted of waves of radiation it could have no weight, and would exert no pressure. Einstein's Theory of Relativity predicted that, on the contrary, light particles have weight and should be subject to gravitation. During the 1918 eclipse of the sun he was proved spectacularly right. Measurements showed that the light rays actually bent as they passed through the sun's gravitational field. Nowadays, scientists design spaceships with "light sails" to exploit the pressure exerted by light waves.

Orthodox science has yet to accept the idea of thought pressure, and decrees that thought is supposed to be an imponderable. There are many scientists who, in the face of much evidence, decline to accept the reality of telepathy. Nevertheless, evidence has continued to accumulate until the point has now come when the only way to deny telepathy is to ignore the facts or to refuse to examine them closely. The only way to explain many of these facts is to assume that thought, like light, can exert its own kind of pressure.

A final question: if we are higher up the evolutionary ladder than other animals, why is it that Brick's lions, like many dogs and other pets, seem to possess more highly developed telepathic powers than we? The answer may be that we have allowed just as powerful faculties in us to fall into disuse. In our most primitive form our capacities may have been as highly developed as those of other animals—more highly developed, probably, or we might not have survived against predators. As we developed tools, the use of fire, and other techniques, we had less and less need for such innate powers. We needed reason and conscious awareness rather than instinct and subconscious awareness.

Humankind seems always to have been more interested in power than in inner awareness. This desire for power is the scarlet thread we shall find running through the history of men of strange powers.

18. Strange Feats

When Louis Jacolliot, an eminent French lawyer and later a chief justice, went to India in the early 1860s, he was a free-thinker with a profound skepticism about religion. However, when his servant announced one morning that a fakir (Hindu holy man) wished to see him, his curiosity got the better of him and he decided to see the man. Jacolliot opened the conversation by saying that he had heard that fakirs possess the power to move objects without touching them—a power that is now called psychokinesis. The fakir—a thin bony little man—replied that he himself possessed no such power, but that spirits lent him their aid. The Frenchman asked if he might see a demonstration of these powers. The Hindu said that he would demonstrate and requested seven flowerpots filled with earth, seven thin wooden rods each a yard long, and seven large leaves from any tree in the garden.

The wooden rods were stuck in the flowerpots so that they were upright. Then a hole was made in the center of each leaf, and the leaves were impaled on each rod so that they fell down and covered the flowerpots. The fakir stood up, joined his hands above his head, and intoned a Hindu prayer. After that he seemed to go into a state of ecstasy, his hands outstretched toward the flowerpots. Suddenly, Jacolliot felt a breeze on his face. During the next 10 minutes, it blew several times. Slowly and gently the leaves began to rise up the wooden rods, then to float downward again. Jacolliot went closer to see if the Hindu could somehow be causing them to move by a trick. But the leaves continued to rise and fall undisturbed as Jacolliot passed between them and the fakir. For the remainder of that morning Jacolliot tried different tests to discover if the fakir used trickery. He arranged

211

the flowerpots and rods himself in case of collusion between his servant and the fakir. He had the rods fixed into holes bored in a plank. It made no difference; the leaves still rose and fell as before.

Finally, the fakir asked Jacolliot if he would like to ask a question of the spirits. In doing so, Jacolliot used an alphabet of brass letters with which he printed his name in his books. Thinking of a dead friend, he began to take letters out of their bag one by one. When he pulled out the letter "A," the leaves moved. He returned the letter to the bag and repeated the process. This time the leaves moved when he pulled out the letter "L." By this process the leaves slowly spelled out the message: "Albain Brunier died at Bourg-en-Bresse January 3, 1856." This was the friend Jacolliot had been thinking of.

Jacolliot concluded that the Hindu had simply read his mind. He thought of a way to test this suspicion and tried it with the fakir next day. As he held the bag containing the letters, he concentrated on changing the name to "Halbin Pruniet." The leaves spelled out "Halbin Pruniet" instead of "Albain Brunier;" but no amount of concentration could change the date of Brunier's death, or the name of the city in which he died.

Jacolliot had experiences in psychokinesis with other fakirs, one of whom was able to hold down a small table so firmly that Jacolliot's attempts to move it only tore off one of its folding leaves. The same fakir dropped a papaw seed into a pot filled with damp earth, went into a trance for two hours, and caused the seed to sprout into an eight-inch-tall plant. Jacolliot's most startling experience was when a fakir named Covindasamy caused a phosphorescent cloud to form in the air. After a moment, white hands appeared in the cloud. One of them held Jacolliot's hand for a moment. At his request, it plucked a flower from a bowl and dropped it at his feet. Next, the fakir conjured up the shade of an old Brahmin priest. When Jacolliot asked it whether it was once alive on earth, the word "Am" (yes) appeared on its breast in glowing letters as if written with phosphorus. Finally, the fakir materialized another shade that moved around the room playing a flute. When the apparition vanished, it left the flute on the ground. It was a flute that Jacolliot had borrowed from a rajah and that he had had in his locked house.

What is so impressive about these stories is that Jacolliot does not write as an occultist. The book in which they appear is a sober study of Hinduism, and these stories of his experiments are added almost as an afterthought. He is merely interested in recording inexplicable events to which he attaches no undue importance. Not being concerned with psychical research, which in the 1860s had not yet attracted much attention, he does not attempt to classify the phenomena as the products of extrasensory perception, telepathy, or psychokinesis. He puts it that, "What we call spirit force is called by the Hindus *artahancarasya* or the force of I." It seems clear that he is referring to what we have called Psi power. The fakirs themselves believe that all such phenomena spring from the same source—the spirits. The fact that Jacolliot actually saw entities that appeared to be spirits suggests that this idea cannot be wholly dismissed.

Most Hindus find nothing strange about such marvels. The ancient Hindu scriptures—the Vedic hymns, the *Upanishads*, the *Bhagavad Gita*—all teach that the human soul, the Atman, is identical with the godhead, Brahman. Thus, if one could penetrate through all a man's outer layers to the very depth of his being, one would find Brahman. Stripped of its religious essence, this echoes the central conviction of occult philosophers: the deeper we penetrate our innermost being, the closer we approach the strange powers that all men possess, but that few can tap or consciously use.

The science of yoga, which is basically a system of meditation, is intended to enable man to gain control over his body and emotions, and to move inward toward the "source of power, meaning, and purpose." A yogi assumes one of the traditional yoga postures, withdraws deep into himself, concentrates his gaze, and attempts to still his mind. The aim is total inner serenity. In attempting yoga, many westerners make the mistake of simply suspending the mind, as if sitting in church. Consequently they find it difficult to prevent it from wandering. The more experienced practitioner soon realizes that, although the posture suggests absolute rest, the mind is actually in gear, concentrating with a certain earnestness as if engaged in some difficult and dangerous operation. In the imagery of the Buddhist scriptures, the mind is like a pond, and the aim is to still the pond until it becomes a perfect mirror reflecting the moon, man's basic divinity. Great importance is attached to *prana*

213

(breathing) because the breath is identified with life, or the spirit.

Eugen Herrigel, a German professor who taught in Japan for many years, determined to attempt to master the secrets of Zen, the peculiarly Japanese form of Buddhism. A central aim of Zen studies is the total integration of one's mental and physical powers. One of Herrigel's spiritual exercises directed toward this end was learning how to draw an archer's bow correctly. He watched his Zen master draw the bow without effort and release the arrow casually. It flew to the center of the target. When Herrigel tried it, he found it almost impossible even to draw the string of the massive bow.

After a long period of frustration, Herrigel was told by the Zen master that he was not breathing correctly. "Press your breath down gently after breathing in so that the abdominal wall is tightly stretched, and hold it there for a while. Then breathe out as slowly and evenly as possible and, after a short pause, draw a quick breath of air again—out and in continually in a rhythm that will gradually settle itself. If it is done properly, you will feel the shooting becoming easier every day. For through this breathing you will not only discover the source of all spiritual strength, but will also cause this source to flow more abundantly, and to pour more easily through your limbs the more relaxed you are." It took Herrigel a year to succeed in drawing the bow with this perfect ease. Then came another long struggle, this time to release the arrow without a jerk, "as if the bow string had cut through the thumb that held it."

The Secret of Zen

What Herrigel had to learn so painfully was to use his whole being, his subconscious as well as his conscious mind, in drawing and releasing the bow. Once this was learned, he had also learned the basic secret of Zen. This union of every part of one's self also enables men and women to begin to grasp the perfect truth about Being. For Zen Buddhism holds that our central problem is that we have become too self-conscious, or rather, that we have developed what the novelist D. H. Lawrence called "head consciousness."

We are all familiar with the sensation of doing some simple physical activity badly because we are thinking about it. For

214

instance, if we are aware of someone staring at the way we walk, we begin to walk awkwardly. If something makes us self-conscious about our accent, we begin to trip over words. According to the mystical tradition, this awkwardness has reached deep into human consciousness so that most of our powers are tied in a knot and unable to find expression. To some extent, relaxation can help to release these powers. For example, the fashionable cult of Transcendental Meditation is basically a kind of self-hypnosis that brings deep relaxation, leading to the release of hidden powers. We are out of tune with ourselves. We oppose ourselves like clumsy adolescents tripping over our own feet. All spiritual disciplines aim at removing this self-division. But, as Zen recognizes, the basic problem is how to arouse our "true will."

All the mystical traditions, Western as well as Eastern, recognize that the awakening of the true will can occur in a single flash. That is why the Zen master may sometimes kick his disciple violently. In one of the Zen stories, the disciple is awakened to a state of total enlightenment by such a kick. Similarly, there is a story told of the 19th-century Hindu saint Ramakrishna. When he was a young priest, Ramakrishna became deeply depressed because he seemed unable either to escape from the boredom of everyday existence or to catch a glimpse of Brahman. One day in despair he seized a sword, and was about to plunge it into himself. Suddenly the Divine Mother revealed herself to him. Ramakrishna was filled with a vision of an endless sea of vitality and self-knowledge, and with such deep ecstasy that he became unconscious. Undoubtedly the threat of death aroused his true will—showed him, as it were, the trick of parting the curtain of everyday existence that obstructs our view of reality.

According to Ramakrishna, such powers as Jacolliot's fakir exhibited are merely the first consequences of this deeper knowledge of reality, and are utterly without value. Again and again he insists on the triviality of the feats that are traditionally ascribed to yogis and fakirs—for example, walking on water, moving objects without touching them, and climbing a rope that hangs unsupported in the air. The yogi who wants to do such things, says Ramakrishna, is at a rudimentary level of spiritual progress. The yogi who has tasted *samadhi*—the moment of absolute union with Brahman, the moment in which he realizes that his own soul is Brahman—cares only to strive for continual union. The conjuring tricks he regards with contempt.

The Tales of Yogananda

Yet these examples of strange powers, called conjuring tricks by Ramakrishna, are a vital part of the Hindu tradition. One of the most extraordinary spiritual autobiographies of this century is Paramhansa Yogananda's *Autobiography of a Yogi*, to which the eminent orientalist W. Y. Evans-Wentz wrote an introduction that vouched for its authenticity. The book breathes the essential spirit of the Hindu religion, yet it is so full of tales of miracles that the skeptical westerner's first reaction is to dismiss it as a pack of lies. At the age of eight, Yogananda was dangerously ill with cholera. He was told by his mother to bow mentally, being too weak to move physically, to a picture of a great yogi on the wall of his room. As he did so, the room seemed to glow with light, and his fever disappeared. Shortly after this, he quarreled with his sister about some ointment she was using to cure a boil. He told her that the following day her boil would be twice as large, and that he would have a boil on his forearm. Both things turned out as he said, and his sister accused him of being a sorcerer.

From this point on the stories become ever more incredible. Yogananda tells of visiting a yogi named Pranabananda. The yogi told him that a certain friend of his was on his way. At exactly the moment foretold, the friend arrived. Yogananda asked him how he had come to be there. The friend explained that Pranabananda had approached him in the street, and told him that Yogananda was waiting in his room. Then the yogi had vanished into the crowd. What baffled Yogananda and his friend was that Pranabananda had been with Yogananda throughout the previous hour. It seems, then, that Pranabananda had been able to project his astral body—the spiritual second body.

In another chapter of his autobiography Yogananda describes visiting the "perfume saint," a yogi able to induce the smell of any perfume. At Yogananda's request, the yogi caused a scentless flower to smell of jasmine. When Yogananda arrived home, his sister was also able to smell the scent of jasmine on the flower,

216

thus allaying any suspicion that the yogi had managed merely to suggest the perfume to Yogananda.

Some of the most incredible of Yogananda's stories are about Babaji, the 19th-century "Yogi-Christ." One tells of how he allowed a disciple to hurl himself from a high crag, and then resurrected him. Another recounts how he materialized an immense golden palace in the Himalayas. Yogananda tells these stories at second hand, and it may be that he intended them to be accepted as myths or parables rather than as literal truth. But the stories he tells of his own *guru* (religious teacher or spiritual adviser) Sri Yukteswar, are almost as astonishing. Yukteswar also appears simultaneously in two places, Calcutta and Serampore. One day when his disciples are about to attend a festival in stifling heat, Yukteswar assures them that a cooling umbrella of cloud will be sent to help them. As he said, the sky clouds over and a gentle rain falls during the festival. However, Yukteswar did not claim to have conjured up the rain himself.

The climax of Yogananda's book is the description of the death and resurrection of Yukteswar. He predicted the time of his death, and died exactly when he had foretold. After his death, he appeared to Yogananda in a hotel room in Bombay, and Yogananda insists that he was there in the flesh. Before vanishing, Yukteswar explained to his disciple at length that his task was now to serve as a savior on an astral plane, or another dimension of the world.

It is possible, of course, to dismiss the whole of Yogananda's book as the invention of a religious crank. But before doing so, it is well to bear in mind that most of the strange powers described in it have been observed and vouched for many times in the records of the reputable Society for Psychical Research. Moreover, we know that many yogis and fakirs have remarkable control over their bodies. Some have survived after being buried alive for some time—a feat that is beyond the understanding of most of us. Until we have a more systematic knowledge of the possibilities of higher states of consciousness, it may be as well to keep an open mind.

How, for example, do we account for the apparently ghastly self-mutilations of the Moslem holy men called the dervishes? Gurdjieff's disciple John G. Bennett has described a Moslem dervish ceremony that he witnessed twice in Istanbul. The dervishes knelt on the floor, swaying as they chanted the name of Allah. At a certain point of intense emotion, they began to drive spikes and skewers through their cheeks and arms. One old man lay down on the ground and placed a sharp sword, edge downward, across his stomach. Another man stepped onto the sword, balancing himself by holding the hands of two men on either side. When the man stepped down, the old dervish raised the sword from his body and revealed that it had not even made a mark. Bennett examined the sword after the ceremony. It was as sharp as a razor and bore no trace of blood.

The Western temperament is more given to intellectual speculation and is less mystical than the Eastern—which partly explains why the technological advances of the West have been so much greater than those of the East.

The Flying Monk

The state of ecstasy can produce remarkable effects. There is reliable evidence that it caused a devoutly religious monk to rise into the air and fly. Giuseppe Desa was born at Apulia, Italy, in 1603. He was feeble and sickly as a child. At the age of 22 he joined the Franciscan order, and soon became well known for his prayers and fasting. One day after Mass, he suddenly rose into the air, floated above the congregation, and hovered over the altar. The candle flames did not burn him. From this time on Father Joseph as he was now known, often levitated and flew considerable distances. Many eminent contemporaries witnessed this strange feat, including the great German philosopher Leibniz. There are so many apparently reliable records of his flights that it seems probable they were not faked. Significantly, when a hostile and envious superior started to bully and humiliate him, Father Joseph ceased to fly. He recovered his spirits, however, and afterward flew through the air and embraced the statue of the virgin above the altar. A century after his death, he was canonized as St. Joseph of Copertino.

Science cannot explain levitation, although there are thousands of well-authenticated cases on record, particularly from India. But then, neither can science explain how John G. Bennett, seriously weakened after a three-day attack of dysentery, could dig furiously for an hour without collapsing. We know little about the powers of the mind because in most of us they are undeveloped. If we lived in a world in which there was only the moon and no sun, no one would believe that light could cause sunburn or make forests burst into flames. We know the universe only to the extent of our as yet feeble attempts to perceive and measure it, and the results are often absurd and contradictory.

One of the most eminent Protestant mystics was also a distinguished scientist and engineer. Emanuel Swedenborg was born in Stockholm in 1688 and began his career as a mathematician. He also studied watchmaking, carpentry, and music. Later he became Assessor of the Swedish board of mines, and demonstrated his engineering skill when he transported five ships overland for 15 miles during his country's war with Denmark.

In 1744 when he was 56, Swedenborg had an overpowering dream in which a roaring wind flung him on his face. Then Jesus appeared and spoke the words: "Well then, do it!" From this time onward, Swedenborg began to go into ecstatic trances and to see visions. His books contain vivid descriptions of journeys he claimed to have made through heaven and hell under the guidance of angelic spirits.

One's first reaction to this is to conclude that Swedenborg must have gone mad. But people who met him and expected to find a lunatic were surprised by his sanity and good humor. Moreover, his powers of clairvoyance were witnessed by many. One night when about to sit down to dinner in Gothenburg, he suddenly turned pale and announced that a great fire had just broken out in Stockholm 250 miles away. It was threatening his own house, he said. For the next two hours he was in a state of agitation. Then he said with relief: "Thank heavens, the fire is under control. It had almost reached my doorstep." The next day he wrote a detailed description of the fire to the governor of Gothenburg, and the day after that, a letter arrived confirming to the last detail all that Swedenborg had said.

One day when Swedenborg was at the royal court, the queen asked him perhaps mockingly if he had seen her deceased brother on his visits to heaven. Swedenborg replied gravely that he had not. The queen then remarked that, if Swedenborg met him, perhaps he would give him her greeting. The next time Swedenborg came to court, he told the queen that he had seen her brother and had given him her message. The brother, he said, sent his apologies for not having answered her last letter to him before he died, but he would now do so through Swedenborg. The scientist then repeated her brother's reply to various points in her letter. The queen was dumbfounded as she declared "No one but God knows this secret."

About this time the Dutch ambassador to the Swedish court died. When his widow afterward received an invoice for a silver tea service, she was convinced that her husband had paid for it shortly before his death. But she could not find the receipt. She asked Swedenborg for help. A few days later as she sat with friends, Swedenborg told her: "Your husband says the receipt is in the bureau upstairs." "Impossible," said the widow, "I have searched it." Swedenborg said that there was a secret drawer, which he described. The widow went to the bureau, found the secret drawer, and opened it. The receipt was inside.

Many of Swedenborg's contemporaries believed that these remarkable demonstrations proved that his visions of heaven and hell must be true. We should be more cautious. One of his books contains a description of Mars and its inhabitants that is wholly nonsensical in the light of our present knowledge of the planet. We can only conclude that if Swedenborg had visions—as he almost certainly did—then some of them were false ones.

The Curé of Ars

Of the more modern European wonder workers, perhaps the most interesting is Jean-Marie-Baptiste Vianney, the curé (parish priest) of Ars. In 1818 at the age of 34, Vianney was appointed to the parish of Ars near Lyon. He was a simple man, not particularly intelligent, and generally narrow-minded. Yet his piety and reported understanding of the human soul soon spread his reputation far afield. He had mystical visions, although he would say little about them—and many seriously ill people who came to see him were cured. His most famous miracle took place during a year of famine when there were only a few cupfuls of wheat left in the village granary. Vianney prayed all night. The next morning when a girl tried to enter the granary, she found the door blocked. Forcing it open, she found the place full of grain—enough to feed most of the parish for months.

This story was not investigated by an independent observer, and one hardly needs to be a skeptic to be suspicious of it. But, even allowing for the credulity of the more devoted members of his flock, Vianney seems to have possessed special powers, particularly of telepathy. As his fame spread, people came from far and wide to attend services at his church.

Powerful religious feelings sometimes seem able to release deep and hidden forces in the human soul. But it is important to realize that many of these powers are little more than by-products of our inner evolution. What is impressive about all the mystics, from Boehme to Yogananda, is not the wonders or visions. It is the sense they all share that the everyday world conceals some tremendous reality that all are capable of seeing if they can discover how to look. We feel something of this kind in the paintings and poetry of William Blake. We feel it in Vincent Van Gogh's evocative painting *Starry Night*, which the artist painted with candles tied around his hat so that he could see the canvas in the dark. Works such as these suggest something of the ecstatic intensity experienced by Boehme when he found himself looking "into the heart of nature," or by Ramakrishna when he was overwhelmed by the vision of the Divine Mother. They give us a glimpse of the source of power, meaning, and purpose that lies deep inside all human beings.

19. Living Witnesses

In Paris in the year 1960 there appeared on the bookstalls a volume with the euphonious title *Le Matin de Magiciens* (The Morning of Magicians) by Louis Pauwels and Jacques Bergier. It is a curious hodgepodge of a book, as the authors themselves recognized, for they wrote in the first chapter: "Skip chapters if you want to; begin where you like, and read in any direction; this book is a multiple-use tool, like the knives campers use . . ." To everyone's astonishment the book became a best seller, running through edition after edition in France. Serious critics were irritated and baffled by its success; they pointed out that the book was merely a series of wild speculations on magic, alchemy, telepathy, prophecy, strange cults, the Great Pyramid, Hitler's astrologers, the Cabala, flying saucers, and a thousand other topics. This mass of eccentricity was held together by one simple theme: the world is a stranger and richer place than science is willing to recognize.

It was a message that apparently had wide appeal in France, especially to the young. They were less interested in the book's argument about the narrowness of science than in the imaginative appeal of its magical wonders. Other writers saw that there was money to be made out of the occult. Books on astrology, reincarnation, and visitors from outer space rolled off the presses, and there was no sign of any loss of interest. The craze spread to other countries, notably Germany, England, and the United States. In 1968 a German book called *Remembrance of the Future* made a fortune and a name for its author, Erich von Daniken. Translated into English as *Chariots of the Gods?* it sold more copies than any other book except the Bible. Daniken's thesis was that the earth was visited thousands of

222

years ago by spacemen who left signs of their presence in many ancient cultures. Stanley Kubrick's film *2001, A Space Odyssey*, was based on the same idea. It became a kind of cult classic, and its admirers went to see it again and again, just as they might attend a religious ceremony. The great occult boom had arrived.

Curiously enough, a powerful resurgence of interest in the occult has occurred toward the end of every century for the past 400 years. Is this pure chance—or is there, as some people believe, a hidden law that governs such apparently cyclic occult revivals? The question is impossible to answer, but it is clear that we are now in the middle of the most widespread occult revival in history. One of its most significant and encouraging features is that it has captured the interest of a large number of scientists. All over the world universities and other institutions have established laboratories of parapsychology—the scientific investigation of extrasensory perception, clairvoyance, psychokinesis, and other psychic phenomena.

The Remarkable Croiset

In the Netherlands a famous Institute of Parapsychology was set up at the University of Utrecht, with Professor Willem H. C. Tenhaeff in charge. Tenhaeff has devoted much time to testing the powers of the psychic Gerard Croiset.

Croiset was born in 1909. He was unfortunate in being an unhealthy child, and in having to spend much of his childhood in foster homes. But from an early age he somehow knew about things that were happening in other places. Once when a teacher returned to school after a day's absence, Croiset was able to tell him that he had spent the day in a distant place with a girl who wore a red rose in her dress, and whom he would shortly marry. The teacher was amazed. He had, in fact, taken the day off to see his fiancée, who had worn a red rose.

When he was 25 years old Croiset visited the house of an acquaintance, and picked up a stick lying on a table. Immediately his mind became crowded with images of an automobile accident, and of a body lying on the roadside in a grassy place. The owner of the stick was astonished: it was an accurate description of an incident that frequently occupied his own mind. He told Croiset that he must be clairvoyant. Croiset now began to develop his faculty, and had clear visions of the future—of the Nazi invasion of the Netherlands, and of the loss of the Dutch East Indies to the Japanese, for example.

In recent years Croiset has become internationally known as a psychometrist—a person with the gift of reading the past associations of objects by holding them in his hand. The authenticity of this faculty in Croiset cannot be doubted, for he has been employed on numerous occasions by the Dutch police—and often with remarkable success. In 1949, for instance, Croiset was asked to help in a case of a sex crime. The police had suspects, but were by no means certain which, if any, was guilty. Croiset was handed two wrapped objects. Without opening the first he declared correctly that it was a tobacco box. He described the house from which it came and the two middle-aged brothers who lived in the house. He went on to give detailed descriptions of the characters of each of the brothers, and he identified them as the rapists. The second package contained a sack. Croiset immediately saw a cow in connection with it and, in fact, it was used as a cow blanket. He described how the two brothers had taken the girl, a mentally retarded child, to a cowshed with hay on the floor, and raped her. After that, the girl had been put into the sack, and the brothers had discussed what to do with her. One wanted to bury her alive, the other to drown her. The brothers quarreled over this, and the girl was allowed to live.

The two men, who had been among the suspects, were tried separately and convicted. Croiset again correctly foretold that one of them would commit suicide within a week or two of conviction. He was also able to tell the police that the brothers had committed other crimes—among them the rape of a Jewish girl in hiding from the Nazis during the war. He was even able to show them the house where this crime had taken place.

Another Dutchman has become even more famous than Gerard Croiset as a psychometrist who occasionally aids the police. He is Pieter van der Hurk, better known as Peter Hurkos. He also has scored some remarkable hits. In 1958 he was asked by the police of Miami, Florida to sit in the cab of a murdered cab driver and give them his impressions of the killer. As he sat there, Hurkos described the murder of the driver in detail. Then he described the killer as tall and thin, with a tattoo on his right arm and a rolling walk like a sailor. His name, Hurkos said, was Smitty, and he had also been responsible for another murder in Miami—that of a man shot to death in his apartment. The police were stunned. There had been such a murder recently but, as far as they knew, it had no connection with the killing of the cab driver. They searched their files and came up with a photograph of an ex-sailor named Charles Smith. Shortly afterward a waitress interviewed by the police recognized the man in the photograph as a drunk sailor who had boasted to her of killing two men. A wanted alert went out for Smith, who was arrested in New Orleans and sent back to Miami. He confessed to the murder of the cab driver and was sentenced to life imprisonment.

Hurkos' Fall

Unlike Croiset, Hurkos was not born clairboyant. He acquired his extraordinary gift in the Netherlands during World War II as the result of an accident. Knocked unconscious after a fall from a ladder, he woke up in the hospital with a fractured skull. As he recovered he found to his amazement that he could read people's thoughts, and seemed to know the future. Once when a nurse took his pulse, he told her to be careful or she might lose a suitcase belonging to a friend. The nurse had, in fact, just arrived at the hospital by train, and had left a friend's suitcase behind in the dining car. Hurkos told another patient that he ought to be ashamed of himself for selling the gold watch his father had left him when he died. This, too, was true.

His new faculty almost cost Hurkos his life. A patient who had been discharged from the hospital came to shake his hand—and, in that moment of contact, Hurkos knew that the man would shortly be murdered in the street. The victim was involved in resistance against the Nazis. When gossip about Hurkos' prediction reached the Dutch underground movement, it was assumed that Hurkos was a German counterespionage agent and a member was sent to kill him. It took Hurkos some fast talking to convince his would-be assassin that he was not in the pay of the Nazis.

When Hurkos came out of the hospital he found that he was unable to do normal work. He no longer possessed the power

225

of concentration required for everyday tasks. This is significant. It may well be that psychic powers are inherent in all of us, but that we unconsciously suppress them—not because they are of little help to us in everyday circumstances, but because they would actually impede our survival in the modern world. Croiset had become bankrupt as a grocer before he began to use his clairvoyant powers. Likewise, it was only after someone suggested that Hurkos exploit his extraordinary gift on the stage that he made enough money to support himself.

It is also interesting that Croiset was frequently sick as a child, and that Hurkos' gifts emerged only after an accident. This is not to suggest that strange powers are necessarily accompanied by sickness but only that sickness may be one of the factors which releases psychic sensitivity. On the other hand, many healthy people have deliberately cultivated their psychic powers because they needed them. The tiger hunter Jim Corbett, whose *Man Eaters of Kumaon* has become a modern classic, recounts how his life was saved again and again by his "jungle sensitiveness"—his sudden intuitive knowledge that a man-eater was lying in wait for him.

Another psychic whom I myself have met is the British dowser Robert Leftwich. Leftwich was described in a magazine article as a man of tremendous energy. The article had discussed his dowsing abilities, which he had successfully demonstrated on television, and also his power to project his astral body. Leftwich had also explained how he had used his psychic powers as a child at school. When the class was instructed to learn a long poem by heart, Leftwich would memorize only a few lines. The teacher customarily looked around the class and chose someone to recite each successive passage of the poem. When the passage that he had learned was coming up, Leftwich would will the teacher to ask him to recite. He claimed that the trick had always worked.

I was anxious to meet a man who seemed to combine psychic abilities with enormous zest and vitality. I visited him at his home in Sussex, and later he came to my home in Cornwall. His dowsing abilities are undoubtedly remarkable. He demonstrated the dowsing in the house. I hid a coin under a carpet while he was out of the room. He came in with his divining rod and walked around. The rod bent downward violently as

226

he stood over the coin. He explained that for him dowsing is a matter of tuning in the mind to the specific object. If he had been looking for some other object—a playing card or a matchbox—the rod would have ignored the coin, and dipped over the card or matches. He further explained that the rod could also be made to react over everything except what he was looking for. To demonstrate he walked around the room again, and this time the rod twisted violently in his hands until he stood above the coin; then it became still.

We also did thought transference tests with playing cards. I chose a card from the deck while Leftwich stood on the other side of the room, and tried to transmit its identity to him. His score was exceptionally high. But he is convinced that his powers do not depend just on telepathy, so we tried another test. I shuffled a deck of cards and threw the cards face down on the table. At a certain point he said, "Stop. That's the ace of clubs." He was right. He scored four our of seven on this test.

Telepathic Dowsing

Leftwich also demonstrated a form of telepathic dowsing. He stood with his back to my wife, and asked her to walk away from him across the garden. We knew where underground waterpipes were located, but he did not. At a certain point, however, he called "Stop!"She had just crossed an underground waterpipe, and he had located it by using her mind as a transmitter.

The usual explanation of dowsing is that the mind tunes in to some form of electric field. This was the explanation put forward by the philosopher Professor C. E. M. Joad in one of the British Broadcasting Corporation's *Brains Trust* broadcasts of 1946. But, after suggesting that water emits some form of electrical radiation that can be detected by the dowser, Joad went on to admit that he had no idea of the explanation of map dowsing. The map dowser holds a pendulum over a map, and the pendulum begins to swing or vibrate when it is held over the substance he is looking for—water, oil, minerals, or even gold. Joad described how he had witnessed map dowsing in action. A large-scale map, from which all rivers and streams had been carefully removed, was laid out on a table. The map dowser went over it with a pendulum, on the end of which was a small bobbin that could spin. The bobbin spun every time the pendulum was suspended over a place where the dowser detected water. At the end of the session, the dowser had located every river, stream, and pond in the area.

Obviously Joad's theory about radiation cannot explain this. Then how can it be explained? Once again, we are driven to return to the hypothesis that the secret lies in our own minds, but not necessarily in the subconscious mind—the Freudian "basement" that is supposed to contain all our most primitive animal impulses. Leftwich, like many other occultists, believes that the answer may lie in a part of the mind which could be called the "superconscious." If the mind can have a subconscious basement, might it not also possess a superconscious "attic"?

It was nearly a century ago that respectable scientists such as Sir William Crookes and Sir Oliver Lodge began to take an interest in the paranormal. At that time it looked as if the answers to the questions raised might rest reassuringly within the concepts of life after death, and of a universe of benevolent spirits doing their best to give help and guidance to the living on earth. But since that time every decade has revealed new mysteries, and the problem of finding a single explanation becomes increasingly difficult.

Let us take a look at some of the experiences of Dr. Andrija Puharich, a researcher whom Aldous Huxley described as "one of the most brilliant minds on parapsychology." In 1952 Dr. Puharich investigated the case of Harry Stone, a young Dutch sculptor. In deep trance states Stone spoke ancient Egyptian and wrote hieroglyphics—neither of which he had the slightest knowledge of in his normal state. The messages purported to come from one Ra Ho Tep, an Egyptian of the Fourth Dynasty about 2700 B.C.

The 'Surgeon of the Rusty Knife'

In 1963 Puharich heard about José Arigó, a Brazilian healer called the "surgeon of the rusty knife." In April of that year he went to Arigó's town to watch the wonder worker in action. The surgeon proved to be a barrel-chested peasant who thought himself possessed by the spirit of a dead German doctor. Puharich watched Arigó deal with 200 patients in four hours, performing many operations without anaesthetic and at great speed. Arigó removed a tumor from Puharich's own arm in a few seconds. Puharich felt nothing, and the flesh healed in four days without disinfectant or antibiotics. In 1971 Arigó was killed in a car accident. Puharich received the news by telephone, but was unable to confirm it from any of the news agencies. Later that day he discovered that Arigó had been killed that morning, as his caller had said. But when Puharich looked for the phone number of the caller, which he had written on a notepad, it had vanished. Moreover, his secretary who had been with him throughout the day could not recollect him taking the phone call.

This anecdote is recounted in Puharich's most baffling book, *Uri, a Journal of the Mystery of Uri Geller.* Puharich was drawn to Geller by accounts of his feats of mind reading, spoon bending, and his curious power over watches. At his first meeting with Geller, Puharich witnessed some remarkable feats. Geller told a woman to hold a ring in her hand, and placed his left hand over her clenched fist for 30 seconds. At the end of that time the ring was found to be broken into two pieces. Geller also demonstrated his powers of telepathy by performing a reading of the future. He wrote three numbers on a pad and placed it face down on the table. Then he asked Puharich to think of three numbers. Puharich selected the numbers 4, 3 and 2. Uri then turned over the pad—on which was written the figures 4, 3, 2. Geller explained that his experiment did not involve precognition, because he had transmitted the numbers to Puharich. In still other demonstrations of his strange powers, Geller change the time on Puharich's watch as Puharich held it in his own hand, and raised the temperature of a metal thermometer by eight degrees without touching it.

If this were all it would be remarkable enough. But Puharich goes on to make such a startling claim that one's first response is to doubt his sincerity. Briefly he says that Geller is a kind of savior or messiah, controlled by beings from outer space that are hovering a few million miles away in a spaceship called *Spectra.* These beings had apparently visited earth on a number of previous occasions, and had also selected the patriarch Abraham and the Pharaoh Imhotep as avatars, or incarnations of a divine being.

Given the present worldwide interest in the occult, one might expect Puharich's book to have created a sensation and become a best seller. Instead, it was received with a mixture of indifference and hostility. This is not to say that most critics thought Puharich was a liar. Many of them obviously felt that Puharich was sincere but mistaken. Geller has told me that everything in Puharich's book is factually accurate, but that he himself does not necessarily accept the notion that he is a messiah. This raises some fascinating questions, not merely about Geller and Puharich but also about the whole subject of the occult. The fact that a person possesses certain powers proves nothing about the source of those powers. Impressive documentary evidence seems to prove beyond all doubt that the Victorian medium Daniel Dunglass Home was able to wash his face in red hot coals without getting singed, and could cause heavy tables to float through the air. But this does not prove, as he claimed, that his powers came from spirits rather than from his own subconscious mind. Joan of Arc declared that she had been ordered to save France by St. Michael and St. Catherine, and the Church that has sanctified her apparently accepts her claim. But did her voices have any greater reality than those of the beings that visited Geller? In the long history of messianic religious movements, dozens of messiahs have astounded their followers by apparently genuine miracles, such as levitating, healing the sick, and conferring immunity against weapons. But as their promises about the end of the world have proven untrue, we must conclude that most of them were self-deceivers, however authentic their strange powers. Similarly, Puharich's claims regarding Geller's gifts may be true—but this does not prove that Geller is a messiah or that the spaceship *Spectra* exists.

The Source of Miraculous Powers

This still leaves us with the basic question: What is the source of energy or power behind these events—and behind so many psychic phenomena? There seem to be two possibilities: what we have called the superconscious, or spirits or celestial intelligences. The problem with the idea of a superconscious is that, while it is easy enough to understand its role in map dowsing or precognition, it is altogether more difficult to understand why it should conceive flying saucers and beings from outer space. Is it possible that the superconscious possesses a sense of humour? Many students of the paranormal would say that this is, indeed, a possibility, to the extent that the activities of the superconscious may be completely freakish and unexplainable.

Consider the curious case of the Abbot Vachère of Mirebeau in France. In 1913 the abbot was regarded as a kindly and conscientious member of the church, well liked by the Pope himself, but without any remarkable talent. He was in his sixtieth year when the first of a series of strange and rather embarrassing events began and drops of reddish moisture began to ooze from the hands and feet of the figure of Jesus in a painting that hung in Vachère's private chapel. Vachère reported the matter to his Bishop who asked to see the picture. It was dispatched to the Bishop, but failed to bleed. When it was returned to its chapel, however, the bleeding started again.

Later, a gang of workmen were building Stations of the Cross near the abbot's home, and Vachère pinned up an ordinary color print of Jesus in their hut. This also began to bleed. The bishop investigated, decided that Vachère was a fraud, and excommunicated the abbot. The bewildered and unhappy Vachère visited his friends at Aix-la-Chapelle; with him·in the house, a statue and a picture belonging to his hostess began to bleed.

Many people felt that the bleeding indicated that Abbot Vachère was a saint—or, at least, that he had been selected by God for some special destiny. The Church had no reason to think so, and refused to investigate the phenomena which, however, continued to occur until the abbot died in 1921.

The evidence leaves little doubt that the phenomena were genuine. On the other hand, the Church probably showed common sense in refusing to accept them as evidence of sanctity. Possibly the bleeding statues and pictures were a trick perpetrated by the abbot's superconscious. In any event, like the fakirs' wonders, the phenomena were spiritually worthless.

This story illustrates the fact that most human beings, churchmen as well as scientists, find supernatural phenomena embarrassing and prefer to ignore them. Such phenomena fail to conform to the laws of nature as we know them. Consequently they tend to be regarded as irrelevant freaks rather than as interesting pieces of some as yet unsolved universal jigsaw puzzle.

Photographs by Means of the Mind?

A similar attitude was shown toward a series of experiments made by Dr. Jule Eisenbud, a psychiatrist and member of the faculty of the University of Colorado Medical School. In 1963 Eisenbud published an article arguing that it is impossible to devise a truly repeatable experiment in the field of paranormal phenomena. A correspondent disagreed and sent him a magazine clipping about a man called Ted Serios. According to the article, Serios could take photographs by means of the mind alone. He would take a polaroid camera in his hands, stare hard into the lens, and somehow produce photographs of recognizable places, of faces or people, or of objects such as cars and buses.

Eisenbud's interest was aroused and he arranged a demonstration. Serios proved to be a bellhop of alcoholic tendencies, who also claimed to have the power of projecting his astral body. But the second claim was unconnected with the ability he demonstrated to Eisenbud. He stared down a small paper tube, which he called his "gismo," toward the camera lens. After a number of failures he succeeded in producing two blurry pictures of a water tower and a hotel. In considerable excitement, Eisenbud immediately got in touch with various scientists and told them what had happened. To his astonishment, they showed only polite interest, and had no wish to see a demonstration. Eisenbud was encountering the reaction we have mentioned above—the embarrassment effect produced by freakish and apparently inexplicable events.

Eisenbud refused to be deterred, however. He continued to test Serios, and some of the resulting "thought photographs" were spectacular. Naturally Eisenbud's first suspicion—like that of everybody else who tested Serios—had been that the trick lay in the gismo. Serios insisted that the tube of paper merely helped him to concentrate, and close examination of the gismo revealed nothing suspicious. Eisenbud concluded that Serios's powers were genuine, even if they made no sense in terms of any scientific law.

Die letzte photographische Aufnahme des blutenden Bildes.

The picture of Christ in the church at Mirebeau, France, which began to bleed in 1913. *(Living Witnesses)*

Charles Reynolds and David Eisendrath, two reporters who had watched Serios at work, were convinced he was a fake. They constructed a small device that could be hidden inside the gismo, with a lens at one end and a piece of unexposed film at the other. When this was pointed at the camer, the result was a picture not unlike those that Serios had produced. The account of their invention was printed in *Popular Photography* in 1967, and it gave all the skeptics fresh ammunition. Since then, their article has been cited by people who believe that Serios is a fake, as evidence that he performed his thought photography by sleight of hand. In March, 1974 *Time* magazine ran an article on the occult·revival, and included a brief account of Serios and the *Popular Photography* article. *Time* concluded: "Many of Serios's followers were shattered. Again, the millennium was deferred."

Now it is certainly possible that Serios is a fraud. But Reynolds and Eisendrath have done nothing to prove the contention. They merely demonstrated that they themselves could construct a gismo fitted with a lens and film. Dr. Eisenbud vainly pointed out that he and other experimenters had examined Serios's gismo for such fraud, and had found none.

My aim here is not to defend Serios—although thought photography is no less extraordinary than paintings that bleed or spoons that bend—but to point out that orthodox science is still a long way from taking a balanced and truly scientific attitude toward paranormal phenomena. There exists a deeply ingrained emotional prejudice that is just as likely to obscure the truth as are the wishful thinking of gullible parapsychologists and the dishonesty of fraudulent psychics.

Finally, if we discard the idea of the superconscious, is it remotely possible that some of these strange forces come from outside man? Might there be other intelligences—either spirits of the dead or creatures from other worlds—that are controlling or influencing the destiny of this planet?

The idea of life outside earth has received support from a number of scientists, but it must be admitted that the evidence is far from convincing. Some scientists have suggested that certain radio signals received from outer space may have been sent by intelligent beings. We also have the curious accounts of people who claim to have been in communication with creatures from flying saucers.

William Paley, a late 18th-century British theologian, used his watch as an argument for the existence of God. He argued that when we open the back and see the works, it is impossible not to recognize that it has been created by an intelligent mind. Therefore when we contemplate the universe, which is far more complex than a watch, how is it possible not to believe that it was created by an intelligent being? The followers of the scientist Charles Darwin were contemptuous of this argument. They insisted that the complexity of the universe—like the complexity of a snow crystal—is due to the operation of natural laws. This argument is not very convincing either, for the complexity of the universe is infinitely greater than that of a snow crystal. Next time you take a walk in the countryside, look at every living thing—trees, flowers, insects, birds, rivers, clouds. Then ask yourself whether you can imagine that they could have been produced by purely mechanical laws.

Intelligences from outer space or the human superconscious mind? Either explanation is possible, and it may be that there is truth in both. But for the human race at this point in history, the most fruitful line of inquiry undoubtedly lies within ourselves. The secret of the powers of shamans, of magicians, of psychics and clairvoyants probably lies in some unexplored part of our inner space. When man invents a spacecraft that will carry him to his own inner moons and planets, he will have discovered the secret that every magician has sought—a secret more fascinating than the Philosopher's Stone or the Elixir of Life.

20. Dream Clairvoyance and Telepathy

Bertha Huse left her home in the early morning of October 31, 1898, and disappeared. When the alarm was raised, 150 men from her home town of Enfield, Vermont, searched the woods and shores around nearby Muscova Lake. The only clue they had was a report from a woman that she had seen a young person who might have been Bertha on Shaker Bridge, which crossed the lake. But the first day's search was fruitless. On the second and third days a diver was brought in to search the lake, but he found no sign of Bertha either. A Mrs. Titus lived in a village some four miles away. During the evening of the second day of the search she dozed off in her rocking chair. When her husband woke her up she said, "George, why didn't you let me be? In the morning I could have told you where the girl lies and all about it." Later that night and during the following night her husband heard her talking about the missing girl in her sleep. Once she seemed to be giving instructions to a diver, saying, "She's not down there but over here to the left." When she awoke on the morning of the fourth day, she told her husband that she had seen where Bertha was, and that they must go to the bridge at Enfield.

A local mill owner who had sponsored the search was so impressed by Mrs. Titus' conviction that he called out the diver again. When Mrs. Titus led him to a spot on the bridge and said, "This looks like the place that I saw last night," the diver protested that he had already searched there. "No," said Mrs. Titus, pointing to two other spots, "you have been down there and there, but not *there*. She is head down in the mud, one foot sticking up and a new rubber on it." The diver reluctantly went down at the spot she indicated. A crowd of villagers watched and

235

waited. After about a minute a woman's hat bobbed to the surface. The anxious crowd surged forward to the rail and nearly knocked the diver's assistant off the bridge. When the diver surfaced some time later, he reported that he had found the body in exactly the position that Mrs. Titus had described.

The diver later reported how he had felt when, in the murky water 18 feet below the surface of the lake, he had first laid his hand upon the corpse. "I stopped short where I was," he said, "It is my business to recover bodies in the water and I am not afraid of them, but in this instance I was afraid of the woman on the bridge. I thought to myself, 'How can any woman come from four miles away and tell me or any other man where I would find the body?'" The psychologist William James, who investigated the case and interviewed and obtained signed statements from all the people involved, could not answer that question. He was as puzzled as the diver, but he committed himself to the statement that "the Titus case . . . is a decidedly solid document in favor of the admission of the supernormal faculty of seership."

"Seership," generally called clairvoyance, is a phenomenon often associated with dreams. There are many recorded cases of people apparently obtaining through dreams information they could not have obtained through any normal means. A skeptic may be able to think up arguments that cast doubt on the authenticity of any individual case. But when the mass of evidence from many different sources is reviewed, it is difficult to avoid the conclusion that some minds possess a faculty for "seeing" objects and events paranormally, and that this faculty sometimes operates through dreams.

The Red Barn Murder

Another well-known tale of dream clairvoyance that solved a mystery is the Red Barn Murder case. In 1827 Maria Marten ran away from her village in Suffolk, England with William Corder, a farmer. Corder got involved with another woman, murdered Maria, and buried her under the floor of a barn. He wrote to the girl's parents, saying that he and Maria were married and keeping well, and for a year nobody had reason to suspect the crime. Then one night Maria's mother had a dream in which she saw the murder and the burial. The experience was so vivid, unexpected, and alarming that her husband decided to investigate. He found the barn that his wife had seen in her dream, broke up the floor, and discovered the decayed body of his daughter in a sack. Corder was arrested, confessed to the crime in prison, and was executed.

Fortunately, most clairvoyant dreams are not so gruesome, and some are even beneficial. If it had not been for a dream of the son of the poet Dante, one of the supreme works of world literature, the *Divine Comedy*, might have remained incomplete forever.

After Dante's death, his friends, followers, and family searched for months for the concluding cantos of the *Paradiso*, the last part of the *Divine Comedy*, but to no avail. They decided that he must not have had time to complete his great work. His two sons Jacopo and Piero, who were poets in a modest way, were persuaded by friends to try to complete the poem. Then one night Jacopo had a dream which, according to another great poet, Boccaccio, "not only induced him to abandon such presumptuous folly but showed him where the 13 cantos were which were wanting to the *Divine Commedia*." Jacopo awoke from his dream, and in the middle of the night rushed to the home of an old friend of his father's, Pier Giardino. In his dream, said Jacopo, his father had taken him by the hand, led him to a room in a house where they had lived and, touching one of the walls, had said, "What you have sought for so much is here." Jacopo's story so excited Giardino that he immediately dressed, and the two went to the house where Dante had died. They roused its owner even though it was still before dawn, and went to the room Jacopo had seen in his dream. There they found a small mat on the wall at the point where the dream-apparition had indicated. Lifting it, they discovered a window alcove in which lay some papers, moldy from the damp. When they were cleaned, these papers turned out to be the 13 missing cantos of the *Divine Comedy*.

Skeptics who seek to explain away dream clairvoyance tend to rest their case on one of two main arguments: the possibility of coincidence, or the probability that the unconscious contains more knowledge and is much more perceptive than we normally suppose. One of the basic principles of Western philosophy is that it is a profitless and futile exercise to multiply hypotheses.

According to this principle, the interests of knowledge are best served when, confronted with a problem, we settle for the solution that does least violence to reason. In the case of apparently clairvoyant dreams, the principle would hold that coincidence, unconscious reasoning or knowledge, or even cynical lying or fraud, would be more acceptable explanations than clairvoyance. Yet sometimes these acceptable explanations are even more unlikely than the paranormal explanation. The Titus case offers fairly sound evidence for the paranormal hypothesis. Moreover it was investigated by William James, the leading psychologist of his age. He was a researcher of unimpeachable integrity, well aware of all the arguments and alternative explanations that the skeptics could muster.

William Stevens' Story

Another strong case for dream clairvoyance is related in William Oliver Stevens' book *The Mystery of Dreams*. The testimony here is first-hand from the author's son.

The young man was late to breakfast one morning and did not respond to a call, so his mother went to his room to see what was wrong. She found him "sitting up in bed, his eyes staring with the air of being shaken by some horror that he had just witnessed." He said he had had a "terrible" dream, unlike any that he had ever had before. In it he had seemed to be in the air about 20 feet above a car traveling along a dirt road. A young man and a young woman were in the car, which suddenly swerved off the road to the left and crashed into a tall pole. The man, who was tall and thin and looked "like a foreigner," got out of the car clutching his stomach. He lay down on the grass and tried to smoke a cigarette, but apparently was in too great pain because the cigarette dropped from his mouth. The dreamer's attention was focused on the man, but he was aware of the girl standing by and knew that she wasn't badly hurt. When he saw the man exhale a puff of vapor he thought of tales he had heard about the soul being seen to leave the body at the moment of death. Although he realized that the exhalation was probably only cigarette smoke, he knew for certain that the man was doomed.

The Stevens family was then staying in their summer home on Nantucket Island. They had no radio contact with the mainland,

238

but did receive the daily newspaper every afternoon. On this particular day the paper's front page had a photograph of a dark-haired man, whom Stevens' son immediately recognized as the man he had seen in his dream. The accompanying report related the circumstances of the death of the Count of Covadonga, former heir to the Spanish throne, in an automobile accident in Florida. The Count had been in the company of a young woman, a cigarette seller in a Miami night club. She had suffered only bruises in the accident. She said that the steering had failed when she swerved to avoid a truck, and that the car had gone off the road on the left side and struck a pole. The Count had been severely injured, but might have survived if his bleeding could have been staunched at the time. He later died in the hospital of haemophilia, and the woman was charged with manslaughter.

The correspondences between the dream and the external event in this case are obvious. One interesting difference was that the truck claimed to have caused the accident did not appear in the dream.

Shared Dreams

There are many recorded cases of telepathy—direct mind-to-mind communication—in dreams. One of the earliest was written down by Saint Augustine, a man who was disinclined to believe in any marvel that was not demonstrably the work of God. Here is Augustine's account of the story.

"A certain gentleman named Prestantius had been entreating a philosopher to solve him a doubt, which he absolutely refused to do. The night following, although Prestantius was broad awake, he saw the philosopher standing full before him, who just explained his doubts to him, and went away the moment after he had done. When Prestantius met this philosopher the next day, he asked him why, since no entreaties could prevail with him the day before to answer his question, he came unasked, and at an unseasonable time of night, and opened every point to his satisfaction. 'Upon my word it was not me that came to you; but in a dream I thought my own self that I was doing you such a service.'"

In this case, a kind of reciprocal telepathy seemed to be operating. The philosopher was aware, in his dream, of appearing

to Prestantius, while the latter, while awake, experienced a telepathic apparition of the philosopher. In other cases, the telepathic link occurs when both parties are asleep and dreaming.
One such case of reciprocal dreaming occurred between two
friends in Elmira, New York in 1892.

Dr. Adele Gleason dreamed that she was in a deserted spot in
the midst of very dark woods. She was suddenly terribly afraid
that a man she knew well might arrive unexpectedly and shake
the tree next to her, causing the leaves to fall and burst into
flames. Dr. Gleason awoke and wrote down the time of her dream
and the initials of John R. Joslyn, the friend who had appeared
in it. When she met Joslyn some days later she said, "I had a
strange dream on Tuesday night." He replied that he had also
had a strange dream that night and had written it down on
awakening. "Let me tell you mine first," he said, and he proceeded to describe the identical dream from a different angle.
His written account of the dream was as follows: "I dreamed
that I was walking at night in a remote spot where I sometimes
go shooting. Soon I saw in the bushes, about 12 yards from the
road, one of my women friends apparently paralyzed with fear
of something that I did not see, rooted to the spot by the feeling
of imminent danger. I came to her and shook the bush, upon
which the leaves that fell from it burst into flames." The two
dreams had occurred at the same time.

A Freudian analyst would no doubt revel in the symbolic
significance of *tree* and *flames* and discover disguised sexual
desire in the shared dream, but he would be at a loss to explain
how the dreams could occur at the same time and contain the
same strange imagery. The case seems a clear demonstration of
the possibility of communication between minds in sleep
independently of any channel of sense.

Such startling cases of shared dreams are fairly rare in the
records of dream research, though they may occur more often
than we know. People generally don't make a point of telling their
dreams to the people who have figured in them. In any case these
dreams, like others, are often forgotten by the time the dreamer
wakes up.

People undergoing psychoanalysis often dream about their
analyst—sometimes as himself, sometimes disguised as another
person. This is not surprising because in the course of analysis a

close relationship builds up between the two people. What has surprised some analysts is the occasional dream in which a patient somehow zeroes in on the analyst's own thoughts or on an event in the analyst's life of which the patient could not possibly be aware. In the book *Dream Telepathy*, which he co-authored with Dr. Stanley Krippner and Alan Vaughan, Dr. Montague Ullman describes several cases of telepathy between analyst and patient. One such case, which he calls the "Chromium Soap Dish Caper," involved Ullman himself.

The patient was a salesman for children's clothes. The book quoted him as follows: " 'I was wrapping up a few of the samples that had been on exhibit and was preparing to leave. Someone gave me, or I took, a chromium soap dish. I held it in my hand and I offered it to him. He took it. I was surprised. I asked him, are you a collector, too? Then I sort of smirked and said, knowingly, well, you're building a house. He blushed. He smirked and kept on smoking his cigar.' "

This trivial dream had little apparent meaning for the patient, but it did mean something to the doctor. On the day of the patient's dream, Ullman had been telling a friend about work he was having done on his house to correct a defect in the original structure. Although Ullman did not mention it to his friend, he was at the time thinking of an incident involving a chromium soap dish. This object was lying unused in the basement, and was spotted by one of the workmen. Ullman explained that it had been delivered by mistake during the building of the house a year and a half earlier. Annoyed by the rising costs of building his home, he had simply kept the dish "in a spirit of belligerent dishonesty." When the workman made a crack about his having gotten away with it, Ullman had been slightly embarrassed and had, he wrote, "managed a sheepish smirk."

The patient, it seemed, had unconsciously discovered a way to strike back at the analyst, whose intrusions into his own psyche he resented. But apart from its analytic significance, the dream demonstrates the extreme subtlety of the telepathic process. Although there existed a strong relationship between the two minds, the subject matter that was transmitted was extremely trivial. This was no life-and-death matter, or even an emotionally charged event—unless Dr. Ullman was more affected by the discovery of his dishonesty than he admitted. In fact, the sender of this particular telepathic message seems to have played a relatively passive role. Instead, in some mysterious way the patient's mind apparently established contact with the mind of his analyst and ferreted out a fragment of thought that—although insignificant in itself—gratified his own subconscious wishes to get a step ahead of the analyst.

Communication between Man and Animal

If the subtlety of such human-to-human telepathy is surprising, even more surprising is telepathic communication between human and animal. The novelist Rider Haggard had a dream in which he believed that he received a crisis telepathic communication from his dog. In his dream he saw the dog lying on its side in rough growth on the edge of water. It was clearly in pain and seemed to be struggling to speak to him. "My own personality," Rider Haggard wrote, "in some mysterious way seemed to me to be rising from the body of the dog, which I knew quite surely to be Bob and no other . . . In my vision the dog was trying to speak to me in words, and, failing, transmitted to my mind in an unidentified fashion the knowledge that it was dying. Then everything vanished and I woke to hear my wife asking why on earth I was making those horrible and weird noises."

The next day he told his dream to five others at the breakfast table. In the afternoon it was discovered that the dog was missing. They all remembered the dream, and a search was organized. Four days later the body of the dog was found against the weir in a nearby river. Inquiries among local people produced the information that a dog had been hit by a train crossing a bridge over the river at 11 o'clock the previous Saturday night. Signs of the accident—some blood and a broken dog collar identified as Bob's—were found on the bridge. It appeared that the dog had for a time lain in the reeds along the river bank, and had later been carried downstream by the current. It was not possible to ascertain the precise moment of death, but it could well have coincided with Rider Haggard's dream, which occurred at one o'clock in the morning about two hours after the accident. Reflecting on the implications of this domestic tragedy, the novelist wrote: "Of the remarkable issues opened by this occurrence I cannot venture to speak further than to say that . . . it does seem to suggest that there is a more intimate ghostly

242

connection between all members of the animal world, including men, than has hitherto been believed, at any rate by Western peoples; that they may be, in short, all of them different manifestations of some central, informing life, though inhabiting the universe in such various shapes."

Statements like this greatly annoy the rational and scientific.

Dr Daim's Experiments

Moreover, most scientists are even reluctant to accept spontaneous cases of clairvoyance and telepathy as evidence that these phenomena exist. If such phenomena exist, they argue, they should be capable of being studied under controlled conditions, and of being produced at will. However, telepathy and clairvoyance appear to depend either on a strong personal attachment between the receiver of the message and the sender, on the intrinsic importance of the material conveyed, or on a combination of these two factors. So it does not seem likely that their occurrence in dreams can be regulated and observed in any systematic way. In recent years, however, the situation has changed. Controlled experiments in dream telepathy have been carried out that satisfy exacting standards of scientific proof. These experiments make use of sophisticated modern techniques for monitoring sleep and dreams, and they have received a good deal of publicity. The credit for devising and first putting into practice the basic method such experiments employ belongs to a Viennese psychologist, Dr. Wilfrid Daim. In the 1940s he independently conducted a series of experiments which he reported in the February 1949 issue of the *Parapsychological Bulletin* of Duke University.

Daim conducted his experiments in the early morning hours and participated in them himself, sometimes as sender and sometimes as receiver. The material to be transmitted was a colored geometric shape, selected at random from a pile of envelopes containing various colored shapes. The sender concentrated on the image with the object of projecting it into the dream consciousness of the receiver. Sender and receiver were sometimes located as far as four miles apart. On one occasion Daim concentrated on a red equilateral triangle on a black background. After a few minutes of concentration, he felt that he had been successful in transmitting the image, and he willed the receiver to wake up. The time he began the experiment was 6:30 a.m.

The receiver later reported that he had awakened at 6:35 a.m. He remembered a dream involving music and soldiers. Suddenly, in the midst of the soldiers, appeared "a three-cornered, glaring-red fir tree . . . ." It "pushes through the whole . . . and remains unmoved for seconds amid all the former dream contents. It is not a fir tree out of nature but such a one as one finds in children's primers, the trunk is black, color distinct, while all the other dream contents are of a colorless gray." In other words, the shape of a red equilateral triangle with a black background interrupted his ongoing dream at the time Daim was attempting to project such a pattern.

Similar experiments were carried out in the 1960s by Dr. Ullman and his colleagues at the Maimonides Medical Center. Their domain at the Medical Center later became known as the "dream laboratory." With machines that could monitor mental activity during sleep, these researchers began a systematic large-scale series of experiments designed to test the hypothesis that information can be communicated to sleeping subjects by extrasensory means. The first experiments used simple geometric shapes as targets. For instance, at 4:30 a.m. on one occasion the experimenter drew three angular shapes as shown on this page. At 6:30 a.m. the subject was awakened from a REM sleep period. He reported a series of dream impressions in the course of which he said: "some people were standing around, and they had in their hands *canes* shaped like hockey sticks, used upside down, the curved part up. But they were shaped more like *free form* than plain hockey sticks." In another session the experimenter drew a circle, and this same subject again produced a report of dream activity that incorporated the image. "I had an image of a . . . it was sort of like being on a round, like the bottom half of a large tube, such as if you would be going into the Holland Tunnel or something . . . I was on a road shaped like the curve of a trough."

More complex target materials were used and thousands of dreams that contained significant correspondences with the targets were recorded by the Maimonides researchers. This extensive work, conducted for more than a decade, has established without doubt and to the satisfaction of many scientists that dream telepathy is a reality.

244

21. The Projection of the Astral Body

Imagine that you were to wake up from a dream, reach out to switch on a bedside lamp, and find yourself grasping at a void. Coming fully awake, you realize that you are suspended in mid-air. You are in command of all your sensory faculties, and can see all the familiar features of your room including your own physical body lying peacefully asleep in the bed below. It is difficult for anyone to imagine how he or she would initially react to such an experience. William Gerhardie, the English novelist whose first astral projection occurred in this way, was neither alarmed nor frightened. He said to himself, "Now this *is* something to tell. And this is *not* a dream." Gerhardie's account of his first astral projection appears in his partly autobiographical novel *Resurrection*, which was published in 1934. Gerhardie is certain of the authenticity of the experience, and his description is a useful one on which to base an examination of out-of-the-body experiences. The author had no prior knowledge of the phenomenon before it happened to him, and he was able to observe it with the professional writer's curiosity, detachment, and eye for detail. The most convincing evidence for the reality of astral projection for a person who has not experienced it is the fact that many of the same characteristics can be found in accounts from widely different sources. Several of these characteristics are to be found in Gerhardie's narrative.

He remained suspended in the air for several minutes, then felt himself pushed forward and placed on his feet. He staggered to the door but was unable to turn the handle because he had no grip in his hand. He became aware of a strange appendage. At his back was a coil of light that resembled "the strong broad ray of dusty light at the back of a dark cinema projecting onto the screen in front." To Gerhardie's astonishment he found that the cable of light "illumined the face on the pillow, as if attached to the brow of the sleeper. The sleeper was myself, not dead, but breathing peacefully, my mouth slightly open." He saw an aspect of his face he had never seen before, because of course he had never seen himself asleep.

"But I was not dead, I consoled myself; my physical body was sleeping under the blankets, while I was apparently on my feet and as good as before. Yet it wasn't my accustomed self, it was as if my mold was walking through a murky heavy space which, however, gave way easily before my emptiness." While wondering how he would get out, he found himself pushed forward so that either he passed through the door, or the door through him. The apartment was in darkness except for a subdued light that seemed to emanate from his own body. He entered the bathroom and from habit tried to switch on the light, but he found he was unable to press the switch. All the time he was aware of the strange tape of light "like an umbilical cord" between his two bodies, "by means of which the body on the bed was kept breathing while its mold wandered about the flat."

Determined to approach the whole matter scientifically, and to prevent himself from later thinking the whole experience had been a dream, he began to make systematic observations. He noted that the bathroom window was open and the curtain drawn, and he registered the existence of a new towel rack. Passing into other rooms, he noted which windows were closed. He attempted to open the linen closet but failed. Then suddenly he was pushed along "like a half-filled balloon." He flew out through the front door and "hovered in the air, feeling an extraordinary lightness of heart." He realized that he could quickly fly anywhere he wished, but he was afraid that something might happen to sever the link with his sleeping body. His new being, registering his anxiety, flew back to his sleeping body. But, Gerhardie writes, when "I felt it hovering over my old body on the bed, drab disappointment came back to me. 'Not yet,' I said. And again I flew off. When I flew thus swiftly, my consciousness seemed to blot out and only returned when again I walked or moved at a reasonable speed . . . Consciousness returned suddenly. I was stepping lightly over an open patch of grass . . . The thought occurred to me: how do I know I am not dreaming this?

and the answer: look for the lighted cord behind you. It was there, but it was very thin ... Then, with a jerk that shook me, I opened my eyes. I was in my bedroom ... Not a detail of my experience had been lost to my mind and there was quite another quality about it all, that of reality, which removed it from the mere memory of a dream ... I got up, and went through the rooms, checking the mental notes I had made about which windows were closed or open, which curtains drawn; and the evidence in all cases proved correct."

The Features of Projection

Gerhardie's narrative is a vivid description of what an out-of-the-body experience is like, and its details are corroborated in other accounts. Dr. Robert Crookall, a leading psychic researcher and authority on astral projection, has collected and compared many such accounts in his various books on the subject. Taking Gerhardie as a starting point, it is illuminating to see how many of the features he describes can be paralleled in the description of other astral projectors.

a) Positions of the astral body after separation. Many people report occupying a horizontal position above the physical body for several minutes after separation, and then having a sensation of being pushed into a vertical position.

b) The "strange appendage." The "silver cord" connecting the physical and astral bodies is mentioned in the biblical *Book of Ecclesiastes*, and has been referred to in accounts of OOBEs by people isolated from outside influences—for example by Basuto tribesmen in South Africa. Gerhardie mentions three characteristics of the cord that tally with numerous other accounts: that it is attached to the brow of the physical body (the pineal gland, or "third eye" of occult physiology is in the middle of the brow); that it is luminous; and that it becomes thinner as the distance traveled from the physical body grows greater.

c) The "murky, heavy space." Numerous accounts speak of the conditions first encountered in the astral in terms of fog, grayness, heaviness, or murkiness. Crookall attributes this to consciousness being "enshrouded by the still-unshed body veil." In other words, consciousness is clouded, confused, and unable at first to adjust to the new conditions.

d) Confusion over relation to physical reality. During their first

OOBE many people try to do things that they would do in the physical body, such as open doors or closets or move objects, and find they are unable to do so. Many projectors are also surprised to find that they can move at will through walls or doors. The second body feels so real and substantial that it takes time to realize that it has neither the capacities nor the limitations of the physical.

e) An attitude of alert attention. On adjusting to the new conditions, projectors frequently move around and make mental notes of their environment for later corroboration. Many report a sense of enhanced alertness, of sharper mental functioning than they have on the physical plane. They feel more alive, more real. This ability to focus and control attention is one of the characteristics of the OOBE that makes it totally undreamlike.

f) Conflicting emotions of exaltation and apprehension. Gerhardie's "extraordinary lightness of heart" when he realized that his subtle body enjoys total freedom of movement is typical. So is his worry lest, possessing such freedom and not knowing the laws that govern this unprecedented experience, he might go too far and sever the link with his physical body.

g) The conscious will as a motor force. Projectors *think* themselves into different locations. Gerhardie realized that he could travel anywhere in the world in a flash simply by willing to do so, and when he thought about his physical self his second body "obeyed and flew back." His observation about the blotting out of consciousness temporarily during high-speed astral travel is confirmed by many other experients.

h) The experience of reentry. Gerhardie speaks of returning to the physical "with a jerk that shook me." The suddenness and shock of the return is an experience reported by many projectors.

Although Gerhardie's account of his first out-of-the-body experience has all the above characteristics in common with the reports of other projectors, it would be misleading to call it a typical case. The list of common characteristics could be considerably extended if we took as points of reference the testimonies of other experients, but OOBEs come in many varieties and no characteristic, however common, necessarily applies to all of them. The commonest are the presence of the silver cord, the sense of enhanced alertness, and the fact that the conscious will can effect transitions in space in a very short time, though not always instantaneously. Different speeds of travel are reported by different projectors.

It is only in recent years that astral projection has been taken seriously by some psychologists, and there remains a great deal of research work to be done to see whether certain physiological and psychological states precede certain types of astral projection. Crookall has noticed differences between enforced, spontaneous, and deliberate projections, and some experienced projectors offer advice on the most suitable conditions for an out-of-the-body experience. But knowledge, at the present time, remains tentative and incomplete. Apart from the work of Crookall, the only substantial contribution to the subject has been made by Celia Green of the Institute of Psychophysical Research in Oxford, England. She published some of the results of her work in 1968 in a book entitled *Out-of-the-Body Experiences.*

Celia Green's Questionnaire

Celia Green's study was based on the testimonies of 326 experients who completed a questionnaire sent out by the Institute. Over 60 percent of the group reported having had only one OOBE, 21 percent had had six or more, and the remaining 18 percent had had between two and five experiences. The group consisted of people of all ages, and showed that the incidence of OOBEs diminished in later life, was common in childhood among subjects who had had more than one experience, and tended to cluster between the ages of 15 and 35 for those who had had only one experience. Most of the cases were not as sustained or full of detailed description as Gerhardie's, but were merely momentary projections. Eighty percent of the subjects reported no awareness of being in a second body, but simply of being a "disembodied consciousness" located at a distance from the physical body. About 32 percent reported that their projections had occurred as a result of an accident or under anesthetic; 12 percent reported them occurring during sleep; 25 percent under conditions of psychological stress; and the rest while awake and active and going about their normal routine.

The very fact that many of the subjects of this study had only one or two fleeting experiences of projection is significant. It suggests that though only a few may undergo prolonged and intense astral journeys, there may be many more who have had some sort of relevant experience at a far less intense level. Two such examples are quoted from the study. The first is a young man who wrote: "During the morning while driving fast along a road the drone of the engine and vibration seemed to lull me into a stupor and I remember I seemed to leave my motorbike like a zoom lens in reverse and was hovering over a hill watching myself and friend tearing along on the road below and I seemed to think "I shouldn't be here, get back on that bike!' and the next instant I was in the saddle again."

The second subject was a waitress who, after working nonstop for 12 hours, left the restaurant to go home and found that she had missed her last bus. She reported:

"However, I started walking as in those days I lived in Jericho, a 15 minute walk at most. I remember feeling so fatigued that I wondered if I'd make it and resolved to myself that I'd 'got to keep going' . . . The next I registered, was of hearing the sound of my heels very hollowly and I looked down and watched myself walk round the bend of Beaumont St. into Walton St. I—the bit of me that counts—was up on a level with Worcester College chapel. I saw myself very clearly—it was a summer evening and I was wearing a sleeveless shantung dress. I remember thinking 'so that's how I look to other people.'"

Both of these reports suggest a slightly altered state of consciousness, precipitated in the one case by the monotony and the vibration of the ride, and in the other by fatigue. Neither mentions a sense of possessing a second body, but as Celia Green remarks, many first-time experients are too preoccupied with the novelty of viewing themselves from an objective viewpoint to pay attention to the attributes of their second self. They nevertheless have a total conviction that the second self, even if it is only a "disembodied consciousness" is, as the waitress wrote, "the bit of me that counts."

The Bonding of Man's Two Bodies

All systems of occult physiology maintain that the physical and astral bodies are normally completely merged and coincident, but that certain circumstances can throw them out of coincidence. In some people, too, the bonding between the two is looser than normal, and separation can take place relatively easily. The most common cause of separation is a crisis or accident. An experience recounted by the biologist and writer Lyall Watson in his book *The Romeo Error* is typical of this kind of out-of-the-body projection.

The author was driving with a safari group in Kenya when their bus skidded and rolled over several times. He lost consciousness for a moment, and in that time had a brief out-of-the-body experience. He was projected outside the bus and saw that it was about to roll over again, and that when it did one of the occupants would almost certainly be killed. He came around at that point, and took immediate steps to rescue the trapped passenger.

This is a good example of an OOBE serving a useful purpose by enabling a person to obtain information paranormally, act on it and, in Lyall Watson's case, save a life. There are a number of other reported cases of lives being saved as a result of a projection. The most dramatic is that related by a well-known medium, the Reverend Max Hoffman.

At the age of five Hoffman was a victim of a cholera epidemic in Germany. He was diagnosed as dead, and duly buried. The night after his burial his mother woke up to find the child's double standing at her bedside. He told her he was not dead, and begged her to recover his physical body from the grave. He said they would find him lying on his side with his right hand under his right cheek. The apparition returned on three successive nights. Though the father was reluctant to apply to have the grave opened on the dubious evidence of what was probably an anxiety dream, his wife finally prevailed upon him to do so. When the grave was opened the child was found in exactly the position his projected double had told his mother that he was in. Doctors were able to resuscitate him. The physical body had been in a state of suspended animation, just clinging to life, while the astral body went in search of help.

Where the psychic link is strong, as between mother and child or husband and wife, life-saving astral experiences frequently occur. Dr. Crookall has recorded a case of a woman who passed out while taking a bath and lay for some time face down in the water. She left her body and went downstairs to the living room where her husband was reading. She tapped him on the shoulder. He did not actually see her apparition, but he had a sudden compulsion to hurry to the bathroom. He was just in time to drag his wife out of the water and bring her around by artificial respiration. Meanwhile she hovered above the scene, and was later able to describe his every move.

Helping and healing are other useful functions frequently performed by projectors. There is a Scottish doctor who is said to project regularly in his second body to give his professional help to people who send out psychic calls at times of distress. One of Crookall's correspondents, a Major Pole, relates how once, when he was desperately ill on a houseboat on the Nile River, the doctor materialized before him, diagnosed his condition, and wrote out a prescription. He chatted meanwhile, as doctors will, telling Major Pole in a matter-of-fact manner about his astral errands of mercy, and mentioning that he always took the precaution of locking his office door when he was projecting so that nobody would disturb his physical body. On returning to England, Major Pole managed to track down his strange benefactor through a radio appeal.

Positive Consequences

The conviction of the astral voyager that his essential self is not identified with his physical body is an aspect of the experience that can itself be of positive and life-preserving value, for example under conditions of torture or extreme physical hardship. A particularly interesting case of this kind is that of Ed Morrell, a man who had many OOBEs while serving a four-year prison sentence in Arizona some 50 years ago. He later wrote about them in his book *The Twenty-Fifth Man*. Morrell used his secret faculty as a weapon in a psychological war with his guards. The guards were incredibly sadistic in attempting to crush his spirit. They beat him brutally and put him in a tight straightjacket that they doused with water so that it would shrink and increase his pain. During one night of intolerable agony, Morrell suddenly experienced a sense of release from his body. He no longer felt pain, and was joyful and elated by his sense of freedom. He found that he could pass through the prison walls and travel at will to any place he thought of. Moreover, when he returned to his physical body he felt refreshed and invigorated. The guards redoubled their efforts to break him, once leaving him in the straightjacket for 126 hours, but the astral travels of Morrell's double continued to sustain and revitalize his spirit and his physical body, and nothing they could devise defeated him.

Of course, such a case could be put down to delusion, or explained as a stratagem of the unconscious to overcome the ravages of pain, but Morrell expresses the conviction, typical of the astral traveler, that his essential conscious self, "the bit that counts," had been able to transcend the limitations of time and space. In addition, during his second-body excursions he witnessed events that he was later able to verify, for example a shipwreck, and he saw people unknown to him at the time whom he later met, including his future wife.

Morrell's astral experiences finished after he was released from prison. When he was happy, healthy, and free from stress he found that he could no longer leave his body. This might suggest that out-of-the-body experiences are compensatory and perform the same function as dreams which, according to the psychologist Carl Jung, help to establish a balance in the psyche and make good certain deficiencies in a person's total life experience. Such a theory might account for some astral experiences, but it clearly does not apply to all cases, and it does not imply that the experience is merely subjective. The fact that Morrell and others have acquired information at a distance during out-of-the-body experiences, information that has later been verified and that could not have been obtained through any of the normal channels of sensory communication, stands as clear evidence that in astral experiences the psyche interacts with the objective physical world.

A Symptom of Sickness?

Other theories try to explain out-of-the-body experiences by suggesting that they occur in people suffering from abnormal or pathological conditions such as epilepsy, brain damage, drug addiction, and chronic alcoholism, or during attacks of migraine, influenza, or typhus. Although this may frequently be the case, there are plenty of examples of astral projection by people whose condition can in no way be classed as abnormal or pathological.

In the same way many nervous and unstable people have had psychic experiences. Their instability does not necessarily make these experiences invalid, nor does it account for the hundreds of experiences undergone by people of stable temperaments.

Various famous writers have written about experiences of the double. Guy de Maupassant's double frequently annoyed him when he was writing, and sometimes sat opposite him at his desk and dictated his stories. Shelley, the English romantic poet, frequently projected his double. Once it was seen walking in the woods by Byron and others when the poet was known to be with other friends elsewhere. On another occasion Shelley reported seeing his double himself, pointing toward the sea where he was later to meet his death. The Swedish dramatist Strindberg, a man who lived perilously near the edge of insanity, had moved to Paris after the breakdown of his second marriage. Desperately longing to be back with his family, he had an astral experience in which he found himself in his home and saw his mother-in-law playing the piano. Soon afterward he received a letter from her saying that she had seen his double appear, and asking if he were ill.

The corroborating testimonies of others, and the fact that verifiable information is sometimes obtained, indicates that though abnormal conditions may facilitate the projection of the double, the double is nevertheless real, and not an hallucination. Some forms of astral projection may arise as psychic compensation, and some may be due to abnormal or pathological conditions, but the phenomenon is so varied and individual that no theory can be all-inclusive. The hale and hearty have out-of-the-body experiences, as well as the ailing and introspective. They can occur spontaneously and for no apparent reason, they can be precipitated by circumstances such as accidents or psychological crises, or they can be deliberately cultivated and induced. Various authors have examined the conditions and methods that are helpful for deliberate astral projections.

The 'Techniques of Ecstasy'

Mircea Eliade in *Shamanism* repeatedly makes the point that shamans are "masters of the techniques of ecstasy," and Dr. Robert Crookall has noticed correspondences between these ancient traditional techniques and the descriptions of modern astral projectors. A strange document was obtained by the American psychologist Prescott Hall through a medium who herself had no knowledge of or interest in astral projection. It was published in the *Journal of the American Society for Psychical Research* in 1961, and purported to be detailed instructions on astral projection from a nonphysical source. Looked at together these accounts seem to provide some kind of guideline for the would-be astral projector.

The right weather conditions seem to be important. The air should be clear and dry, the temperature between 70° and 80°F. Conditions of humidity and electrical storms are not favorable. The would-be projector should not eat anything for several hours before an attempt, and should try to avoid a high protein intake for a considerable period before. Favorable physiological conditions are also created by breathing exercises. Heavy rhythmical breathing is said to assist the loosening of the double, and the ancient yogic technique of pranayama, or holding the breath in, is practiced by some projectors to wing the astral body on its way.

Shamans often dance and whirl to the point of exhaustion to induce ecstasy and start the second body on its journey, but less strenuous means are generally recommended for the novice. Relaxation, quiet, deliberate reduction of muscle tension, a mental state of reverie or unfocused consciousness, of withdrawal of attention from the physical world, are essential psychological preconditions. Hall's article also offered a number of images for contemplation in the progressive stages of projection exercises, revealed through the medium's informers. To loosen the astral from the physical body they suggest imagining oneself "as a point in space floating, or as a piece of cloud or as steam." To initiate movement in the astral body they suggest contemplation of the image of a twirling star suspended in space, or images of oneself flying, swinging, or rocking. For the final stage of separation and release of the astral body they gave a number of visualization techniques. For example, they suggest concentrating on the image of a whirlpool or going down through a whirlpool. This gives practice in the exercise of contracting to a point and then expanding. A cone is another image used. The projector must visualize passing through a waterspout or hourglass shape, constructing a cone of circles becoming large or smaller, and turning such a cone inside out. Another exercise is to visualize a tank gradually filling with water, with oneself floating on the top as a point of light. The object is to find a small hole in the side of the tank through which one can pass out.

Robert Monroe, an American businessman who has been having astral experiences regularly for more than 15 years and has learned to control them at will, writes in his book of 1971,

Journeys Out of the Body: "I believe that anyone can experience existence in a Second Body if the desire is great enough." He also recommends a sequence of exercises to help in astral projection, the key feature of which, as in all methods, is visualization.

But the questions still remain. What is the point of astral projection? What rewards are to be expected from it, and what dangers are incurred? The best way to examine these questions is to consider the accounts of those who are experienced in the techniques of astral projection.

22. Astral Experts

Sylvan Muldoon had his first experience of spontaneous projection at the age of 12, so when he was 21 and had the experience he later described as "the most unusual I ever had," he was already a seasoned projector. At the time he lived in a small quiet town in Wisconsin. One moonlit summer evening in 1924 he went out for a walk after dinner, and fell into that mood of listlessness, loneliness, and philosophical perplexity that introspective and impressionable young men are prone to. He returned home in disgust, went into his room, locked the door, and flung himself on the bed. When his physical body began to turn numb and his sensory functions deserted him, he recognized the signs of an imminent projection and gave himself over to the experience.

He felt himself rise in the air, then outward and into a vertical position. Gradually the misty atmosphere cleared and he was able to move freely. He walked about indoors for a short time, and then went out into the street. There a bewildering thing happened. He was whipped away at supernormal speed and suddenly found himself in a strange house. There were four people in the room, one of them an attractive girl of about 17, who was sewing a black dress. He found himself propelled without any effort to a position directly in front of the girl, where he remained for a short time watching her. Then he moved around the room, making mental notes of the furniture and various objects. He could see no reason for his being in this place, so he willed himself back to his physical body, taking a last look around before he left and noting from outside that the house was a farmhouse.

Some six weeks later Muldoon was on his way home one

257

afternoon when he saw a girl get out of a car and go into a house. He immediately recognized her as the girl he had seen on his astral excursion, and knowing that she did not live in the house she had entered, he waited for her to come out. When she did he accosted her and asked her bluntly where she lived. The girl said it was none of his business, and would have brushed him off and gone on her way had he not to her amazement started to describe her home, inside and out, in great detail. Muldoon does not record the girl's reaction to his uncanny intelligence, but he states that as a result of this meeting she became a very close friend. He visited her home, which was 15 miles from his own, several times, and recognized all the features and details he had noted on his previous astral visit. He confessed to the girl how he had come by his knowledge, and further convinced her by projecting his visible double into her room. She later participated with him in several experiments.

The thought of disembodied voyeurs hovering around is enough to give any normally modest young women the creeps. Muldoon and Oliver Fox, a British scientist and another experienced projector, are careful to portray themselves as gentlemen of the utmost propriety, both in the body and out of it; but their records are of events of 50 years ago, and in the permissive 1970s it wouldn't be surprising if there were to appear the confessions of a lecherous astral projector. It requires little imagination to conceive how the following experience related by Oliver Fox in his book *Astral Projection* would appear in an updated version.

Oliver Fox's Visit

It was an autumn afternoon in 1913, and Fox lay down in his room "intending to experiment." He was soon able to leave his body and go out into the street. He had walked for about 100 yards when he was "caught up in some strong current and borne away with great velocity." He came to rest in a beautiful small park which he did not recognize. A school party seemed to be in progress, and children dressed in white were playing games and having refreshments under the trees. "Bluish smoke rose from the fires they had lit, and a magnificent amber sunset cast a mellow glow upon the peaceful scene."

Fox walked on till he came to some houses. The front door of one of them was open and he went in, curious to know whether the occupants would become aware of his presence. He mounted a flight of richly carpeted stairs and entered a bedroom on the first landing. "A young lady, dressed in claret-colored velvet, was standing with her back to me, tidying her hair before a mirror. I could see the radiant amber sky through the window by the dressing table, and the girl's rich auburn tresses were gleaming redly in the glamorous light. I noticed that the coverlet of the bed had a crumpled appearance and that there was water in a basin on the washstand. 'Ah, my lady,' I thought, 'you too have been lying down, and now you are making yourself presentable for tea—or is it dinner?' . . ."

Fox moved behind her and stood looking over her shoulder into the mirror. He could see the reflection of her attractive face, but not a trace of his own was visible. Realizing that she could not see him, he wondered whether she would be able to feel him. "I laid a hand upon her shoulder. I distinctly felt the softness of her velvet dress, and then she gave a violent start—so violent that I in my turn was startled too. Instantly my body drew me back and I was awake. . . . The western sky had been blue when I lay down; but on breaking the trance I saw that it was actually the same glorious amber color that it had been in my out-of-the-body experience. . . ."

Both Muldoon's and Fox's narratives could be dismissed as a young man's romantic fantasies if they stood alone, but in the context of the total work of these two men they are perfectly credible descriptions. Muldoon and Fox independently discovered their ability to project, cultivated and developed it, and gradually learned some of the rules governing this strange experience. They were both well aware that the experiences they reported would appear to others to be nothing more than extremely vivid dreams. They wanted to demonstrate that OOBEs were more than dreams, and to encourage others to experiment for themselves and prove the point.

Muldoon Writes to Carrington

Muldoon's material was written with the encouragement of the distinguished psychical research Hereward Carrington. Carrington had published a book, *Modern Psychical Phenomena*, in which he had a chapter on astral projection based on the testimony of a French projector Charles Lancelin. Shortly after its publication he received a letter from Muldoon, who was then unknown to him. Muldoon said that, judging from the material in the book, he doubted whether Lancelin was a conscious projector, and that he could write a book on the things that Lancelin did not know. He gave so many details of his intimate knowledge of the subject in his letter that Carrington eagerly followed up the proposal. Two years later in 1929 their book, *The Projection of the Astral Body*, was published. Most of it was written by Muldoon, and it remains to this day the most informative single work on the subject written by someone who had actually experienced the phenomenon of astral projection.

Carrington makes the point in his Introduction that Muldoon's material is convincing because in fact his claims are modest. He does not profess to have visited distant planets, to have projected into the past, the future, or the spirit world, or to have relived his own past incarnations. "He asserts, merely," says Carrington, "that he has been enabled to leave his physical body at will, and travel about in the present, in his immediate vicinity, in some vehicle or other, while fully conscious. This is perfectly rational. . . ." The skeptic may not consider it rational, but it is certainly modest compared with the claims of some other projectors.

Muldoon's first out-of-the-body experience occurred in an environment conducive to the manifestation of paranormal phenomena. His mother was interested in Spiritualism, and one summer she took him and his younger brother to a Spiritualist Association camp in Iowa. They stayed in a rooming house where half a dozen well-known mediums were also staying. In the middle of their first night there the 12-year-old Sylvan awoke after sleeping deeply for several hours. He found himself in a "bewildering stupor," unable either to arouse himself into normal waking consciousness or to fall back to sleep. He couldn't ascertain where he was. He was aware that he was lying somewhere, but when he tried to move he found that he was powerless. He felt as if he were stuck to whatever he was lying on. He was in a condition that he later defined as "astral catalepsy." In medical terms, *catalepsy* is a trancelike condition that sometimes lasts for several weeks. Astral catalepsy, according to Muldoon, is an unpleasant state in which one is fully conscious but completely unable to move.

Other unpleasant sensations followed. He felt that he was floating, that his entire rigid body started vibrating up and down at great speed, and that there was a tremendous pressure at the back of his head which came in spasms. "Amid this pandemonium of bizarre sensations—floating, vibratory, zigzagging, and head-pulling—I began to hear somewhat familiar and seemingly far-distant sounds," he wrote. His senses began to function again, first hearing, then sight. Things seemed hazy at first, then gradually cleared until he saw his surroundings and knew where he was. To his astonishment, however, he found that he was floating toward the ceiling. "It was too unnatural for me to understand, yet too real to deny," he wrote. He had neither experienced nor heard of the existence of the second body at the time, and he assumed that he was in his physical body while mysteriously defying gravity. He was still cataleptic, and remained so for about two minutes after he was "uprighted from the horizontal position to the perpendicular, and placed standing upon the floor of the room."

Suddenly he felt free and able to move. He turned and saw his physical body lying on the bed. An "elastic-like cable" extended between the center of the brow of the physical body and the back of the head of its "astral counterpart." He was swaying from side to side and had difficulty keeping his balance. He was understandably alarmed because he thought that he had died. His first instinct was to go to his mother and awaken her. He went to the door and tried to open it, and was further astonished to find that he just passed through it. He then went around the house trying to shake people and call to them, but his hands passed through them "as though they were but vapors." It was uncanny. All his senses seemed normal except that of touch. He started to cry. He saw an automobile pass the house and heard the clock strike two. He prowled disconsolately about for 15 minutes, then began to feel a pull on the cable. He became cataleptic again, and was drawn back toward his physical body and into a horizontal position above it. With a shock that shuddered painfully through his entire frame his two bodies came together again and he found himself awake—alive and filled with sensations of awe, amazement, and fear.

The correspondences between Muldoon's and Gerhardie's

accounts of their first projections will be obvious. Both found themselves cataleptic and suspended in midair for some time before some force moved them into a standing position. Both were unsteady on their feet at first, but when able to move felt the second body to be substantial enough to attempt to open a door, and were surprised to find that they could pass through doors and walls. Both saw the cable connecting the two bodies and attached to the brow of the physical one, and on returning to the physical both experienced a sudden jerk or shudder. Gerhardie was more adventurous and inquisitive on his first excursion, and learned more about the potentials of distant projection, but Muldoon was only 12 years old and his reaction of fear, loneliness, and anxiety to contact other people is only to be expected.

When he became accustomed to the experience of astral projection, Muldoon began to investigate the phenomenon in a systematic way and to develop his own theories about it. He came to the conclusion that prolonged projection from a state of sleep, such as he had experienced the first time, was probably rare, but that "instantaneous projection" was not uncommon and might happen to people without their realizing it. He wrote: "When something unusual or unnatural occurs to upset the harmony of the physical—a shock, a jolt, a broken habit, an intense unappeased desire, sickness—in fact, anything which would cause a lack of perfect material coordination there is always a jar to the astral." Even so commonplace an event as the jolt a person experiences when he descends a staircase in the dark and, at the bottom tries to take an extra step, can momentarily jar the astral body out of coincidence with the physical. In sleep, Muldoon maintained, the astral body always moves slightly out of coincidence, perhaps only a fraction of an inch, but often much more. "If you could hold consciousness up to the very last moment, in the hypnagogic state," Muldoon says, "you could feel this act of discoincidence, as indeed nervous and fatigued people often do."

The Theory of Discoincidence

Muldoon's theory of the purpose of what he calls discoincidence during sleep is interesting, particularly in the light of modern Soviet research into the "energy body" through means of electrophotography. The astral body, he claims, is a "condenser" of cosmic energy, and it regularly discoincides from the physical in order to become recharged with energy. So in the person who is fatigued or run down discoincidence will be more pronounced, and will occur more frequently than in people of more robust constitution. This theory has a certain logic and appeal, for it would explain the fact that people who have OOBEs are often frail. Muldoon himself was of delicate health throughout his life. Eliade remarks that shamans are usually recruited from among the delicate and sickly, and a true shaman is "a sick man who has succeeded in curing himself." It would also explain the fact that many projectors, for example Ed Morrell, report that they return from their astral travels feeling refreshed and revitalized.

"If you ask me which is the most pleasant way to promote astral projection," Muldoon wrote, "I should answer by saying 'dream control.'" The astral body may be called the "dream body," he said, "for it is in that body that we dream—even though we may be in coincidence or completely separated from the physical." The first stage of the dream control method of promoting projection involves holding consciousness up to the very moment of falling asleep, or as Muldoon calls it, "rising to sleep." To do this he recommends holding an arm in the air so that it will begin to sway and tend to fall when sleep comes, resulting in a slight awakening. The next stage is to construct an appropriate dream, to dwell on it and hold it clearly in mind so that it continues when the body completely succumbs to sleep. The dream should be one that involves an upward and outward movement of the body, a dream of flying or of going up in an elevator, for example. Muldoon claims that "a properly constructed dream is sure to move the astral body out," and explains that "the astral naturally moves out of coincidence at the moment of sleep; it naturally starts itself, and that is just the moment when you must mentally project yourself into the up-going elevator (or whatever the dream may be) and 'keep going.' . . . In such a dream the astral body acts out exactly whatever the dream may be. . . . If you become *completely* conscious in such a dream, you would usually find yourself in some place corresponding to the place of action which was last seen in the dream."

263

Oliver Fox also maintained the reality of the dream world and the possibility of projecting the astral body by means of dream control. His own research, he wrote, began with a dream.

"I dreamed that I was standing on the pavement outside my home. The sun was rising behind the Roman wall, and the waters of Bletchingden Bay were sparkling in the morning light. I could see the tall trees at the corner of the road and the top of the old gray tower beyond the Forty Steps. . . . Now the pavement was not of the ordinary type, but consisted of small, bluish-gray rectangular stones, with their long sides at right-angles to the white kerb. I was about to enter the house when, on glancing casually at these stones, my attention became riveted by a passing strange phenomenon so extraordinary that I could not believe my eyes—they had seemingly all changed their position in the night, and the long sides were now parallel to the kerb! Then the solution flashed upon me: though this glorious summer morning seemed as real as could be, I was *dreaming*."

Dreams of Knowledge

Fox called the kind of dream in which one is conscious of dreaming a "Dream of Knowledge," and he discovered that with practice he could prolong and control such dreams. He also found that in a Dream of Knowledge he could do some curious things. "I could glide along the surface of the ground, passing through seemingly solid walls, etc., at a great speed, or I could levitate to a height of about 100 feet and then glide. . . . I could also do some intriguing little tricks at will, such as moving objects without visible contact, and molding the plastic matter into new forms." He found that the effort of prolonging a Dream of Knowledge produced a pain in the head, which he realized was a warning "to resist no longer the call of my body." As the call of the body grew stronger he experienced a period of dual consciousness, in which he could simultaneously feel himself standing in his dream body and lying on his bed, and see both the dream scenery and his bedroom.

What, he wondered, would happen if he tried to resist the call back to the body and disregarded the pain in his head? He screwed up his courage to make the experiment, and had "a never-to-be-forgotten adventure."

He dreamed that he was walking beside the sea. "It was

morning; the sky a light blue; the foam-flecked waves were greenish in the sunshine." He became aware that he was dreaming, and when he felt the pull back to the body he exerted his will to continue in the dream. "A battle ensued; now my bedroom became clearly visible and the shore-line brighter." The pain in his head became increasingly intense and he fought against it, resolutely willing to remain in the dream world. Then suddenly the pain ceased, something seemed to go click in his brain, and he felt delightfully free. He continued his walk, "reveling in the beauty of the morning. . . . It seemed to me that the apparently solid shore and sunlit waves were not the physical land and sea; that my body was lying in bed, half a mile away at Forest View; but I could not feel the *truth* of this. I seemed to be completely severed from that physical body. At this point I became aware of a man and boy approaching. As they passed me they were talking together; they did not seem to see me, but I was not quite sure. A little later, however, when I met another man and asked him the time, he took no notice and was evidently unaware of my presence."

He began to get worried. When he willed to end the dream and wake up nothing happened. He didn't know how much time had elapsed in the physical world. He wondered whether he was dead, and then began to worry lest, if he were alive, he should be prematurely buried. He desperately willed to get back to the physical, but the shore-scene remained vividly before him. He tried to hold down a mounting feeling of panic. He willed and willed, and suddenly something seemed to snap, he felt another click in his brain, and he found that he was awake and in his bedroom—but he was completely paralyzed. After some time he managed to move a little finger, then other fingers, then his hand, and at last he emerged with relief from his state of catalepsy.

The Pineal Door

Fox attributed the click in the head to the passage of the astral body through what he called the "pineal door." He later found that he could go into a trance state and induce projection by concentrating on the pineal gland and willing to ascend through it. He imagined the process as one of gathering up and compressing the "incorporeal self," rushing it to a point in the pineal gland, and hurling it against a kind of trap door that would briefly be forced open and then click shut after the astral body had passed through. He stressed, however, that though this was what he felt happened in projection, his readers were at liberty to take it as a figurative description.

Fox tended to experience more adventurous and far-flung projections than Muldoon. Once he found himself in an oriental city and saw street bazaars and a huge black sculptured elephant in a kneeling position. On another terrifying occasion he was bound, bleeding and naked, to an X-shaped framework and saw robed figures moving about in the dimness. He roamed through an astral counterpart of London where among all the familiar features there were buildings and monuments that he did not recognize and thought must belong to the past or future of the city. Sometimes he practiced *skrying*, which he described as "like gliding, but in a vertical direction," or as "rising through the planes."

The idea of the existence of several planes or dimensions of the astral world was central in the conceptual scheme of Yram, a mysterious French contemporary of Fox, whose true identity remains unknown. The English version of his book was published in 1900 under the title *Practical Astral Projection*. Yram believed that humans have not merely two but several bodies, and that "as the conscious will penetrates into new dimensions it uses a corresponding body." The bodies were of different degrees of density, and Yram sometimes experienced difficulty in passing through walls when he was "using a double of too material a quality." At other times he could pass through them as if they were not there at all because, he said, he had "exteriorized a less material double." His travels were as dramatic as Fox's, and they took him to several parts of the material world as well as through the several planes of the astral. On the lower planes he sometimes was attacked by "rather unpleasant entities," and once he was hardly out of his body when he "received a terrific slap in the face without being able to find whence it came."

Higher Planes

To compensate for such unpleasant experiences, Yram sometimes projected to higher spiritual planes where the beings he met and the visions he had were of great beauty and religious intensity. On one stratum he would meet and chat with deceased friends. Explaining this he wrote: "In order to appreciate this properly you must remember that I am not telling you a dream, not a vision, I am telling you of a real fact, a conscious act accomplished with an absolutely clear mind, with perfect freedom, and without any trace of sleep. You are there near your friends, talking affectionately, fully conscious of your double state, which you can terminate immediately whenever you wish. As all your psychical elements are active, a thought is all that is needed to bring you straight back to your body with a lucidity equal to that of any moment of the day."

Yram's writing style tends to be as ethereal and lacking substance as his double, and of all the virtuosi of astral projection, his approach is the least critical and scientific. His narrative would not convince any skeptic that his experiences were anything more than vivid dreams or nightmares, though anyone familiar with the literature of projection will recognize in it elements that suggest that at least some of his OOBEs were authentic. At the opposite extreme is Robert Monroe who, as a result of having had many OOBEs, established a Mind Research Institute in Virginia. His book is the most level-headed and analytical of all experients' records.

Monroe recalls two out-of-body experiences from his childhood, one of which involved an apparent projection 30 years into the future and a foresight of television before it was invented. But it was not until much later in life that he began to have OOBEs regularly. It started alarmingly. On several occasions when he lay down he suffered a severe and inexplicable abdominal cramp. Then his entire body began vibrating. The condition lasted for some time, then ceased abruptly. Monroe consulted a physician and a psychologist, but neither could offer any explanation of the experience. He got accustomed to simply waiting patiently for the pain and the vibrations to pass. One evening as the pain occurred, he happened to let his arm fall loosely over the side of the bed. His fingers were resting on the bedside rug, but when he moved them slightly they seemed to pass through the rug to the floor beneath, and when he pushed they seemed to penetrate the floor as well. Curious, he pushed deeper until his entire arm was through the floor and his hand through the ceiling of the room below. He was sure that he was fully awake, and made careful mental notes of the familiar features of his room and the moonlit landscape through the window, but the sensation persisted. His fingers splashed about in a pool of water. When the vibrations began to abate he snatched his arm back onto the bed for fear that the floor might close and sever it.

Some four weeks after this incident, Monroe again experienced the vibrations, and while he was waiting for them to pass he "just happened to think how nice it would be to take a glider up and fly the next afternoon." Soon after this he felt something pressing against his shoulder and back, and thought at first that he had fallen out of bed and was leaning against a wall. Then he realized that it was not the wall but the ceiling. He was floating against it like a balloon, and down below he could see his wife in bed with someone. When he looked closer and saw that the other person was himself, his first thought was that he had died, but when in a panic he tried to get back into his physical body, he found that he had no difficulty in doing so.

This experience started Monroe on a long program of research. In his book he reports several experiments undertaken with the cooperation of other people in which he projected his second body to a distant location and returned with correct information about what those people were doing at the time. Once he projected to visit a woman friend who was on vacation somewhere on the New Jersey coast. He didn't know exactly where she was, and she was not aware that he was going to attempt an experiment. About three o'clock on a Saturday afternoon he lay down and employed one of the techniques he had developed to separate his second body, at the same time willing it to visit his friend wherever she was. He saw a scene in what appeared to be a kitchen. His friend and two teenage girls were sitting there chatting. They held glasses in their hands. He remained a while, and then decided to try something he had never attempted before. He went over to the woman and pinched her just below her ribcage. He was somewhat surprised when she let out a loud "Ow!" Well, he thought, he had given her something to remember the occasion by, and he waited impatiently for Monday, when they would meet again at work. Asked what she had been doing between three and four on Saturday, the woman answered after some thought that she had been sitting in the kitchen of a beach cottage with her niece and her niece's friend. They had been doing nothing in particular, she said, mostly talking and drinking cola. Monroe had to prompt her to remember the pinch, but when he mentioned it she asked in amazement, "Was that you?" She showed him two bruise marks on her side at exactly the spot where he had pinched her.

Monroe's Locales

Monroe does not use the term "astral" when he writes about his OOBEs, but he firmly believes he has visited different planes of reality that he calls "Locales I, II, and III." Locale I is the here-and-now physical world. Locale II is a "thought world" and is "the *natural* environment of the Second Body." Locale III, Monroe writes, "seems to interpenetrate our physical world, yet spans limitless reaches beyond comprehension." In it "reality is composed of deepest desires and most frantic fears. Thought is action . . . it is the well-spring of existence . . . the vital creative force that produces energy, assembles 'matter' into form, and provides channels of perception and communication." What we call heaven and hell are located in Locale II, which is inhabited by various entities and creatures that are really "thought forms." Monroe states that on visits to Locale II he has met the dead, and he believes that "human personality survives the transition of death and continues in Locale II." Locale III is a physical and material world weirdly like, but at the same time in many details unlike, the world we know. There is a natural environment similar to the Earth's. There are people, cities, roads, businesses, all the signs of a civilization. But it is a civilization based on different technologies and with different customs. There are no electrical devices, no signs of the use of oil or the principle of internal combustion as power sources. Scientific development is apparently less advanced than on Earth, but Locale III cannot be a period of our past history because our science was never at the Locale III stage. On visits there, Monroe has inhabited a different body and lived a different life from his earthly one.

When Monroe writes about his experiences in Locale III he strains his readers' credulity to the utmost. It is interesting, though, and perhaps relevant to note that since 1971 when his book was first published, theoretical physicists working in the field of advanced quantum mechanics have come up with the hypothesis that there exist multiple Universes, all basically

269

similar but with slight differences, and that "transition events"—which could take the form of OOBEs—between these Universes can and do occur. In fact, in the light of these recent developments in theoretical physics, even the convinced skeptic should hesitate before dismissing accounts of astral projection as nothing more than mere fantasy.

23. The Evidence for Reincarnation

In 1962 Professor Ian Stevenson met a young Lebanese who told him that in his home village of Kornayel there were several children who remembered previous incarnations. He gave Stevenson a letter of introduction to his brother. Two years later Stevenson had an opportunity to visit Lebanon and follow up his interest in reincarnation. He was able to investigate personally the curious case of Imad Elawar, and he tells the fascinating story in an article entitled "Twenty Cases Suggestive of Reincarnation," published in 1966. Imad was born in Kornayel in 1958. As soon as he began to talk, he repeatedly mentioned the names "Jamile" and "Mahmoud," although no members of his family had such names. He also talked about Khriby, a village some 30 kilometers from Kornayel across the mountains. One day when he was two years old, he was out for a walk with his grandmother. Suddenly he rushed up to a stranger in the street and hugged him. The bewildered man asked, "Do you know me?" and little Imad answered, "Yes, you were my neighbor." It turned out that the stranger was from Khriby.

Though the Elawar family belonged to an Islamic sect that believes in reincarnation, Imad's father did not like the suggestion that his son was a reincarnate. He became angry when Imad talked about his previous life in Khriby and said he belonged to the Bouhamzy family. So the boy suppressed such talk in his father's presence, but continued to tell his mother and grandparents about his memories. He talked a great deal about the beauty of Jamile. He mentioned an accident in which a man had had both his legs crushed beneath the wheels of a truck, and had died soon afterward. He remembered the accident very vividly, he

271

said, but he had not been the man who was killed. This statement was puzzling, because as Imad grew older he repeatedly expressed delight in the fact that he was able to walk. He also repeatedly begged his parents to take him to Khriby, but his father refused.

When Professor Stevenson arrived in Kornayel, Imad was just over five years old, and had been describing memories of his former life for the past three years. He had never left the village. Stevenson collected all the facts he could. He talked to members of Imad's family and to Imad himself. Among other information, the boy gave him a detailed description of the house he had lived in in Khriby. Stevenson then traveled the rough mountain road to Khriby to check the information he had received.

He soon learned that Bouhamzy was the name of a local family, and that in 1943 Said Bouhamzy had been run over by a truck, had both his legs crushed, and had died after an unsuccessful operation. He was shown the house where Said had lived, but it did not correspond with Imad's description of his former home, nor did the facts he managed to learn about Said's life match Imad's memories of his previous existence.

Stevenson continued his investigations, however, and discovered that Said had had a cousin and close friend named Ibrahim Bouhamzy. Ibrahim had scandalized the village by openly living with his mistress, the beautiful young Jamile. His happiness had been short, though. In 1949 at the age of 25, he had died of tuberculosis. He had spent the last six months of his life bedridden and unable to walk, which had distressed him greatly. Like his cousin Said, Ibrahim had been a truck driver. He had himself been involved in a couple of accidents, and he had never gotten over Said's death. Mahmoud was the name of an uncle of Ibrahim.

On his first visit to Khriby, Stevenson was also able to confirm that the house Ibrahim had lived in matched Imad's description, and that the man who lived in the neighboring house was the person Imad had embraced on the street in Kornayel three years before. In all, Stevenson on this visit confirmed that out of 47 facts Imad had given him about his previous life, a total of 44 matched exactly with facts about the life of Ibrahim Bouhamzy.

He returned to Kornayel and persuaded Imad's father to let him take the boy to Khriby. The three of them went, and during the drive Imad produced seven correct statements about the route, which he had never traveled before. In Khriby, Imad produced a further 16 facts about Ibrahim's life and his home, and Stevenson was able to confirm 14 of these as completely correct. Ibrahim's house had been locked up for several years and was opened especially for their visit, so Stevenson was able to check immediately statements that Imad made about its furnishings. In his former life as Ibrahim, the boy said, he had owned two rifles, one of them double-barreled. This proved to be correct, and when they entered the house he was able to go directly to a place where Ibrahim had hidden one of the rifles.

1000 Suggestive Cases

Stevenson has collected reports of over 1000 cases that are, as he cautiously puts it, "suggestive of reincarnation." The Imad Elawar case is one of the strongest, not just because of the quantity of corroborative evidence, but also because of the circumstances in which the evidence was obtained. Stevenson stumbled upon the case by a lucky chance. He arrived in Kornayel unannounced and began his investigation immediately, so there could be no question of fraud or deception because such an elaborate hoax would have taken some time to set up. Nor could there be any question of misconstruing and subsequently distorting the child's information to match the verification, consciously or unconsciously. In this case Stevenson collected the facts at first hand and not by hearsay, and wrote them down before attempting verification.

There seems to be no doubt that, for whatever reason, the mind of the child Imad Elawar contained memories and impressions that corresponded with experiences in the life of the dead Ibrahim Bouhamzy. Whether this suggests that Imad was a reincarnation of Bouhamzy is, of course, another question.

Belief in reincarnation is fundamental in the Hindu and Buddhist religions, so it is not surprising that some of the classic cases on record come from India. In 1961 and again in 1964 Stevenson visited the village of Rasulpur in Uttar Pradesh, India, to interview people and collect facts that might corroborate an apparent reincarnation case that had been brought to his attention. In 1954 a child of the village, Jasbir Jat, had fallen ill with smallpox at the age of three and a half, and had apparently died. Preparations for burial were made, but the child began to show faint signs of life. Some weeks passed before he was fully recovered, and when he was able to express himself clearly again, Jasbir spoke and behaved in a manner that distressed his family. He insisted that his name was Sobha Ram and that he was the son of a Brahmin, Shankar Lil Tyagi, of the village of Vehedi, which is about 20 miles from Rasulpur. He introduced into his speech sophisticated words characteristic of the Brahmin caste, and he refused to eat his family's food. Fortunately, a Brahmin woman heard about him and volunteered to cook Brahmin food for him.

This situation continued for several years. Communication between the villages of Rasulpur and Vehedi were virtually nonexistent. In 1957, however, a Vehedi woman who had been born in Rasulpur paid a visit to her home village. She had not been back since 1952, when Jasbir was only 18 months old, but he recognized her. From others she learned the story of his strange claim and behavior, which she repeated to her own family when she returned to Vehedi. When the family of the late Sobha Ram Tyagi heard about it, they paid a visit to Rasulpur to meet Jasbir. The child greeted them all by name, showing that he knew the relationship of each to Sobha Ram and many facts about their life in Vehedi. He also gave an exact account of how Sobha Ram had died, which was as a result of a fall from a carriage during a marriage procession. After the visit, Jasbir was allowed to go to Vehedi several times and stay with the Tyagi family. He was much happier than in Rasulpur, and showed intimate familiarity with the family life and past history.

When Stevenson investigated this case he did not have the good fortune he had had in the Imad Elawar case of being present when the verifications took place. But by visiting the two villages and talking to the people involved he compiled a list of 39 facts about Sobha Ram's life that Jasbir had mentioned before he paid his first visit to Vehedi. Of these, 38 could be corroborated. The one that could not be verified was the most intriguing of all. Jasbir stated that Sobha Ram's fatal fall had been caused because he had been poisoned, and he even named the murderer. There was no way of proving this, but Stevenson discovered that the Tyagi family had suspected that Sobha Ram had been murdered. Furthermore, he found that the time of Sobha Ram's death had coincided with the time of Jasbir's smallpox illness, during which he too had almost died.

274

Violent Ends

In a significant number of apparent reincarnation cases the previous life ended violently or prematurely. Believers maintain that this does not mean that only those that meet violent deaths are reincarnated, but simply that those who die a natural death, particularly in old age, do not carry over distinct memories from one life to another. Violent death, it seems, can leave strong impressions not only on the soul, but also in some cases on the physical body. Several researchers have noted birthmarks in alleged reincarnates situated where fatal wounds were apparently sustained in the previous life.

Guy Playfair quotes such a case in his book *The Flying Cow*. It is from the records of the Brazilian Institute for Psycho-Biophysical Research and concerns a woman named Tina. She was born in the town of Araraquara, 175 miles from São Paulo, and still works there as a lawyer with a public utility company. Tina is an unusual reincarnate in that as an adult today she clearly remembers incidents from her previous life. Normally such memories fade in childhood.

Tina remembers that she lived in France and that her name was Alex Amadado Barralouf. Her father's name was Jean Paris and her mother's Angala. She believes that she came from the town of Vichy, and remembers shopping with her mother, a tall, blonde, well-dressed woman. When she was two and a half years old she recalls being taken to Le Havre and seeing the ships tied up on the quay. She learned French easily and has a strong sense of identification with France. She detests everything German because she believes she had been shot and killed by a German soldier during World War II. On the front and back of her left side are two marks that she has had from birth. They correspond with the positions that would have been marked if a bullet aimed at her heart had gone in and out.

Family anecdotes such as this one cannot be regarded as providing the same kind of evidence as Professor Stevenson's scrupulously objective investigations. But they are common in parts of the world where reincarnation is widely believed in, and they give an interesting insight into the belief.

Although belief in reincarnation is far less frequently found in the contemporary Western world, most people at some time have had a strange type of experience that is sometimes explained by the idea of reincarnation. This experience is generally known by the French term *déjà vu* which means "already seen." It refers to those instances in which a person has a strong feeling of having been in a place or a situation before. Various psychological explanations have been put forward to account for this. It has been suggested that the experience is a hallucination, or that it is an evocation of a memory that seemed to have been completely forgotten. Physiological explanations have also been advocated. One is that the brain receives two visual signals from the retina within a split second of each other, and that the so-called memory is implanted by the first of these two signals.

Although such explanations may be relevant to many ephemeral and rather vague sensations of *déjà vu*, they do not explain cases in which detailed knowledge, which could not have been acquired by normal means, is possessed. An example is if a person visiting a place for the first time can correctly describe present or former features of the town or landscape before actually seeing them.

Jacobson's Patient

Nils Jacobson, a Swedish psychiatrist, cites the following case in his book *Life Without Death?*, published in English in 1974. A patient had from time to time experienced throughout his adult life a kind of trance vision in which he was a World War I soldier who met his death in Flanders. The experience was always preceded by a sensation of profound depression and dullness, and began with an OOBE. He felt himself leave his body and glide out "into a milky-white, dense mist where everything was deathly silent." Then he was on a crowded railroad station with a lot of soldiers amid great scenes of emotion and distress as relatives said goodbye to the men embarking for the front. When he was aboard the train he hung out of the window, clasping the hands of a pretty young woman who gazed desperately into his eyes and whispered repeatedly, "Marcel, o mon Marcel," to which he replied, "Catherine, ma Cathy. . . ." Then the train pulled away and he experienced a long clattering journey through the dark. Finally the train arrived at a destination that he learned was near Arras. With hordes of other soldiers he disembarked and trudged through rain and mud to an encampment near the front line.

276

Time passed—he couldn't tell how long—and a day came when it was the turn of his company to attempt to take a village by storm on a height in front of them. He wormed his way with other soldiers along the trough of a deep ravine at the bottom of which a stream flowed. This afforded the only protected approach to the village. They finally arrived at the point from which the attack was to be launched, and at a given signal he went over the top and ran toward the village, which he saw clearly in front of him. He was suddenly stopped by a powerful blow and burning pain in his chest, and everything went blank.

Jacobson's patient had experienced this harrowing vision several times before 1966 when, during a journey, he found himself near Arras. He decided to take the opportunity to discover whether the vision had any foundation in reality. He drove into and around the town, but everything was unfamiliar. Then he came to a crossroads and saw a signpost with the name "Bapaume," and his heart rose in his throat. About three miles down that road he began to recognize features, and when they arrived at the village his recall became crystal clear. He was able to take his family through the maze of narrow streets to a field. There he pointed out the winding ravine from which rose steep slopes toward another village beyond, the place where in his vision he had died. When they went to this village he was disappointed to find it unfamiliar. Neither the church nor the buildings were as in his vision. But his son, by chatting to an elderly inhabitant, learned that the village had been completely destroyed during violent fighting between French and German forces in November 1914, and that the church and the buildings around it had been rebuilt in the 1930s.

Déjà Vu?

This case is interesting not only because the subject had told others about his vision before some of its details were confirmed, but also because others were present at the time of verification. *Déjà vu* is not normally preceded by a visionary experience that the person consciously remembers, and cases in which paranormally obtained knowledge is communicated to another before the event are rare. This may partly be, however, because people are reluctant to communicate such apparently baseless information for fear of being proved wrong and thought foolish.

A 26-year-old German woman recorded a strange *déjà vu* experience in 1967. Her husband became impatient with her when, during a journey by car through a part of Germany which neither had previously visited, she suddenly exclaimed that she knew the area because she had lived there before. Although he knew that it was the first time she had been in that part of the country, she insisted that it was familiar to her. She pointed out a house where, she said, she had lived with her parents and two brothers in a previous life when her name had been Maria D. They stopped at a village tavern and she immediately recognized the proprietor as someone who, when much younger, had served her family. This finally made her husband wonder whether her talk had been more than mere fantasy, and he casually inquired of the old man about the "D. family." The parents, the older son, and the daughter were all dead, he told them sadly, and the death of "poor little Maria" had been most tragic. She had been savagely kicked to death by a horse in a stable. This information awakened what seemed like vivid and terrifying memories in the wife, who broke down and cried as she recalled the details of her previous death.

All the cases we have looked at are, in Stevenson's phrase, "suggestive of reincarnation." But there may be other explanations. The first that springs to mind is that they are all due to fraud or some sort of delusion. However, there are too many anecdotes and too many carefully investigated cases on record for this easy solution to be acceptable. The only other explanation that seems at all tenable is that the alleged memories of former lives are acquired by extrasensory perception.

Modern parapsychological research has established fairly conclusively that telepathy, clairvoyance, and precognition do take place, particularly in heightened states of consciousness. It is theoretically possible that information in the mind of any living person may be paranormally acquired by another, or that past, present, or future events or scenes can be clairvoyantly experienced. But the conditions that normally facilitate ESP, such as the existence of a bond between sender and receiver, or circumstances of crisis, or the development of a general psychic faculty, are not to be found in the experiences described in this chapter. None of the subjects had any connection with or prior knowledge of the deceased, and none of them showed any ability to acquire information paranormally about any other facts except those about their former life experience. Imad and Jasbir had no knowledge of events in Khriby and Vehedi after the deaths of Ibrahim and Sobha Ram, and the knowledge that they possessed had a continuity and coherence that suggests the functioning of memory rather than ESP. ESP tends to supply fragmentary and discontinuous information, and to mix information received from the external source with contents of the consciousness of the receiver. The ESP hypothesis is also inadequate to explain the existence of, for example, birthmarks on the skin of an alleged reincarnate that correspond exactly with wounds received in an alleged previous life. Nor can it account for sustained creative work such as, for example, the extraordinary novels of Joan Grant.

The Novels of Joan Grant

Joan Grant was born in England in 1907, and as a child became aware that she possessed memories of previous lives in other centuries and other lands. Her claims were an embarassment to her family, and she did not fully develop her psychic gifts until adulthood, when a visit to Egypt brought a flood of intense and detailed memories of that land in ancient times. She wrote down the memories as they came to her, which made a great deal of fragmentary material. With the cooperation of her husband, a psychiatrist, she put the fragments into a novel that was published in 1937 under the title *Winged Pharaoh*. She had done no research before or while writing the book, which was presented as the story of the life of Sekeeta, the daughter of an Egyptian pharaoh who had lived 3000 years ago. When scholars, critics, and Egyptologists evaluated the novel, they unanimously praised the accuracy of its historical detail, though they were understandably dubious about Joan Grant's claim that her accuracy was due to the fact that she *was* Sekeeta. Other books followed, and in her autobiography, *Far Memory*, she wrote: "During the last 20 years, seven books of mine have been published as historical novels which to me are biographies of previous lives I have known." It is a seemingly outlandish claim, but to attempt to apply the ESP hypothesis to the Joan Grant case only produces the scarcely less fantastic explanation that she acquired her information by telepathically picking the minds of Egyptian scholars unknown to her, and focusing and sustaining her telepathic powers in a manner without precedent in ESP research.

When all the evidence has been examined, it seems that the ancient and widespread belief in reincarnation offers an explanation for many otherwise incomprehensible occurrences. Hindus and Buddhists, among others, believe that a single human lifetime is only one stage in the development of a soul, which has to return to Earth many times in many different bodies before it can attain perfection. They believe that a person's actions generate a force known as *karma*, which determines his destiny in the next existence. If the soul brings with it into life an accumulation of bad karma acquired through wrong action in a previous life, it will have to spend a lifetime expiating it in order to advance its process of growth. Such a belief accounts for the apparent injustices and inequalities of earthly life. It explains differences of personality and endowment, precocity in some children and special gifts in people of genius. And it serves, as no other philosophical or religious concept does, to reconcile man to his fate while at the same time encouraging him to change himself. It also may account for many of the strange memories described in this chapter. It is a belief that is surely worthy of more serious consideration than it has been given.

Part 4

24. Servants of Satan

The recent revival of witchcraft has not yet had time to affect the popular conception of a witch. Most people see the witch as the child-eating crone in Grimms' Fairy Tales (and in Walt Disney's treatments of them), or beak-nosed hags wearing conical hats and riding broomsticks, or the Weird Sisters in *Macbeth*. We picture the witch mostly as a female, casting spells on her enemies, stirring loathsome animal parts into a cauldron, and dancing on stormy mountain tops in the moonlight. Like most stereotypes this image is a complex blend of fact and fantasy. One misconception that can be disposed of immediately is that witches were invariably women—old, ugly, and misshapen women at that. Female witches always outnumbered the men, but at the height of the witchcraft persecutions in the first decades of the 17th century, vast numbers of men were also burned as witches. So were children, some as young as eight. Even before the Great Witch Panic men feature prominently in the recorded cases. In one of the earliest witch trials, held in the French Alps in 1436, Thomas Bègue confessed to conjuring up the demon Mermet by calling "Mermet diable!" three times. The demon appeared before him, first as a black cat and then as an old black man dressed in black with horns on his feet.

The reason why women predominate in the history of witchcraft is probably connected with their position in society. Because women were for so long thought to be inferior beings, they were considered to be more susceptible to foolishness and sin than men. Sixteenth-century writers felt that women would be more easily tempted by the Devil, and that Satan, as a male personification of evil, would prefer woman assistants. Certainly women were less able to protect themselves against accusations leveled at them by the entirely male and officially celibate Church and Inquisition. Even so, there were many male witches in the past, just as there are many male mediums today.

As for the broomsticks, the night flying, the eating of babies, and the worship of Satan, these are all details that emerged at the time of the great witch trials. By that time the stereotype of the witch had been fully formed from its different sources in folklore, in earlier trials for heresy, and in the ingenious minds of the prosecutors.

At the beginning of the Christian era beliefs about witches were less sharply defined. The distinction between *sorcerers* who directed their magical powers for their own benefit, and *witches* who only served the Devil's purposes, had not yet been established. Witches and sorcerers were both regarded as the Devil's emissaries, and the confusion between the two lasted for centuries. Most of the pre-Christian beliefs about sorcery were attributed to the enemy of the Christian God—the Devil, with his legions of fallen angels. In the same way, the pagan deities came to be identified with Satan and his demons among the early Christians. The biography of the 3rd-century Saint Martin of Tours records that "when Martin exorcised the demons, one would admit he was Jupiter, another Mercury . . ." It followed that continuing worship of the old Greek and Roman gods was equal to Devil worship.

Saint Augustine, the most influential of the early theologians, condemned amulets, horoscopes, and the practice of healing the sick by means of charms, all of which he considered to be achieved with the aid of demons.

Christian Legislation

Naturally the early Christian authorities legislated against such activities. Christian emperors who ruled over the crumbling ruins of the Roman Empire passed laws like that of Theodosius in 381, forbidding meetings and magical sacrifices in old temples. These laws reflected the confusion between witchcraft and remnants of the old Greco-Roman religion. In England in 690 Theodore, Archbishop of Canterbury, issued edicts against sacrificing to demons and casting spells. Throughout the newly founded kingdoms of Europe, similar laws opposed witchcraft.

The penalties were sometimes severe. When the two sons of

284

the Frankish Queen Fredegond died of dysentery in 580 she was persuaded that her stepson Clovis had asked the mother of his mistress to cast an evil spell on the two young princes. Fredegond ordered the woman to be tortured until she confessed. Clovis was then stabbed to death, and the woman was bound to a stake and burned alive. The savagery of these sentences was probably because the alleged crime was against royalty. Generally in 6th-century France, as in other parts of Europe, a witch who had killed by magic was merely required to pay a specified fine—though if the fine was not paid, the witch could be burned.

In its campaign to defeat the lingering beliefs of paganism, the Church even tried to discredit certain popular ideas about the powers of witches. Saint Boniface, the 8th-century English monk and missionary to Germany, preached that it was not true that a person could turn himself into a wolf, as witches were supposed to do. A century later Saint Agobard, Bishop of Lyons, declared it was not true that witches could call up storms and destroy harvests. Nor could they devour people from within nor kill them by the "evil eye." Most significant of all, in view of later developments, are the words of a 10th-century canon of Church law concerning the widespread belief that certain women—"a numberless multitude"—were in the habit of riding out on beasts in the dead of night and crossing many great lands before daybreak. According to the canon, any person who believed in night flying was "beyond doubt an infidel and a pagan." Only a few generations later any person who did *not* believe in night flying and witches as the Church defined them was in danger of being burned as a heretic.

What had happened in the intervening years to change the Church's attitude? First, the threat of heresy, which was undermining the Church's all-powerful position in society. Secondly, the Church had come to take a more careful look at the idea of magic, particularly as practiced by the richer and better educated members of society. Some practitioners of this ritual magic were to be found in the papal court itself. Scarcely had the French Pope John XXII been elected in 1317 than he arrested the elderly Bishop of Cahors and put him on trial for attempting to kill him by magic means. Under torture the bishop admitted his guilt. Though such confessions prove nothing, he was scourged, burned at the stake, and his ashes scattered in the Rhone River.

Few if any of the ritual magicians of this period worshiped Satan. In their search for wisdom, wealth, or power they believed they could command devils to serve them by invoking the name and power of God. They usually considered themselves devout Christians. But gradually the Church authorities came to the conclusion that magic performed by these means could occur only with Satan's permission. The practitioners must therefore somehow be in league with the Devil and in opposition to God and His Church. So the practice of magic and witchcraft came to be considered a heresy, and could be investigated and punished with the ruthlessness reserved for heretics.

The Heretics

Heresy can be defined as religious error persistently adhered to in the face of the truth as laid down by the Church. In the 13th century the Inquisition was established especially to combat heresy. To escape from the Inquisitors, the heretics of that time—mainly the Albigensians and Waldensians of southern France, neither of whom had any connection with witchcraft—took refuge in the mountainous valleys of the Pyrenees and the Alps. For the next 200 years the Inquisition directed its efforts to rooting them out of the mountains and executing them. Then in 1484 came the bull of Pope Innocent VIII that unequivocally defined witchcraft in all its aspects and practices as a heresy. The Inquisitors came down from the mountains with two centuries of experience behind them, and carried their techniques throughout Europe. The attack on witchcraft had begun.

We shall return to the Inquisition and its pursuit of heresies when we deal in detail with witch hunting and the witch trials. The main point at the moment is that it was consorting with the Devil that branded witches as heretics. A conscious and willing pact made with Satan was the principal means, the witch hunters believed, by which a person acquired a witch's powers. These pacts were not the written contracts signed in blood that feature in the legends of selling one's soul to the Devil in return for riches or power. The witches were not Satan's customers, but his servants. They were committing themselves, body and soul, before and after death, to the Devil's work. Their pacts were thought to take the form of a ceremonial entry into a kind of secret society devoted to evil.

The novice witch would be taken along to a Witches' Sabbat and there presented to the Devil, who was alleged to preside at these meetings. The ceremony of initiation varied from place to place but always included sacrilegious and obscene elements. One of the simplest ceremonies on record comes from the testimony of a young French girl given at her trial in 1594. When she was presented to the Devil by her lover, who was a witch, she was required merely to make the sign of the cross with her *left* hand. This entitled her to join in the orgiastic adoration of the Devil that followed.

A more complex ritual was described by a 17th-century Italian demonologist, Francesco-Maria Guazzo. He lists 11 separate stages as follows:

1. A spoken denial of the Christian faith.
2. Rebaptism in the Devil's name, after which the novice was given a new name in place of his Christian one.
3. Symbolic removal of the baptismal *chrism* (consecrated oil mixed with balm) by the Devil's touch.
4. Denial of godparents and the gaining of new sponsors.
5. The gift of a piece of clothing to the Devil as a token of submission.
6. An oath of allegiance made to the Devil while standing in a magic circle.
7. Inclusion of the initiate's name in the "Book of Death."
8. A promise to sacrifice children to the Devil.
9. A promise to pay an annual tribute to the Devil of black-colored gifts.
10. Marking the initiate with the Devil's mark—a strangely shaped area of the skin that became insensitive.
11. Various vows of special service to the Devil, including the destruction of holy relics and keeping the secrets of the Sabbat.

Sex played an essential part in all witch celebrations. The witch trials established that female witches regularly received the attentions of their Satanic master, as a reaffirmation of the evil bond between them. It was emphasized, however, that these attentions gave the witch no pleasure. In fact, they were said to be highly painful, the Devil's touch being of a "freezing cold-ness." By stressing the discomfort of these proceedings the prosecutors may have been trying to ensure that devil-worship did not get linked with sexual pleasure.

Incubi and Succubi

The Devil was also thought to empower certain of his demons to have sexual intercourse with witches, and the prosecutors were unable to deny that this sometimes brought pleasure. To a female witch the Devil would send a demon called an *incubus*, to a male witch a *succubus*. Some witches confessed that they had been visited by their demon lover regularly for years. It was generally believed that the same demon could act sometimes as incubus and sometimes as succubus, assuming human form as required.

Incubi and succubi sometimes visited people who were not witches in order, it was believed, to lead them into sexual sin and conscript their souls for the Devil. It was generally thought that the incubi outnumbered the succubi nine to one—probably because chastity was considered more important in women, though perhaps because women were thought to be more licentious than men. Usually a distinction was drawn between the witches who were willing partners of the demons, and the innocent who resisted and were raped. Rape could be hard to prove, however, and the alleged victims were often punished whether they submitted willingly or not—especially if the attacker was an incubus.

The idea of incubi and succubi arose from the highly charged erotic imaginations of the prosecutors and their victims. Sex is a perennial human obsession, but it was especially so in an age of repression like the Middle Ages. The witch hunters insisted that sexual malpractices be a main feature of an accused witch's confession, and were obsessively concerned to find out every detail of such activities.

The Devil's other way of gaining control of a human being was *demonic possession*. The Devil, or one of his demons, would enter a person's body without displacing the soul, and make the person speak and act as the evil spirit wished. The victim of a demonic possession was seldom held responsible for his or her actions while in this state. Nor was the victim held responsible in the rarer cases of *obsession*, in which the Devil and his agents harassed a person without entering the body. A case in point is that of Saint Anthony, who was terrifyingly and subtly tempted by devils in the desert.

Virtuous people were usually thought to be immune from demonic possession unless witchcraft was involved. A witch's evil spell was believed to force an entry for the demon, who would drive the victim to the most blasphemous and obscene speech and actions. This theory was used to account for the violent attacks of demonic possession that erupted in monasteries and convents where the inmates were presumed to live blameless lives.

When a demon took control, a certain pattern of behavior resulted. The victim's face and body would go into startling contortions. The expression would take on a fiendish look. The voice would become coarse and gruff, even in young girls. In this new voice the victim would often shriek invective against God in the foulest of language, or speak gibberish, or foam at the mouth. Other extraordinary things were reputed to happen. Victims would vomit quantities of strange objects—needles and pins, broken glass or pottery, hair, bark, and stones. They would also make animal noises and perform feats of superhuman strength.

All theses signs of possession have since been recognized as the symptoms of hysteria, including the compulsion to swallow stones and vomit them up. Among some religious sects all over the world, the effects of hypnotic oratory and chanting can send the individual into hysterical convulsions of ecstasy. It is hardly surprising, then, that hysterical possession was rife in the Middle Ages when priests preached constantly on the sternness of God, the certainty of hellfire, and the remorseless presence of the Devil at everyone's side. The persecution of the witches was itself a mass hysteria to which the entire population—prosecutors, accusers, and victims—succumbed.

Even so, widespread hysteria cannot be held solely responsible for the frequency of cases of possession. Often fraud was practiced and found out. Presumably it was just as often practiced successfully. People might pretend to be possessed if they felt they were in danger of being accused of witchcraft, because strange actions would not be held against them if they were seen to be in Satan's control. They might simulate possession so as to bring a charge of witchcraft against an enemy. Or they might do so merely in order to draw attention to themselves.

As far as nonfraudulent cases of possession are concerned, some authorities today, especially within organized religion, reject the "hysteria" explanation and continue to hold the Devil and his minions responsible. They point out that many cases of possession still occur today, and that the Church deals with such cases just as it did centuries ago—by exorcism. Others would argue that where exorcism succeeds, it does so in the same way that various forms of psychoanalysis and psychotherapy succeed. For certain individuals, religious exorcism seems to be the correct method of relieving mental disturbance. Accounts of dialogues between psychiatrists and schizophrenics, for example, show a marked similarity to dialogues between exorcists and the possessed. The point is, that what the Middle Ages called demonic possession still exists, but we call it hysteria or schizophrenia.

Just as witches were believed to lend the Devil a helping hand in cases of demonic possession, so their many other magical powers were used for the purposes of harming humanity, scorning God, and worshiping Satan. A witch could bring disease, insanity, accidents, or death upon anyone she wished. She could wreck marriages, and cause barrenness or stillbirths in women, impotence or sterility in men. Witches were also blamed for damage to a person's house or property. They were thought capable of injuring or killing cattle, and they could destroy crops by calling up mighty storms of rain or hail. The storms were produced by stirring or splashing water, if not in a pond, then in a small hole filled with water. Even the witch's own urine, stirred with a finger, would do.

Witches were also thought to kill babies, because the flesh of a baby was considered to possess supernatural power. It was the principal ingredient of "Devil's grease," the ointment that enabled witches to fly. Whether they used a broomstick or not, most authorities agreed that they could not leave the ground without first applying this magic unguent. The witch hunters were usually vague about the exact composition of the ointment, although it was said to include such noxious ingredients as toads, lizards, spiders, and poisonous herbs. The resulting mixture was supposed to be either black or a repulsive green in color. A similar ointment was thought to enable the witch to assume animal shape, the better to escape recognition while doing evil deeds.

The Dutch physician Johan Weyer, one of the few sane voices raised against the witch hunts in the 16th century, named several formulas for flying ointment. In addition to such ingredients as

bat's blood, baby's fat, and soot, these included aconite, belladonna, opium, and sometimes hashish. The effect of these drugs,
Weyer pointed out, was to induce hallucinations and vivid
dreams. Like some authorities today, he thought it possible that
under the influence of drugs witches merely imagined or dreamed
they had flown—and for that matter, that they had taken part in
a Sabbat. Even a few confirmed witch hunters subscribed to this
view—although they considered the dream as bad as the act.
The Dominican friar and Inquisitor Johannes Nider tells of a
peasant woman who offered to show a visiting Dominican how
she was able to fly. She climbed into a basket, rubbed her body
with an ointment, and fell into a stupor from which nothing
could rouse her. When at last she did awake, she assured the onlookers that she had been out flying. She could hardly be persuaded that she had remained in the basket the whole time.

Aconite produces excessive excitement, and belladonna causes
delirium. Rubbing such substances into the skin would, experts
say, be as effective as swallowing them. Norman Cohn, a British
professor, recently wrote a study of events leading up to the great
witch hunt. In this book, called *Europe's Inner Demons*, he refers
to the witches' use of these substances, and says that, "Some bold
spirits, notably in Germany, recently tried them out on themselves—and promptly experienced very much what the witches
are supposed to have experienced."

The Familiar

Of course, few of the witches' enemies would have accepted
this explanation—or if they did, would simply have claimed it all
was the Devil's work anyway. Some played down the idea of the
ointment in their theories of witches' flight, and played up the
idea of a demon who acted as beast of burden. Often this role
was thought to be part of the job of the witch's personal demon,
her *familiar*. Though as a demon the familiar was capable of
performing harmful magic itself, its primary function seems to
have been to focus and strengthen the witch's power.

Most witches had only one familiar—often a dog, a cat (not
necessarily black), or a rabbit, but sometimes a more unpre-
possessing creature like an insect or a toad. The stories of
familiars were most widespread in Britain, traditionally the land
of animal lovers and pet owners. It is unlikely that anyone har-

bored the more unpleasant animals as pets, but few poverty-stricken old women in 16th-century England would have been able to keep all spiders, beetles, or even toads out of their hovels. According to the tales, the familiar was rewarded for its work by food—ordinary food, or special tidbits, or most often some of the witch's blood sucked from her body. The place on the witch's body from which the familiar fed was known as the "witch's mark" (not to be confused with the "Devil's mark" of initiation). Both the mark and the presence of an animal, however small, were considered incontrovertible proof of witchery.

When a married witch went to a Sabbat, whether on a familiar, a cleft stick, a shovel, a broomstick, or unaided, she would previously have placed in her bed a stick that magically took on her form. In this way she deceived her husband into thinking she was still beside him. This done, the witch slipped out of the room through a keyhole or up the chimney, and was away.

At this point a word of warning is necessary. Almost all the information about witches comes from the witch trials, which offered evidence extracted by severe torture. The details concerning familiars, Sabbats, and the rest are therefore not "the truth about witchcraft." They are simply the truth about *what people believed* about witchcraft. The Inquisitors and witch hunters were firmly convinced that certain blasphemous horrors always formed part of a witch's activities. Any accused witch was tortured until she agreed to the whole story put to her. It seldom occurred to them that the accused might be innocent. It never crossed their minds that their own beliefs might be false.

The Witches' Sabbat

No witch trial was complete without a lascivious account of proceedings at a Witches' Sabbat. The word *Sabbat* is derived from the Sabbath of the Jews, who were the stereotypes for the enemies of Christ before the witches. In fact, the term first applied to a gathering of witches was *synagoga*, from synagogue. Sabbats could be held on any day of the week, although Thursdays and Fridays occur most often in the accounts. These were local Sabbats, for which a small group of witches from one neighborhood assembled. There were also large-scale Sabbats, held on certain days of the year and attended by witches from a far wider area. These large Sabbats were supposed to take place on the nights of four seasonal festivals: February 2, the winter festival of Candlemas; June 23, the spring festival of the Eve of Saint John the Baptist; August 1, the summer festival of Lammas Day; and December 21, the autumn festival of Saint Thomas.

Aside from these seasonal dates, two special nights would have been heavily marked on any witch's calendar: April 30, the eve of May Day, and October 31, All Hallows' Eve or Halloween. The night of April 30 was the Grand Sabbat known as *Walpurgis-nacht*, Walpurgis Night. It is so called because it is the eve of the feast day of the English Saint Walpurga, who accompanied Saint Boniface on his mission to Germany and died there in about 777.

The small Sabbats were held at some desolate spot such as the foot of a gallows or a forest clearing. But for the big festivals the witches flew to a faraway mountain peak like the Brocken in the Harz Mountains of Germany, or the top of the Puy-de-Dôme in Auvergne, France, or to the "delicate large meadow" in Sweden called the Blåkulla.

No special number of witches was required at a Sabbat. Some accounts describe village meetings where fewer than 10 attended. Others give enormous figures. Near Ferrara, according to a witch's confession in the mid-16th century, the congregation numbered 6000. The 17th-century French demonologist Pierre de Lancre spoke of Sabbats gathering "some 100,000 devotees of Satan."

This consideration of numbers leads us to the question of the *coven*, a term largely invented and popularized by Dr. Margaret Murray some 50 years ago. She held the view that witches always organized themselves in covens composed of 12 witches led by a devil, or a man disguised as a devil. The parody of Christ and the apostles is obvious.

Covens certainly exist in the 20th century. That is, people calling themselves witches band together in groups of 13. If these people call their groups covens, they are covens. But despite the evidence put forward by Dr. Murray, it is extremely doubtful that covens flourished at the time of the witch hunts. Dr. Murray herself admits that "there is only one trial in which the number 13 is specially mentioned," and that is as late as 1662 when the persecutions were virtually over. She draws the remainder of her evidence from only 18 other trials in which she has simply added up the number of accused and reached a figure of 13. However, the British writer Alex Keiller and others who have checked her sources have found that in many cases she had added up incorrectly. The British historian G. L. Kittredge has stated flatly: "There is not the slightest evidence that [witches] were ever organized at all," let alone in groups of 13.

Although we must reject the antiquity of the coven for lack of evidence, there is a vast amount of factual detail concerning the Sabbat. The imagination of the witch hunters was preoccupied to the point of obsession by the thought of the witches gathered together, their naked bodies greased with flying ointment and shining in the light of a fire or of black candles held in their hands.

Satan was supposed to preside in person at the greater Sabbats. At other times a lesser demon might take his place, or even an important witch masked as the Devil and acting as the Devil's deputy. Satan appeared as a huge black bearded man, or as a black goat with light shining from his horns, or sometimes as a gigantic toad. He sat on an ebony throne or stood on an altar around which his witches gathered.

Usually the Devil started the proceedings by reading a roll call. If any novice witches were present, they would be brought forward and initiated. Delinquent witches who had missed a Sabbat or performed insufficient curses were then punished, usually by a whipping. After this the entire company would line up to pay homage to the Devil. They presented him with gifts such as black cakes, black candles, or black fowls, and performed the ultimate act of abasement: kissing his buttocks. This was known as the *osculum infame*, the kiss of shame. It features in practically every account of the Sabbat.

When the homage was concluded, the witches proceeded to a banquet at which they gorged themselves gluttonously. In this instance also the Church authorities were anxious to avoid any suggestion that such devilish pleasures gave satisfaction. The food was always described as cold and disgusting, with the meat tasting of rotton wood and the wine like manure juice. No matter how much the witches ate they always stayed hungry. Salt, an essential ingredient of white magic, was invariably absent.

The feasting over, the witches began the dancing that formed the central feature of the Sabbat and led up to its climax. The witches were generally said to perform various kinds of ring dances around a central object, usually the Devil himself or a phallic pillar or maypole. They danced in a state of high excitement and moved *widdershins* or counterclockwise, a detail considered to be especially sinful. As an indication of how customs change, the ballroom dancing of today is danced widdershins. Indeed, the waltz derives from the *volta*, a dance associated with witches.

The Sabbat concluded with a frenzied and uninhibited sexual orgy. The Devil copulated with every man, woman, and child present. Then all the witches indulged in indiscriminate copulation with one another. In the confessions and the demonological treatises, no variety of sexual activity was excluded. Incest, sodomy, and bestiality feature in almost every account to satisfy the expectations of the witch hunters.

The crowing of the cock before dawn usually brought the Sabbat to an end, and the presumably exhausted witches returned to their houses till next time—or until they were caught, interrogated, dressed in the "uniform of a heretic," and burned at the stake.

25. The Black Mass

On January 4, 1679, the Police Commissioner of Paris, Nicolas de la Reynie, began an investigation that was to implicate many of the leading figures of France in the gravest scandal of Louis XIV's long reign. La Reynie discovered that members of the nobility were poisoning people on a colossal scale, usually in order to obtain inheritances or to remove an unwanted spouse. Members of the court were deeply involved with a sinister network of poison-pushers and Satanists, and persons in the intimate confidence of the king were regularly seeking the Devil's aid by sacrificing babies at Satanic Masses. The Satanic or Black Mass is a sacrilegious travesty of the Church's most sacred ritual. It developed partly from accounts of heretical practices that were said to take place at Witches' Sabbats, and partly from the special-purpose Masses that were a feature of the early Christian Church. Among the early Christians it was not uncommon for people to pay a priest to say a special Mass designed to secure the death of an enemy or to ensure financial or sexual success for the petitioner. During the witchcraft persecutions witches were frequently accused of indulging in all kinds of inversions or parodies of Christian ritual, and this led to the mistaken idea that the Black Mass was a regular feature of the Sabbat. In fact, only a very few confessions refer to the performance of such a ceremony, and the Black Mass did not really come into its own until after the witch frenzy was over. The term Black Mass first appears in English as late as 1896.

Nevertheless, because many modern newspapers and probably most of their readers continually confuse witchcraft with the Black Mass and Satanism, it might be helpful to clarify the essential differences between these activities. The Black Mass is a blasphemous and obscene perversion of the Mass indulged in ostensibly for the purpose of mocking God and worshiping Satan, although it may be celebrated in the hope of achieving some evil end. Witchcraft, as defined at the time of the persecutions, included Devil worship, but that rarely involved the performance of a full-scale Black Mass. Satanism is a later development, and is a complete reversal of orthodox Christianity. Satanists believe that the Devil stands for good and God represents evil, and the Black Mass is a central feature of their ritual.

The affair uncovered by Nicolas de la Reynie in 1679 is one of the few cases that link witchcraft with the Black Mass, insofar as several alleged witches were among the poison-pushers who had infiltrated Louis XIV's palace at Versailles.

The France of Louis XIV was a setting in which extremes of elegance coexisted with extremes of vice. Exquisitely dressed courtiers occupied themselves with the minutest niceties of etiquette and behavior, yet were capable of brutal cruelty to further their ambitions. Louis XIV, "the Sun King," was the center around which everything revolved. He was the golden fount of wealth and honors. To secure his continuing favor was the aim of everyone at court. Commissioner La Reynie brought into the light of day the seamy underside of that glittering world.

The Chambre Ardente

When several suppliers of poison named members of the court as their customers, the king appointed a special commission to continue the investigation and judge the accused. It was popularly called the *Chambre ardente*, or fiery chamber, because it met in a room hung with black drapes and lit by candles. The commission sat in secret and allowed no appeal. Many people were arrested, of whom Catherine Monvoisin was to become the most celebrated. Familiarly known as La Voisin, she was a successful fortune teller frequently consulted by the nobility, and an expert in numerous occult sciences including the craft of fashioning love-charms and death-charms. Two priests were arrested along with her, but their role in the drama was not immediately clear. La Reynie's immediate job was to find and arrest as many of the poison-pushers and their clients as he could.

By the end of the year several suppliers of poison had been

burned. A pretty young duchess had been banished for trying to kill her old and wealthy husband by means of a shirt soaked in arsenic. Other aristocrats had been imprisoned in the Bastille or fled the country. The king personally urged his commissioners "to penetrate as deeply as possible the abominable traffic in poisons; to do strict justice, without distinction of person, rank, or sex."

By the following October, however, the king had ordered certain evidence to be removed from the records. The sittings of the *Chambre ardente* had been suspended and the investigation reduced to the most private, though intense, inquiry by La Reynie and a single companion. The reason for this complete about-turn was the closeness of the scandal to the king. Of all the members of the court who had been clients of the fortune tellers and poison-pushers, none was more guilty than the woman who had been his own mistress for 12 years: Françoise Athénais de Rochechouart, Marquise de Montespan. She was more influential than the queen, and the most brilliant jewel of the Age of Louis XIV. The inquiry revealed the murderous methods by which she had achieved and retained her position.

The story begins 13 years earlier, in 1667. Madame de Montespan, then 25 years old, was a lady-in-waiting to the queen. The king was beginning to tire of his current mistress, Louise de la Vallière, and Madame de Montespan determined to take her place. She sought the help of La Voisin, who introduced her to the Abbé Mariette. She agreed to try the effect of a special kind of magic Mass that was reputed to further success in love. Known as the Mass of the Holy Spirit, it was a less extreme variation of the Black Mass.

The Mass was celebrated in a house in Paris. The Abbé in full vestments spoke the rite, invoking the Holy Spirit in a Latin hymn. Madame de Montespan knelt before him and recited incantations against her rival. "I ask for the affection of the king," she intoned, "that it may be continued, that the queen may be barren, that the king leave her bed and table for me, that I obtain from him all that I ask for myself and my relatives; that, beloved and respected by great nobles, I may be called to the councils of the king and know what passes there; and that the king may leave La Vallière and look no more upon her."

The rite was repeated in the Abbé's own church over the hearts of two doves, symbols of Venus, that were solemnly consecrated in the names of the king and Madame de Montespan. A third Mass, designed to procure the death of the rival, was made upon human bones.

These Masses seemed to bring the ambitious lady-in-waiting all she desired. The star of La Vallière paled, and Madame de Montespan became the ruling favorite. The king built her a chateau in the country, and showered her and her relatives with wealth and honors. In a court packed with schemers, however, Madame de Montespan could not afford to rest on her triumph. The fear of being superseded by a rival and the changing moods of the king sent her back again and again to La Voisin for supernatural aid. La Voisin's daughter Marguerite told the judges of the *Chambre ardente*, "Everytime that anything fresh happened to Madame de Montespan, or she feared some diminution in the favor of the king, she told my mother, so that she might provide a remedy; and my mother at once had recourse to priests whom she got to say Masses, and gave my mother powders to be given to the king."

Madame de Montespan's Love-charms

These powders were love-charms, composed according to the various formulas of sorcery and containing the dust of dried moles, bat's blood, the famous aphrodisiac *cantharides*—made of finely ground blister beetles, especially the Spanish fly—and sundry other noxious substances. The resulting mixture was placed under the chalice on the altar at a Black Mass and blessed by the priest at the moment of the consecration. Madame de Montespan sprinkled the powders into the king's food, and he swallowed them without realizing it.

On one occasion the king was overcome with remorse for his adultery, and Madame de Montespan was exiled from court. She immediately had recourse to the charms and Masses, and after a mere month in exile she was summoned back to the king's side. More dangerous than the king's occasional religious scruples, however, was the roving eye he sometimes cast upon the other beauties of the court. In 1672 Madame de Montespan returned to La Voisin, this time in need of stronger magic. She was passed from the Abbé Mariette to the more sinister hands of the Abbé Guibourg.

299

Guibourg claimed to be the illegitimate son of a nobleman. He was nearing 70, ugly, bloated, and disfigured by a fierce squint. His specialty was a truly Satanic version of the Black Mass.

To produce the desired effect, the Mass had to be celebrated three times in succession. Madame de Montespan and the Abbé Guibourg met for the first Mass at the secluded and deeply moated Chateau de Villebousin, between Paris and Orleans. In the chapel of the chateau Madame de Montespan disrobed and lay across the altar, holding a candle in each hand. Father Guibourg celebrated the Mass upon her naked body, placing the chalice upon her belly. At the moment of consecration he lifted up a small infant and stabbed it in the throat with a penknife, letting the blood pour into the chalice. He and Madame de Montespan then recited the following incantation, invoking two of the chief demons of hell: "Astaroth, Asmodeus, Princes of Affection, I conjure you to accept the sacrifice I present to you of this child for the things I àsk of you, which are that the affection of the king for me may be continued; and that, honored by the princes and princesses of the court, nothing be denied me of all that I shall ask the king."

The second Mass, also involving the sacrifice of a child, was held in a tumbledown hut in the countryside, and the third Mass was said in a house in Paris. It is hardly surprising that Madame de Montespan became convinced of the power of the princes of hell. Her murderous invocations of them were followed by the king's renewed devotion to her.

But crises continually recurred. In 1675 the Masses had to be said again; and La Voisin's daughter later described how she had helped her mother prepare a room in their house for the ceremony. She spread a mattress on seats with a stool at either end. The Abbé Guibourg came out of a sideroom wearing a white chasuble spotted with black fir cones. Madame de Montespan entered and lay down "stark naked on the mattress, with her head hanging down, supported by a pillow on an overturned chair, the legs too hanging over, a napkin on the belly, a cross on the napkin, and the chalice on the belly."

One grisly detail concerned the child to be sacrificed, which on this occasion was a prematurely born baby. When its throat was cut the blood would not flow, and Guibourg had to cut open the heart to obtain some clotted blood. Madame de Montespan took some of this blood back to the court to put in the king's food.

By 1679 Louis had tired of Madame de Montespan and took a new mistress, Mademoiselle de Fontanges. At that point, Madame de Montespan or one of her associates tried to murder the king and his new mistress by means of another series of Black Masses. The ceremonies failed to achieve the desired effect, and before any further attempts could be made La Reynie had begun making his arrests.

A Halt to the Enquiries

In view of the shocking revelations that followed, it is hardly surprising that the king abruptly halted the inquiries of the *Chambre ardente*. The splendid court that reflected his own inordinate self-love could not be exposed as a vicious and blasphemous sham. He confronted Madame de Montespan privately with her crimes, but his pride forbade him to disgrace her publicly. For 10 years he continued to visit her daily, to avoid scandal. What passed between them on these occasions will never be known.

La Reynie arrested 360 people, of whom 110 were tried and 36 burned or hanged. Several priests admitted celebrating Black Masses. On at least two occasions a woman present sacrificed her own newborn baby and the priest said Mass over the placenta. One priest publicly lay with a girl on the altar while celebrating a Mass of the Holy Spirit. Frightful though these offenses were, it was impossible to put many of the people concerned on trial for fear that their evidence would implicate Madame de Montespan. The only solution was to keep them in prison without trial. This fate was suffered by 150 people who were kept in strict isolation from all other prisoners until their deaths. The last of them died in 1724, forty years after the investigation had closed. The king himself burned the documents of the case, and it is only because La Reynie's notes survived that we have any record of the most genuine, and influential, Black Masses ever known to have taken place.

Perhaps some outbreak of this sort was inevitable. For centuries witches and heretics had been accused of sacrificing babies to the Devil—with little or no evidence that such crimes ever occurred. So when certain ruthless people genuinely wished to obtain the Devil's aid, it was almost natural they should do so according to the "rules" laid down by the witch hunters. Even Rossell Hope Robbins, that exploder of popular delusions, observes that the *Chambre ardente* affair "is probably the only witch trial based on some element of factual truth, rather than on the wild imaginings of young neurotics or the morbid logic of perverse witch judges and inquisitors."

In a case so full of fantastic incidents, perhaps the most significant is that the rituals of infanticide and appeals to hell were followed, at least for a number of years, by success. No doubt the love-charms compounded of aphrodisiacs also played their part; but recent theories concerning the power of thought—especially malevolent thought—suggest that concentrated thought pressure of the kind that would have been exerted during a Black Mass may have the power to affect the minds of others.

The Hell Fire Clubs

Since the 17th century the Black Mass has been periodically revived, often by people in sophisticated circles looking for a new thrill. This was true of the members of England's notorious Hell Fire Clubs. They were mostly young men who dabbled in Satanism, and who met to indulge in various obscene and blasphemous activities in order to entertain themselves. There were several Hell Fire Clubs throughout England, Ireland, and Scotland, but the principal one met at fashionable addresses in London in the 1720s. Thirty years later 12 wealthy young rakes formed themselves into a sacrilegious brotherhood of "monks," and met twice a month in the suitably refurbished chapter house of Medmenham Abbey on the upper reaches of the River Thames. Only seven of the 12 have ever been positively identified, but they include the scandalous son of an Archbishop of Canterbury and Sir Francis Dashwood, who rented the Abbey and became the first "abbot." Above the portal of the chapter house a quotation from Rabelais can still be read: *Fay ce que vouldras* (do what you wish). The walls were lined with salacious books bound as works of devotion, and the "monks" had a gallery of rare pornographic paintings. Master chefs prepared exotic dishes, and girls were brought from London especially to satisfy other appetites. At their meetings the "monks" sacrificed to Bacchus, the god of wine, and Venus, goddess of love, and presumably also to the Devil, though how serious they were about this worship it is hard to say. One of the "monks" is reputed to have released a baboon during a Black Mass.

In the latter half of the 19th century there was a renewal of interest in every branch of the occult. In France a defrocked priest, Joseph Antoine Boullan from Lyons, preached that the way to salvation lay through copulation, both with human beings and with angels and spirits of the dead. Knowingly or not, he was reviving the medieval idea of demon lovers, according to which the Devil sent to his female witches a demon called an *incubus* and to his male witches a *succubus*. Along with a nun who became his mistress, Boullan headed a Satanist group that specialized in exorcising demons from supposedly possessed nuns by the administration of consecrated Hosts mixed with excrement. He almost certainly celebrated a number of Black Masses in which he is said to have crucified small babies, the offspring of the group's sexual excesses. He is reputed to have sacrificed his own child at one Black Mass. His activities were first exposed by a rival magician, the Marquis Stanislas de Guaita, who is reputed to have celebrated a Black Mass against Boullan. Later Joris-Karl Huysmans, an occultist turned Christian, wrote a book titled *Là-bas*. In it he revealed details of a number of Satanist groups operating in France in the late 19th century, including that of Boullan. Huysmans describes one Black Mass in which the priest, wearing blood-red vestments embroidered with obscene symbols, chanted the Mass backward, defiled the Host, and called on the Devil to grant the congregation virility, glory, riches, and power. The acolytes were heavily made-up male prostitutes, and the Mass terminated in a sexual orgy. Huysmans' book caused a sensation, and undoubtedly inspired much subsequent occult fiction. Boullan, who is said to have forecast his imminent death in conversation with Huysmans, died two years after the publication of *Là-bas*, in 1893.

A Literary Creation

Because of the lack of a continuous tradition, the Black Mass is largely a literary creation in which Satanists of one period of revival reconstruct a ritual from the surviving records of a previous one. Black Masses vary immensely in different accounts, largely because some writers and practitioners stress the sacrilege and others the obscenity.

For example, different substances have been used in different places for the sacramental wafer, the Host. One mock ceremony elevated a slice of turnip stained black. Others used ordinary bread "consecrated" in the Devil's name. Still others went to the length of making their own wafers stamped with the name of Satan. Some Satanists preferred direct desecration. They would attend a real Mass, sometimes with alum in their mouths to prevent salivation, and retain the consecrated Host in their mouths. Later they used it for profanation in a Black Mass. The profanation might be accomplished by mixing the Host with urine or excrement, or tearing it to pieces with pincers. The reasoning behind this last practice is that if the Host is truly the body of Christ, it can be made to suffer pain.

The Black Masses celebrated in the first half of the 20th century were probably much as the American author W. B. Seabrook has described them. He witnessed ceremonies in New York, Paris, Lyons, and London, and in his accounts the basic pattern is clear. The ritual required an unfrocked or renegade priest, a consecrated Host, a prostitute, and a virgin. The virgin was stretched naked on the altar and a crucifix was placed upside down over her. Parts of the true Mass were repeated backward, with "evil" substituted for "good" and "Satan" for "God." The prostitute served as acolyte, assisting the priest. A goblet of wine was placed between the virgin's breasts or between her thighs, and some wine was spilled over her. The Host was debased, not elevated, and then defiled.

In versions from other sources, variations occur. Sometimes the Mass is held in a ruined church, sometimes in a cellar or an ordinary room. The virgin is a standard feature, but, as in the Black Mass described in the Marquis de Sade's *Justine*, she seldom stays unviolated. Various parodies of holy water are used, and various nauseous mixtures replace the wine in Seabrook's account. The celebrant may be clothed in a black cope with no cross woven in it. The sign of the cross is made but with the left hand, or on the ground with the left foot. The variations within the ceremony are infinite and depend on how far the participants are willing to go, the extremity of their hatred for Christianity, and the intensity of their erotic imaginations.

When interest again turned to the occult in the 1960s, Satanism and the Black Mass began to flourish as never before. In Western

Europe and notably in the United States, Satanist groups are now well established. Anton La Vey's Church of Satan, founded in San Francisco in 1966, is the most widely known of these. It claims members in Europe and Australia as well as many thousands in the United States. La Vey's book *The Satanic Bible* became a best seller on many college campuses.

La Vey tries to look like Satan, but the majority of his followers are indistinguishable from fellow members of society. For instance, two important members of the Church of Satan in Louisville, Kentucky, are a young married couple, he with the rank of "bishop," she a "priestess." They have two children, a boy and a girl. They both have bachelor-of-arts degrees, he in political science, she in nursing. "My husband and I look like Mr. and Mrs. America," she says. In the ranch-style home of this Mr. and Mrs. America the basement has become the ritual chamber where the Louisville "grotto" (congregation) of Satanists meets to call upon the power of the Devil.

They celebrate a Satanic Mass, during which a naked woman is placed upon the altar to represent the Earth Mother. Ritual items include candles, incense, a bell, a chalice, a sword symbolizing power, and a phallic symbol "representing generation, virility, and aggression." According to the "bishop," "Anyone who is a Satanist has no doubts about his virility." His wife adds that they have toned down the early excesses of blasphemy and sexual activity. The blasphemy is limited to stamping on a sesame seed wafer symbolizing the Host. "The Mass used to be very dirty, very lewd," she says. "Now it's just a way one can release inhibitions."

A newly enrolled member wears a red baphomet, a symbol associated with Satan, a five-pointed, star-shaped figure drawn on a red disk and worn on a chain around the neck. Ninety percent of the Church's membership belong to this first degree. If a member demonstrates proficiency in Satanism he or she can take an examination and be elevated to the second degree—warlock for men, witch for women. The third degree is the priesthood of Mendes, named for a city in ancient Egypt where a sacred ram, or some say a he-goat, was worshiped. At the fourth level a member can become either *magister caverni*, *magister templi*, or *magister magis*—ranks roughly equivalent to bishop, archbishop, and cardinal. The fifth degree has been

305

achieved only by La Vey and is that of *magister satanis* or satanic master.

The essential beliefs of the modern Satanist are difficult to establish. One of the aims of the Church of Satan is to re-establish Satan as a divinity worthy of worship; but the reasons for turning to him rather than away from him are not wholly convincing. According to *The Satanic Bible*:

"Satan represents kindness to those who deserve it, instead of love wasted on ingrates!

"Satan represents vengeance, instead of turning the other cheek!

"Satan represents vital existence, instead of spiritual pipe dreams!

"Satan represents all of the so-called sins, as they all lead to physical, mental, or emotional gratification!"

Such theories have understandably been called "the echo of Nazism," and have been linked with torture murders such as the Manson killings.

It is still too early to say whether the revival of Satanism is here to stay or just another passing cult. Unlike similar manifestations in the past, La Vey's version has a firmly imposed hierarchy and a fixed ritual, although this probably varies a little from place to place to accommodate the tastes of particular grottoes. Satanism is inevitably a reaction cult, deriving its impetus from its contempt for Christianity just as the character of Satan evolved as the antithesis of God. The life of such reaction cults, whether religious or political, is usually short if they offer nothing more than the spirit of opposition. What Satanism appears to satisfy is a wish to participate in an enthusiastic and erotic ritual. It also provides spiritual approval of material pleasures, as Christianity does not. It remains to be seen whether these satisfactions prove to be enough.

It is worth noting that modern Satanists actually perform most of what the medieval witch was only accused of doing. They may not go in for killing babies but they worship the Devil, include sexual activity in their ceremonies, have rituals for pronouncing curses on their enemies, and are internationally organized. They are therefore much closer to the Inquisitors' idea of a witch than any of the tens of thousands whom the Inquisition actually burned.

306

The frontispiece of Matthew Hopkins's *Discovery of Witches* (1647),
showing Hopkins himself and witches with their familiars. During the
16th and 17th centuries, the persecution of witches reached a level of
mass hysteria throughout Europe and America, engulfing prosecutors,
accusers and victims alike. (*Servants of Satan*)

An engraving of the Witches' Sabbat, illustrating all the practices an extravagant mind could conceive, including powers of flight *(top left)*, an incubus *(bottom left)*, a witch's cauldron *(centre)*, and a magic circle *(right)*. Large-scale sabbats took place on the nights of four seasonal festivals and the Grand Sabbat was held on 30 April, also known as *Walpurgisnacht. (Servants of Satan)*

The Cornish witch, Cait Sidh. Most contemporary witches conduct their ceremonies naked, or "sky-clad" as they call it, believing their power resides in their bodies and will be obstructed and dissipated if clothes are worn. *(White Witches)*

26. White Witches

In a basement room in London a male witch is initiating a girl of
20 into the local coven. When the ceremony began she was
wearing a loose robe. This has now been removed and the girl
stands naked within a nine-foot circle drawn on the floor with
chalk. Earlier in the ceremony the girl swore oaths of loyalty and
secrecy, and was ritually purified by the strokes of a scourge.
Now the air is heavy with the smell of burning incense. The witch
in charge of the initiation stands naked. So do the other witches,
male and female, who wait attentively outside the circle. They
have danced around it to raise power, and are now directing that
power upon the girl standing, rather nervously, in the circle. The
inducting witch kisses her feet, saying:
"Blessed be thy feet, which have led you here."
He kisses her knees:
"Blessed be thy knees, which will kneel at the sacred altar."
He kisses her abdomen:
"Blessed be thy womb, without which we would not be."
He kisses her breasts:
'Blessed be thy breasts, formed in beauty."
He kisses her mouth:
"Blessed be thy lips, which will utter the sacred names."
The girl will next be ritually washed with oil and wine, and in-
troduced to the eight "weapons" of the craft. These are the
black-handled knife known as the *athame*, the white-handled
knife, the censer, the sword, the cauldron, the scourge, the wand,
and the cord.
After she has been led around the circle and presented to the
other members of the coven, she will be entitled to join in the
closing ceremony, the ritual meal of cakes and wine eaten within

307

the circle. By then she will have become a witch.

Allowing for minor variations between different covens, this is the procedure followed throughout the Western world for the initiation of a white witch.

Strictly speaking, a white witch is a contradiction. If we hold to our definition of a witch as someone who worships Satan and performs evil in his service, to talk of a witch performing white— or good—magic is like talking of a friendly rattlesnake! However, since modern practitioners of the craft call themselves witches, that is the word we must use, remembering that its enlarged meaning embraces both good and evil. Present-day Satanists are also known as witches, albeit "black" witches, and the fact that they have their own definition of evil merely adds to the confusion. By far the most helpful distinction between the two kinds of modern witch is to be found in the object of their worship. The black witch or Satanist worships Şatan, the adversary of the Christian God. The deities of the white witch, on the other hand, are pre-Christian, because white witches claim to be the inheritors of a pagan tradition that antedates almost any known religion.

The Great Mother

Modern white witches worship the Great Mother, the Earth Mother. She is the symbol of fertility, and the oldest and most elemental of the ancient gods. In most cases the white witches also worship the Horned God, that malè deity written of by Margaret Murray: Dianus or Janus, god of the hunt. He is the primitive symbol of power, but not evil—much closer to the Greek god Pan than to Satan.

In pre-Christian times the cult of the Great Mother was found throughout the world, and her names were as innumerable as the aspects under which she was worshiped. The home of a modern witch is likely to contain figurines, images, and other representations of many of these aspects of the goddess: Rhea, the barebreasted snake-goddess of Crete; Isis of Egypt with her horned headdress; Babylonian Ishtar, "goddess of the morn and goddess of the evening;" Phrygian Cybele; Astarte, the goddess worshiped by the Phoenicians and the Canaanites; Diana, the ancient Italian moon goddess; Hecate, goddess of the earth and the underworld; and the Irish goddess Brigit who survives in

Christianity under the name of Saint Brigid. White witchcraft is able to draw on the legends of all these goddesses, seeing each as an aspect of the same truth.

The emergence of witchcraft in modern times cannot be precisely dated. Many scholars consider that the revival began about 1921 with the publication of Margaret Murray's influential book *The Witch-Cult in Western Europe*, which identified witchcraft as the survival of an ancient religion. But it was not until the early 1950s that the revival really took off. That was when Gerald Gardner published his version of Margaret Murray's views along with his own account of witchcraft rituals. Gardner maintained that he had been initiated into a coven in England's New Forest in 1946.

Although doubt has been cast on many of Gerald Gardner's statements about his introduction to witchcraft, there is independent evidence that a coven did exist in that part of England, an area rich in folklore and legend. The British writer and occultist Louis Umfraville Wilkinson claimed to have known members of a coven operating in the New Forest in the late 1930s. He described the group as an "amalgam of middle-class intellectuals with the local peasantry," and the ceremonies as a blend of folk tradition with a more sophisticated occultism.

Further evidence comes from Sybil Leek, now one of the most famous witches in the United States of America. In her book *Diary of a Witch*, she states that she was at one time the high priestess of a modern coven of witches in the New Forest area.

Aradia — Daughter of Lucifer

The story of the coven or covens named by Gardner, Wilkinson, and Leek remains unwritten, but the evidence suggests that the New Forest was probably the cradle of the white witchcraft revival. A book written by the American Charles G. Leland may have influenced the rituals of the New Forest witches. Leland was a folklore student interested in sorcery and the survival of pagan mythology. While staying in Florence in the 1880s he got to know an Italian witch named Maddalena. She told him that in Italy the religion of the witches was known as *la vecchia religione*, "the old religion." This religion was said to derive from Diana, the moon goddess. According to the Italian tradition, Diana fell in love with her brother Lucifer, and as a result of their union gave birth to a daughter named Aradia. Diana took pity on the poor and oppressed people of the earth— particularly the gypsies—and sent Aradia to help them and teach them the arts of witchcraft. In effect, Aradia became a Savior— and an alternative to her Christian rival.

The precise age of this tradition is not known but, except in the Alpine valleys of the north, witchcraft in Italy certainly developed in a manner unique to itself—probably because the social usefulness of the Italian witch, or *strega*, became well-established at an early date. As the Swiss historian Jacob Burckhardt observed, "the business of the *strega* was to provide for other people's pleasure." People of all classes sought her aid to help the course of a love affair, procure an abortion, or get rid of an unwanted lover. Especially in such urban areas as Rome and Naples, the world of the *strega* shaded into the world of the prostitute.

In 1899 Leland published his book *Aradia, or the Gospel of the Witches*. It contains lengthy rituals and detailed accounts of a variety of witchcraft ceremonies, but makes the point that, according to Maddalena, the prime purpose of "the old religion" was ritual magic. Membership was open to men and women, and certain rituals required nudity and sexual intercourse between the witches.

Most contemporary witches conduct their ceremonies naked, or "sky-clad," as they call it. According to Leland this was a sign that all were equal and free. Modern witches add that the wearing of clothes hinders their efforts to release and direct their power. They believe that this power resides in their own bodies, and will be obstructed and dissipated if clothes are worn. If the power is imagined as a current of psychic force akin to electricity, the clothing "earths" the current in some way. White witches believe that the religious ecstasy their rituals can produce enables them to raise their power and that, by acting together, they can strengthen and direct this power in order to achieve their beneficent ends.

White witches are traditionally organized in covens of 13, although in practice the number may vary from three or five to perhaps 25, made up of a leader and an equal number of men and women. In some covens the priestess is the dominant figure, as one would expect in a cult of the Great Mother. Others have a male leader, known as the magister. In her book *Witchcraft, the Sixth Sense* the British writer Justine Glass explains the apparent anomaly of a male leader as "a symbolism of the esoteric truth that the outer world is a world of illusion, a mirror reflection. A mirror always reflects opposites; what is seen on the external must be the opposite of the inner reality."

That quotation serves as a reminder that the rituals of witchcraft are designed to bring the worshiper to an increased state of understanding and unity with the mysteries of existence. Its practitioners stress the fact that the word witchcraft is derived from the Anglo-Saxon *wiccecraeft*, craft of the wise. In its search for wisdom, witchcraft merges into magical practices.

In fact, it is impossible to draw the line between present-day witchcraft and magic. Both can be seen as activities of an intense psychic character used to influence invisible forces in some way. The distinction between spells and charms on the one hand and elaborate ceremonies of ritual magic on the other is one of degree, not of kind.

Levels of Initiation

A witch who has achieved the first level of initiation has the opportunity and usually the desire to study for a higher level. Here is one version of the Great Oath a witch must take on initiation to the second level: "I swear upon my mother's womb and by my honor among men and my brothers and sisters of the art, that I will never reveal to any at all any of the secrets of the Art, except it be to a worthy person, properly prepared, in the center of a circle, such as I am now in. This I swear by my hopes of salvation, my past lives and my hope of future ones to come, and I devote myself to utter destruction if I break my solemn oath."

A third level exists, and the initiation to this may include a sex rite. Some covens say they consider this level unnecessary and do not use it. In those that do, according to Justine Glass, the rite "must be carried out only by two people who love one another." To misuse the rite is rated "a sin which could carry the death penalty in this world and oblivion in the next." From other accounts, however, it would seem that the word "love" is interpreted freely. In the heady, semitrance state that can develop at some ceremonies—particularly during the initiation rites— it is easy to understand how participants can feel transfigured by a general love for all present.

Covens assemble on a Saturday evening to celebrate the Sabbat. In addition to these weekly gatherings, most covens meet for eight other Sabbats during the year. The four lesser Sabbats are held on the days that mark the four seasonal changes, the Spring and Autumn Equinoxes and the Summer and Winter Solstices. The other four are the great Sabbats: All Hallows' Eve or Halloween (October 31), Candlemas (February 2), May Eve or Walpurgis Night (April 30), and Lammas (August 1). Ostensibly Christian festivals, all are pagan in origin.

All Hallows' Eve, the day preceding All Saints Day, was the last day of the Celtic year and an ancient festival of the dead. Candlemas owes its name to the Roman Catholic custom of blessing on that day all the candles that will be used in the coming year. The day commemorates the purification of the Virgin Mary 40 days after the birth of Jesus, but this Christian feast cloaks the significance of the *preceding* day, now the feast of Saint Brigid but once that of Brigit, the mother-goddess of the Irish. Walpurgis Night is so called because it is the eve of the feast day of Saint Walpurga, but her feast, May Day, was another great festival of the Celts, who called it Beltane. Last of the four is Lammas, originally Loaf-mass, the day on which in Anglo-Saxon times the first fruits of the harvest were offered. It is also associated with the legendary Welsh hero Llew Llaw Gyffes (Lion with the Steady Hand), who is said to have been worshiped until the 19th century in parts of Wales. His death was commemorated on the first Sunday in August by a feast called Lughmass.

In ideal circumstances a coven would meet out of doors, but both the weather and the law might be adverse. Covens therefore generally meet indoors, usually in the home of the priestess or magister. In the United States the meetinghouse is sometimes referred to as the covenstead.

A few days before Candlemas, one British witch was asked if she would be celebrating in the open. She replied that she certainly did not propose to go leaping about on a cold February night in darkness and probably rain. She found it hard to believe that witches had ever gone in for outdoor activities in winter—though if they did, she added, it would explain the popular idea of the witch as a bent old crone, "crippled with arthritis and riddled with rheumatism!"

The Devil's Grease

According to Louis Wilkinson, the New Forest coven in England used an ointment to protect their naked bodies from the cold at open-air gatherings. It consisted largely of bear's fat, and was similar to the heavy grease used by long-distance swimmers. If something of this sort was used by devotees of a similar cult in medieval times, it may have given rise to the idea of "Devil's grease," the magic ointment that was believed to give witches the power of flight.

A number of writers on medieval witchcraft have remarked that this "flying ointment" sometimes contained drugs such as aconite, belladonna, and opium, and these may well have caused the witches to imagine or dream that they were flying. It is not known if the New Forest witches mixed hallucinogens with the bear's fat for their ointment, but they are reported to have swallowed small doses of fly agaric, which contains a powerful hallucinogen. Fly agaric is the common red and white spotted toadstool *Amanita muscaria*, familiar from nursery pictures. Viking warriors used to eat it to go berserk while mounting an attack, and shamans and tribesmen of Siberia use it to achieve a state of trance. Fly agaric is poisonous, and although a small dose may not prove fatal to a person in good health, it is extremely unwise to eat it because there can be considerable variation in the amount of poison present.

When the members of a coven have assembled, a circle nine feet in diameter is drawn on the floor with chalk or charcoal, and then symbolically redrawn with the athame. According to Gerald Gardner, the evil magician draws a circle to protect himself from the spirits he calls up to help him in his work, but the white witches draw their circle to focus their own power—not to keep spirits out but to keep magic in.

Inside the circle is an altar covered with a white cloth. On it stand a censer for burning incense, containers of water and salt, *The Book of Shadows*—the litany for the rites—and the weapons or tools of the craft. The tools may differ in detail from one coven to another but usually include the athame, the cauldron, the wand, and a copper pentacle, symbolizing the four elements of air, water, fire, and earth. They have their equivalents in the

313

Tarot deck of cards, in which a cup takes the place of the cauldron. It has been suggested that witches stopped using a cup in case it was mistaken for the chalice of the Catholic Mass and so gave rise to accusations of blasphemy.

The Purpose of Being a Witch

The Sabbat rituals are secret of course, but the ceremony is made up of four parts followed by a symbolic meal. First comes the blessing of the coven; then the ritual dance; then the initiation of a new member if any; finally the invocations and requests to the goddess. This is the answer to the frequently asked question, "What is the purpose of being a witch?" In return for worship of the goddess the participants hope for supernatural aid. Because they are white witches their requests are usually for cures for illness or help in difficulties, undertaken for people outside the coven who are friends of one of the members. Most witches will tell of skin diseases and internal complaints cured after the full coven had concentrated their power on the absent person and his trouble. Presumably suggestion plays a part in these cures, as it does in most healing. White witches admit that in certain circumstances they might direct their power to cause hurt—"but generally only to harm someone who is harming others." They refuse to be drawn on this point, stating only that the harm would probably be limited to causing disruption and discord in the life of the victim.

Doing harm, or *maleficia*, is one of the acts of which the medieval witch was accused. But white witches set the occasional occurrence of this sort into the context of the greater good. They are therefore in line with the solitary sorceresses who still practice in some rural areas of Europe. A French example, recounted in the *Parisien Libéré* in 1963, featured a 72-year-old woman, Marie Moreau. She was accused of using witchcraft to create discord within a family in her small village. She denied the charge, asserting that she had never committed an evil deed. Her work, which was reportedly much in demand, involved only good deeds like curing sick people and animals, removing spells from fields, stables, and houses, and so on. She used salt to work her magic—ordinary salt, which she infused with power through incantations. Although most of her customers regarded her as a genuine witch, they referred to her—perhaps nervously—as "the good lady of Château-Ponsac."

In many parts of Europe and the United States white magic is still considered to be the surest shield against misfortune. A variety of gestures, amulets, and charms are traditionally used to ward off harm. Widely used objects include horse brasses, horseshoes, and "witch balls" (spheres of green glass). In Britain, stones with holes in them, typically found in chalk deposits, have been worn as amulets. Nowadays these are much favored by witches themselves, who thread them together into necklaces. In Germany and Switzerland in particular, a considerable number of country people continue to place their faith in supernatural healing, especially for minor ailments. A German report published in the early 1970s estimated that there were around 10,000 sorceresses practicing in the village communities of rural Germany. Their age-old remedies included a mixture of seven beetles and six laurel berries to cure rheumatism, the tooth of a mouse to be worn around the neck of a sufferer from toothache, and a piece of black bread dipped in cat's blood to reduce fever.

Another power attributed to the medieval witch and her pagan predecessor was the ability to control the weather, and modern white witches also claim to be able to do this. Witch Hazel, a young American witch living near New York, was asked how she brought rain by an effort of will. "Well, first," she explained, "the concentration is on water itself—or rain and wind. I have to bring myself to a state where I can smell rain, literally. Have you ever thought about something so strongly, like remembering summertime so that you could actually feel the sensation of the heat? I have to concentrate on clouds, not visually but in my mind, and draw them toward me. I pull them in with my mind. I envision them to the point where they are crystal clear in my mind. I see them. I feel them coming. I feel the wind rising. Then I add the sensation of smelling rain. There is a certain smell to rain water. I smell this very deeply. It is an intensely strong sensation and I pull this to me. If I am doing it correctly, with a sufficient amount of concentration, it will occur. I feel the wind rising. I will begin to see clouds move in and I will eventually smell the rain because it will be all over me. It works."

A striking example of the witch's alleged power over the weather occurred in Ethiopia in 1964. In the middle of the rainy season not a drop fell in the capital Addis Ababa on the day the British Embassy celebrated the Queen's Birthday. Ambassador John Russell told the London *Evening Standard* that the good day was by courtesy of a local witch. "I paid him eleven dollars" [then around $3 U.S. or a little over £1], he said, "to keep the rain off. It rained for two weeks before the day and two weeks after the day, but on the day itself the weather was perfect. The Foreign Office had the impertinence to query it when I put it down in my expenses, so I returned it to them under the word 'insurance.'"

There is no agreement as to the nature of the power that modern witches believe they can command. Many study the Egyptian, Chaldean, and Tibetan mysteries because the priests who practiced those are considered to have understood more fully the secret nature of supernatural power. Another hopeful, though tantalizingly fragmentary, field of study is the wisdom of the *kahunas* of Hawaii.

The Kahunas of Hawaii

Huna was the old religion of Hawaii and means secret. The *kahunas* (priests) were keepers of the secret, and their knowledge seems to have given them remarkable powers. By the effort of thought alone they could bring about events in the material world such as healing, materializing the dead, and keeping away sharks. But the core of Huna was a profound understanding of human consciousness. The priests' technique for resolving inner conflict and for expanding consciousness enabled people to live their lives happily and without guilt. Unfortunately, these beliefs brought the kahunas into conflict with Christian missionaries who did all they could to suppress them and had virtually eliminated them by the end of the 19th century. The American anthropologist William Tufts Brigham was able to make contact with the last of the kahunas, but though they demonstrated some of their skills such as fire-walking—and taught him how to walk barefoot over red-hot lava—they would not reveal how they made contact with the force they said was the source of their power. Max Freedom Long, founder of the Huna Research Association, has rediscovered some of their secrets, but others may now be lost forever.

Since the revival of witchcraft, the movement has split into a

number of sects. Gardnerian witchcraft has been repudiated by
some covens that do not share his masochistic taste for scourging.
Others emphasize the sexual element. One of these, according
to the British writer Francis King, "has an extraordinary 'death-
spell' which involves the Priest and Priestess indulging in the
no doubt very uncomfortable process of having intercourse
through the hole drilled through the middle of an allegedly neolithic stone relic!"

Some covens deny that sex ever played a significant part in
witchcraft, although this is not borne out by Vance Randolph's
research into the Ozark witch society in Arkansas. In this remote
mountain countryside, an unbroken tradition of witchcraft
appears to have existed back through the generations to the time
when the area was settled in the 18th century. The witches, mostly
women, instruct their daughters in the craft, but there are also
male witches. At least until recently, initiations involved sexual
intercourse witnessed by the group.

White witchcraft is still at the stage of being able to offer all
things to all men and women. Some people join a coven for
kicks. For others it is a fashionable alternative to bridge. But if
these hangers-on are discounted, there remains an increasingly
large core of people who hope to find in witchcraft the satisfaction that is lacking in a technological culture, and that they have
failed to encounter in orthodox religion.

The revival of witchcraft in the United States received a remarkable boost in 1961 with the publication of Robert Heinlein's
best-seller *Stranger in a Strange Land*. In this science fiction
classic, an earthman raised by Martians returns to Earth. There
he is distressed to discover mankind locked in resentments,
envies, jealousies, and hate. He studies the currently flourishing
religions, finds all of them unsatisfactory, and founds his own,
using his Martian powers of telepathy, telekinesis, and teleporta-
tion to build up a following of dedicated disciples.

He teaches an intimate, loving relationship with the Universe
and all within it, a relationship expressed by the Martian word
grok, meaning something like *feel, understand, love*, and *merge*
all rolled into one. "Thou art God, I am God, all that groks is
God." Men and women become "brothers" through a rite of
watersharing, and married members of a "nest" make love with
other "brothers" without jealousy.

The Church of All Worlds

Heinlein's book took some satirical swipes at materialism, politics, and established religion, and it inspired a group of young people at Westminster College, Missouri, to found a "water brotherhood fraternity." They hoped it might form the nucleus for an alternative society. With ideas borrowed from Heinlein and others, they went on to establish the Church of All Worlds, or CAW, "a Neo-Pagan Earth Religion dedicated to the celebration of Life, the maximal actualization of Human potential, and the realization of ultimate individual freedom and personal responsibility in harmonious eco-psychic relationship with the total Biosphere of Holy Mother Earth."

The Neo-Pagans seek a guilt-free harmony within mankind and a nonexploiting relationship of harmony between mankind and Nature. In the words of Lance Christie, one of the founders of CAW and subsequently High Priest of a nest in Venice, California, "There seems to be a profound relationship between seeing nature as an enemy and battling oneself as well. Both battles are ultimately self-destructive."

By 1974 the Yellow Pages Directory of *Green Egg*, the publication of the Church of All Worlds, was able to list 78 Neo-Pagan religious organizations and their branches. Despite their differences of emphasis, the various sects overlap in many respects and all worship the Goddess under one of her numerous aspects and the Horned God. Rituals are adapted or devised to suit the inclinations of a particular nest or coven.

Neo-Pagan witches are robustly anti-Christian but not Satanist. They consider the Judaic-Christian tradition of sin, sacrifice, and atonement to be anti-sex and anti-life. Neo-Pagans and allied witches study all branches of the occult, believing that The Way embraces many ways. A basic bibliography published in *Green Egg* lists nearly 200 relevant books, grouped in 18 categories such as Occult Practices, Planetary Ecology, and Human History We Were Never Taught. Because such a wide spectrum of subjects is considered to have a bearing on the modern witch's beliefs, the current state of witchcraft is one of active development. An article in the *Christian Science Monitor* in November 1974 sums up the situation like this: "Cults such as CAW serve as a means of reacting against dehumanizing and conformist social pressures." If those strong pressures relax, the urgently felt need for the alternative will gradually diminish. But if the dehumanizing trend persists, the continuing growth of white witchcraft seems assured.

27. Psychic Healing

"His psychological terms and description of the nervous anatomy would do credit to any professor of nervous anatomy. There is no faltering in his speech and all his statements are clear and concise. He handles the most complex jawbreakers with as much ease as any Boston physician, which to me is quite wonderful, in view of the fact that while in his normal state he is an illiterate man, especially along the line of medicine, surgery or pharmacy, of which he knows nothing."

This description of Edgar Cayce, perhaps the most celebrated psychic diagnostician of modern times, was given by a skilled and successful doctor who worked alongside him for many years, using the guidance Cayce gave while in trance to help him treat his most intractable cases. One of these was a college boy, the son of a wealthy family. For no apparent reason he had suddenly gone out of his mind. He could only mutter a few words, was prone to violent seizures, and otherwise would sit speechless, staring in front of him for hours on end. With money no object, his distraught parents consulted specialists from all over the country. His condition was pronounced hopeless and deteriorating. When Cayce was given his name and address—the only information he ever required about a patient—and went into trance, he diagnosed the boy's illness and prescribed a little-known drug. The drug was administered—and within a month the boy had recovered.

He had almost no formal education. As he grew up it became apparent that he had certain psychic faculties. However, it was not until his early twenties, when he came into contact with a hypnotist named Al Layne, that he himself recognized the full extent of his own extraordinary powers. Cayce suffered from a

320

severe throat condition that doctors had been unable to cure.
Layne took the unusual step of putting him to sleep, and then
telling him to diagnose his own complaint. From his trance
Edgar Cayce began his own diagnosis with the words, "Yes we
can see the body," a phrase that was to be repeated thousands
of times in his subsequent work. He went on in a clear voice to
pinpoint his own trouble as partial paralysis of the vocal
chords, and to suggest that the problem could be cured by an
increase of blood circulation in the area for a short time. Still
in trance, Cayce used self-hypnosis to cause the circulation to be
increased at that particular point, and then to return to normal.
In a few moments he came round. He remembered nothing, but
his voice was restored.

Layne, who had been ill for years, then persuaded Cayce to
diagnose him, although Cayce was still unconvinced of his own
ability. From his trance state Cayce was able to describe all
Layne's symptoms, and prescribe treatment in medical terms
that in his waking state he was unable to understand. It seemed
as if some strange power were talking through him. Later he
was to demonstrate, in trance, knowledge of languages and of
scientific and historical facts that in his conscious mind he knew
nothing of. When he began to give regular readings, as his
trance diagnoses were called, he usually had someone skilled in
medicine present to make sure that none of the remedies he
prescribed in his readings were harmful.

Because of attempts to exploit his clairvoyant powers in
order to make money, Cayce also insisted that his wife be
present at all sessions to supervise the questions put to him.
He would lie down on a couch, having loosened his collar,
cuffs, and laces. His wife would touch his cheek, and he would
close his eyes and begin to breathe deeply. His wife and his
secretary would close their eyes in prayer, and then Mrs. Cayce
would initiate the reading by giving him the name and address
of the subject. Cayce would then visualize the state of health of
the subject, wherever he was, and also his surroundings. In
recommending treatment Cayce would often direct patients to
therapists or doctors whom he did not know outside his trance
condition. One Staten Island mother, consulting him for a sick
child, was told to "Find Dobbins." Eventually she traced a
young osteopath named Frank Dobbins who had just arrived in

Staten Island, and whose name was not yet in the phone directory. Cayce had never heard of him nor he of Cayce.

Incomprehensible Prescriptions

The prescriptions Cayce gave while in trance were often incomprehensible to a pharmacist. They contained a strange mixture of ingredients of which some were totally unfamiliar. Sometimes the unusual ingredients were not yet on the market. Other times they were substances that had fallen out of use. At one time Cayce prescribed balsam of sulphur. The druggists who were to fill the prescription were unable to find it in any current list of therapeutic drugs. Finally they unearthed from an attic a 50-year-old catalog. In this they found balsam of sulphur mentioned. On another occasion Cayce recommended the use of clary water for rheumatism. As no druggist had ever heard of it, the patient advertised for anyone who could give any information on the subject. A man from Paris replied that his father had developed the product, but that it had been out of use for nearly 50 years. He enclosed a copy of the original prescription. Without prior knowledge of this prescription, Cayce asked himself in a trance state how clary water could be made. His answer tallied exactly with the original directions.

As his fame grew he was inundated with requests for help, and a fully staffed hospital was set up for him in Virginia Beach. In 1931 the Association for Research and Enlightenment began to keep records of the thousands of cases he had treated. Although Cayce died in 1945, his readings on file at the Association continue to be studied for the insight they give into the treatment and diagnosis of illness, and many followers of Cayce carry out the ideas he put forward while in trance.

How could he do it? And if he could do it, could anyone? These are the kinds of questions that present themselves time and again in the world of spirit healing. Strictly speaking Cayce, who has been called the outstanding sensitive of the century, was a diagnostician and not a healer. He did not possess in himself the power to cure, but his psychic perceptions showed the way back to health for thousands who consulted him.

Many modern faith healers are Spiritualists. Why is this so? Spiritualists believe that the human personality outlives the death of the physical body, a belief they share with most of the world's great and small religions. But Spiritualists go further in believing that the spirits of the dead can and do communicate with the living.

The ancient Egyptians feared the spirits of the dead as envious bringers of disease. Among the California and Oregon Indians a strict tribal law forbade the speaking of any person's name after his death for fear it brought back his ghost. In parts of Indonesia some names given to people were also the names of common objects such as "fowl" and "fire." With the death of a man who bore such a name, the name of the object had to be changed. This led to great difficulties in communication.

All these measures were designed to protect the living from the dead. Spiritualists, on the other hand, believe that the dead, far from harming us, want to help us. The spirits of those who have died retain their human personality, and seek out the opportunity to return to earth and continue their work.

A Contemporary British Healer

To return to the physical plane, the spirits normally require the agency of a sensitive intermediary, a medium who can serve as a junction and channel between the two worlds. Prominent among those who seek to return, it seems, are men who practiced healing when they were alive. Many of the Chinese and Indian spirit guides that featured strongly in early Spiritualist lore are thought to have been physicians or medicine men knowledgeable in healing arts unfamiliar to Western man. Harry Edwards, the most celebrated contemporary British healer, believes the spirits of Louis Pasteur and Lord Lister direct his work.

Edwards' first healings occurred in the Middle East during World War I when he was in charge of a crew of Arabs building a railroad. They were inexperienced laborers, and accidents were frequent. Those who smashed their fingers with hammers found their wounds healed unexpectedly quickly if Edwards treated them. He attributed this to the hardiness of their race, but they recognized his unusual power and called him the *hakim*—healer. Edwards returned from the war believing his gift was nothing special, and for the next 15 years concentrated on the family's printing business. Not until 1935 when he was over 40, did he turn his attention to Spiritualism and healing.

323

As an amateur conjurer his interest was at first limited to reproducing Spiritualistic phenomena by trickery. But he soon decided there was more to Spiritualism. Mediums at several of the Spiritualist circles he attended told him he was "born to heal," and a succession of events gradually persuaded him that he did in fact possess the healing gift. In one instance he and two friends were sitting quietly in meditation one day concentrating their thoughts on a man they knew to be in London's Brompton Hospital. He was dying of advanced tuberculosis. Edwards became aware that he was gazing down a long hospital ward with his attention fixed on a man in the last bed but one. When he afterward checked what he had "seen" with someone who had visited the patient, he discovered his description was accurate in every detail. It was Edwards' first experience of astral traveling.

Within a day of his vision, the friend's hemorrhage ceased and his temperature was almost down to normal. He recovered and remained in good health for many years.

Convinced by this and other like experiences that he could be used as a medium for healing, Edwards began to follow the Spiritualist healing methods then in use. He soon found, however, that it was unnecessary for him to go into trance as most Spiritualist healers did. The spirit guides seemed to work through him just as well when he was in a state of receptive meditation. Sometimes he would just sit and let the healing force flow through him to a sufferer, perhaps many hundreds of miles away. At other times he might feel moved to manipulate the arthritic joints of a patient. Till well into his 70s, Edwards held large public demonstrations of healing at which sufferers from disabilities such as rheumatism, curvature of the spine, and paralysis would come forward to be helped or cured by him and his team of assistants. As his successes became more and more widely known, so his mail increased, until thousands of letters began to pour in every year with requests for absent healing. Edwards came to believe that absent healing, often without the patient's knowledge, was more effective than direct healing.

At one time Edwards felt his duties should include convincing the medical and church authorities that spiritual healing worked. He gathered details of several hundred cases, and provided X-ray data and surgeons' reports. He placed special hopes on their being finally convinced by the case of Mr. R. B., cured of cancer in 1953.

This was a case in which it had been proved by a *biopsy*, which is the medical term for the removal and examination of a small portion of the tissue thought to be diseased, that Mr. B. was suffering from a malignant cancerous condition of the throat. All the usual symptoms were present. He had severe pain and swelling, he was unable to swallow, and his voice had deteriorated into a hoarse whisper. He was due to be operated on in two weeks.

When Mr. B. learned of this decision he telephoned Edwards for absent healing. "In the immediate days following," Edwards says, "the pains left him and the swellings subsided; and his voice returned to normal." Two days before the operation was due to take place Mr. B. requested a further examination by the two specialists who had conducted the previous examinations. "After exhaustive tests and a fresh biopsy, they declared that all symptoms of the cancer had disappeared."

This seemed to Edwards proof enough that a cure by spirit healing had occurred. But the two specialists disputed this. Their explanation was that by a fortunate coincidence the section of tissue removed for the first examination contained all the diseased tissue.

The Aura
As a result of experiences like this Edwards decided against further attempts to prove spirit healing. The proof that mattered was to be found in the healings themselves—healings, incidentally, for which Edwards himself takes no credit. "I myself have never 'cured' anyone," he says. "My part is simply that of a channel for the healing powers."

As to how these powers operate, the British healer Gordon Turner has put forward some ideas in his book *An Outline of Spiritual Healing*, published in 1963. It is based on his study of the *aura*, a field of energy believed to surround all living creatures. Turner possesses considerable psychic powers. He has described the aura around an ant's nest as a faintly pinkish glow, becoming darker around the body of each ant. A pet budgerigar was surrounded by a faint blue light about twice the size of the bird's body. The aura that surrounds a human body is necessarily more complex. Turner sees it as an ever-changing pattern of rippling color, densest where close to the physical body and faintest at the outer edge. Emotions are registered in the aura as changes in color. The effect of illness is to make the aura duller or to mark it with patches of new color

"When a healer places his hands upon a patient," Turner explains, "there is an immediate blending together of their auras. Within a few minutes all other colors that were previously observable become subordinated by a prevailing blue, which extends greatly beyond normal and seems to fill the room in which treatment is being carried out. . . . It is still possible to see the colors that had denoted symptoms, but these float away from the body of the patient and become surrounded by a yellow colored light which seems to be spinning. What follows is for all the world like the action of a 'spiritual penicillin.' The yellow light gradually overcomes the duller color of the disease and it becomes flattened out and much less intense."

Many patients have spoken of the feelings of energy and warmth that pass into them during the moments of healing. Turner describes an interesting experiment in which unexposed film was placed between the healer's hands and the patient in a darkened room. When the film was developed, markings were discovered on it similar to those that can be made by holding film close to an electric stove in a darkened kitchen. A control experiment was performed using someone who lacked the power to heal. No markings were visible.

Many healers now perform much of their work by the method known as "absent" healing. One way is to ask the patients who cannot get to the healer to sit quietly each day at a certain time. At the same time the healer will slowly read out each patient's name asking that healing may be given. He might then make a general request for healing for all the other people on his absent healing list whose conditions are less severe. After a period of meditation the intercession, or appeal by the healer on behalf of the sick, is over.

Distance between healer and patient appears to have no adverse effect on treatment. The healer projects his thoughts both toward the sick person and toward the spiritual world, and once the link has been established the healing forces flow where they are directed. Turner contrasts the success of this method with the relatively poor results obtained when people pray directly for themselves. It is as though the healing process requires someone else to appeal on a person's behalf.

In 1944 Harry Edwards' house was wrecked by a German bomb, and his record book and healing register destroyed. "In losing that register," he says, "it was as if the very bottom had fallen out of life itself, for I knew that absent healing work had received a very heavy blow. All I could then do was to recall from my memory as many cases as I could for directive intercession for the remainder."

He expected a marked falling off in the good progress his patients were reporting, but to his astonishment he found that the percentage of improvements was actually increasing. This caused him to review his manner of work, and from that period on he stopped making timed absent healing appointments except in emergency cases. The explanation for the unexpectedly good reports may be that his quality as a receiving and transmitting agent for the healing powers had reached such a high degree of development that he could become an open channel. All that he does today is to make a mental note of the names of the patients as he reads their letters requesting treatment. The healing force then flows directly to them by this simple act.

Controlling Spirits

Healers like Edwards and Turner are *directed* by their spirit guides. Another type of healer will enter a trance and while in that state be *controlled* by a spirit. One of the most interesting of these is George Chapman, an ex-fireman from Liverpool, England. He turned to Spiritualism after the death of his baby daughter in 1945. The messages he received proved to his satisfaction that life continued after death, and also led him to become a medium. In his trance state he received messages from a spiritual healing band that included "Lone Star," a member of the Cree tribe of Indians, and a Chinese surgeon named Chang. But these slipped into the background after the spirit of Dr. William Lang presented itself.

The association between Chapman and Dr. Lang is one of the most enigmatic in spirit healing. Lang was born in 1852. He

327

became an eminent eye doctor, and published several works concerning diseases of the eye. He died in 1937 at the age of 84. Chapman was then a boy of 16. Ten years later Lang's voice began speaking through Chapman's mouth, and he was eventually able to assume complete control of Chapman while he was in trance.

When this occurs Chapman's face becomes wrinkled, his body hunches slightly, and he speaks in an "elderly, old-fashioned" voice that Lang's old associates have recognized as the voice of their former colleague. If Lang thinks an operation is necessary Chapman, controlled by Lang, moves his fingers over the body of the patient who remains conscious and fully clothed. He uses invisible spirit surgical instruments to perform an invisible operation on the spirit body.

Chapman believes the spirit body he and Dr. Lang operate on to be composed of electric cells supplying energy to the physical body. When illness develops in the physical body a corresponding change occurs in the spirit body. In the same way an operation performed on the spirit body can alter the condition of the physical body.

Once Chapman is in trance his own spirit self is temporarily withdrawn from his body, and Dr. Lang takes over. Mrs. Kathleen Vaughan, transport officer of the Red Cross Ambulance Service in Croydon, London, described Chapman's state when he does a trance healing. She drove a patient the 40 miles to see Chapman in Aylesbury, Buckinghamshire, and then stayed to watch. Here is what she says in *Extraordinary Encounters* (1973), collected by George Chapman.

"His eyes were closed," she reports, "and during the whole time we were with him they never moved, whereas in sleep there is usually some movement of the eyeball . . . He asked the patient how he could help her and she gave a very simple description of her immediate failing. He examined her sitting upright in a chair less than an arm's length away from me. He diagnosed a trapped artery to the spine and said he would operate.

"I helped her onto the couch and straightened her clothing. He told her to close her eyes and breathe deeply, and then he said, 'Come on, Basil,' snapped his fingers, and appeared to be handed what he needed for the operation. I stood right behind

328

him, watching every movement. He said to me, 'I must operate
on the heart, but don't worry, fortunately it is very strong.' He
then started to operate in silence, except for the snap of his
fingers indicating the instrument he required. All this took
place about an inch above the patient's body. I was amazed at
the precision and skill of the whole thing. Then he told me he
would try to change the chemical action of the fluid to the spine.
We brought the patient back to the chair, so that I could see
all that was going on, and Dr. Lang gave her an injection on
every vertebra right up to the brain.

"I had seen Dr. Lang make about 60 stitches after operating,
but without touching the patient. When I told her this she could
not believe it. She said she felt every move that was made. The
stitching was very apparent to her, though not painfully so, as
she had felt the flesh drawing together."

Several patients have commented on Dr. Lang's habit of
snapping and clicking his fingers. Madame Siri Biro, the distinguished concert pianist, was treated by Chapman for an
illness brought on by her allergy to penicillin. She says, "Dr.
Lang explained to me that he has invisible helpers who know,
by the way he clicks his fingers, which instrument he requires."

Lang's son Basil is one of these helpers, and in conversation
with Dr. Robert W. Laidlaw, member of the American Society
for Psychical Research, Lang explained that his son is being
trained in the spirit world to take over from him. After George
Chapman dies, the healing association will be continued between
Basil Lang and Chapman's son Michael.

Healers of Brazil and the Philippines

A determined materialist finds such phenomena hard to
credit. Yet healing acts considerably more bizarre are performed
daily as a matter of course in Brazil and in the Philippines. The
psychic operations performed by the late José Arigó, Edivaldo
Silva, and Lourival de Freitas in Brazil, and by Antonio Agpaoa,
Mercardo, and their compatriots in the Philippines, have been
the subject of much speculation in recent years. Accusations
of trickery abound. People who have not witnessed psychic
surgery maintain it is impossible for an invisible scalpel to produce visible spurts of blood, and that an abdomen roughly
opened for an operation cannot heal in an instant and leave

the skin unscarred.

Guy Playfair, an English writer who lived in Brazil for many years, gives an account of his own psychic operation in his book *The Flying Cow*, published in 1975. His healer was Edivaldo Silva, known generally as Edivaldo, a schoolteacher whose spirit controls include doctors from several countries. The operation took place in Rio de Janeiro in an old ramshackle building—for though psychic surgery is tolerated by the law it is still illegal. Playfair reported that he was aware of Edivaldo's thumbs penetrating his abdominal wall, but felt no pain. When he looked at his stomach afterward the only sign of the operation was a thin jagged line about three inches long, which disappeared overnight, and two bright red dots that have never faded.

Like the other healing mediums Edivaldo works in a trance state, and has no idea why his treatments work. Playfair came across so much paranormal activity in Brazil—"the world's most psychic country"—that he felt he had to find the explanation. He does not exclude the possibility of occasional fraud, although he feels that healers only fall back on this when, as must sometimes happen, the spirit fails them.

Harold Sherman, the veteran ESP researcher from Arkansas, closely studied the working methods of Antonio Agpaoa in Manila and, since he seems to have liked Agpaoa personally, regretfully recorded the evidence against his wonder cures. More recently, a British television team examined the work of another Filipino healer who appeared to remove bleeding pieces of tissue from gaping incisions that left no scar. These wonders were shown to be the work of a skilled illusionist. Two doctors, one an amateur conjurer, posed as patients and recognized the tricks.

It is possible that some of these tricks are window dressing, intended to make a patient feel he has undergone an operation even though his illness has been treated by other means, perhaps by suggestion. This possibility is considered by Dr. Lyall Watson who describes Filipino psychic healing in his book *The Romeo Error*, published in 1974. In this connection it is interesting that Edivaldo should have told Guy Playfair the spirits were already treating his patients while they waited in the queue to see him.

Theories that rely on suggestion and hypnotism, however, leave too much unexplained. Playfair suggests that there may be a preexistent biological model for all living structures, located outside our physical world but connected to it possibly through the brain. Since this model would not represent diseased or damaged tissue, any person who obtained access to it might possess the means to recreate living tissue. Research is continuing in Brazil and has recently been taken up in Czechoslovakia and the Soviet Union. Until the outcome of such research is known, the principles governing the work of the Brazilian Spiritists must remain tantalizingly unexplained.

28. Mysterious Rays

It was probably as far back as 2000 B.C. that certain people found they had the power to locate underground water by dowsing. They would traverse an area holding a forked twig in their hands, and if they passed over water, seemingly involuntary movements in their muscles would cause the rod to move in a certain way. This indicated the presence of water. Later this skill was adapted to prospecting for minerals. In our own day it is also used to discover the location of buried pipes and cables on building sites, to trace missing persons, and to diagnose illness. Dowsers nowadays use a variety of instruments. Some use the traditional forked hazel twig, some a whalebone rod. Others find that a small pendulum on a thread gives a more accurate response, while still others rely only on their bare hands. These last feel that it is the movement of the dowser's muscles that seems all-important, and the rods or pendulums are merely devices to help the dowser interpret such movements.

What actually causes the dowser's muscles to contract remains a mystery. Many dowsers believe that all substances give off different radiations which the human mind is capable of picking up, though it has to a large degree lost this ability as a result of relying on verbal communication. As Brian Inglis explains in his book *Fringe Medicine*: "Most people when discussing one of the phenomena of ESP, such as clairvoyance or telepathy, think of it (whether they believe in it or not) as a mental process, but diviners assume that it will eventually be accounted for by radiations. Every form of matter radiates on its own wavelength; the human mind, they believe, contains a built-in receiving station capable of tuning in to these broadcasts, in certain conditions; and when the set is properly tuned in, a force is exerted which generates neuro-muscular energy of the kind that can be seen working on the dowser's twig."

Map Dowsing

Even if this idea is accepted, the whole question is made more complex and difficult to grasp by the strange ability many dowsers possess of tracing the whereabouts of underground water or minerals from a map. By holding their dowsing instrument over a plan of an area, they are able to get accurate responses, which afterward are verified on the site. Since the map itself could not give off the radiations, we must look for a further explanation. Perhaps the map helps the dowser to focus his responses, and so pick up the radiations from the area shown in the map in a way that we are at present unable to understand. An analogy might be seen in the work of Edgar Cayce. He only needed the name and address of a patient to be able to tune in to him, however many miles away, to visualize his surroundings, and to diagnose his complaint. He was only able to do this while in trance, when there was no interference from his conscious mind. Dowsers also seem to be using some sixth sense or faculty outside the normal human range of consciousness. We may tend to dismiss this power because it is so outside our everyday experience, but our ancestors would have dismissed radio, television, and space flights in just the same way.

When prospecting for minerals, some dowsers carry small samples of the mineral with them. Whether this acts as an actual guide or merely serves to concentrate the dowser's faculties, rather like the map, is not clear. However, in the 19th century it was discovered that dowsers could distinguish between pure and polluted water, and dowsers made use of different samples of water to help them establish the different reactions to the different impurities. From this it was only a short step to using the dowsing instruments, most often the pendulum, for medical diagnosis to distinguish between healthy and unhealthy parts of the body. A pendulum swung over a healthy organ would have one reaction; swung over an unhealthy organ it would have a different reaction. In this way it was often possible to locate the source of various complaints. Some practitioners went further and used the technique to suggest remedies. Samples of different remedies, usually homeopathic, were held by the operator, and the pendulum was swung over the patient's body until a certain movement of the pendulum indicated that the correct medicine to use had been found.

The Abbé Mermet, who used the term *radiesthesia* to describe diagnosis with a pendulum, did much in France at the end of the 19th century to give these ideas respectability. He was a highly regarded member of the Church, and his careful scientific studies did much to put the work on a firm footing. His ideas were taken up and practiced in France and Italy, and gained an acceptance they have never enjoyed in either England or America. The Abbé Mermet himself often assisted the police in tracing missing persons. All he needed was an article belonging to the missing person that had not been excessively handled by other people. This was believed to contain the person's unique radiations, and could be used as a guide in finding the right response to the person who was missing from the pendulum.

Radiesthesia received an impetus from the research and experiments of Albert Abrams, an eminent neurologist who was born in San Francisco in 1863. He had studied extensively in Europe under some of the greatest scientists of the time and, most unusual for a medical specialist, had acquired a knowledge of the newest developments in modern physics. Much of his later research was to be governed by an attempt to reconcile the laws of physics with those of biology. On his return to San Francisco he embarked on a brilliant medical career, achieving an international reputation and making many important contributions in his own field of neurology. But his work also had its unorthodox side. In 1898 the French scientists Pierre and Marie Curie had discovered the radioactive element radium, and Abrams soon became interested in the nature of radioactivity and the use of radium in the treatment of patients. A chance examination of a patient early in the century set him off on a long line of research which lasted until his death in 1924. It laid the foundation for what at first was known as the Electronic Reactions of Abrams, or ERA, and later became established as radionics.

The patient who set off this chain of research was a middle-aged man suffering from a chronic ulcer on his lip—technically known as an *epithelioma*, a form of cancer. While giving him a thorough checkup Abrams discovered that one small area in the region of the man's stomach sounded dull instead of hollow when tapped. What puzzled him was that it only sounded dull when the man faced west. If he faced any other direction or lay down on a couch, that small area of the body gave the normal hollow note.

Abrams' guess was that this puzzle had some connection with the earth's magnetic field, and he embarked on a program of research to solve this biophysical mystery. He examined other people suffering from the early stages of cancer, as well as those in good health and those suffering from numerous other diseases. His findings led him to the conclusion that when a patient faced west, the atoms in the diseased tissue emanated some kind of radiation that affected certain groups of nerve fibers. These then produced the muscular contractions he was able to hear as a dulled sound in certain parts of a patient's body. When he found that the different sounding points were specific to each disease, he realized the diagnostic value of his discovery. A dull note just below the navel, for instance, indicated the presence of tuberculosis; the place for detecting the presence of malaria was located to the left of the navel, and so on.

Other discoveries were to follow. He placed a small container holding a cancer specimen against the forehead of a healthy young man. Within two seconds the hollow note Abrams had been obtaining from the subject's abdomen became dull. When the cancer specimen was removed the normal hollow note of health returned. Evidently the radiation from diseased tissue could affect a person's reactions even though the tissue did not come from his own body. Later, when he began to construct machines to help in diagnosis, Abrams also discovered that a drop of blood from a patient gave as definite a reading as a piece of tissue. Today practitioners in radionics generally use blood spots for convenience sake. The spots are sometimes called "witnesses."

Gradually Abrams began to formulate a theory to account for the astonishing results of his experiments. Long before it was a generally accepted fact, he concluded that radiation was a universal property of matter. He then went on to argue that if matter and energy were indistinguishable at the atomic level, the basis of disease was electronic and not cellular. If, as seemed to be apparent from his experiments, healthy and diseased tissue gave out different radiations, then it should be possible to build equipment to receive and diagnose these radiations, somewhat on the lines of a radio receiving set. It ought also to be possible to construct equipment on the same lines to treat and cure abnormal radiations, he believed.

In order to distinguish the different types of radiation emitted by different diseases, Abrams used an old-fashioned variable resistance box. This was the first of the notorious "magic boxes."

This was not Abrams' name for them, of course. He called them *reflexophones*. Later more refined versions were known as *sphygmobiometers* or *sphygmophones*. They were used principally for diagnosis. To cure the patient Abrams invented the *oscilloclast*, which is often known as the "black box." Its aim was to produce measured vibrations that would destroy infection in the patient.

One of Abrams' early students, Dr. Eric Perkins, recalls an incident during a postgraduate course on Abrams' methods. Another doctor on the course was beginning to suffer from chest pains, and asked Abrams to diagnose in front of the class. Abrams warned him that the results of an examination were sometimes embarrassing, but the doctor told him to go ahead. It wasn't, he said, as though he was the least likely to have a venereal disease.

From the blood sample Abrams immediately got a strong reaction for syphilis. When he revealed this the doctor became very angry. "That's all bunk!" he shouted. "I don't care what your readings say! I tell you I've never had it!"

This incensed Abrams. "My work's all bunk, is it?" he growled. "I'll tell you if you caught it from a male or female and the site of the inoculation."

According to Perkins, the dials of the machine were then set to "sex combination." Abrams tapped both sides of his reluctant patient's abdomen and got a dull note on what he designated as the male side.

"He caught it from a male," Abrams announced. "Now we

have to find where he caught it. Let's try the hands first—
medical men often get infected on the hands."

Once again the angry doctor was examined, this time on his
hands where an electrode from the machine was pointed at
each finger in turn. Abrams got a reaction from the end of the
middle finger of the left hand and there, on inspection, he
found a scar.

"You've got me, Doctor Abrams!" confessed his patient. "I
jabbed that finger with a needle when sewing up a man after an
operation, and it did not heal for a long time. I never thought it
was a chancre."

With an electrode held over the man's chest Abrams diagnosed syphilitic aortitis as the cause of the chest pains. Fortunately, he was able to be reassuring about the prospects of a
cure provided treatment began at once.

Without Abrams' box the condition might well have remained
undiagnosed for a considerably longer time.

Great interest was aroused by such diagnoses and by treatments suggested by the machine and successfully carried out.
Patients and doctors flocked to San Francisco to study the ERA.
Upton Sinclair, the celebrated American novelist, called Abrams'
laboratory a "House of Wonders."

The British Investigation

Interest was also aroused in Britain, and in 1924 a committee
of the British Medical Association was appointed to investigate
the phenomenon. Sir Thomas Horder, later the king's physician,
was in the chair. Among medical circles it was confidently
expected that the demonstrations arranged for the committee
would be a failure, and ERA dismissed as a fraud. The succinct
report quoted by Brian Inglis in *Fringe Medicine* is worth
repeating. It said:

"The Committee's report was startling. Tests, it said, had
been arranged under suitable supervision; the results had been
carefully evaluated; and the Committee had come to the conclusion that 'no more convincing exposition of the reality of
the phenomena could reasonably be desired.' Not merely was
it satisfied that the claims about the diagnostic value of the
method were proven: two of its members, Horder being one,
had actually felt an alteration in their abdominal muscles at the

time when—if the therapeutic claims are to be believed—they should have expected to feel them. As they had not been told what to expect, this could not have been from suggestion—not, at least, on a conscious level."

This seemed like a clear endorsement for Abrams. Unfortunately, however, the demonstration was conducted by Dr. W. E. Boyd of Glasgow who used a machine of his own called an *emanometer*. This was a development of the Abrams box, and Boyd was always careful to acknowledge his debt to Abrams. But the difference enabled the BMA committee to maintain that they were examining a different box entirely. Horder even made a point of criticizing all who employed the "scientifically unsound" paraphernalia of Abrams.

Thus the committee managed to praise and dismiss Abrams' work in the same statement. Orthodox medicine was able to interpret these findings as a general condemnation. Abrams himself died about this time—some say of a broken heart—and further development of his ideas slowed down.

Not for long, however. Ruth Beymer Drown, a chiropractor who had been Abrams' secretary, kept the infant science alive in the difficult period after its inventor's death. She began to devise new instruments and soon discarded external currents in her machines, believing that her task was to focus the life force which she held was present in everything. "It cannot be too strongly stressed," she wrote, "that the individual's own body energy is the only force or current used by the Drown Method in diagnosis, remedy selection, or treatment." She used the same instruments for diagnosing and treating, but in different ways. For diagnosis, the machine received and dealt with energy emanating from the diseased part of the body. For treatment, on the other hand, the whole of the body's energy was channeled through vibrations to act on the diseased part.

Ruth Drown was the first to regularly treat patients at a distance by means of a blood spot or other specimen. Abrams had found that a patient's blood spot gave off all the radiation necessary for diagnosing a disease. Ruth Drown applied this by using the blood spot as a way of tuning in with the distant patient. The right vibrations were focused on the blood spot, and it was held that these would be picked up by the patient.

Ruth Drown built up a large practice in the 1930s and 40s.

She also worked out a list of treatment rates for most parts of the body and nearly all the ailments that can afflict it. These treatment rates were based on the number and intensity of vibrations applied by the Drown machine to cure bodily disorders. In 1950 her supporters persuaded her to demonstrate the power of her instruments at the University of Chicago. Ten blood specimens were given to her, but her diagnosis of the first three was so inaccurate that she did not continue with the test. The following year the Food and Drugs Administration (FDA) arranged for her arrest on charges of fraud and medical quackery. Despite the bulk of evidence presented in her defense she was sentenced and her instruments seized and destroyed. Shortly afterward she died. Practitioners of radionics look on her as their first—and it is hoped their only—martyr.

The practice of radionics is still a technically illegal act in the United States. The English author and editor Edward W. Russell wrote to the FDA in 1973 to ascertain their current attitude. He was told in effect that since they were required to insure that all devices were "safe, effective, and properly labeled" they knew "of no way of labeling a device so that it would bear adequate directions for use for Radionic Medicine."

The Instruments of de la Warr

Investigation into radionics is now concentrated in Britain—although it may also be taking place in the Soviet Union where there is vigorous research into all manifestations of parapsychology. The diagnostic instruments most used in Britain are those designed by George de la Warr in his Oxford laboratories. During World War II de la Warr was asked to copy one of the Drown instruments for someone who was unable to obtain it. His interest in radionics was immediately aroused, and he began to devote most of his time and energy to experimenting and researching in the field. He was the first to produce standardized, highly accurate instruments. Working in close cooperation with his wife Marjorie, he devised a new diagnostic instrument. It resembled a large portable radio with nine tuning knobs. Blood spots or other samples were placed in two small cups above the knobs. A master index of 5000 rates was compiled by testing different diseases. To diagnose a sample the knobs were tuned until the correct rate was found. This could then be identified by checking against the index. The method of determining the rate was a strange one, with some similarities to dowsing. A thin rubber membrane was fixed to the base of the instrument. The operator would rotate the dials and stroke the membrane. Most of the time there was no reaction, but if the rubber became sticky, it meant that some of the dials were tuned to a correct rate. Confirmation or more details could be obtained by further tuning. After diagnosis the patient would be treated with specific remedies, by a treatment instrument, or both. To use the treatment instrument, the complementary rate to the diagnosis was worked out, the machine tuned in to the patient's blood spot, and treatment broadcast through the ether to distant patients. In 1960 an action in the High Court was brought against the de la Warrs by a dissatisfied purchaser of a machine. However, they were cleared of all charges of fraud and their honesty and sincerity were publicly established by what came out in their trial.

The successful radionics practitioner has to have some of the talents of a dowser and be sensitive to ESP, but the Delawarr Laboratories estimate that six people out of ten are able to operate the box to some extent, and three of those six can do so extremely well. The chief drawback is that the operator's ability can be disturbed by certain states of mind. The presence of a skeptic is said to be inhibiting, but nervousness also has a damaging effect.

Several mocking tales are told about radionics. One recounts the hoax played on Abrams by a Michigan doctor who sent in a blood sample from a Plymouth Rock rooster, and got back a diagnosis of malaria, cancer, diabetes, and two venereal diseases. But radionics has continued to have its successes, and our knowledge of the life force—by whatever name we choose to call it— is still so incomplete that it is unwise to dismiss any method which seeks to understand it.

The history of healing is filled with examples of methods used for healing before the principles by which they operated were known. Color therapy from the 13th century provides a notable case. When a son of King Edward I caught smallpox, the royal physician, John of Gaddesden, hung red cloth all around his bed. By doing so he reduced the disfiguring effect of pitting considerably. John of Gaddesden may have had mystical reasons for choosing the color red, but the treatment worked. Nearly 600 years were to pass before Niels Finsen, the Danish pioneer of phototherapy, showed that the success of the treatment was the result of preventing ultraviolet light from reaching the patient's skin.

In cases other than smallpox, the beneficial effect of the full spectrum of the sun's rays are well known. Deprived of sunlight the body is unable to convert the fat present in the skin into Vitamin D. The effect of different colors on illness is still the subject of experimental tests, but already it is thought advisable that the colors red and orange should not be used in mental wards—however cheerful they may appear to visitors. Some colortherapists irradiate their patients with light shining through colored glass, and claim that certain colors and color combinations are of benefit to definite diseases—yellow for indigestion, blue for skin troubles, violet for ease in childbirth, for instance. Finsen showed that a tubercular condition of the skin, known as lupus, is improved when subjected to ultraviolet rays.

Music for Healing

As with rays of light, so with sound. Music has been used in healing since ancient times. Sounds and music were thought to be of magic origin, and could therefore communicate directly with the spirits. The music played by the witch doctor or medicine man was not designed to calm or comfort the patient, but to break the resistance of the spirit by means of its own magic power. Juliette Alvin, a professional cellist and founder in 1958 of the British Society for Music Therapy, explains that while the beat of "magic music" can seem monotonous, the music in fact goes through different emotional moods as it tries to persuade, flatter, cajole, or threaten the evil spirit responsible for disease to go away and leave the patient cured.

In biblical times we find David the harp player calming the madness of Saul. Greek and Arab medicine recommended soothing songs and the playing of flutes for certain complaints. To treat sciatica musicians played close to the patient's body to make his flesh move. The Greek mathematician Pythagoras used loud music to treat mental patients, calling this his "musical medicine." The voice has also been used for this purpose, notably by the great 18th-century Neapolitan singer Farinelli. In 1737 he paid a visit to Spain where he found the moody and melancholy King Philip V suffering another of his lengthy depressions. He was hiding away from his court—unshaven, slovenly, and slumped in lethargy. The Queen invited Farinelli to sing in an adjoining room, and asked him to choose some of his more expressive and poignant songs. Farinelli sang four, including one entitled *Pallido il sole—Pale is the Sun.* These expressed the King's melancholy so perfectly that he emerged from his depression and resumed the business of state upon hearing them. Farinelli remained in Spain until King Philip's death nine years later. Every evening the King asked him to sing the same four plaintive and melodic songs and no others.

A unique form of madness raged in Southern Italy toward the end of the Middle Ages for which the only cure seemed to be music, and only a certain kind of fast music. The madness centered around the ancient town of Taranto in the Apulian heel of southern Italy. It was said to be caused by the bite of a local spider, the tarantula. The madness was therefore named tarantism, and the frantic music that caused the people to dance wildly until they were cured was called the tarantella.

In the intense summer heat a peasant would suddenly jump up, cry out that a spider had bitten him, and run to the market place. There he would find other sufferers lying slumped by the roadside while neighbors desperately searched the countryside for musicians to come and play the tarantella. Bands of musicians wandered the countryside throughout the summer for this very purpose, carrying violins, pipes, and small drums. They played the tarantella, repeating the same tune again and again. Gradually sufferers would revive and move a limb. Then they started to dance faster and faster, going through the night and even the following day until they dropped exhausted and the madness was cured.

One strange feature of the disease was that people's madness returned year after year on the anniversary of the bite, whereupon they would have to repeat their frenzied dancing. Other things were puzzling too. If a tarantula was taken out of Apulia its bite became harmless. What was special about Apulia?

The probable explanation is that the wild dancing was an

Dowsing has an ancient history, probably going back as far as 2000 B.C. This 16th-century print shows dowsing for metals. (*Mysterious Rays*)

Many modern dowsers believe that every form of matter radiates on its own wavelength and that the human mind contains a built-in "receiving station" which can "tune in" to the radiations and allow them to affect the dowser's body. Here, Geoff Blundell, developer of the Mind Mirror EEG device, monitors Leslie Banks at the Rollright Stones, Oxfordshire. (*Mysterious Rays*)

Bust of Wilhelm Reich at Rangeley, Maine, U.S.A., with his "cloud buster" in the background. Reich is best known for his books, *The Sexual Revolution* and *The Function of the Orgasm*, and for his identification of sexual energy with the life force, which he called "orgone energy". He believed "orgone energy" could be stored in boxes and used to cure illnesses, including cancer. Eventually he fell foul of the US Food and Drugs Administration (FDA) and was arrested and imprisoned. He died in a prison hospital in 1957. (*Mysterious Rays*)

essential safety valve, a hysterical release of energies pent up by the miseries and fears of medieval life. As to why it should occur in Apulia and nowhere else, here is one interesting explanation. Pythagoras went to Apulia with his musical medicine in the 6th century B.C., and lived in Taranto until his death. Christianity was slow to take root in the far south of Italy, and it is thought that the orgiastic rites of Bacchus, the god of wine, celebrated in Pythagoras' time, probably survived in secret—to reemerge into the light of day as the dancing madness of Apulia in the Middle Ages.

Tarantism faded away in the 17th century and is now extinct. It had served its purpose. But many people today still have little tolerance for strange ideas and practices that they do not understand, even if the practices do no harm and they themselves are not directly affected by them. Five years after the arrest of Ruth Drown the FDA moved against a more celebrated figure, the internationally known therapist Wilhelm Reich.

Reich and the Sexual Revolution

Since Reich's death in a prison hospital in 1957, the last years of his life have become encrusted with legend. To the young generation his work is expressed in the slogan, "Make Love Not War." The connection of this slogan with his ideas is aided by the titles of his most significant books, *The Sexual Revolution* and *The Function of the Orgasm*. He is seen as a forerunner of the Permissive Society.

Reich believed that virtually all mental disturbances and a great many physical illnesses are the result of sexual repression in infancy and in puberty. Men and women become trapped within a "character armor" of unhealthy submissions and resentment. This armor expresses itself in muscular rigidity, tensions, and stereotyped facial expressions. Reich's novel approach to his patients was to draw attention to these repeatedly, and this appears to have had considerable success as a means of uncovering some of their childhood crises. Even the many psychotherapists who feel that Reich stressed the effects of sexual repression to the neglect of other factors admire his work on character analysis. It is largely through his influence that many therapists discarded the role of anonymous wise man and reach out to a patient as one human being to another.

More controversial are his views on sexual energy. According to Reich a man or woman imprisoned within a character armor becomes unable to discharge sexual energy completely during orgasm. Unexpressed sexual energy emerges as neurotic symptoms, anxiety, and sadism, making the person less able to achieve satisfactory orgasm the next time. The process continues in a vicious circle.

Reich uses the word orgasm to express more than is commonly meant. The individual must "surrender to the flow of biological energy without any inhibition. There must be no trace of sadism in the male nor of masochism in the female, no smug satisfaction in the male, no talking either, except words of tenderness, and no laughing." In *The Function of the Orgasm* he describes the "orgiastically satisfying sexual act" in great detail. Coming as it did six years before the Kinsey Report and its startling revelations of American sex habits, it was an undertaking of some courage.

According to Reich, very few individuals achieve full orgiastic potency. All neurotics and most civilized people fail. But the importance of achieving it lay in the fact that Reich identified sexual energy with the life force, present throughout Nature and filling the Universe. He called this force "primordial cosmic energy" or "orgone energy." He claimed to have observed the units of this energy—called "bions"—under a microscope and detected them by Geiger counter. The spots we sometimes see in front of our eyes are said to be examples of it. He believed that cancer is caused by bions which had degenerated through stagnation.

Reich fell foul of the FDA when he declared that orgone energy could be stored in boxes, known as orgone energy accumulators. These boxes, about the size of narrow telephone booths or coffins were made of steel encased in wood. They were said to act like greenhouses, letting in the orgone energy and storing and concentrating it. The sick were to sit within the boxes to be irradiated with orgone energy. By these means Reich claimed to be able to cure cancer. For these ideas and practices, he was arrested, imprisoned, and his books destroyed.

There is today no scientific agreement about the radiation said to be detected by diagnostic boxes, or the energy stored in accumulation boxes. Nor is there certainty that the life force in man can be identified with any force that fills the Universe and moves the stars. But a belief in a life force of some kind is central to many successful methods of healing. If its existence has not yet been proved, it may be because scientific instruments are simply not sensitive enough for the task. The end of this particular story lies in the future.

29. Alchemy

It is late at night. In a room hidden away from prying eyes, an old man bends over a flask of bubbling colored liquid. All around is a clutter of jars, bottles, and apparatus that looks somewhat like the equipment in a modern school chemistry laboratory. The walls are hung with animal skulls and astrologers' charts. A stuffed owl sits amid a jumble of thick leather-bound books with iron clasps. From time to time he stirs the liquid, muttering strange words to himself. His fur-collared cloak is in tatters, and he shivers slightly from the chill draft leaking through a broken window. His supper, entirely forgotten and long cold, lies untouched on a nearby bench. Nothing disturbs his concentration as he patiently watches the liquid evaporate. Then disappointment clouds his face. Something has gone wrong. He pores over an old manuscript, puzzling at the strange language and symbols. With a sigh, he sets up some more apparatus. Perhaps a grain more of this and a grain less of that? His excitement returns. The years have slipped by unnoticed. His whole life has been dedicated to one task. He is determined to discover the secret of turning ordinary metals into gold.

Although there is some truth in this popular description of an alchemist, it is by no means the whole story. There is far more to alchemy than a desire to make gold, and serious alchemists were not crazy old men. They were often among the leading scientific and religious thinkers of their time.

The word *alchemy* is an Arabic one. but no one is wholly sure where it came from. The most popular explanation is that it originally meant "the art of the land of Khem." *Khem* was the name the Arabs gave to Egypt, and it was from Egypt that they acquired their knowledge of this strange science, which they later transmitted to the West. Another possibility is that the word derives from the Greek *chymia*, which means the art of melting and alloying metals.

Alchemy is extremely complicated. It is based on the practical skills of early metalworkers and craftsmen, on Greek philosophy, and on Eastern mystic cults that sprang up in the first centuries after Christ and influenced so much of magic and occult thought. It must be remembered that when alchemy flourished there was no dividing line between science and magic. Ideas such as the influence of the planets and the effect of certain numbers or letters on people's lives might today be regarded as superstitions. At that time they were perfectly acceptable to those who were making the kind of accurate observations about the material world that paved the way for modern science.

Long before the beginning of alchemy gold was regarded as the most valuable metal. Its possession indicated wealth and power, and it was prized for its beauty. Known as the most perfect metal, it soon acquired symbolic meaning. It came to stand for excellence, wisdom, light, and perfection. For serious alchemists gold had both a real and a symbolic significance, which at first seems confusing. The reason is that alchemists embarked on two different and difficult quests at the same time, and success in one meant success in the other. The first aim is the one that most people know about. The alchemist was attempting to find a way of transmuting, or changing, ordinary metals into the most perfect metal, gold. The second aim is less well-known but was far more important. The alchemist was trying to make the soul progress from its ordinary state to one of spiritual perfection.

The Philosopher's Stone

For many centuries Western alchemists ceaselessly searched for the Philosopher's Stone. What was this elusive object? It was not some giant boulder on which ancient sages sat and meditated. Nor was it a closely guarded tablet inscribed with words of wisdom. It was a substance that alchemists were convinced they could make, with divine assistance, by subjecting certain raw materials to complex and lengthy chemical processes. The problem was to find the right raw materials and the correct chemical processes. It was a widely held belief that the

Universe was permeated by a spirit that linked everything together. Alchemists thought that this spirit could somehow be reproduced and compressed into a magical substance which they named the Philosopher's Stone. Once discovered, a small quantity of this magical substance added to ordinary metal would change it into gold. Taken as a medicine, the Stone would act as a miraculous cure. It was even believed by some to confer immortality, and was often called the Elixir of Life.

All the patient experiments that alchemists carried out in their laboratories over the centuries were motivated by one overwhelming desire—to produce the Philosopher's Stone. In the course of their painstaking and dedicated work they established many important chemical facts which, even if they did not lead to the Philosopher's Stone, helped to form the basis of chemistry as we know it today.

The greatest alchemists were skilled in many fields. The scope of knowledge in those days was small enough that a person might hope to master all there was to know about subjects as diverse as medicine and religion, philosophy and alchemy, logic and magic. The seeker of knowledge would see nothing incompatible in the different fields of study. Magic would not conflict with medicine, or philosophy with religion. Knowledge was thought of as a unity, and all the different branches were different aspects of this unity. They all led toward a greater understanding of the Universe.

Famous Alchemists

The greatest Arab alchemist, Jabir, who lived from about A.D. 722 to 815, was a widely read scholar who wrote treatises on an enormous variety of subjects including geometry, poetry, magic squares, and logic. Although his main concern as an alchemist was discovering how to convert ordinary metals to gold, he also recorded many important chemical observations, and his design of apparatus led to the development of the modern still.

Al-Razi, the celebrated Persian alchemist and physician who lived from about A.D. 866 to 925, wrote books on medicine, natural science, mathematics, astronomy, logic, philosophy, and theology, as well as many works on alchemy. For the first time in the history of chemistry, facts about chemical substances, reactions, and apparatus are carefully observed and verified in

An early print showing the popular idea of the alchemist at work, trying to turn ordinary metals into gold. The greatest alchemists, however, were skilled in many fields, including medicine, religion, philosophy, logic and magic. The most important aspect of alchemy to them was the search for spiritual perfection. *(Alchemy)*

his books.

When we come to 13th-century Europe we find Albertus Magnus among a distinguished selection of alchemists. He was one of the greatest scholars and teachers of the Middle Ages, and as recently as 1932 was canonized as a Catholic saint. Among his many works were treatises on alchemy, and he was the first to describe the chemical composition of such substances as cinnabar, white lead, and minium.

Paracelsus was one of the most notable scientific figures of the 15th century. From his knowledge of alchemy he was able to introduce a whole new range of medicines for medical treatment. Until that time remedies had been almost exclusively herbal.

One of the greatest difficulties encountered in exploring the development of alchemy is that the books and manuscripts describing the substances to be used and the chemical processes to be followed were written in such obscure, symbolic language. They were often open to many different interpretations, and were puzzling even to an experienced alchemist. An ordinary reader would be floundering after the first sentence. Because the books that the alchemists consulted are incomprehensible to all but an initiated few, most of our knowledge of alchemy is based on legends of transmutations. Many of these have been handed down and greatly embroidered in the course of time. At this distance it is impossible to gauge how much truth there might have been in these stories, and how much trickery. However, there are some accounts that appear convincing. These are ones in which the narrator has an established professional reputation and little to gain from deceiving others. One such man was the well-known Dutch physician Johann Friedrich Schweitzer, who lived in the 17th century.

Helvetius's Story

Schweitzer, who was born in 1625, was a distinguished doctor. He numbered Prince William of Orange, the future King of England, among his patients. In the fashion of his day, he was generally known by the Latin version of his name, Helvetius. In 1666 when he was 41 years of age, Helvetius received a strange Christmas present: the ability to turn lead into gold. He later wrote down an account of what happened. On December 27, in the late afternoon, a stranger came to his house. He described

349

him as being "of a mean stature, a little long face, with a few small pock holes, and most black hair, not at all curled, a beardless chin, about three or four and forty years of age (as I guessed) and born in North Holland." The stranger told Helvetius that he had read several of his pamphlets, and in particular one that was highly critical of an English experimenter who had claimed to have invented a universal medicine. Did Helvetius think, asked the stranger, that it was impossible?

The two argued in a friendly fashion for some time. Then the stranger took out of his inner pocket a carved ivory box and showed Helvetius its contents—three heavy pieces of stone "each about the bigness of a small walnut, transparent, of a pale brimstone color." This, said he, was enough to turn some 20 tons of lead into gold. Helvetius handled a piece greedily, and begged the stranger to give him just a little. When the stranger told him that this was impossible, he contrived to scrape a speck under his fingernail surreptitiously.

After telling Helvetius how he himself had learned the art, the stranger demonstrated "some curious arts in the fire," and promised to return in three weeks' time. As soon as he was gone, Helvetius excitedly got out a crucible and melted some lead in it. When he added the tiny crumb of stone, however, "almost the whole mass of lead flew away," leaving only a dull residue.

The physician impatiently awaited the return of the stranger, more than half convinced that he would not come again; but in three weeks exactly the man of mystery once more came to his house. "But," said Helvetius, "he was very sparing in speaking of the great elixir, gravely asserting, that was only to magnify the sweet fame of the most glorious God." Again the physician begged him for some of the stone, and at last the stranger relented. According to Helvetius: "He gave me a crumb as big as a rape or turnip seed, saying, receive this small parcel of the greatest treasure in the world, which truly few kings or princes have ever known or seen." Ungratefully Helvetius protested that this was hardly enough to transmute four grains of lead, whereupon the stranger took it back, divided it in half, and flung half in the fire saying, "It is yet sufficient for thee."

Helvetius confessed his former theft, and recounted his lack of success. The stranger laughed and said: "Thou art more dextrous to commit theft, than to apply thy Tincture; for if thou hadst only wrapped up thy stolen prey in yellow wax, to preserve it from the arising fumes of lead, it would have penetrated to the bottom of the lead, and transmuted it to gold." He promised to come again the next morning at nine to show Helvetius the proper procedure.

"But the next day he came not, nor ever since; only he sent an excuse at half an hour past nine that morning, by reason of his great business, and promised to come at three in the afternoon, but never came, nor have I heard of him since; whereupon I began to doubt of the whole matter. Nevertheless late that night my wife . . . came soliciting and vexing me to make experiment of that little spark of his bounty in that art, whereby to be more assured of the truth; saying to me, unless this be done, I shall have no rest nor sleep all this night . . . She being so earnest, I commanded a fire to be made (thinking alas) now is this man (though so divine in discourse) found guilty of falsehood . . . My wife wrapped the said matter in wax, and I cut half an ounce or six drams of old lead, and put it into a crucible in the fire, which being melted, my wife put in the said Medicine made up into a small pill or button, which presently made such a hissing and bubbling in its perfect operation, that within a quarter of an hour all the mass of lead was totally transmuted into the best and finest gold . . ."

The philosopher Spinoza, who lived nearby, came to examine the gold, and was convinced of the truth of Helvetius' story. The Assay Master of the province, a certain Mr. Porelius, tested the metal and pronounced it genuine.

What Helvetius implied in his story was that the strange visitor was an alchemist who had given him some of the Philosopher's Stone. Although we may find the idea incredible, and wonder whether Helvetius was the perpetrator of a giant hoax, none of his contemporaries saw it in that light. To them, alchemy was perfectly acceptable, and they saw no reason to doubt Helvetius' integrity.

30. Two Mysterious Frenchmen

At least as late as the year 1742, there stood in the cemetery of the Holy Innocents in Paris an old arch with remarkable paintings on its walls. It had been built and decorated on the instructions of Nicholas Flamel, a man whose profession it was to copy out manuscripts and documents in the days before printing. The paintings showed the figure of Nicholas Flamel dressed as a pilgrim, strange symbolic scenes, and the various stages of a successful transmutation of ordinary metals into gold. Flamel explained the transmutation scenes as follows: "In the year of our Lord 1382, April 25, at five in the afternoon, this mercury I truly transmuted into almost as much gold, much better, indeed, than common gold, more soft also, and more pliable. I may speak it with truth, I have made it three times, with the help of Perrenelle [his wife] who understood it as well as I, because she helped me in my operations . . ."

Flamel wrote an account of his lengthy alchemical quest in 1413. His devoted wife and companion, Perrenelle, had died in 1399, and for a long time he had been inconsolable. They were a thrifty, industrious, and charitable couple, and Flamel's narrative, with its sober enthusiasm, has an authentic ring. His tale begins in the year 1357 when he purchased a very old and very large gilded book. "It was not of paper, nor parchment, as other books be, but was only made of delicate rinds (as it seemed unto me) of tender young trees; the cover of it was of brass, well bound, all engraven with letters or strange figures . . . this I know that I could not read them nor were they either Latin or French letters, of which I understand something. As to the matter which was written within, it was engraved (as I suppose) with an iron pencil or graver upon the said bark leaves,

352

done admirably well and in neat Latin letters, and curiously colored." The manuscript contained 21 leaves. The seventh, fourteenth, and twenty-first leaves were blank, apart from some strange illustrations. The seventh leaf showed "a Virgin and serpents swallowing her up," the fourteenth a cross with a serpent crucified on it, and the twenty-first "a desert with many springs out of which serpents writhed."

On the first page was written in capital letters in gold: "Abraham the Jew, Priest, Prince, Levite, Astrologer, and Philosopher, to the nation of the Jews dispersed by the wrath of God in France, wisheth health." Flamel afterward referred to the manuscript as the *Book of Abraham the Jew*. The dedication was followed by lengthy curses and execrations against anyone who might read the book who was neither a priest nor scribe. Flamel, who was a copyist or scribe, was exempt from these curses and felt emboldened to read further. On the third leaf and in all the following writings were instructions for the transmutation of metals to gold. The author wished to help the dispersed Jews pay their taxes to the Roman emperors. The instructions were clear and easy to follow. The only problem was that they referred to the later stages of the transmutation. There were no written instructions given as to what the *prima materia*, or first matter, consisted of, and so it seemed impossible to carry out the essential first stages of the transmutation.

The only clue the author gave to the identity of the first matter was that he had depicted it in the illustrations on the fourth and fifth leaves of the book. Flamel found to his disappointment that, although these pictures were clear and singularly well painted, "yet by that could no man ever have been able to understand it without being well skilled in their [the Hebrews'] Cabala, which is a series of old traditions, and also to have been well studied in their books." Flamel had the pictures copied and showed them to various people in the hope that someone would be able to interpret them. One one side of the fourth page was a painting of a young man with wings at his ankles. In his hand he held the *caduceus*, the snake entwined rod of Mercury, messenger of the gods. Running and flying at him with open wings came an old man with an hourglass on his head and a scythe in his hands, as if he were about to cut off the young man's feet. On the other side of the page was a picture of a high mountain.

On its summit was a blue plant with gold leaves and white and red flowers, shaking in the strong north wind, "and round about it the dragons and griffins of the north made their nest and abode."

On the first side of the fifth leaf was a rose tree in flower against the side of a hollow oak. A pure spring bubbled up at the foot of the oak and ran down through a garden to disappear into the depths. It ran through the hands of many blind people who were digging for it, but who could not recognize it except for a few who could feel its weight. On the other side of this leaf the painting showed a king with a broad sword ordering his soldiers to slaughter hundreds of babies, while their mothers flung themselves weeping at his feet. The soldiers collected the infants' blood into a bath, where the Sun and Moon came to bathe themselves.

The Search for a Meaning

No one who saw the pictures could understand them. At last, a man named Anselm, who was deeply interested in alchemy, claimed to be able to interpret them. Unfortunately, he started Flamel off on the wrong track. "This strange and foreign discourse to the matter was the cause of my erring, and made me wander for the space of one and twenty years in a perfect meander from the verity; in which space of time I went through a thousand labyrinths or processes, but all in vain."

Finally, Flamel's wife Perrenelle suggested that, since the manuscript came from a Jewish source, he should seek the advice of a learned Jew in interpreting it. Many Jews had at that time settled in Spain. Flamel decided to go on a pilgrimage to Saint James of Compostella, and at the same time seek help in the synagogues. Attired as a pilgrim, and carrying careful copies of the mystifying illustrations, he set off for his journey to Spain.

After he had made his devotions at the Shrine of Saint James of Compostella, Flamel tried without success to find someone who could enlighten him as to the true meaning of the pictures. He traveled on to León, where quite by chance he was introduced to a certain Master Canches, who was well-versed in the secrets of the Cabala and other Jewish mysteries. When he saw Flamel's copies of the illustrations he was "ravished with great astonishment and joy." He recognized them as part of a book which it was believed had been completely lost. Master Canches immediately resolved to return with Flamel to France to find out more about the manuscript. On the journey he interpreted Flamel's illustrations with such accuracy, even to the smallest detail, that Flamel was able to find out what he needed to know about the nature of the first matter. Unfortunately, Master Canches fell sick and died when they reached Orléans. Flamel buried him as well as he could afford, and sadly returned to Paris. But nothing could stifle his joy when at last he came in sight of his small house and was reunited with his wife Perrenelle. He put up a painting on the door of the chapel next to his home. It showed him kneeling with his wife and giving thanks to God for granting him the desired knowledge.

However, Flamel's troubles were not yet over. "Well, I had now the *prima materia*, the first principles, yet not their first preparation, which is a thing most difficult, above all the things in the world; but in the end I had that also, after long errors of three years, or thereabouts . . . Finally, I found that which I desired, which I also soon knew by the strong scent and odor thereof. Having this, I easily accomplished the Mastery, for knowing the preparation of the first Agents, and after following my Book according to the letter, I could not have missed it though I would. Then the first time that I made projection was upon Mercury, whereof I turned half a pound, or thereabouts, into pure silver, better than that of the Mine, as I myself assayed [tested], and made others assay many times. This was upon a Monday, the 17 of January about noon, in my home, Perrenelle only being present, in the year of the restoring of mankind 1382."

Transmutation into Gold

Three months later, Flamel made his first transmutation into gold. For a long time he was worried that Perrenelle, who was overjoyed at the final outcome of so many years of experiments, would let some word slip among her family and reveal the secret of their sudden wealth. "But the goodness of the most great God had not only given and filled me with this blessing, to give me a chaste and sober wife, but she was also a wise and prudent woman, not only capable of reason but also to do what was reasonable, and was more discreet and secret than ordinarily other women are."

Because she was now well past the age for bearing children, Perrenelle suggested that their riches should be devoted to charity. She and Flamel founded and endowed "fourteen hospitals, three chapels, and seven churches, in the city of Paris, all which we had new built from the ground, and enriched with great gifts and revenues, with many reparations in their church-yards. We also have done at Boulogne about as much as we have done at Paris, not to speak of the charitable acts which we both did to particular poor people, principally to widows and orphans . . ."

The arch built by Flamel in the cemetery of the Holy Inno-cents, with its strange alchemical paintings, disappeared some time in the 18th century. The painting of Flamel and his wife giving thanks to God on the door of the chapel next to their home has also vanished. But one day in the mid-19th century, a herbalist in one of the streets near where Flamel used to live turned over the finely polished marble slab on which he had for years been chopping his dried herbs, and found it to be Flamel's tombstone. It is now preserved in the Museum of Cluny in Paris, and the inscription reads: "Nicholas Flamel, formerly a scrivener, left in his will for the administration of this church certain rents and houses which he acquired and bought during his lifetime to provide for masses and distribution of alms each year, in particular the Quinze-Vingts [a hospital in Paris for blind men] cathedral and other churches and hospitals of Paris." The will of Perrenelle, dated 1399, survives, and so does Flamel's, which he signed on November 22, 1416. Three years later he died.

After Flamel's death, many people thought that some of the Philosopher's Stone must still be hidden in one of his houses. His property was searched over and over again, and so thorough-ly that one house was reduced to a pile of rubble with only the cellars remaining. By about 1560 the local magistrate, in the name of the king, took possession of all property that had once belonged to Flamel, so that a final thorough search could be made. But nobody ever admitted to having found anything.

There were those, of course, who insisted that Flamel, having discovered the secret of the Philosopher's Stone, had also dis-

covered the secret of immortality. The 17th-century traveler
Paul Lucas, during a discussion on alchemy and magic with a
Turkish philosopher from Asia Minor, was told "that true
philosophers had the secret of prolonging life for anything up to
a thousand years."

"At last I took the liberty of naming the celebrated Flamel,
who, it was said, possessed the Philosopher's Stone, yet was
certainly dead. He smiled at my simplicity, and asked with an
air of mirth: 'Do you really believe this? No, no, my friend,
Flamel is still living; neither he nor his wife has yet tasted death.
It is not above three years since I left both the one and the other
in India; he is one of my best friends.' "

According to the Turk, Flamel had realized the danger he was
in if ever the news got out that he possessed the Philosopher's
Stone. Perrenelle had therefore feigned illness and had gone to
Switzerland, leaving Nicholas to announce her death. He buried
a log in her grave. After several years he in his turn carried out
the same deception. Nearly a century later, in 1761, Flamel and
his wife were reported to have attended a performance of the
opera in Paris, and there were many other stories of a similar
nature.

One of the most detailed and most fantastic of such tales
appears in the little-known work of *Le Corbeau Menteur* (The
Lying Raven) by the 19th-century French writer Ninian Bres. He
wrote: "He was a little less than middle height, stooping somewhat with the weight of years, but still with a firm step and a
clear eye, and with a complexion strangely smooth and almost
transparent, like fine alabaster. Both he and the woman with
him—clearly his wife, although she appeared almost imper-
ceptibly the older and more decisive of the two were dressed
in a style that seemed only a few years out of fashion and yet
had an indefinable air of antiquity about it. I stood, half concealed in a little archway toward the end of the boulevard du
Temple: my hands were stained with acid, and my topcoat
stank of the furnace. As the couple came abreast of the spot
where I stood, Flamel turned toward me and seemed about to
speak, but Perrenelle drew him quickly on, and they were
almost at once lost in the crowd. You ask how I am so confident
that this was Nicholas Flamel? I tell you that I have spent
many hours in the Bibliothèque Nationale, poring over the

Figures d'Abraham Juif [*Pictures of Abraham the Jew*]: look carefully at the first side of the fifth leaf and there, in the lower right-hand corner of the representation of those who seek for gold in the garden, you will see the face that searched mine that evening on the boulevard du Temple, and that has haunted my dreams ever since."

The illustration to which Bres refers is from a manuscript previously thought to be of Flamel's day but now considered to be of the 17th century. It is only one of many different attempts to reproduce the book that Flamel described so carefully. In different but obviously similar forms these pictures have appeared over and over again in alchemical works through the centuries. The manuscript also attempts an explanation of the meaning of the illustrations that puzzled Flamel for so long, and this interpretation has been expanded by numerous later writers. For example, take the illustration of the young man with wings on his ankles being attacked by an old man with a scythe. The first stage in the explanation was that these two figures stood for Mercury and Saturn. The second stage was that Mercury, in alchemical terms, represented an impure form of silver, and Saturn meant lead. When imperfect silver and lead are heated together in a cupel, the inpurities of the silver are absorbed into the material of the crucible, and the resulting silver is said to be "fixed" in the sense of stable or permanent. This illustration, represented in symbolic terms, is the alchemical process necessary for the fixing of silver.

Fulcanelli's Beliefs

From the time of Flamel on, alchemy became increasingly symbolical. The mysterious 20th-century alchemist Fulcanelli, in fact, suggested that the whole of Flamel's story was pure symbolism. He wrote: "We are prepared to certify—if our sincerity is to be trusted—that Flamel never quitted the cellar where his furnaces roared. Anyone who knows the significance of the pilgrim's staff, the begging bowl and the cockleshell in Saint James' hat will also know that we are speaking the truth. By substituting himself for the material and modeling himself upon other secret workers, the great Adept was obeying the rules of philosophic discipline and following the example of his predecessors."

The true identity of Fulcanelli himself is uncertain. He is best known as the alleged author of a book in French, *The Mystery of the Cathedrals*. In this he claims to show that all the secrets of alchemy are concealed in the carvings of the central porch of Notre Dame and various of the porches of the cathedral in Amiens. Fulcanelli proposes that gothic art, *l'art goth*, of which the French cathedrals are outstanding examples, is really *argot*, the language of the common people. They in turn are descendants of those intrepid adventurers who sought the Golden Fleece, the sailors aboard the *Argo*. In all this he claims to discover what he has called "the phonetic Cabala."

One example must suffice. In writing of the labyrinth, Fulcanelli refers to the thread of Ariadne in the Greek myth. Ariadne is Ariane in French. "Ariane is a forme of *airagne* (*araignée*, the spider) by metathesis [transposition] of the i," he said. ". . . Is not our soul the spider, which weaves our own body? But this word appears in other forms. The verb *airo* (Greek) means to take, to seize, to draw, to attract; whence *airen*, that which takes, seizes, attracts. Thus *airen* is the lodestone, that virtue shut up in the body, which the wise call their Magnesia . . . In Provençal iron is called *aran* and *iran*, according to the different dialects. This is the masonic Hiram, the divine ram, the architect of the Temple of Solomon . . . Compare all that with the Greek *Sideros*, which may mean either iron or lodestone. Nor is this all. The verb *aruo* means the rising star from out of the sea, whence *aryan*, the star which rises out of the sea; our *ariane* is thus the Orient, by the permutation of vowels. Further *arua* has also the sense to attract; thus *aryan* is also the lodestone. If we now compare *Sideros*, which has given the Latin *sidus, sideris*, a star, we shall recognize our Provençal *aran*, *iran, airan*—the Greek *aryan*, the rising sun."

Who was Fulcanelli?

Is this genuine, or is it some heavy-handed hoax? Scholars have argued for and against the existence of Fulcanelli ever since the publication of his book in 1925. In his preface to the first edition, Eugene Canseliet, a well-known writer on alchemy, wrote: "For a long time now the author of this book has not been among us . . . My Master . . . disappeared when the fatal hour struck, when the Sign was accomplished . . . Fulcanelli is no more." Then in March 1953 the French writer Louis Pauwels met an alchemist in the Café Procope in Paris. "How old can he be? He says 35. That seems surprising. He has white curly hair, trimmed so as to look like a wig. Lots of deep wrinkles in a pink skin and full features. Few gestures, but slow, calculated and effective when he does make them. A calm, keen smile; eyes that laugh, but in a detached sort of way. Everything about him suggests another age . . . I asked him about Fulcanelli, and he gave me to understand that Fulcanelli is not dead . . ."

A few weeks later Pauwels met Jacques Bergier, a scientist, with whom he later collaborated in writing on the occult. Bergier told Pauwels of his own meeting with a man whom he guessed to be Fulcanelli. It happened one afternoon in June 1937. Bergier said that he met the alchemist by appointment in a laboratory of the Gas Board in Paris Bergier at that time was working as research assistant to André Helbronner, the French atomic physicist. Fulcanelli (if it was he) told Bergier: "You are on the brink of success, as indeed are several other of our scientists today. May I be allowed to warn you to be careful? . . . The liberation of atomic energy is easier than you think, and the radioactivity artificially produced can poison the atmosphere of our planet in the space of a few years. Moreover, atomic explosives can be produced from a few grains of metal powerful enough to destroy whole cities. I am telling you this for a fact: the alchemists have known it for a very long time . . .

"I shall not attempt to prove to you what I am now going to say, but I ask you to repeat it to M. Helbronner: certain geometrical arrangements of highly purified materials are enough to release atomic forces without having recourse to either electricity or vacuum techniques . . . The secret of alchemy is this: there is a way of manipulating matter and energy so as to produce what modern scientists call a *field of force*. This field acts on the observer and puts him in a privileged position vis-à-vis the Universe. From this position he has access to the realities which are ordinarily hidden from us by time and space, matter and energy. This is what we call the Great Work."

In an introduction to the English edition of *The Mystery of the Cathedrals* Walter Lang carries the Fulcanelli legend further, reporting that "after a lapse of many years, Canseliet received a message from the alchemist and met him at a prearranged rendezvous. The reunion was brief, for Fulcanelli once again severed contact and once again disappeared without leaving a trace of his whereabouts." But, says Lang, Fulcanelli had grown younger, for whereas he had been an old man of 80 when Canseliet had first met him, 30 years later he appeared to be a man of 50.

Says Louis Pauwels: "All that we know of him is that he survived the war and disappeared completely after the Liberation. Every attempt to find him failed." It is difficult to decide how deliberate these attempts to find Fulcanelli were. In August 1945 the American intelligence services asked Bergier to contact urgently a certain anonymous major who worked for an organization searching out German research reports on atomic energy. This major desperately wanted to know the whereabouts of Fulcanelli—but he appears to have been satisfied when Bergier assured him that the veteran alchemist had once more disappeared. After 50 years, we know no more of Fulcanelli now than we knew in 1925. Perhaps, with Nicholas Flamel, he lives the life of an Indian Mahatma in the distant hills. Perhaps, who knows, he *is* Nicholas Flamel.

31. Modern Alchemy

After the physical and chemical discoveries of the 18th and 19th centuries, it would have seemed natural for alchemy in the 20th century to have advanced ever farther into the realms of symbolism and mysticism, and away from anything to do with physical transmutation. But in 1919 the eminent English physicist Lord Rutherford succeeded in transmuting nitrogen into oxygen in the laboratory, and every aspiring alchemist took new heart. Admittedly, the quantity of oxygen produced was hardly impressive, and the experiment involved the use of high-energy radioactivity. But at least it refuted the continual insistence by scientists that transmutation was an impossibility. One of the first to take inspiration and renewed hope from this experiment was Franz Tausend, a 36-year-old chemical assistant in Munich. He had developed his own theories about the structure of chemical elements. These were a strange mixture of the beliefs of the Greek philosopher Pythagoras about the structure of the Universe, and the findings of the Russian chemist Mendeleev in 1863. Mendeleev devised a way of classifying chemical elements by arranging them in order of their atomic weights, and discovered that chemically similar elements recurred at approximately equal intervals or periods. This became known as the *Periodic System*. Tausend wrote a pamphlet, *180 Elements, the Atomic Weight, and their incorporation in the System of Harmonic Periods*, on his theories. His belief was the every atom of an element had a characteristic frequency of vibration, which was related to the atomic weight of the nucleus and the various orbital rings of electrons around it. Later research was to show that this part of Tausend's theory was true. He went on, however, to suggest that matter could be as it were "orchestrated." By this he meant adding a carefully selected substance to one element to change its vibration frequency into that of another.

At about this time in 1924 Adolf Hitler was sent to jail for organizing an armed rising in Munich. His fellow conspirator, General Erich von Ludendorff, was acquitted. In the following year Ludendorff ran for election as president of the German republic, but he was heavily defeated in the polls by General Hindenburg. He then turned his attention to fund-raising for the Nazis. He heard the rumors that a certain Tausend in Munich had succeeded in making gold, and got together a party of associates to visit Tausend. The group consisted of Kummer, a chemical engineer, Alfred Mannesmann, a business magnate, Osthoff, a banker, Stremmel, a merchant, and a fifth man known as Franz von Rebay. Stremmel had bought the necessary substances, largely iron oxide and quartz, on Tausend's instructions. He had them melted down by Kummer and von Rebay, and took the crucible to his hotel bedroom in Munich for the night so that no one could tamper with it. In the morning, Tausend heated the crucible again in the electric furnace, added a small quantity of a white powder to the molten mass, and allowed it to cool. When the crucible was broken, a nugget of gold weighing seven grams was found inside.

Ludendorff than formed a company called Company 164 with himself at its head. He was to receive 75 percent of the profits, and Tausend five percent. Investments poured in, of which Ludendorff succeeded in diverting some 400,000 marks "to patriotic ends"—the financing of the Nazi party. This affected the company adversely. In December 1926 he resigned as the company head and restored all rights to Tausend, but left him to shoulder all the debts. Tausend continued to raise money, however, and on June 16, 1928 is said to have made 723 grams of gold in a single large-scale operation. No doubt it was this success that encouraged him to issue a series of share certificates, each to the value of 10 kilograms of gold.

But time was running out for Tausend. A year later, when no more gold had been produced, he was arrested for fraud. After a long wait in prison and a sensational trial, he was found guilty on February 5, 1931, and sentenced to nearly four years' imprisonment. While awaiting trial, he had allegedly made gold under supervision at the Munich Mint—but experts disagreed so violently on what had happened that the evidence was of no value in court.

Dunikovski's Z Rays

In the same year, a Polish engineer named Dunikovski announced in Paris that he had discovered a new kind of radiation that he named "Z rays." He said these rays would transmute sand or quartz into gold. The mineral was ground up, spread on copper plates, and melted by application of 110,000 volts. Then it was irradiated by Dunikovski's Z rays.

The engineer succeeded in raising an investment of some two million francs. When after a few months he had not produced any gold, he, like Tausend, was brought to trial for fraud. In due course he was found guilty and sent to jail for four years. After two years his lawyer succeeded in obtaining his release, and in 1934 Dunikovski took his family to San Remo, a seaside town in Italy, where he renewed his experiments.

Soon rumors began to reach Paris that the engineer was supporting his wife and children by the occasional sale of lumps of gold. His lawyer, accompanied by the well-known French chemist Albert Bonn, traveled to San Remo to see for himself. They discovered that the sand that Dunikovski was using in his experiments contained a small proportion of gold, but whereas normal methods of extraction yielded only some 10 grams of gold per ton, Dunikovski's method produced nearly 100 times as much. This sounds impressive, but it must be remembered that, since each experiment involved only a few hundred grams of sand, the quantity of gold being extracted was extremely small.

Nevertheless, the two Frenchmen were sufficiently impressed to ask the French government to reopen the Dunikovski case. On March 26, 1935, Dunikovski himself addressed an open letter to the prime minister, offering the French government a first option on his invention. The French newspapers, however, opposed the idea vociferously.

In October 1936 Dunikovski gave a demonstration to an audience of invited scientists. He was naturally secretive about the details of his apparatus, but the theoretical explanation he gave is interesting in that it went right back to the primitive beginnings of alchemy. He believed that all minerals contained atoms in the course of transformation, a process that takes thousands of years in nature. He called these atoms "embryonic atoms," and claimed that his process accelerated the growth of the embryonic gold in quartz.

The demonstration attracted a great deal of attention. Mussolini instructed an Italian professor to look into the process. Paris financiers retained the chemist Coupie. An Anglo-French syndicate was formed. Sand was to be brought from Africa and treated in a big new laboratory in England.

Then came World War II. There were stories that a factory for transmuting base metals into gold had been established in Saint Blaise on the French–Swiss border. Rumor further insisted that the Germans had found some way to bolster their sinking economy by the manufacture of gold. But no proof has ever been found. Meanwhile in England, in a crammed laboratory in the center of London, a modern alchemist claimed to have made the Philosopher's Stone.

Archibald Cockren

His name was Archibald Cockren. He had qualified as an osteopath in London in 1904. During World War I he had been in charge of the department of electrical massage and remedial treatment, first at the Russian Hospital in London, and then at the Prisoners of War Hospital. Later he had been attached to the Australian Army, and served on the staff of the Australian prime minister at the peace conference. He was clearly a respected and responsible practitioner.

He spent the next 20 years in private practice. During this period it became fairly common to inject gold salts as a cure for rheumatism and arthritis, and Cockren became very interested in such gold therapy. He also experimented with homeopathic methods of healing by making use of microscopic doses of gold. Looking for new ways to make solutions of compounds of gold, he decided to try to prepare the "oil of gold" of which so many alchemists had written.

Cockren had read *The Triumphal Chariot of Antimony* by Basil Valentine, a strange figure whose true identity lies hidden in the alchemical legends of the 15th and 16th centuries. Valentine is credited with the discovery of the element antimony. He was supposed to have given it the name *antimoine*, which in French would mean "against a monk," because he had used it successfully to poison several monks. Whatever the truth of the legend, Cockren decided to begin his experiments with antimony. He managed to produce a "fragrant golden liquid." Then he went on to work with iron and copper. "The oil of these metals was obtained, a few drops of which used singly, or in conjunction, proved very efficacious in cases of anemia and debility." He related how, on one occasion, he took a few drops of the oil himself after a particularly laborious day, and found himself reinvigorated. The prospect of a "bout of fairly strenuous mental effort held no terrors at all."

After continuing his experiments with silver and mercury, Cockren finally turned his attention to gold; but he found that his watery mixture would not retain gold in solution. He realized that what he lacked was the "alkahest of the philosophers," the universal solvent that alchemists believed would dissolve all matter. Only with this, thought Cockren, could he achieve the real oil of gold. He plunged into a study of alchemical writings, anxious to find a clue to the identity of this strange solvent. The experiments he had already made helped considerably. One day, while sitting quietly in a state of deep concentration, the solution to the problem was revealed to him in a flash, and he suddenly understood many of the puzzling statements of the alchemists.

"Here, then, I entered upon a new course of experiment with a metal for experimental purposes with which I had no previous experience. The metal, after being reduced to its salts and undergoing special preparation and distillation, delivered up the Mercury of the Philosophers."

The first intimation Cockren had that he had been successful was a violent hissing. Jets of vapor poured from the retort and into the receiver "like sharp bursts from a machine gun." Then there was a violent explosion and "a very potent and subtle odor filled the laboratory and its surroundings." A friend of Cockren's described this odor as resembling "the dry earth on a June morning with the hint of growing flowers in the air, the breath of wind over heather and hill, and the sweet smell of rain on the parched earth."

Cockren's next problem was to find a way of storing this "subtle gas" without endangering anything. He achieved this by an arrangement of coils of glass piping in water joined up with the receiver, and a carefully regulated system of heating. The result was that the gas gradually condensed into a clear golden "water" that was extremely inflammable and volatile. The water then had to be separated by distillation, "the outcome being the white mercurial water." This mercurial water, added Cockren, was absolutely essential to the production of the oil of gold. It was added to the salts of gold after the salts had been washed several times with distilled water to remove the acidity of the Aqua Regia, a mixture of nitric and hydrochloric acid that had been used to dissolve the gold. He found that when the mercurial water was added to the salts of gold, there was a slight hissing sound and in increase in temperature, after which the gold became a deep red liquid. When this was distilled the oil of gold, a deep amber liquid of an oily consistency, was produced. "From the golden water I have described can be obtained this white water, and a deep red tincture which deepens in color the longer it is kept; these two are the mercury and the sulfur described by the alchemists."

To make the Philosopher's Stone, Cockren took the black dregs of the metal left after the extraction of the golden water, heated it to red hot, and then treated it until it became a white salt. He then took a certain quantity of this "salt" and of the "mercury" and "sulfur" that he had already produced, and put them in a hermetically sealed flask over a moderate heat. The mixture looked at first like leaden mud, which slowly rose like dough until it produced a crystalline formation "rather like a coral plant in growth." Edward Garstin, a writer and friend of Cockren's, visited him at this time and saw "a glass vessel of oval shape containing layer upon layer of basic matter in the traditional colors of black, white, gray, and yellow. At the top these had blossomed into a flower-like form, a pattern arranged like petals around a center, all of a glowing orange-scarlet."

The heat was gradually raised until this formation melted into an amber-colored liquid, which then thickened and sank into a black earth on the bottom of the glass. "When more mercury was added, the black powder dissolved and from this conjunction it seems that a new substance is born . . . As the black color abates, color after color comes and goes until the mixture becomes white and shining; the White Elixir. The heat is gradually raised yet more, and from white the color changes to citrine and finally to red—the Elixir Vitae, the Philosopher's Stone, the medicine of men and metals."

Soon after this, Cockren was killed in the blitz of London, and his secret perished with him. He left many who believed in the curative powers of his oil of gold. Mrs. Maiya Tranchell Hayes, who headed a surviving temple of the Golden Dawn, swore by it, as did Mrs. Meyer Sassoon, widow of a well-known financier. As late as 1965 there were elderly people in London who still took small doses of Cockren's elixir.

Barbault's Methods

Since the war, most alchemical speculation seems to have taken place in France. Eugene Canseliet, who has written many books on alchemy, has been seen on television at work in his laboratory. Others, like the author Roger Caro and the painter Louis Cattiaux, have also established laboratories. But the most famous French alchemist is probably Armand Barbault, author of *Gold of a Thousand Mornings*. He carries out his work only at times that he has determined by detailed astrological calculation.

Perhaps Barbault gained his initial inspiration from a well-known theory that the name of the Rosicrucians is derived not from *rosa*, the Latin word for rose, but from *ros*, the Latin word for dew. An essential part of his process, for example, is the gathering of dew in canvas sheets every morning from March 21 to June 24. The idea of gathering dew was first put forward at the end of the 17th century in a mysterious book of engravings without captions entitled *Mutus Liber*, the *Wordless Book*. The author of another book of about the same date, the *Polygraphice*, writes: "Gather Dew in the Month of May, with a clean white Linnen Cloth spread upon the Grass." When this filtered dew has been left for 14 days in horse dung, and then distilled to a quarter of its bulk four times running, it yields a potent Spirit of Dew. "And if you are indeed an Artist, you may by this turn all Metals into their first matter."

Barbault describes his first matter as a germ, growing a few centimeters below the surface in black earth in a woodland clearing. This substance, whatever it is, is placed in a closed flask, kept at a steady temperature of 40°C (104°F). Dew, in which the tips of young plants have been fermented for 40 days, is added through a faucet. As far as it is possible to make out from Barbault's erratic account, the final ingredient is a "mother plant." There are detailed instructions on how to draw this plant whole from the ground by tying one end of a string to it, and the other end·of the string to a nearby bush that has been bent over. The bush is then released, and as it springs back to place, it pulls the plant out.

The flask is kept at the temperature of 40°C (104°F) for 40 days, extra dew being added as necessary. Later, the temperature is raised until a dry ash is obtained. This is then put into long test tubes, together with about 2.5 grams of powdered gold and some dew, and the tubes are sealed with a rubber stopper. Barbault has a thermostatically controlled oven maintained at a temperature between 150° and 200°C (302° and 392°F)—that is, substantially above the boiling point of water—and 12 test tubes are inserted partway into this oven so that the contents boil. The steam condenses in the upper part of the tubes, which are outside the oven, and liquid returns to solid matter below. After four hours of boiling, and four hours of standing, repeated seven times, the liquor in the tubes is a clear golden color—but, says Barbault, spectrum analysis does not reveal the presence of any gold in solution.

Armand Barbault regards this liquor as the alchemists' elixir, and calls it vegetable gold. It seems, in fact, to be a typical homeopathic remedy effective in microscopic doses. Dr. Ruth Jensen Hillringhaus of Freiburg, Germany claimed to have used it to cure a woman paralyzed by multiple sclerosis. Another doctor tried several drops of the elixir each morning and reported a marked reduction in tiredness, increase in initiative, and improved urination. Others reported miracle cures of uremia and syphilis. Barbault, who found it too expensive to continue adding gold to his liquors, was last reported to be employing the "Blood of the Green Lion"—extracted vegetable sap.

The story of alchemy is like a detective novel. But, although in this last chapter it is possible to unravel some of the tangled threads and make some deductions, there can be no dramatic last-minute revelation. We can only guess at the possible nature of first matter and the Philosopher's Stone.

We do not know whether seemingly objective scientific wit-

369

nesses ever saw a real transmutation in an alchemist's laboratory, but we do know that transmutation is possible. It goes on
naturally all the time as radioactive elements decay and give off
radiation—and the end-product of this "putrefaction" is lead.
Transmutation is also possible in a modern laboratory. Apart
from the changes from one known element to another, as in
Rutherford's experiment, there are more than a dozen new
elements known to science which do not occur naturally at all,
but which have been made in the course of experiments in
nuclear energy. The only limitation to laboratory transmutation
at the moment is that subatomic particles that travel at high
speeds and with immense energies are needed.

Alchemical tests are full of tantalizing information about the
nature of first matter. This desirable substance is, apparently, to
be found everywhere, is walked on by everybody, prized by
nobody. Quartz and sand, the essential ingredients of both
Tausend's and Dunikovski's process, answer well to this description. These minerals are almost pure silicon dioxide, and it is
possible that when Cockren spoke of using "a metal . . . with
which I had had no previous experience," he was referring to
silicon. This element is not in fact a metal. However it is known
as a metalloid because in its physical nature and chemical properties it belongs to a group of elements including germanium,
tin, and lead, and of which the first member is carbon. Silicon
is of particular interest in that it can take the place of carbon
in a great number of chemical compounds, producing silicones.
It has even been suggested that life, which on Earth is sustained
by compounds of carbon, may be sustained by silicones on
some other planet in another galaxy.

This is as far as the clues in our detective story lead us. It is
disappointing not to be able to conclude by unmasking an
alchemical "butler," but our present-day knowledge of the
nature of matter is still too sketchy. It may be naive to suppose
that any alchemist ever succeeded in preparing gold by transmutation, although the possibility exists; but there seems every
reason to believe that, by some means that we still call magic,
men were able to perceive a vision of what we are only just beginning to discover by experiment. They told their vision in a
succession of charming allegorical stories. The birth of metals
and their progression through seven stages to the perfection of

gold paralleled the seven ages of man, or the passing of the soul through the seven planetary spheres to heaven. The quest for the Philosopher's Stone and the Elixir of Life obsessed and impoverished many alchemists—but it is possible that they knew something that our modern scientists are only just beginning to discover.

Part 5

32. The Poltergeist

To all appearances Shirley Hitchins was an ordinary teenager. She lived with her parents, Mr. and Mrs. Walter Hitchins in one of a row of identical houses that lined Wycliffe Road, a thoroughfare in a working class area of London. Like many of her friends she had left secondary school early to go to work, and she seemed happy enough with the position she found as a salesgirl in a London department store. Then in 1956, a few months after her 15th birthday, Shirley ceased to be ordinary.

Her troubles started one morning when she woke up to find a shiny new key lying on her bedspread. She had never seen it before, her parents knew nothing about it, and it did not fit any of the doors in her home. During the following nights her bedclothes were brusquely yanked from her as she lay asleep, and thunderous knockings sounded on her bedroom walls. During the day such knockings were accompanied by tappings and scratchings in other parts of the house, and heavy pieces of furniture moved mysteriously around the rooms.

Within a few days the girl was haggard through lack of sleep, and arranged to stay a night with neighbor Mrs. Lily Love in an attempt to get some rest, away from it all. "It" followed her. An alarm clock and some china ornaments were shuffled around a shelf in Mrs. Love's house by an invisible agency, a poker was hurled across a room, and Shirley's wristwatch was pulled from her arm and thrown to the floor.

After this her father, a London Transport motorman, decided to sit up one night to see exactly what went on. He was accompanied by his brother. Shirley went to bed in her mother's room. All was quiet for a while, and then a resonant tapping began to shake the bed in which she lay. She was still wide awake, lying with her hands outside the covers. After a while she called to her father and uncle to say that the bedclothes were moving. The two men grabbed the bedclothes and found they were being tugged with considerable force toward the foot of the bed. As they struggled with the invisible force, they and Shirley's mother saw the girl suddenly go rigid. To their astonishment her stiff body rose six inches into the air without any support whatever.

Fighting back their fear, the Hitchins brothers lifted the floating body clear of the bed. Shirley, who had seemed dazed at the time, later said that she had felt a tremendous pressure in the small of her back, lifting her up. The levitation occurred only once and seemed to mark the peak of the strange events, for the following day the disturbances reverted to the form of rapping noises. These went with the girl everywhere, even onto the bus that took her to work. At the store her co-workers persuaded her to see the store doctor. Skeptical at first, the doctor was finally persuaded that "something was going on" when the knockings began in his own consulting room. He was still puzzling over the mystery when, almost a month to the day after the first mysterious appearance of the key, all the phenomena abated, and then ceased for good.

Today, some 20 years later, it is impossible to judge the happenings in Wycliffe Road with total objectivity, for we have only the contemporary newspaper stories and reporters' interviews with witnesses as evidence. From these, however, we can infer that Shirley Hitchins, her parents, Mrs. Love and her family, and the doctor who examined the girl were all rational down-to-earth people, none of whom had ever previously experienced any form of psychic phenomena.

It seems probable that the Shirley Hitchins case was a genuine example of poltergeist phenomena. The German word poltergeist, meaning a "noisy spirit," is today commonly used by psychic investigators to describe certain apparently supernormal physical effects—whether or not the investigator believes that they are caused by a spirit.

Definitions

In his book *Can We Explain the Poltergeist?*, Dr. A. R. G. Owen clearly defines the term. It is, he says, the occurrence of one or both of the following taking place in an apparently spontaneous, often sporadic way: (a) production of noises, such as tappings, sawings, bumpings; (b) movement of objects by no known physical means.

These two kinds of phenomena include a host of distinct effects. The noises, for example, may be impersonal in character, such as the rappings that followed Shirley Hitchins around, or they may suggest a human or superhuman agent. The movement of objects may take many forms: pictures may fall from the wall, vases fly across the room, heavy pieces of furniture be moved. On rare occasions, poltergeist activity may involve levitation, like that experienced by Shirley Hitchins.

The poltergeist has a long history. One of the earliest recorded cases took place in the German town of Bingen-am-Rhein in A.D. 355. Stones whizzed through the air, apparently of their own volition; sleepers were tossed out of their beds; and banging and crashing noises echoed in the streets. Since then many other cases have been reported in other parts of the world.

In a book entitled *The Story of the Poltergeist*, the late psychical researcher Hereward Carrington listed 375 cases of alleged poltergeist activity, from the Bingen-am-Rhein case to one in 1949, a few years before the book was published. After analyzing the cases Carrington concluded that 26 were undoubtedly fraudulent, and 19 were "doubtful." Assuming that all the doubtful cases were fraudulent as well, 330 cases remained "unexplained." In other words, they were apparently caused by some supernatural force.

Carrington admitted that the standard of evidence varied greatly, and that in many cases it was not high. In fact, such substandard evidence, coupled with the proven frauds, has always strengthened the arguments of the skeptics. As early as 1584 Reginald Scot in his *Discoverie of Witchcraft* was writing: "I could recite a great Number of Tales, how Men have even forsaken their Houses, because of apparitions and Noises; and all has been by meer and rank Knavery; and wheresoever you shall hear that there are such rumbling and fearful Noises, be you assured, that it is flat Knavery, performed by some that seem most to complain, and are least suspected . . ."

Scot was a remarkable man who, in an age of superstition, hit out with considerable force against those who believed in witchcraft; but his strong skepticism on the subject of the occult in general seems to have led him to throw the baby out with the bath water. Today most psychic investigators would agree that there have been many instances of genuine poltergeist effects.

One characteristic that most poltergeists have in common is that they generally occur in a household containing an adolescent. It seems possible that the onset of puberty may in some way generate the forces that produce the poltergeist effects.

The Wesleys and Old Jeffrey

This factor was certainly present in the case of the Wesley poltergeist. John Wesley, the founder of the Methodist Church, was a boy of 13 when in 1715 strange knocking noises began to be heard in the family's house, Epworth Rectory, in Lincolnshire, England. The Wesleys were a large family. Besides John there were 18 other children including Molly, aged 20; Hetty, 19; Nancy, 15; Patty, 10; and Kezzy, 7. In a letter to her eldest son Samuel, Mrs. Wesley described the beginning of the events: "On the first of December our maid heard, at the door of the dining room, several dismal groans, like a person in extremes, at the point of death." When the maid looked behind the door she found no one there.

The following day various raps were heard, and on the third day Molly heard the rustle of a silken gown passing quite close to her. The same evening something began to knock on the dining table, and footsteps were heard on the stairs. As the days passed other noises were added: the sound of a cradle rocking; another like the turning of a windmill; another like a carpenter planing wood. The poltergeist frequently interrupted family prayers.

Gradually the Wesleys became accustomed to the disturbances, and even jocularly nicknamed the unseen presence "Old Jeffrey." In the record he kept of the events, John Wesley wrote: "Kezzy desired no better diversion than to pursue Old Jeffrey from room to room."

Suddenly, after a visit of two months, Old Jeffrey left the Wesleys, and the Rectory at Epworth has been quiet ever since.

The Wesley poltergeist attracted the attention of no less a scientist than Joseph Priestley, a Fellow of the Royal Society for the Advancement of Science, and the discoverer of oxygen. Priestley mulled over the facts of the Wesley case, and in 1784 reported his findings in the *Arminian Magazine*. His article showed that he suspected Hetty Wesley of some unconscious part in the phenomena. It was significant, said Priestley, that "the disturbances were centered around Hetty's bed, and were marked by Hetty's trembling in her sleep."

The Wesley case was typical of most poltergeists in that it harmed no one. The Wesleys were also fortunate in that Old Jeffrey confined itself to noises. Many poltergeists have a destructive streak, and hurl crockery about with reckless abandon. Oddly, though, these flying objects rarely strike anyone, and when they do their impact is slight—even when they appear to travel at great speed. Occasionally poltergeist activity takes the form of showers of stones—or even coins, or shoes.

The Bell Witch

Although poltergeists rarely hurt anyone, there is one striking exception to the rule. This was the notorious "Bell Witch," a malevolent force that tormented the Bell family of Robertson County, Tennessee, for nearly four years. It apparently caused the death of the father, John Bell. The word "poltergeist" was not widely known in the United States in 1817 when the phenomena first occurred. Neither the family nor their neighbors knew what to call the thing that plagued them. The birth of Spiritualism was 30 years in the future, and in any case, once the thing began to talk, it asserted that it was not the spirit of someone who had died, but "a spirit from everywhere." Once it called itself a witch, and that was the term that stuck.

John Bell was a prosperous farmer, well-liked and respected by his neighbors, who lived with his wife Luce and his nine children in a large farmhouse surrounded by outbuildings and slave quarters. At the time of the first outbreak Bell's daughter Betsy, who figured prominently in the case, was a robust, apparently contented girl of 12. Richard Williams Bell, who later wrote an account of the disturbances entitled *Our Family Trouble*, was a boy of six.

The disturbances began with knockings and scrapings that seemed to come from the outside of the walls and windows of the house. Later the sounds entered the house, taking the form of gnawing noises on bedposts, scratchings on the floorboards, and flappings on the ceiling. Gradually the noise increased until at times it seemed to shake the house. The Witch continually added new sounds to its repertoire: chairs being overturned, stones raining on the roof, heavy chains being dragged across the floor. According to Richard Williams' book the noises bothered Betsy more than the other members of the family.

It began to show physical strength. Richard Williams Bell was awakened one night by something pulling at his hair. "Immediately Joel [one of the children] yelled out in great fright, and next Elizabeth [Betsy] was screaming in her room, and after that something was continually pulling at her hair after she retired to bed."

Up to this point the family had kept their curious troubles to themselves, but now they decided to ask the advice of a friend and neighbor, James Johnson. Johnson listened attentively to the noises, and concluded that some intelligence lay behind them. He performed a simple exorcism, which helped for a while.

When the Witch returned it did so with renewed vigor, and concentrated on Betsy to such an extent that her parents became seriously worried. It slapped her face, leaving crimson patches on her cheeks, and it pulled her hair with such force that she screamed in agony.

By this time Johnson was convinced that whatever the thing was, it could understand human language and ought to be capable of communication. He advised John Bell to call in more neighbors to form an investigating committee. Unfortunately, the committee seems to have done more harm than good. The members, fascinated by the effects and presumably safe enough themselves, invited it to "rap on the wall, smack its mouth, etc., and in this way," wrote Richard Williams, "the phenomena were gradually developed."

The Witch began to throw sticks and stones at the Bell children as they went to and from school. Apparently the children soon became accustomed to this and they developed a game with it. When a stick was thrown at them, they would mark it and throw it back. "Invariably," wrote Richard Williams, "the same sticks would be hurled back at us."

This sort of thing was harmless enough, but the Witch was now becoming more violent. Occasionally it struck people in the face with what felt like a clenched fist. Meanwhile Betsy, who had always been robust, began to suffer fainting fits and shortness of breath, each spell lasting for about half an hour. During these attacks the Witch remained silent, but as soon as the girl had recovered her composure it began to whistle and talk again. Its voice, which had been faint and inarticulate at first, gradually developed to a low but distinct whisper. Because the talking never occurred while Betsy was suffering a seizure, someone suggested that she might be producing the voice herself, by ventriloquism. A doctor "placed his hand over Betsy's mouth and soon satisfied himself that she was in no way connected with these sounds."

The Witch's first utterances tended to be of a pious nature. It showed an astonishing ability to reproduce, word for word, the Sunday sermons of the two local parsons, even imitating their voices. In a commentary on the case, included in *The Story of the Poltergeist*, psychoanalyst Nandor Fodor observes that the Witch "would have made a grand 'spirit communicator' if it had been imbued with mediumistic ideas." After its pious phase, however, the Witch began uttering obscenities—very distressing to a Bible Belt family. It also declared its hatred for "old Jack Bell" and said it would torment him for all his life.

From that time onward the farmer began to decline. He complained of stiffness in his mouth and of something punching either side of his jaw. His tongue became so swollen that he could neither eat nor speak. These attacks sometimes lasted as long as 15 hours. Then he developed a nervous tic in his cheek. It seemed to spread to the rest of his body so that eventually he was permanently bedridden, twitching in a kind of constant delirium.

The Witch seemed to have mixed feelings toward the rest of the family. The mother, whom Betsy adored, was showered with presents of fruit and nuts which appeared from nowhere. Joel, Richard, and Drewry were frequently thrashed by the Witch, but never seriously hurt. As for Betsy herself, after her fainting spells ceased she seemed to be left in peace—at least physically. But the Witch began persecuting the girl emotionally. She had already become engaged in her early teens to a neighbor, Joshua Gardner. The Witch relentlessly sought to break up the engagement, whispering into the girl's ear, "Please, Betsy Bell, don't have Joshua Gardner, please, Betsy Bell, don't marry Joshua Gardner," and adding that if she married the boy she would never know a moment's peace. Eventually it succeeded in breaking up the relationship.

John Bell Dies

In the autumn of 1820 John Bell managed to rouse himself from his bed and go about the farm business. But the Witch was not about to allow this. Richard Williams recalled how his father staggered suddenly, as if stunned by a heavy blow to the head, and slumped pathetically onto a log by the side of the road while "his face commenced jerking with fearful contortions." The father's shoes would fly off as fast as the boy could put them on. All the while "the reviling sound of derisive songs" and "demoniac shrieks" rang around them. Finally the shrieks faded away, the contortions ceased, and the boy saw tears running down his father's quivering cheeks.

Defeated, John Bell returned to his bed. On December 19, 1820, he was discovered in a deep stupor and could not be roused. His son John Jr. went to the medicine cabinet, but instead of Bell's prescribed medicine found a "smoky looking vial, which was about one-third full of dark colored liquid."

The doctor was sent for, but when he arrived the Witch was heard crowing: "It's useless for you to try and relieve old Jack— I have got him this time; he will never get up from that bed again." Bell died the next morning. As his coffin was lowered into the grave, the Witch had a final gloat: its voice could be heard singing a raucous song, "Row me up some brandy, O."

The family doctor tested the potion found in the medicine bottle on a cat, and the cat immediately went into convulsions and died. Instead of analyzing the liquid, the doctor threw it into the fire. No satisfactory medical explanation of John Bell's death was ever given.

After his death the phenomena gradually faded. As his family was sitting down to supper one evening, a kind of smoke bomb burst in the room and a voice announced that it was going but would return in seven years. The return took place as promised, after Betsy had left to marry another man and only Mrs. Bell, Joel, and Richard Williams remained in the house—but consisted only of a brief scuffling and twitching of bedclothes. After that the Witch vanished forever.

Although some of the peripheral aspects of the Bell Witch case may have become distorted with the passing of the years, it seems certain that the principal phenomena did take place. The case is still regarded as worthy of serious study, and it has been explored at length in several works on parapsychology.

The most interesting psychological aspect of the Bell Witch mystery lies in the relationship between Betsy Bell and her father. First of all, let's consider the symptoms experienced by the girl. Dr. Fodor points out that Betsy's fainting fits and dizzy spells— immediately followed by the voice of the Witch—are very similar to the symptoms exhibited by a medium while going into trance. He also notes that the girl was healthy and sexually precocious.

Her father, on the other hand, showed all signs of what a modern psychiatrist would recognize as acute guilt expressed in physical ways: the nervous tic, the inability to eat or speak, and the general withdrawal from the world. Despite some evidence that an unknown person might have administered the poison that finally killed him, the strong possibility remains that he killed himself—goaded beyond endurance by the phantom.

Describing the Bell Witch, Dr. Fodor notes that the entity could not account for itself or its strange powers when asked by the committee of neighbors. It was singularly human in its emotional behavior, playing pranks, imitating people, occasionally showing great solicitude for Luce Bell.

It also loathed John Bell with the most profound loathing.

Dr. Fodor concluded that Betsy Bell suffered from a split personality—that in some mysterious way part of her subconscious mind had taken on a life of its own. This renegade part of Betsy's psyche methodically plagued her father to death.

The psychology of such a split is still a mystery. Only very rarely do cases of multiple personality appear, but when they do, some powerful emotional shock is usually the triggering factor. Drawing on cases of neurosis and psychosis with which he was familiar, Dr. Fodor made a "purely speculative guess" at the origin of the Bell Witch. Noting that the onset of puberty and budding sexuality would tend to be traumatic in the puritanical surroundings in which Betsy grew up, he speculated that in her case the shock might have been aggravated by the awakening of long-suppressed memories. What were these memories? Dr. Fodor's theory was, as he put it, "not for the grim and prudish." He thought that in childhood Betsy may have been molested by her father.

The theory may sound far-fetched, but incest is not as uncommon as we tend to assume—particularly in rural communities. Dr. Fodor points to the fact that the first appearance of Bell's severe guilt symptoms coincided with Betsy's puberty. Perhaps Bell's guilt was so extreme that to some extent he co-operated with the Witch in causing his own illness.

As to why the Witch persecuted Betsy, this is comprehensible if we accept the premise that it was part of the girl's own sub-conscious. If part of Betsy's psyche was determined to kill John Bell, it would at the same time have terrible guilt feelings about this, and would exact some penance from her conscious self. This took the form of blighting her youthful romance. "The sacrifice [of her engagement] came first," says Fodor, "but the murder, mentally, had been envisioned long before."

The Laboratory of Dr Rhine

Had the Bell Witch case occurred in the first part of the 20th century instead of 100 years earlier, we would be in a better position to evaluate it, both psychologically and psychically. Today psychical research is becoming more and more sophisticated. The Parapsychology Laboratory at Duke University, founded by Dr. J. B. Rhine, is perhaps the best equipped psychical research unit in the world. The staff members go to painstaking lengths in examining many paranormal phenomena, including cases of poltergeist activity. Dr. Rhine's assistant, J. Gaither Pratt, described some of the laboratory's methods in his book *Parapsychology*. In one chapter he tells of the Seaford Poltergeist, which troubled a middle-class Long Island family and was investigated by Dr. Pratt and William G. Roll, another psychical researcher, during February and March 1958.

Mr. and Mrs. James M. Herrmann lived with their two children James, age 12, and Lucille, 13, at their home in Seaford, Nassau County, New York. Over a period of two months, 67 recorded disturbances were investigated not only by the Duke University team but also by the Nassau County Police. The phenomena fell into two categories: the unscrewing of bottle caps followed by the spilling of the bottles' contents; and the moving of furniture and small objects.

Although Dr. Pratt states that no firm conclusion could be reached as to the cause of the Seaford poltergeist, he observes that nothing ever happened when all the family were out of the house, when they were fast asleep, or when the children were both at school. He also notes that the disturbances usually took place nearer to James than to any other member of the family.

Dr. Pratt's account is of interest mainly in showing to what lengths a psychical researcher must go before concluding that an alleged poltergeist is genuine. Between them Dr. Pratt, Roll, and Detective Joseph Tozzi first ruled out the possibility of hoax by one or more members of the family. Observing the tangible evidence of the force—the smashed objects and spilled liquids—they could quickly rule out collective hallucination. Next, they checked the possibility that the disturbances could be caused by high frequency radio waves, vibrations, chemical interference (in the case of the spilled liquids), faulty electrical wiring, drafts, water level alteration in a well near the house, possible underground streams, radio frequencies outside the house, and subsidence of the land under the house. They held a conference at nearby Adelphi College with members of the science departments, and they called in structural, civil, and electrical engineers from the Nassau Society of Engineers. They examined the possibility that takeoffs and landings at nearby Mitchell Air Field might be causing the events, and they checked the house's plumbing installations from top to bottom.

All of their findings were negative. After almost two months on the spot, Dr. Pratt tentatively gave his opinion that they were not dealing with the "kind of impersonal psychical force which perhaps sometime in the future will fall within the scope of physics . . . If the Seaford disturbances were not fraudulent—and no evidence of fraud was found—they clearly make a proper claim upon the interests of parapsychologists." In other words, in his opinion some intelligence lay behind the disturbance.

Dr. Pratt did not overlook the fact that in the Seaford case, as in most poltergeist cases, adolescent children were on the scene. So far as he could tell during his short visit, neither of the Herrmann children had psychological problems. Perhaps no such problem is required; perhaps puberty itself can trigger off poltergeist phenomena as its energies react with other forces.

The existence of other forces can't be completely dismissed, for there have been some poltergeist cases in which no adolescents were involved. This was true in the case of the poltergeist phenomena at Killakee Arts Center in Ireland, which was also haunted by a phantom black cat. Margaret O'Brien, the only person who lived on the premises throughout the entire disturbance period—from the late 1960s to the end of 1970—is a mature and intelligent woman. Furthermore, she was absent from the house on several occasions when phenomena occurred. It's impossible, therefore, to link the trouble with any one person.

It does seem possible, though, that the Killakee poltergeist may have been goaded into activity—perhaps even created—by some amateur psychic investigators. It's worth remembering that the Bell Witch investigating committee helped to develop the phenomena by urging the presence to "smack its mouth" and make other noises. Old Jeffrey, the Wesley poltergeist, was encouraged to some extent by Kezzy following it from room to room, teasing it. A poltergeist may be an unhuman force, but it often seems capable of reacting to human interference.

After the appearance of a monstrous black cat during the renovation of Killakee House, several other apparitions were reported, though none of them was as vivid as the cat.

Following reports of these strange events in the Irish press, a group of show business personalities from Dublin persuaded Margaret O'Brien to let them try a seance at the house. They arranged letters of the alphabet in a circle on a table and used a glass turned upside down as a pointer that could be controlled by any psychic forces present. The results of the seance were inconclusive—although the lights failed, apparently without cause, at one point during the evening. Within a couple of days of the seance, however, serious disturbances began.

They began sporadically at first with bumps and rappings in the night, and lights being switched on and off. Then some of the artists living in the Center began to suffer sleepless nights, kept awake by the chiming of bells, although there were no bells in the neighborhood. The next stage of activity was more vigorous. Heavy pieces of furniture in locked rooms were found overturned, a stout oak chair was pulled apart joint from joint, and another solid chair was smashed to slivers.

For a few weeks after the chair smashing, peace descended. Then the disturbances began again. This time crockery was flung about and shattered, wide areas of the walls were smeared with glue, and several of the paintings were ripped to shreds.

Toward the end of 1970 the most peculiar of all the incidents occurred. They followed an attempt at exorcism by a Dublin

386

priest.

At this time Mr. and Mrs. O'Brien were still making improvements to the premises, and had not yet installed a refrigerator. Consequently the milkman made use of a natural "icebox" in the form of a cool stream that runs through the grounds. He left the milk bottles standing in its shallow water. One morning when Mrs. O'Brien went to the stream to get a bottle, she found that the foil caps of all the bottles had been removed, though the milk inside was undisturbed. This continued for several days.

At first the O'Briens assumed that birds were pecking off the tops, although no trace of foil was ever found. To stop the nuisance Mr. O'Brien built a four-sided box of heavy stone on the stream bed, covered it with a massive slab of slate, and instructed the milkman to place the bottles in the box and replace the slate lid. Still the caps disappeared.

As if in compensation, though, other kinds of caps began to appear inside the house. In view of the various disturbances, the O'Briens naturally enough made a practice of locking all doors and windows before retiring for the night. Despite this, caps and hats began to appear all over the house. There were Derby hats and opera hats, children's knitted hats with woolly pom poms on top, and men's and women's straw sun hats. The pride of the collection was a lady's linen cap with drawstrings which was identified as 19th-century in style, although it appeared new.

This peculiar activity ceased suddenly at the end of 1970, and although occasional knockings and footsteps are still reported, Killakee Arts Center has settled down to a relatively quiet life. It was investigated at the height of its activity, but only in a limited way in the course of preparing a television program on the strange occurrences. It seems a pity that no thorough scientific investigation was conducted at Killakee, for it certainly ranks among the most fascinating poltergeist mysteries.

33. Haunted Battlefields

Lieutenant John Scollay was normally an even-tempered man, but at the moment he was losing patience with his sergeant-major. Here, in a little wood outside Dunkirk, Scollay was trying to hold his company together in the face of sporadic but deadly German sniper fire. Too many of the green-kilted Scottish Highlanders had crumpled into the undergrowth that day in June 1940, and now, as night fell, the sergeant-major's absurd notion cracked Scollay's calm.

"What the bloody hell do you mean, *haunted*?" he snapped. "This wood is haunted by Huns, laddie, that's all you need to know and think about at the moment."

The sergeant-major was persistent. "The wood is haunted, sir," he whispered. "I know it and the lads know it. For the love of God, sir, we're no' scared of Germans. If we have to we'll advance, or we'll force a way through the Jerries on our flank—but we canna stay here another night!"

Ridiculous as the idea sounded, Scollay couldn't entirely dismiss it. For the past 48 hours his company had been holed up in this straggling thicket. They were surrounded by fields in which German soldiers were entrenched awaiting the arrival of tanks, which would mean the end for the little band of Scots. During those two days, the Highlanders had fought with their usual cheerful savagery, raking the enemy with Bren gun fire and cracking off rifle shots at any moving shadow. Now they seemed to be losing their morale—an unheard of occurrence among the 51st Highlanders. Because of *ghosts*?

"It's just a presence, sir," explained the sergeant-major, "but we've all felt it. It's a kind of force pushing us away. And it's something that none of us can fight sir—something uncanny."

Eventually the 51st dropped back, joining the other British troops in the disastrous retreat from Dunkirk. Once clear of the "haunted wood" Scollay's men regained their determination and high spirits, but against the Panzer tanks and Stuka dive-bombers they could do nothing. Most of them were either slain or taken prisoner on the dunes of Dunkirk.

Scollay himself spent the duration of the war in a German P.O.W. camp, where he occasionally pondered the words of the sergeant-major on that night in June. When the war ended, he went back to the "haunted wood." Some research in a Dunkirk library uncovered a significant fact: in the summer of 1415, a few months before the Battle of Agincourt, English soldiers had fought the French in that same thicket.

Had the spirits of the slain English and French soldiers whose bodies had lain in the underbrush somehow come back to haunt their successors, more than 500 years later? Or was the area permeated with an aura of death, which the Scots began to sense after two days of exposure to it? There was no local tradition of haunting on that spot, but perhaps the psychic force had lain dormant for five centuries to manifest only under the stimulus of fresh violence.

Scollay is not sure what that force was, but he is convinced of its existence. "There could never be any question of the courage of those men in battle," he says. "Their valor is a matter of record. But something more than gunfire frightened the hell out of them that day."

If that little wood in northern France is haunted, it is only one of the battlefields with supernatural reputations. According to legend, the battlefield of Marathon was such a place. For several years following the Greeks' victory over the Persians there in 492 B.C., the battle was mysteriously repeated every night. Anyone visiting the field after sunset heard the clash of steel upon steel and the screams of the wounded and dying, and smelled the odor of blood. Those who were unfortunate enough actually to see the ghostly warriors reportedly died within the year.

Spectral battles are a dramatic example of the kind of apparition we call a haunting. When most people think of ghosts they think of the kind that appear over and over in the same place. The "single-appearance" apparition, such as a crisis apparition, is less familiar. A ghost that appears to one person—or even a group of people—at one time only is a private kind of ghost. But a ghost that is associated with a particular place and has been seen there more than once is a ghost that might be seen by anyone. Moreover, the haunting ghost usually has a dramatic story behind it—some reason why the person's spirit, or image, seems to be fixed there. The supposed reason for the haunt is usually found to be either great unhappiness experienced by the person in that place, or great emotional attachment to the place, or some form of violence.

Following this line of thought, we can assume that if *any* place is haunted, a battlefield surely would be. The pain and terror once concentrated there, the pride in victory and shame in defeat, not to mention the prodigious energy expended by the men would somehow be impressed on the spot, capable of being sensed or even seen and heard by people with sufficient psychic awareness. If this theory is correct, one would expect all battlefields to be haunted, but relatively few of them have this reputation.

The Shepherds of Edgehill
Of such battlefield hauntings, one of the most famous took place in England at Edgehill, Warwickshire. There, on October 23, 1643, Royalist troops commanded by the King's nephew, Prince Rupert, and Parliamentarian troops under Oliver Cromwell fought the first battle of the English Civil War. After the battle, which was indecisive, the bodies of some 5000 men lay on the frozen ground of Edgehill.

A month after the battle some local shepherds saw a strange sight—the soldiers of King and Parliament locked once more in struggle, drums beating, harnesses creaking, cannons belching shot and smoke. This time, however, there were no bodies left on the ground. When the phantom armies were seen again, on Christmas Eve, news of the phenomenon was sent to Charles I. The King ordered several officers, some of whom had fought at Edgehill, to go and investigate.

On their return the officers brought detailed confirmation of the news. Not only had they interviewed the shepherds and recorded their accounts in detail, but they had also on two occasions seen the battle themselves. They recognized some of

390

the men known to have died at Edgehill. They also recognized the figure of Prince Rupert, who was very much alive. Whether or not anyone took notice of it at the time, this particular observation was a strong piece of evidence for the theory that ghosts are not the spirits of the departed, but rather a kind of recording of a scene that is left to be replayed under certain circumstances.

King Charles interpreted the ghostly battle as an omen that the rebellion against him would soon be put down—an interpretation that was proved wrong six years later when Cromwell's party assumed power and had the King beheaded.

The American Civil War was perhaps the greatest tragedy in the history of the United States, and we might expect its battlefields to echo with this terrible conflict that swallowed up the lives of nearly half a million men. Yet the Civil War battlefields remain, for the most part, silent. Occasionally a story surfaces about phantom troops at Gettysburg, but the only Civil War battlefield widely reputed to be haunted is Shiloh. This spot in Tennessee was where General Johnston's Confederates surprised the encamped army of General Grant on April 6, 1862. After two days' fighting, in which more than 24,000 men were killed, the Union Army defeated the Confederates. The river is said to have run deep pink with blood for days afterward. As soon as the terrible debris of battle had been cleared away, rumors began to circulate of phantom armies appearing on the field every now and then—rumors that persist even today.

Britain is often said to be the most haunted country in the world. Actually, it is probably no more or less haunted than any other country, but as a people who cherish their traditions, the British do more than other nations to keep their ghosts alive so to speak. There is scarcely a country house from one tip of the island to the other without its resident phantom.

The ghosts of Littlecote, a manor in Wiltshire, recall a tragic and gory incident of Elizabethan days. In the 16th century the mansion belonged to "Wicked" Will Darrell. One stormy night in 1575, Darrell sent for the midwife Mrs. Barnes, who lived in a village some distance away. She was offered a large fee to attend a lady in childbirth, but was blindfolded by Darrell's servants so that she would not remember the route to the house.

Arriving at Littlecote, Mrs. Barnes was led upstairs by the

master of the house to a richly furnished bedchamber where she found a woman in labor, wearing a mask. Darrell told the midwife that if the woman were delivered safely, she would be handsomely rewarded, but that if the woman died, she herself would lose her life. The terrified midwife did her work, and soon the lady gave birth to a son. When Mrs. Barnes showed the baby to Darrell, he led her to a fireplace on the landing and commanded her to throw the child into the fire. On her knees the distraught woman begged him to let her keep the child herself, but Darrell snatched the baby from her and hurled it into the flames. In the morning Mrs. Barnes was blindfolded again and returned to her home.

While she had awaited the baby's birth, however, Mrs. Barnes had stealthily cut a piece of cloth from the bed curtains and sewn them up again. With this scrap of evidence and her description of the house, she went to the local magistrates, who were able to identify the house as Littlecote. Because of his wealth and influence, however, Darrell was able to escape justice by bribing the judge.

Ultimately another kind of justice dealt with Will Darrell, for one day when he was riding to hounds, he was thrown from his horse and his neck was broken. According to legend the place where he fell was haunted by the image of a child enveloped in flames—like the innocent baby he had murdered.

Within the house itself, the bedchamber where the unknown lady gave birth, and the landing where the murder took place have occasionally echoed with the screams of midwife, mother, and baby, and some people claim to have seen the figure of the anguished midwife clutching the child.

Leaving aside the specters who were victims of violence, let's consider a haunting that took place a few years ago in a charming and comfortable rectory in the village of Yattendon in Berkshire, England. Part of the house was built in the 18th century, but extensive alterations were made around 1900. One of the two ghosts that haunted the house—a pleasant-faced elderly lady—was sometimes seen to follow the path of a staircase removed during the alterations. This kind of behavior is common to many haunts; a part of a wall through which a ghost habitually disappears, for example, often turns out to be the site of a former doorway.

A detailed account of the haunting at Yattendon Rectory appears in Dennis Bardens' book *Ghosts and Hauntings*. Bardens visited the house some years ago and talked to four people who had seen the ghosts: the Reverend A. B. Farmer, the former Rector; his wife; their daughter; and a Mrs. Barton who had stayed with them for several months. Mrs. Barton saw the younger looking of the two ghosts, and described her as "rather pretty" and dressed in a "silvery gray frock" of 18th-century design. A "light seemed to be shining around her." Both Mrs. Barton and Mrs. Farmer, who had seen the figure on another occasion, noticed that she walked above the level of the floor.

This rather elegant lady was not so frequent a visitor as "Mrs. It," whose appearances, said the rector's wife, were quite a "usual occurrence." The figure varied in its distinctness, sometimes resembling a cloud of dark gray smoke, at other times appearing nearly human. She too was dressed in 18th-century clothing. Her skirt, said Mrs. Farmer, was "of thick, black, watered silk. It has a full round bottom, is very voluminous, and the top part of her is covered by a dark shawl, probably wool, under which she carries a basket or handle — her head is covered by a hat (with cap underneath) which is tied on with ribbon under her chin."

Mrs. It seemed to take an interest in the doings of the family. "During the preparation for my daughter's wedding," said Mrs. Farmer, "she was seen inspecting the wedding presents and the arrangements in the kitchen." Was the ghost really aware of what was going on around her? If so, why did she walk up a stairway that no longer existed? But then, ghosts are obviously not bound by the limitations of our world, and perhaps Mrs. It had had a fondness for the stairway when she lived in the rectory some two centuries ago.

Eventually the Farmers left the house, and a new rector came to live there. The new family was not enthusiastic about spectral visitors, and they asked Mr. Farmer to conduct a service of exorcism. He obliged, and the ladies have not been seen since.

The popular notion that graveyards are apt to be haunted has not been confirmed by psychical research. Traditional stories of picturesquely draped figures, clanking chains, and sepulchral voices issuing from the graves are just that — stories. A phantom is much more likely to appear in the places the person frequented while alive.

There is at least one graveyard, however, that does seem to be haunted—by what exactly no one has yet been able to determine. The cemetery lies on a hill in the Wet Mountain Valley area of Colorado, and its phantoms—whatever they are—appear nearly every night for all to see.

In 1880 the township of Silver Cliff enjoyed a "silver rush." Miners and their families invaded the area, and by the end of the year the town's inhabitants numbered more than 5000. The boom did not last, however, and today Silver Cliff is a ghost town in more ways than one, having a living population of only about 100, slightly less than the town's old graveyard.

The strange phenomena that haunt this graveyard were first seen in 1880, when a group of drunken miners returning to their diggings reported seeing eerie blue lights hovering over each grave. Nor were these lights just a by-product of whiskey— they appeared on other nights to sober observers. Many years later in 1956 the ghost lights were written up in the *Wet Mountain Tribune*, and in 1967 they attracted the attention of the *New York Times*. Hundreds of tourists came to see the uncanny spectacle. Two years later, in an article about Colorado in the *National Geographic*, assistant editor Edward J. Linehan described his first look at the lights.

Linehan drove out to the graveyard accompanied by local resident Bill Kleine. It was dark when they reached the place, and Kleine told Linehan to switch off the headlights. They got out of the car, and Kleine pointed: "There! See them? And over there!"

Linehan saw them—"dim, round spots of blue-white light" glowing above the graves. He stepped forward for a better look at one, but it vanished, then slowly reappeared. He switched on his flashlight and aimed it at one of the lights. The beam of the flashlight revealed only a tombstone. For 15 minutes the men pursued the elusive ghost lights among the graves.

Kleine told Linehan that some people theorized that the lights were caused by the reflections of the town lights of Silver Cliff and nearby Westcliff. Linehan turned to look back at the two small towns in the distance. The tiny clusters of their lights seemed far too faint to produce the effect in the graveyard. What's more, Kleine remarked that both he and his wife had seen the ghost lights "when the fog was so thick you couldn't see the towns at all."

Other theories have been advanced to explain the phenomenon. One is that the ghost lights are caused by radioactive ore; but a Geiger counter test of the whole area revealed no trace of radioactivity. Another says the ghost lights are luminous paint, daubed on the tombs by hoaxers; but no evidence has ever been found to support this charge. Still another theory is that the ghost lights reflect the mercury vapor of the Westcliff streetlights; but there were no mercury vapor lights until recently, and once when a power failure shut off every light in town, the graveyard lights still shone.

An entirely different approach to the puzzle has been offered by the anthropologist and folklorist Dale Ferguson. He notes that the Cheyenne and other Plains Indians laid their dead to rest on hilltops "sacred to the spirits." Sometimes a particularly powerful medicine man would feel his own death approaching, walk to the "dead men's hill," and lie down there until his soul was "taken." A number of Indian tales, he says, mention "dancing blue spirits" on such sites.

Among the old-timers of Silver Cliff only one explanation holds good: the blue-white spots are the helmet lamps of long dead miners, still seeking frantically for silver on the hillside.

"No doubt someone, someday, will prove there's nothing at all supernatural in the luminous manifestations of Silver Cliff's cemetery," concludes Linehan. "And I will feel a tinge of disappointment."

34. The Cry of the Banshee

"It started low at first like, then it mounted up into a crescendo; there was definitely some human element in the voice . . . the door to the bakery where I worked was open too, and the men stopped to listen. Well, it rose as I told you to a crescendo, and you could almost make out one or two Gaelic words in it; then gradually it went away slowly. Well, we talked about it for a few minutes and at last, coming on to morning, about five o'clock, one of the bread servers came in and he says to me, 'I'm afraid they'll need you to take out the cart, for I just got word of the death of an aunt of mine.' It was at his cart that the bansidhe had keened."

More commonly spelled "banshee," as it is pronounced, "bansidhe" is the Gaelic word for "fairy woman," a creature whose mournful cry is said to foretell death. The above quotation was taken from a British Broadcasting Corporation program that Irish psychical researcher Sheila St. Clair conducted with several people who claimed to have themselves experienced the hideous wail of the banshee. In the same program an elderly man from County Down described the fairy death wail in more detail. "It was a mournful sound" he said; "it would have put ye in mind of them ould yard cats on the wall, but it wasn't cats, I know it meself; I thought it was a bird in torment or something . . . a mournful cry it was, and then it was going a wee bit further back, and further until it died away altogether . . . "

The banshee cried for ancient Irish heroes. It wailed for King Connor McNessa, Finn MacCool, and the great Brian Boru, whose victory over the Danes in 1014 ended their sovereignty over Ireland. More recently its eerie voice is said to have echoed in the Cork village of Sam's Cross when General Michael Collins, commander-in-chief of the Irish Free State Army, was killed in an ambush near there in 1922. A few months later when Commandant Sean Dalton was shot in Tralee, a song recalls: "When Dalton died sure the bansidhe cried, in the Valley of Knockanure."

Although its name translates as "fairy woman," most authorities define the banshee as a spirit rather·than a fairy. In some families—the O'Briens, for example—the banshee is considered to be almost a guardian angel, silently watching over the fortunes of the family and guiding its members along safe and profitable paths. When an O'Brien dies this guardian performs her last service, keening for the departing soul.

A County Antrim man gave his interpretation of the banshee to Sheila St. Clair. He claimed that the Irish, as a reward for their piety, had been blessed with guardian spirits to take care of their individual clans. Because these celestial beings were not normally able to express themselves in human terms and yet became involved with the family under their care, God allowed them to show their deep feeling only when one of their charges died. Then the banshee was permitted to howl out its sorrow.

The Banshee in the U.S.A.

James O'Barry was the pseudonym used by a Boston businessman who wrote to the author on the subject, and if O'Barry's testimony is to be believed the banshee, like some other creatures of European folklore, has crossed the Atlantic.

Like many of Boston's Irish Catholics, O'Barry is descended from a family that arrived in Massachusetts in 1848, fleeing the great famine that decimated Ireland's population in the 19th century. His great-great grandfather started a small grocery business, and today O'Barry and his two brothers run a supermarket chain which has branches throughout New England.

"When I was a very small boy," O'Barry recalls, "I was lying in bed one morning when I heard a weird noise, like a demented woman crying. It was spring, and outside the window the birds were singing, the sun was shining, and the sky was blue. I thought for a moment or two that a wind had sprung up, but a glance at the barely stirring trees told me that this was not so.

"I got up, dressed, and went downstairs, and there was my father sitting at the kitchen table with tears in his eyes. I had never seen him weep before. My mother told me that they had just heard, by telephone, that my grandfather had died in New York. Although he was an old man, he was fit as a fiddle, and his death was unexpected."

It was some years before O'Barry learned the legend of the banshee, and he then recalled the wailing noise he had heard on the death of his grandfather. In 1946 he was to hear it for the second time. In May of that year he was an administrative officer serving with the U.S. Air Force in the Far East. One morning at six o'clock he was awakened by a low howl.

"That time," he said, "I was instantly aware of what it was. I sat bolt upright in my bed, and the hair on the back of my neck prickled. The noise got louder, rising and falling like an air-raid siren. Then it died away, and I realized that I was terribly depressed. I knew my father was dead. A few days later I had notification that this was so."

Seventeen years later, O'Barry heard the hair-stiffening voice of the banshee a third time. He was in Toronto, Canada, by himself, enjoying a combined holiday and business trip.

"Again I was in bed, reading the morning papers," he said, "when the dreadful noise was suddenly filling my ears. I thought of my wife, my young son, my two brothers, and I thought 'Good God, don't let it be one of them.' But for some reason I knew it wasn't."

The date was November 22, 1963, the time shortly after noon, and the Irish banshee was bewailing the death of an acquaintance of O'Barry's—John F. Kennedy, President of the United States.

Sightings

The banshee is rarely seen as an apparition, but when she does appear she takes the form of a red-haired, green-eyed woman. The Welsh have their own harbinger of death, a revolting old woman known as "The Dribbling Hag." In Scotland, "death women" can sometimes be seen on the banks of westward-running streams, washing the clothing of those about to die. One Scottish family, the Ewens of the Isle of Mull, Argyllshire, preserve a curious legend concerning their own death spirit. In the early 16th century Eoghan a' Chin Bhig—Ewen of the Little Head—lived at Loch Sguabain Castle, Isle of Mull, as clan chief. His wife was the daughter of another chief, The MacLaine, and Ewen and his father-in-law were forever quarreling. In 1538 matters reached serious proportions, and both sides collected followers for a showdown.

The evening before the battle, Ewen was walking near Loch Sguabain when he came across an old woman washing a bundle of blood-stained shirts in a stream. She was dressed from head to foot in green and Ewen knew that she was a death woman, and that the shirts were those of the men who would die in the morning. He asked if his own shirt was among them, and she said that it was. "But," she added, "if your wife offers you bread and cheese with her own hand, without you asking for it, you will be victorious."

As dawn broke and Ewen buckled on his sword he waited anxiously for his wife to offer him the food. She failed to do so. Demoralized, Ewen led his followers to defeat at the hands of the MacLaines. At the height of the battle a swinging ax cut off his head clean from his shoulders. His black horse galloped away, its headless rider still sitting upright in the saddle. From that day onward, the dead chief himself became his clan's death warning, for when a Ewen was to die the phantom horse and headless rider were seen and heard thundering down Glen More on the shores of Loch Sguabain.

Three members of the Ewen family within living memory have reported seeing the phantom. At Lochbuie, home of the present clan chief, the vision is said to herald serious illness in the family as well as death itself.

Sheila St. Clair offers a theory to account for the banshee. In her book *Psychic Phenomena in Ireland* she says: "I would suggest that just as we inherit physical characteristics—for instance red hair, blue eyes—we also inherit memory cells, and that those of us with strong tribal lineages riddled with inter-marriage have the 'bansidhe' as part of an inherited memory. The symbolic form of a weeping woman may well be stamped on our racial consciousness. Ireland's women are experts at weeping over their slain sons and daughters. And just as our other levels of consciousness are not answerable to the limitations of time in our conscious mind, so a particular part of the mind throws up a symbolic hereditary pattern that has in the past been associated with tragedy in the tribe, be it woman, hare, or bird, as a kind of subliminal 'four-minute warning' so that we may prepare ourselves for that tragedy."

399

Essentially this theory agrees with psychiatrist C. G. Jung's theory of the "collective unconscious," an inherited storehouse of memories of mankind's early experiences.

Other eminent families are afflicted with different kinds of ghosts. Perhaps the most haunted family in Britain is that of the Bowes-Lyons, Earls of Strathmore, the family of the present queen's mother. Their ancestral home, Glamis Castle in County Angus, was the setting of Shakespeare's *Macbeth*—although King Duncan may not have even visited the castle, let alone been murdered there. Glamis (pronounced "Glahms") was, however, the place where King Malcolm II was stabbed to death in the 11th century. A stain said to have been caused by his blood still marks the floor in one of the castle's myriad rooms. Several ghosts haunt Glamis—a little black boy, a lady in gray, a former earl who supposedly played cards with the Devil and lost. But the most celebrated—and chilling—of all the castle's legends is the "Horror" of Glamis.

No one outside the Strathmore family knows what form the Horror takes, but evidence suggests that it is not merely an old wives' tale, and that some terrible mystery does lurk within the grim stone walls. The most frequent story is that a monster child was born to the Strathmores, so hideous that to look upon it was to invite madness. The thing lived to an unnaturally old age— and some say that it still lives locked away in a hidden room.

The possible existence of a hidden room in which the monster could be kept intrigued a party of house guests at Glamis some years ago, and they organized a search for it. Methodically the guests hung a piece of linen from every window they could find. When they went outside, they discovered that over a dozen windows were unaccounted for. The then-Lord Strathmore, who had been away during the experiment, returned unexpectedly and, realizing what his guests had been up to, flew into an uncharacteristically furious temper.

It was he who some years later told a friend who asked about the Horror: "If you could know of it, you would thank God you were not me."

Another theory about the Glamis Horror is presented by Eric Maple in his book *The Realm of Ghosts*. According to Maple, centuries ago during a clan feud some members of the Ogilvie Clan fleeing from the Lindsays, sought refuge at Glamis. The

Earl of Strathmore was bound by the laws of hospitality to admit them, but not wishing to appear partisan he took them to a remote room of the castle, locked them in, and left them to starve. Many years after they had died, their screams continued to echo occasionally in that part of the castle. Eventually one earl decided to investigate, and he made his way to the room from which the noises seemed to come. On opening the door and glimpsing the scene within, he fell backward in a faint into the arms of his companion. The earl refused to tell anyone what he had seen, but he had the door to the room bricked up. "There is a tradition," writes Maple, "that the spectacle within the haunted room was unbelievably horrible, for some of the starving men had actually died in the act of gnawing the flesh from their arms."

Both this story and the monster child story may be mere speculation. The truth of the matter is known only to the Earl of Strathmore. Tradition has it that each Strathmore heir is told the secret by his father on his 21st birthday. Lady Granville, a member of the Bowes-Lyon family, told ghost hunter J. Wentworth Day that female members of the family are never let in on the mystery. "We were never allowed to talk about it when we were children," she said. "My father and grandfather refused absolutely to discuss it."

There, as far as outsiders are concerned, the matter rests.

Some less prominent families have a more tangible form of ancestral Horror. Skulls kept as guardians and treated with a mixture of awe and affection were almost a fashion at one time, according to Celtic folklore—and again the custom seems to have crossed the Atlantic to America. The late A. J. Pew, a journalist from California, told the author of his family's own skull.

Pew's family was French, and arrived in the Louisiana Territory during the late 17th century. Family records from the earliest days of their settlement told of a skull, supposedly that of an ancestor who had been burned as a heretic in the Middle Ages, which was kept in a carved wooden box.

Like other such cranial family heirlooms, the skull—affectionately called "Ferdinand" by the Pews—showed an apparent sensitivity to its surroundings. "It had to be kept in the family house," wrote Pew, "and if it was taken off the premises it screamed. If it screamed *indoors*, it meant a death among us."

Apparently, however, Pew's father suspected the story to be a myth. He had the skull examined by a surgeon, who stated that in his opinion it had all the characteristics of an Indian skull, possibly one from the Florida area.

"I've rather lost touch with the relic and the branch of the family who owned it," Pew said, "but from that evidence I would guess that it came into the hands of the Pew family after their arrival in America, not before. Possibly some ancestor wanted to establish himself in this country, and cooked up the skull story to add an air of mystery to himself. Certainly my father never found concrete evidence of the skull actually screaming—only people who remembered people who had heard it scream."

The Pew family skull is not the only one of its kind. Several English families have possessed—sometimes reluctantly—bony relics that resist any attempts to give them a decent burial.

Burton Agnes Hall, a beautifully restored Elizabethan house, was for many years haunted by the apparition of Anne Griffith, the daughter of Sir Henry. Griffith who had built the house around 1590. Anne particularly loved Burton Agnés, and on her deathbed, according to the story, she asked that her head be cut off after she died and kept inside the house. Several subsequent owners of the house apparently disobeyed her request and removed the skull for burial, whereupon it would begin to scream. The fact that "Awd Nance"—as she was known to the Yorkshire locals—was frequently seen walking through the house was taken as an indication of her sense of insecurity about the resting place of her skull. Around 1900, the occupant of Burton Agnes Hall had the skull sealed into one of the walls to prevent its being removed. Since then Awd Nance has appeared infrequently.

At Wardley Hall, near Manchester, the resident skull is supposed to be that of a Catholic priest executed for treason in 1641. After being displayed on a Manchester church tower as a sinister warning to sympathizers, the priest's head was secretly removed and taken to Wardley Hall, the home of a Catholic family. For many years the skull was kept on view at the head of the staircase. Occasional attempts to remove it for burial brought repercussions in the form of violent storms and other disturbances. Once it was thrown into a pond but, in the words of ghost hunter Eric Maple, "managed to find its way back to the Hall again."

The folklore surrounding family skulls is full of such bizarre images. The best-known of them all, the Bettiscombe Manor Skull, was once buried nine feet deep in the earth by an owner who wanted to be rid of it. The owner was appalled on the following day to discover that the skull had worked its way to the surface, and was lying there apparently waiting to return home.

The Bettiscombe skull case is a classic example of the confusion and distortion that go into making a ghost legend. One version says that the skull is that of a black slave brought to Bettiscombe, Dorset, in the 18th century. In 1685 the owner of the manor, Azariah Pinney, had been exiled for political reasons and sent to the West Indies. The Pinneys prospered in the New World, and Azariah's grandson, John Frederick, eventually returned to Bettiscombe, bringing with him a black slave as his manservant. Pinney seems to have treated his slave well, and when the man asked that on his death his body be returned to Africa for burial, the master gave his promise.

After the black man's death, however, Pinney broke his promise, and had the man buried in the village churchyard not far from the manor house. During the course of the following weeks neither Pinney nor his family were able to sleep because of mysterious groans, shrieks, and bumps in the night. Finally the master disinterred the body and brought it back to his own loft. This seemed to satisfy it, for no more noises occurred.

The body remained in the loft for years until at some point—no one seems to know when or how—it disappeared. Except for the skull. That remained, minus its jawbone, and has been kept in the house almost continuously ever since. In 1847 a visitor at the house was shown the relic by a housekeeper, who told him: "While this skull is kept, no ghost will invade the premises." This was the first recorded mention of its supernatural qualities.

While investigating the Bettiscombe story in the mid-1960s, Maple found that the local people had plenty of tales to tell about the skull. He learned that on several occasions it had been removed from the Hall, only to bring various disasters on the area: thunderstorms that destroyed crops at harvest time, for example, and the wholesale death of cattle and other livestock. It was even asserted that several owners of Bettiscombe who had removed the skull had died within a year.

One man remembered as a youth hearing the skull "screaming like a trapped rat" in the attic—which somewhat contradicts the idea that it objects only to being removed from the house. Others mentioned peculiar rattling noises coming from the attic, believed to be "them" playing ninepins with the skull. Exactly who "they" were was left to the imagination.

The black slave has lingered in the folk-memory of the villagers 200 years after his death. Tales are told of a screaming black man "kept prisoner in a secret room and fed through a grating." And yet, other versions of the story say that John Pinney treated his slave kindly. Who can say what was the truth? A completely different legend says that the skull is that of a white girl who "long ago"—a favorite phrase of the legend-spinners— was kept prisoner in the house and then murdered.

Neither of these stories is likely to be true, for when the skull was examined by Professor Gilbert Causey of the Royal College of Surgeons, he pronounced it to be much older than anyone had suspected. It was, he said, the skull of a prehistoric woman.

The present owner of Bettiscombe Manor, Michael Pinney, believes it to be the relic of some foundation sacrifice which was placed in the building originally constructed on the site in order to propitiate the gods and bring good fortune. The later story of the black man was somehow grafted onto the original story of this sacrifice.

Although Pinney and his wife claim to regard their strange heirloom merely as a conversation piece, he has so far refused to allow it to be taken out of doors. Both he and his wife were slightly shaken when a visitor who stayed with them during World War II, and who knew the history of the skull, inquired: "Did it sweat blood in 1939, as it did in 1914?"

African or Caucasian, curse or good luck charm, the yellowing relic continues to keep a firm grasp on the imaginations of the Dorset farmers of the neighborhood. If it is, in fact, a reminder of ancient sacrifice, its hold on people's minds for more than 2000 years is scarcely less remarkable than that of the wailing banshee, that "symbolic form, stamped on our racial consciousness."

35. The Medium and the Message

Two days after the huge British airship, the R101, had crashed in flames on a hillside in Beauvais, France—killing 48 of its 54 passengers—the hesitant, anxious voice of a man claiming to be its captain spoke through the lips of a medium in London. In short disjointed sentences he described the horrifying last moments before his incineration. His account of the crash included a wealth of technical information that was confirmed six months later by an official inquiry. The disaster, which occurred on October 5, 1930, included two high ranking aviation officials among its victims. It shook the government's confidence in dirigibles, and ended British efforts to develop the lighter-than-air craft for commercial use.

The seance in which the dramatic communication was received took place at the National Laboratory of Psychical Research set up four years earlier by Harry Price, a well-known psychic investigator. Price, his secretary, and journalist Ian D. Coster, had arranged a sitting with the talented young medium Eileen Garrett. The purpose was to attempt a spirit contact with the recently deceased writer Sir Arthur Conan Doyle, the report of which was to be published in a magazine. Sir Arthur, the creator of Sherlock Holmes, was also a Spiritualist.

Shortly after the sitters had gathered in the seance room, Eileen Garrett went into a trance. Instead of making contact with the novelist, however, the sitters heard a voice announcing himself as Flight Lieutenant H. Carmichael Irwin. In anguished tones, the voice said: "I must do something about it . . . The whole bulk of the dirigible was entirely and absolutely too much for her engines' capacity. Engines too heavy. It was this that made me on five occasions have to scuttle to safety.

Useful lift too small. Gross lift computed badly—inform control panel. And this idea of new elevators totally mad. Elevator jammed. Oil pipe plugged . . . Flying too low altitude and never could rise. Disposable lift could not be utilized. Load too great for long flight . . . Cruising speed bad and ship badly swinging. Severe tension on the fabric which is chafing . . . Engines wrong—too heavy—cannot rise. Never reached cruising altitude—same in trials. Too short trials. No one knew the ship properly. Weather bad for long flight. Fabric all waterlogged and ship's nose is down. Impossible to rise. Cannot trim. Almost scraped the roofs of Achy. Kept to railway. At enquiry to be held later it will be found that the superstructure of the envelope contained no resilience and had far too much weight in envelope. The added middle section was entirely wrong . . . too heavy, too much overweighted for the capacity of engines . . . ."

The reporter who took this amazing communication in shorthand at first resented the intrusion of Irwin, captain of the R101, when he had expected the voice of Sir Arthur Conan Doyle. But he was soon to realize that he had unwittingly been part of a dramatic moment in psychic history. He published the story, and it was read by, among others, a Mr. Charlton, who had been involved in the R101's construction. Charlton asked Harry Price for a copy of the seance report. After studying it he and his colleagues described it as "an astounding document," containing more than 40 highly technical and confidential details of what occurred on the airship's fatal flight. "It appeared very evident," said Charlton, "that for anyone present at the seance to have obtained information beforehand was grotesquely absurd."

Charlton was so impressed by the evidence that he began his own psychic investigation, and ultimately became a Spiritualist. The only hypothesis that he could put forward to explain all the evidence was that "Irwin did actually communicate with those present at the seance, after his physical death."

Before the official enquiry into the crash, Major Oliver Villiers of the Ministry of Civil Aviation participated in a seance with Eileen Garrett. Through the medium he heard the testimony of others who had lost their lives in the disaster. Here is part of the verbatim account of the conversation during the seance between Villiers and crew member Scott, one of the victims:

"Villiers: What was the trouble? Irwin mentioned the nose."

"Scott: Yes. Girder trouble and engine."

"Villiers: I must get this right. Can you describe exactly where? We have the long struts numbered from A to G."

"Scott: The top one is O, and then A, B, C, and so on downward. Look at your drawing. It was the starboard of 5C. On our second flight after we had finished we found the girder had been strained, not cracked, and this caused trouble to the cover . . ."

Later Villiers asked Scott if the girder had broken and gone through the airship's covering:

"Scott: No, not broke, but cracked badly and it split the outer cover . . . The bad rent in the cover on the starboard side of 5C brought about an unnatural pressure, forced us into our first dive. The second was even worse. The pressure on the gas bags was terrific, and the gusts of wind were tremendous. This external pressure, coupled with the fact that the valve was weak, blew the valve right off, and at the same time the released gas was ignited by a backfire from the engine."

The Court of Inquiry report showed that practically every one of these statements was correct; none were incorrect.

Jarman's Investigations

One important aspect of Eileen Garrett's work is that she respected psychical investigators and actively encouraged their work. In fact, she founded the New York-based Parapsychology Foundation, which was financed by a wealthy woman politician, Congresswoman Frances Payne Bolton of Ohio. On Eileen Garrett's death in 1970 at the age of 77, Archie Jarman, a researcher and writer who had known her for nearly 40 years, paid tribute to her in the columns of *Psychic News*. He revealed that she had asked him to "dig into the famous R101 airship case as deep as I could delve." He agreed to do so and pledged he would take neither fee nor expenses, so that whatever his investigation disclosed, it would be seen that he had worked "without fear or favor." He continued:

"The completed saga, so often briefly mentioned, turned out to be a pretty massive affair. It took nearly six months and finally filled 455 pages of typescript and blueprints. It involved two trips to France, seeking the few remaining witnesses at

Beauvais where the R101 crashed. There were conferences with aeronautical experts, such as the designer of the R101's heavy diesel engines (which were partly responsible for the fatal crash), and with the aging but active captain of the sister-ship, R100.

"Technical witnesses were interrogated; ordnance maps scrutinized; Eileen's own aeronautical knowledge investigated (result, nil, she knew hardly enough to float a toy balloon). At close range I became familiar with meteorology, geodetics, with prewar political maneuvering and with certain conspiracy at a Ministry, with aerodynamics and with scandalous decisions which took nearly 50 brave men to their deaths.

"It was the technical aspect of this case which makes it unique in psychic history—and I mean *unique* . . . My opinion is that greater credulity is demanded to believe that Eileen obtained her obscure and specialized data by mundane means than to accept that, in some paranormal manner, she had contact with the remembering psyche of the 'dead' Captain Irwin to the moment of his incineration with his vast airship."

No one materialized in Eileen Garrett's presence. There were no physical manifestations such as raps or levitations, so beloved of early Spiritualists and psychical investigators. Why, then, is the R101 case so important to the Spiritualist case? The reason is that many of the scientists who risked ridicule by declaring their belief in materialized figures were equally adamant that these seance phantoms were not proof of an afterlife. They felt that mental mediumship might provide the proof.

Professor Charles Richet, a French physiologist and psychical researcher, for example, eventually came to believe in the genuineness of some physical phenomena—after having first ridiculed the idea. But Richet found it difficult to believe in life after death. He described materialization phenomena as "absurd but true," and argued: "Even if (which is not the case) a form identical with that of a deceased person could be photographed I should not understand how an individual 200 years dead, whose body has become a skeleton, could live again with this vanished body any more than with any other materialized form."

Baron A. von Schrenck-Notzing, German pioneer in investigation of psychic phenomena, conducted experiments with every leading medium until his death in 1929. He discovered the

408

amazing powers of Willi and Rudi Schneider. One hundred formerly skeptical and often hostile scientists who witnessed his tests with Willi Schneider signed a statement that they were convinced of the reality of telekinesis—the moving of objects by mental power—and of ectoplasm. Yet the Baron maintained: "I am of the opinion that the hypothesis of spirits not only fails to explain the least detail of these processes, but in every way it obstructs and shakes serious scientific research."

Other scientists accepted materializations as proof of an afterlife. But who was to say they were right? Richet and Schrenck-Notzing believed that, in a way we do not understand, and probably subconsciously, the medium shaped the phantom forms from the ectoplasmic material exuding from his or her body, controlling it through an extension of the nervous system. That may seem to be a far-fetched or fantastic theory, but to some it is more satisfactory than to admit the existence of a soul and the far-fetched idea of a soul materializing itself.

If, however, a medium were to communicate information known only to the dead person and to the sitter, this would be more convincing evidence that the person's spirit had survived death. Still, many investigators would maintain that the medium received the information from the sitter, either from a hint given unconsciously by the sitter or by telepathy. More conclusive would be information *unknown to both medium and sitter, and later established as known to the dead person when alive*. One of the most gifted mediums for such phenomena was Mrs. Leonore Piper, and one of her most extraordinary contacts was George Pelham.

The Survival of George Pelham

"The case of George Pelham," said Richet, "though there was no materialization, is vastly more evidential for survival than all the materializations yet known."

Pelham was the pseudonym of George Pellew, a young New York lawyer who had given up the law to become a writer. He had known Dr. Richard Hodgson of the SPR—a brilliant researcher who devoted much of his life to the study of Mrs. Piper's mediumship—and the two men had often discussed survival. Pelham argued that the idea of life after death was not only improbable but inconceivable. Hodgson said that if it was not probable it was at least conceivable. Pelham then promised that if he died first, he would return and "make things lively." He apparently kept his promise, and much sooner than he could have anticipated; for in February 1892 at the age of 32, he was killed in a fall from his horse.

A month later the first of a series of communications from Pelham began. Dr. Hodgson had arranged a⁻ sitting with Mrs. Piper for an intimate friend of Pelham's, using the pseudonym "John Hart" for the sitter. Mrs. Piper went into a trance; her spirit control Phinuit made various vague statements before announcing that there was a "George" present who wanted to speak. According to Dr. Hodgson, who took notes, Pelham took over the seance, giving his real name in full as well as the first names and surnames of several of his most intimate friends, including the one under an assumed name at the seance. He mentioned in particular a Mr. and Mrs. Howard and gave a message to Katherine, their daughter. When the Howards were told of the message, it was instantly recognized by the family as a reference to a conversation he had had with the girl some years earlier. The Howards later attended sittings with Mrs. Piper, and plied George Pelham with questions. His answers were full and detailed in most cases, but Mr. Howard pointed out that Pelham had failed to answer some points. This failure caused him to have doubt about the identity of the alleged spirit. He therefore challenged George Pelham to "tell me something in our past that you and I alone know."

Mrs. Piper's hand then began writing a message which Dr. Hodgson later said contained too much of the personal element in Pelham's life to be made public. Hodgson watched as the medium's hand rapidly covered the paper, and Mrs. Piper allowed him to read what was written until the word "private" appeared. At that point she gently pushed Dr. Hodgson away.

"I retired to the other side of the room, and Mr. Howard took my place close to the hand where he could read the writing," Dr Hodgson recounted. "He did not, of course, read it aloud, and it was too private for my perusal. The hand, as it reached the end of each sheet, tore it off from the block book and thrust it wildly at Mr. Howard, and then continued writing. The circumstances narrated, Mr. Howard informed me, contained precisely the kind of test for which he had asked, and he said he was 'perfectly satisfied, perfectly.' "

Having apparently established his identity, George Pelham stayed on as one of Mrs. Piper's regular spirit controls along with Phinuit. During a six-year period he spoke to 150 sitters, 30 of whom were old friends. He recognized all 30, although each had been introduced to the medium under a pseudonym. He not only addressed them all by name, but also used with each the tone and manner he was accustomed to use with that person when alive. Never once did he mistake a stranger for a friend. When his father and stepmother heard of Pelham's alleged posthumous activities, they decided to attend a seance. They used false names, but the moment George Pelham spoke through the medium he said, "Hello, father and mother, I am George." The conversation that followed was, according to the father, exactly what he would have expected from his living son.

A Systematic Study

Dr. Richard Hodgson was one of the mainstays of the SPR in its early days. He had a reputation as a talented investigator with a critical and skeptical mind. In 1887 he was sent to America by the SPR to act as secretary for the American Society for Psychical Research in Boston—a post he held for the rest of his life. He became a close friend of the American philosopher and psychologist William James, who brought him and Leonore Piper together. Professor James had been persuaded to attend one of Mrs. Piper's seances by some female relatives who had been greatly impressed by her. James expected to be able to explain the medium's feats logically, but was soon convinced that she possessed supernormal powers. He began a systematic study of Mrs. Piper, and introduced her to Hodgson. When James had to terminate his studies temporarily because of pressure of other work, Hodgson took up the project. Being extremely skeptical, he had Mrs. Piper watched by private detectives to learn whether she tried to collect information she could use at seances. He also took every precaution to prevent her from acquiring knowledge about her sitters in advance, and introduced them anonymously or by pseudonyms to protect their identities. Hodgson finally became convinced not only that Leonore Piper was genuine but also that spirit beings were communicating through her mediumship.

411

Typical of the evidence which helped him reach this decision was that provided at a seance attended by Professor Herbert Nichols of Harvard University. The sitting with Mrs. Piper was arranged by Hodgson at the request of Professor James. Professor Nichols was extremely skeptical at the outset. After the seance he wrote a letter of praise to James declaring, "she is the greatest marvel I have ever met ... I asked her scarcely a question, but she ran on for three-quarters of an hour, telling me names, places, events, in a most startling manner. Then she suddenly stopped talking and began writing—this was far less satisfactory and about an entirely different set of matters— mostly about Mamma (who recently fell and was killed) and messages to her grandchildren. One thing here, however, will interest you. Mamma and I one Christmas exchanged rings. Each had engraved in their gift the *first word* of their favorite proverb. The ring given me I lost many years ago. When Mamma died a year ago the ring I had given her was, at her request, taken from her finger and sent to me. Now I asked Mrs. Piper. 'What was written in Mamma's ring?' and as I asked the question I held the ring in my hand and had in mind *only that ring*, but I had hardly got the words from my mouth till she slapped down on paper the word on the *other ring*—the one Mamma had given me, and which had been lost years ago while traveling. As the word was a peculiar one, doubtfully ever written in any ring before, and as she wrote it in a flash, it was surely curious."

Time and again, Dr. Hodgson witnessed similar astonishing phenomena produced by Mrs. Piper. In his second report on her mediumship, published in 1897, he stated:

"At the present time I cannot profess to have any doubt that the chief communicators to whom I have referred in the foregoing pages are veritably the personages that they claim to be, that they have survived the change we call death, and that they have directly communicated with us whom we call living, through Mrs. Piper's entranced organism."

On Hodgson's death in 1905 the investigation into Leonore Piper's psychic powers was continued by James Hervey Hyslop, Professor of Logic and Ethics at Columbia University, New York. Within days of taking up the task he was studying communications received from his former colleague Dr. Hodgson,

The Polish medium Franek Kluski at a seance in Warsaw, 25 December 1919.
(*The Medium and the Message*)

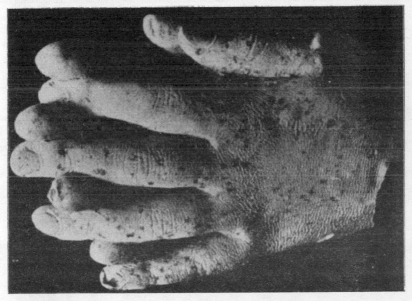

Wax gloves, made by hands materializing and leaving their impression in wax
in the presence of Franek Kluksi. (*The Medium and the Message*)

who became a regular communicator. Professor Hyslop had first encountered Mrs. Piper in 1888, and his initial skepticism about her mediumship soon dissolved. After 12 sittings, the personalities of the communicators who spoke through Mrs. Piper—and the evidence they provided—were so strong that he declared: "I have been talking with my father, my brother, my uncles. Whatever supernormal powers we may be pleased to attribute to Mrs. Piper's secondary personalities, it would be difficult to make me believe that these secondary personalities could have thus completely reconstituted the mental personality of my dead relatives. To admit this would involve me in too many improbabilities. I prefer to believe that I have been talking to my dead relatives in person; it is simpler."

The same conclusion was reached by the vast majority of Mrs. Piper's sitters. Because her mediumship was so accurate and detailed, and because men with critical and skeptical natures believed that fraud had been ruled out, the case of Mrs. Leonore Piper has become one of the most significant in psychic history. It established within 40 years of Spiritualism's beginnings that evidence for an afterlife could be provided through the mind of a medium, without the need for darkness, raps, levitations, or spirit forms. What is more, the quality of the evidence was in most cases far superior to the laboriously spelled out messages that were banged out by tilting tables, or the indistinct materializations that appeared at many seances.

Telephones and Telepathy

At its best, mental mediumship appears to offer a kind of psychic telephone link between this world and the next, using the medium as a receiver. In some cases, the medium goes into a trance and speaks with the voice of the communicator. More often mediums remain conscious and relate in their normal voice what they are hearing mentally. The telephone analogy is a useful one, for it points to some of the difficulties that can occur. Suppose, for example, that you had been abroad for 20 years and, on returning home, decided to call up some friends. They would not be able to see you, so to establish that it really was you, you would probably talk about events in your life before you had left, and about which they knew or in which they had shared. This is what most spirit communicators do.

This raises an immediate objection, however. The communications seem trivial, and the sitters usually know the facts that are given to establish identity. Therefore, telepathy between sitter and medium is postulated as the explanation. Also, sometimes the evidence provided is not right, dates or names are wrong, and doubt is thrown on the authenticity of the entire communication. Here is where the comparison with telephoning breaks down, for conveying information through a medium is not as simple as the telephone analogy indicates. F. W. H. Myers, an early SPR researcher, is supposed to have spoken through a famous medium to give this posthumous description of his efforts to communicate:

"The nearest simile I can find to express the difficulties of sending a message—is that I appear to be standing behind a sheet of frosted glass which blurs sights and deadens sound—dictating feebly—to a reluctant and somewhat obtuse secretary. A feeling of terrible impotence burdens me—I am so powerless to tell what means so much."

We are used to atmospheric interference in television and radio communications and more or less accept it. So perhaps we should allow for distortions through mediumistic communication. Spirit communicators indicate that—in a way we do not understand—they have to use the medium's mind to control vocal cords or move a hand to write a message. The medium's own mind can therefore color the communications. It seems reasonable that if contact really is established between the living and another realm of existence, then difficulties could easily arise. If we accept this, the wonder is not that inaccuracies and misunderstandings creep into many seance messages, but that on occasion a communicator is able to convey accurate information at length—as in the R101 seances.

A set of seance messages called the Cummins-Willett Scripts provide us with the best evidence of this kind. They were received through the mediumship of one of the best modern exponents of automatic writing, an Irishwoman named Geraldine Cummins. The presumed sender of the messages was Mrs. Winifred Coombe Tennant who, during her life, also produced automatic writing under the pseudonym of "Mrs. Willett." Her real name came to light as a result of what she wrote through Geraldine Cummins.

Mrs. Winifred Coombe Tennant was an energetic, practical, and highly intelligent person. She was appointed a Justice of the Peace in 1920, and was the first woman magistrate to sit on the Glamorganshire, Wales, County bench. In 1922 she ran unsuccessfully as a Liberal Party candidate for Parliament. Later, however, she became the first woman to be appointed by the British Government as a delegate to the League of Nations Assembly. With this background, it is perhaps not surprising that she kept her psychic talents secret, and her work as a medium, under the name Mrs. Willett, became known only when she communicated with Geraldine Cummins.

Mrs. Winifred Coombe Tennant died in August 1956. A year later W. H. Salter, honorary secretary of the SPR, wrote to Geraldine Cummins asking if she would cooperate in an experiment. She agreed to do so, but only after she had returned to her home in County Cork, Eire. Two weeks later Mr. Salter sent a second letter to her in Ireland. In it he gave her the name of Major Henry Tennant, who hoped to receive a message from his mother.

Swan on a Black Sea

During the next two years Geraldine Cummins received 40 scripts, ostensibly from Mrs. Tennant, Major Tennant's mother. Most of them she included in her book *Swan on a Black Sea,* published in 1965 and edited by Signe Toksvig. These scripts represent one of the most important contributions to psychical research in the last few decades. In them, the spirit of Mrs. Tennant discusses her life, her relationships with others, and her involvement in psychic work. The writings are peppered with names, dates, and details which, with few exceptions, were found to be accurate.

Skeptics might claim that Geraldine Cummins could have researched all or most of this material when she got the name of Major Tennant, or that she was acquainted with the family. Either theory is questionable in view of comments in a letter that Geraldine Cummins wrote to Signe Toksvig on August 31, 1957, a few days after receiving Salter's second letter. She refers to the experiment, saying in an aside that the letter from Salter contained the name of a major. "The name meant nothing to me. But I realized I must tackle the job the next day.

Otherwise these critical people would say I spent time making inquiries about this blasted major." The first communication from Mrs. Winifred Coombe Tennant was received on August 28, 1957, five days after Salter's second letter. The medium was not happy with the result, and she commented: "I don't care if it's all wrong. It seemed to me an impossible task." She referred to the test scripts in another letter four days later adding, "I'm sure the script message is a failure." In her introduction to *Swan on a Black Sea*, Signe Toksvig observes: "It can be seen that Miss Cummins is by no means an automatic believer in her automatic or transmitted scripts."

Professor C. D. Broad, Fellow of Trinity College, Cambridge, wrote a long and masterly foreword to the Cummins/Toksvig book. He examines many alternative explanations for the scripts and comments: "I found them of great interest, and I believe that these automatic scripts are a very important addition to the vast mass of such material which *prima facie* suggests rather strongly that certain human beings have survived the death of their physical bodies . . ."

The scripts are too long and complicated to condense meaningfully. Instead, here is part of one of the scripts addressed to her son Major Tennant, dated October 29, 1958:

"I am back again in my married life. It is different, though in appearance to my perceptions it is the same outer world of reason, order, and sensible arrangements. But it is different, humanly speaking. I am much with Christopher [another son], who is a darling, while your father pairs off with Daff [her daughter]. That is a new experience to me.

"What is novel also is that I appear to be in a kind of kindergarten, and in my working hours I relive in memory what earth time has snatched away from me. So in the study of memory I do not remain at Cadoxton [their home in Gloucestershire]. I enter the film of past events and make excursions into different times in my past earth life so as to assimilate it.

"I perceive again my budding public life, my immense enthusiasm for the Welsh Wizard, Lloyd George. He has even visited me in the disguise of his past earthly personality so blazing with fire and force when in its prime. . . ."

Major Henry Tennant, initially a skeptic, wrote to Geraldine Cummins after receiving the first communication to say, "The more I study these scripts the more deeply I am impressed by them." He pointed out only one incorrect name and added, "every other name and reference is accurate, and to me very evidential and at times surprising. There was no tapping of my mind because much appears that I never knew."

Geraldine Cummins was highly critical of her own gift. She admitted shortly before her death in 1969 that it was not until she had received the Willett scripts that she felt she had produced what she demanded as irrefutable proof of survival. It had taken her 35 years of mediumship to achieve that goal.

36. Understanding Ghosts

What is really going on when a person sees an apparition? When several people at the same time see the same apparition? When the same apparition is seen again and again in the same place by different people? When an apparition is reflected in a mirror? When photographic film registers an apparition not seen by the person who took the picture? When a person is touched by a hand he cannot touch himself?

These and numerous other questions have been raised again and again in the hundred years or so since serious psychical research got underway, and we are still far from having a satisfactory answer that will cover all of them. Instead we have several answers, each with certain limitations. We are a lot nearer to understanding the nature of apparitions than we were a century ago, but we are still a long way from understanding them completely.

Before picking up the thorny question of ghosts as possible evidence of life after death, let's consider what happens when we see an apparition of a living person. Evidence gathered in the Census of Hallucinations, taken by the SPR in 1889, indicated that in most cases the person whose apparition appeared was at that time undergoing some crisis, such as a severe illness, an accident, or death. The correlation between the crisis and the apparition in so many cases led the researchers to conclude that the apparition was telepathic. That is, the person undergoing the crisis was thinking about the percipient in such a way as to generate a kind of telepathic message that took the form of a picture of himself.

How telepathic information is communicated is still a mystery, and a telepathic picture is certainly the most mysterious of such communications, particularly when the image appears as a solid, living person. Those of us who have never seen an apparition tend to assume that no one can see anything that is not actually physically present in space. But seeing is much more complex than we normally suppose. We often see things vividly in our dreams, even though we're receiving no visual information through our eyes. While awake, most people can readily see in their mind's eye anything they choose to see, mentally superimposed on what their eyes are looking at at that moment.

The peculiarities of perception are well illustrated in the case of hypnosis. Experiments have shown that if a highly suggestible person in a hypnotic trance is told that on awakening he will see only the hypnotist—even though there are other people in the room—he will, on awakening, be unable to see those other people until the hypnotist removes the suggestion.

The hypnotist can tell a subject what he will see and what he won't see. Astonishing as such cases may be, they are not quite as remarkable as the case of a person *spontaneously* seeing the image of someone else, as lifelike as if he were there in the flesh. It seems incredible that the agent, or person sending the telepathic hallucination, should be able to achieve at a distance—and in many cases while he is unconscious—what the hypnotist achieves by giving his subject explicit instructions.

The evidence suggests, however, that the agent's mind plays a smaller part in creating the apparition than does the mind of the percipient. This conclusion becomes obvious when we look at details of reported crisis apparitions. Rarely does the figure manifest itself in the agent's form as it is at the moment of crisis—lying on his or her deathbed, for example, or mangled in an auto accident, or falling into a river. Almost always the apparition appears detached from its surroundings at that time. Instead it enters the percipient's surroundings—with which the agent may not even be familiar—and relates to these surroundings just as the agent would if there in the flesh.

Adaption to Physical Conditions

In his book *Apparitions*, G. N. M. Tyrrell devotes considerable attention to the ways in which apparitions behave like material persons. For example, he cites cases in which an apparition standing in front of a lamp has cast a shadow. An apparition may also enter a room by apparently opening a door which is later found to be locked. In some cases an apparition has been reflected in a mirror. Apparitions, says Tyrrell, "adapt themselves almost miraculously to the physical conditions of the percipient's surroundings, of which the agent as a rule can know little or nothing. These facts reveal the apparition to be a piece of stage-machinery which the percipient must have a large hand in creating and some of the details for which he must supply—that is to say, an apparition cannot be merely a direct expression of the agent's *idea*; it must be a drama worked out with that idea as its *motif*."

In other words, some part of the agent's mind telepathically transmits an idea of himself to the percipient, and some level of the percipient's mind is then stimulated to produce not merely a recognizable image of the agent, but an image that behaves in a lifelike natural way. It is natural for a real human to be reflected in a mirror; consequently that part of the percipient's mind that helps to create the apparition—Tyrrell calls this the "stage carpenter"—produces a figure that is reflected in a mirror.

Such fidelity to natural laws is not a feature of all apparitions. Tyrrell mentions a case in which an apparition close to a mirror did not have a reflection. Another case collected by the SPR illustrates the unrealistic features of some of these apparitional dramas. One day about a hundred years ago, an English clergyman, Canon Bourne, went out fox hunting with his two daughters. After a time the daughters decided to return home with their coachman while their father continued hunting, but they were delayed for several minutes when a friend rode up to talk to them. "As we were turning to go home," reported Louisa Bourne in an account confirmed by her sister, "we distinctly saw my father, waving his hat to us and signing us to follow him. He was on the side of a small hill, and there was a dip between him and us. My sister, the coachman, and myself all recognized my father, and also the horse [the only white horse in the field that day]. The horse looked so dirty and shaken that the coachman remarked he thought there had been a nasty accident. As my father waved his hat I clearly saw the Lincoln and Bennett [hatter's] mark inside, though from the distance we were apart it ought to have been utterly impossible for me to have seen it . . ."

The girls and the coachman quickly rode toward Canon

Bourne, losing sight of him as they rode into the dip in the terrain. When they emerged from the dip and approached the place where he had been, he was nowhere to be seen. After riding around looking for him, they finally went home. Later Canon Bourne—who arrived home shortly after them—told them that he had not even been near the place they had seen him.

One peculiarity of this case, apart from the odd feature of the clarity of the hatter's mark, is that no crisis occurred. Canon Bourne suffered no accident, as his daughters and the coachman feared, nor, apparently, did he even narrowly escape having one —which might have triggered an unconscious telepathic call for help. There is a slim possibility that the hallucination was a subjective one, created by the percipients themselves, who may have had some fear that he might have met with an accident.

The trouble with this hypothesis is that the apparition of Canon Bourne was *collective*—that is, it was seen by more than one person at the same time. According to Tyrrell, "those hallucinations which we have best reason to regard as purely subjective are never collective; so that collectivity would seem to be a sign that the case is in one way or another telepathic."

Collective apparitions present problems. A great many have been reported; 130 had been collected by the SPR by 1943 when Tyrrell published *Apparitions*. It's unlikely that all of these can be dismissed as cases of one percipient verbally persuading others that they see what he sees. On the other hand it also seems unlikely that the agent could convey exactly the same image of himself to several people at the same time. (We are still assuming that the apparition is wholly mental, that it does not exist in the space where it appears to exist.) Tyrrell believes that in collective cases there is a principal percipient who receives the apparition telepathically from the agent, and at the same time telepathically and involuntarily conveys this visual information to the other people present. Of course, not all people are capable of perceiving apparitions, and so in some cases an apparition may be seen by several people at once while someone else nearby sees nothing.

One of the best-known cases of collective apparitions in the history of psychical research is that of Captain Towns of Sydney, Australia. The incident occurred in the Towns' residence in the late 19th century, about six weeks after Captain Towns died, and

421

was reported to the SPR by Charles Lett, the son-in-law of the deceased man. One evening about nine o'clock, Mrs. Lett entered one of the rooms, along with a Miss Berthon. The gaslight was burning. "They were amazed to see, reflected as it were on the polished surface of the wardrobe, the image of Captain Towns. It was . . . like an ordinary medallion portrait, but lifesize. The face appeared wan and pale . . . and he wore a kind of gray flannel jacket, in which he had been accustomed to sleep. Surprised and half alarmed at what they saw, their first idea was that a portrait had been hung in the room, and that what they saw was its reflection—but there was no picture of the kind. Whilst they were looking and wondering, my wife's sister, Miss Towns, came into the room and before any of the others had time to speak she exclaimed, 'Good gracious! Do you see papa!'"

One of the housemaids passing by was called into the room. Immediately she cried, "Oh Miss! The master!" The Captain's own servant, the butler, and the nurse were also called in and also immediately recognized him. "Finally Mrs. Towns was sent for, and, seeing the apparition, she advanced toward it with her arm extended as if to touch it, and as she passed her hand over the panel of the wardrobe the figure gradually faded away, and never again appeared." Lett adds that he was in the house at the time, but did not hear when he was called and so did not see the apparition himself.

We can account for the collectivity of this apparition with the theory that a principal percipient—either Mrs. Lett or Miss Berthon—passed it along to the others. But the question then remains: Who was the original source of the apparition?

Here we arrive at a central problem facing the skeptical psychical researcher: many apparitions are of people who have been dead for some time. These are called "post-mortem" apparitions. A scientifically inclined researcher, reluctant to assume the existence of life after death, finds it difficult to account for such cases. Myers, Gurney, and Podmore, the authors of *Phantasms of the Living*, came to the conclusion after studying hundreds of cases that an apparition seen up to 12 hours after the person's death could be counted a crisis apparition sent by a living but moribund person. They reasoned that the percipient might not see the apparition at the moment it was transmitted. He might be busy or preoccupied at the exact time the agent sent the message, so that its visualization was delayed until a moment when the percipient's mind was relaxed and more receptive.

The Unknown Moment of Death

In addition, as Lyall Watson has shown in his book *The Romeo Error*, death is not as clear-cut as we commonly assume. If by "death" we mean the complete cessation of biologic activity in the whole body, its exact moment of occurrence is impossible to pinpoint, for many bodily processes continue after the heart has stopped. Conceivably, that part of the brain that sends telepathic impulses might continue to function for some time after a person is pronounced clinically dead.

Thus we do not have to believe in life after death in order to account for an apparition of a person who has been dead for several hours. Deferred telepathy might explain it—or temporarily continuing brain activity. Still we are left with a great many apparitions of people who have been dead for days, weeks —as in the case of Captain Towns—and even years. Some of these can be explained as subjective hallucinations. In other cases, however, the person seen is not known to the percipient but is later identified as an actual person. In such cases it is virtually impossible to claim that the percipient created the image all by himself with no external stimulus. The following case is a dramatic example of a post-mortem apparition of a person unknown to the percipient.

In 1964 in a Detroit automobile factory a motor fitter suddenly lurched out of the path of a giant body press, which had been accidentally activated during the lunch hour. Shaken but uninjured, the man told his co-workers that he had been thrust out of the way by a tall black man with a scarred face, dressed in grease-stained denims. He had never seen the man before, but some of the older workers recognized the description. In 1944 a tall black man with a scarred left cheek had been decapitated while working in the same area of the shop floor. He had been pressing out parts for bombers. A subsequent inquiry had revealed that although the dead man was skilled at his job and totally familiar with his machine, long periods of overtime had made him sleepy and incautious.

Telling of his miraculous escape, the motor fitter commented: "The colored guy was real enough to me. He had enormous strength, and just pushed me out of the way like I was a feather-weight. I never believed in spooks before, but if this was a spook I take my hat off to him."

One possible explanation is that one of the fitter's older co-workers, seeing him in danger, but perhaps too far away to pull him to safety or even to shout a warning, suddenly had a powerful subconscious image of the dead man which he telepathically transmitted to the endangered man. It is possible to convey the image of another person, although such cases are rare.

We must also consider the physical impact of the push. Hallucinations of touch occasionally accompany a visual hal-lucination. *Phantasms of the Living* and the *Proceedings* of the SPR include many such cases. For example, one account of an apparition written by the percipient to the person she had seen includes these words: ". . . someone touched my shoulder with such force that I immediately turned. You were there as plainly to be seen as if in the body . . ." Oddly, however, there are no cases of the percipient being able to touch the apparition (if we exclude the supposed materializations of Spiritualist seances). Either the figure moves just out of reach, or the percipient's hand passes right through it.

Following Tyrrell's theory that apparitions duplicate reality, short of becoming substantial, we can accept the possibility that a spectral hand placed on the percipient's shoulder will be felt by the percipient. This is simply the percipient's subconscious effort to create a realistic apparition.

In the case of the dead man pushing the auto worker out of danger we can't easily use this explanation. What the worker felt was not a mere touch but a strong push. Someone—either the man who died 20 years earlier or a living bystander—exerted psychokinetic force.

Psychokinesis

Psychokinesis, or PK as it is often called, is the movement of objects by mental energy. The existence of such a force has been tested and proven in laboratory experiments—notably at Dr. J. B. Rhine's Parapsychology Laboratory. Some gamblers have demonstrated the ability to will dice to fall in a certain way. Other tests have shown that some people can mentally influence the growth of plants or the behavior of single-celled organisms. Even animals have demonstrated powers of PK. Unconscious PK exerted by humans would seem to account for many cases of poltergeist activity. The fact that such disturbances usually, though not always, occur in the vicinity of an adolescent girl or boy suggests that there may be a connection between awakening sexual energy and PK.

The PK activity encountered in most poltergeist cases is capricious and sometimes destructive in character. A gentler kind of PK apparently caused some peculiar events in a bakery in England, described by Andrew Green in *Ghost Hunting*.

The bakery was purchased from a local family who had operated it for several generations. "Shortly after moving in, the wife of the new owner reported that she could 'feel the presence of someone in the bakery.' This phenomenon developed to a stage where doors were seen to open, baking equipment moved and the woman felt 'the entity push past her on numerous occasions.' Both her husband and son began to experience the haunting. Disturbed, they visited the former owners in an attempt to find out more about the ghost, but were assured that the premises were not haunted and never had been during the entire occupation of the original family.

"It was noticed, during the visit, that 'the old man' [one of the family that had formerly run the bakery] had said little during the conversation and 'seemed half asleep most of the time.'"

Green reports that the phenomena continued to disturb the new owners for about two years. "Suddenly, one Tuesday, 'the place seemed different.'" From that time onward there were no more incidents. On that particular Tuesday, the old man had died. The inference seems clear: having retired from the business, the old man had nothing to occupy his mind except thoughts of his former work. He would sit half-dozing, recollecting the activities that he had once performed every day: kneading the dough, cutting and shaping it, putting the loaves onto the trays, and sliding them into the oven. While yet alive, he was a haunting ghost.

Haunting ghosts often seem to be different in kind from apparitions that appear only once, and they are generally considered to be different by psychical researchers. An apparition may be seen in a place unknown to the agent, and almost always appears to a person with whom the agent has some relationship. Often the apparition will seem to communicate with the percipient in some way—by a look, a touch, even speech. By contrast, a haunting ghost almost always seems unaware of the people around it. The place itself—and not any particular human—seems to attract the ghost.

Various theories have been advanced to explain the haunting type of ghost. One of these is the psychometric theory first proposed by Eleanor Sidgwick, an early member of the SPR and the wife of another well-known researcher, Henry Sidgwick. *Psychometry* is the ability shown by certain sensitive persons to receive psychic impressions of a person by touching or holding an object connected in some way with that person. It may be that people who are sensitive in this way can inadvertently psychometrize a building or locality simply by coming into contact with it, so that they will see, hear, or merely sense someone who has been closely associated with it in the past. The apparition would thus be an entirely subjective experience.

One argument against this theory is that almost all dwellings have been inhabited by several, and in some cases, hundreds of people. If a haunting depends on the psychometric abilities of the observer, and not on any action past or present of the persons seen, the observer should be able to see most or all of the people who lived in that place for any length of time. Instead of only seeing the unfortunate Lady L. who committed suicide in 1784, the person would see Lord L., their children, their servants, and scores of people who had lived in the house since that time. Occasionally groups of phantoms are seen— processions of chanting monks, spectral armies—but these are the exception to the rule. Most haunting ghosts haunt alone.

Reactions of Animals

The evidence suggests that one's ability to see a phantom or sense a presence depends partly on some lingering aspect of the person seen or sensed. This possibility is supported by the reactions of animals in cases of haunting. Dr. Robert Morris, a psychologist, has reported various investigations of hauntings using animals. One investigator known to Dr. Morris examined a house in Kentucky containing an allegedly haunted room in which a tragedy had occurred. Instead of the usual team of human investigators, he used a dog, cat, rat, and rattlesnake.

426

Headless ghost dog photographed at Tingewick, Buckinghamshire, about 1916 by Arthur Springer, a retired CID Inspector from Scotland Yard. He did not see the ghost when taking the picture. (*Understanding Ghosts*)

This ghost photograph was taken in Newby church, near Ripon, North Yorkshire by the Revd. K. F. Lord in the early 1960s. Again, he saw nothing unusual when taking the picture. (*Understanding Ghosts*)

The so-called Brown Lady of Raynham, known to haunt Raynham Hall, Norfolk, photographed in 1936. (*Understanding Ghosts*)

The animals were brought into one of the haunted rooms one at a time. "The dog upon being taken about two or three feet into the room immediately snarled at its owner and backed out the door. No amount of cajoling could prevent the dog from struggling to get out and it refused to reenter. The cat was brought into the room carried in the owner's arms. When the cat got a similar distance into the room, it immediately leaped upon the owner's shoulders, dug in, then leaped to the ground, orienting itself toward a chair. It spent several minutes hissing and spitting and staring at the unoccupied chair in a corner of the room until it was finally removed . . ."

The rat showed no reaction to whatever had disturbed the dog and cat, but the rattlesnake "immediately assumed an attack posture focusing on the same chair that had been of interest to the cat. After a couple of minutes it slowly moved its head toward a window, then moved back and receded into its alert posture about five minutes later . . ."

The four animals were tested separately in a control room in which no tragedy had occurred. In this room they behaved normally. Apparently, the animals were reacting to some invisible presence in the first room.

What exactly is the lingering aspect of a person capable of being perceived by certain humans and animals? According to Reverend Neil-Smith, it represents the soul of that person. "For the most part," he says, "I believe that the soul of a person who dies a 'natural' death leaves the body for another place. The soul, or spirit, of one who dies violently may not immediately do so; it is bewildered by the sudden transition, and remains earthbound. If you examine cases of haunting which are well authenticated, you generally find that a sudden or unnatural death lies behind the events."

Reverend Neil-Smith thinks that these baffled ghosts tend to develop either a "place reference" or a "person reference." In the first case they haunt a house; in the second case they either possess or consistently appear to a particular person. Reverend Neil-Smith claims to have used exorcism to release many people from possession by a haunting spirit. Most psychical researchers, however, would reserve judgment in such cases on the grounds that there is usually a possible psychiatric explanation for the behavior of the supposedly possessed person. But they would

427

certainly agree with Reverend Neil-Smith's comments on haunting apparitions: ". . . you get the distinct impression that the apparitions are pointless, rather stupid. They wander around, don't say anything in particular, and for the most part don't really frighten anyone. In these cases, I believe, the ghosts are merely trying to call attention to their trapped plight . . ."

Without going so far as to attribute "mind" to the lingering aspect of a person seen, heard, or felt in a haunting, many researchers believe that it consists of some kind of psychic energy generated by the person while still alive. The Oxford philosopher H. H. Price suggested the existence of a "psychic ether" permeating all matter and space. This ether could be impressed with certain mental images. Such an impression would be most likely to occur in traumatic circumstances—violent death, or great emotional suffering. Thus the correlation often noted between unnatural death and subsequent haunting need not be attributed to a trapped soul. The thing trapped in the haunted place would be a kind of recording made on the medium of psychic ether, capable of being perceived in the form of an image, sound, or touch by a sensitive person.

Such a theory has the advantage of bringing the haunting apparition under the same umbrella with the telepathic apparition. If a person is capable of sending a psychic impulse telepathically to a particular person, it seems equally possible that he could project a psychic impulse with no particular receiver in mind, and that that impulse might remain free-floating in the area where the person is at the time he projects the impulse.

Certain cases of hauntings suggest that the generating force behind this impulse may not necessarily be a traumatic incident. Some phantoms have been identified as images of people who lived apparently happy lives and died natural deaths. In such cases, repetition of their presence over a long period of time may suffice to imprint their image on the psychic ether.

A Plausible Theory?

The concept of a psychic ether carrying psychic impressions left by various people alive and dead could lead to a plausible and coherent theory of haunting. If psychic impressions can be left in a place, we would have an explanation for those rare cases in which photographic film picked up an image that people present

428

at the time did not see. In such a case the observers were presumably undersensitive compared to the film. In other cases, in which the phantom is seen but does not show up on film, the observers are presumably hypersensitive.

If we continue on the assumption that a haunting apparition was originally imprinted on the scene by some human agent, we encounter yet another problem: what about those cases in which the haunting includes coach and horses or other nonhuman phantoms? We may without too much trouble imagine the agent unconsciously projecting a picture of himself wearing certain clothes, but it strains credulity to imagine his projecting an image of himself borne in a horse-drawn coach.

At this point one of Tyrrell's suggestions may provide an answer. Tyrrell raises the possibility that the latent images—what he calls the "idea-pattern"—may sometimes have a collective origin. He cites the case of persistent legends such as the ancient belief in the god Pan, "half human and half goat-like, haunting certain places in the woods and uplands and playing his pipe. The widely spread idea that this happened might conceivably sink into the mid-levels [Tyrrell's term for the parts of the mind that govern perception] of the personalities of a whole community, and there form a telepathic idea-pattern, having a multiple agency. Anyone (suitably sensitive) going to the places which, according to the idea-pattern, Pan was especially supposed to inhabit would then see and hear Pan with the same reality that a person going into a haunted house sees and hears a ghost."

One might extend this idea to suggest that unhuman phantoms such as coaches may have been generated and perpetuated in this way by the percipients themselves.

While some phantoms may be in a sense renewed by the unconscious efforts of the percipients, other phantoms seemingly fade away over a period of time. Andrew Green in *Ghost Hunting* refers to the "ghost of a woman in red shoes, a red gown and a black headdress" which was seen during the 18th century in a remote corridor of an English mansion. "Many years passed before the apparition was seen again, and by then . . . it appeared as a female in a pink dress, pink shoes, and a gray headdress. She was not witnessed again until the mid-19th century, when the figure had dwindled down to 'a lady in a white gown and with gray hair.' Just before the last war all that was reported was 'the sound of a woman walking along the corridor and the swish of her dress.' In 1971, shortly before the demolition of the property involved, workmen 'felt a presence in one of the old corridors.' "

Whether an apparition fades away or remains vivid for centuries, we can usually account for its activities without supposing that they are governed by the surviving spirit of the person it represents. F. W. H. Myers, who devoted considerable effort to the study of the survival question, was careful not to let his wish to believe in survival affect his conclusion. In his book *Human Personality and its Survival of Bodily Death*, he defines a ghost as "*a manifestation of persistent personal energy*, or . . . an indication that some kind of force is being exercised after death in some way connected with a person previously known on earth." He goes on to add that "this force or influence, which after a man's death creates a phantasmal impression of him, may indicate no continuing action on his part, but may be some residue of the force or energy which he generated while yet alive." Myers' hypothesis agrees fundamentally with H. H. Price's concept of mental images being impressed upon a psychic ether.

Yet Myers and other serious psychical researchers have occasionally come across cases that strongly suggest that a post-mortem apparition may be more than a remnant of an extinct consciousness. To quote Lyall Watson, "behind every ghost there may be a conscious projector." Watson is not entirely convinced of the likelihood of survival, but in *The Romeo Error* he includes this interesting case relevant to the question:

"In 1921, James Chaffin of North Carolina died, leaving all his property to one of his four sons who himself died intestate a year later. In 1925, the second son was visited by his dead father dressed in a black overcoat, who said 'You will find my will in my overcoat pocket.' When the real coat was examined, a roll of paper was found sewn into the lining with instructions to read the 27th chapter of Genesis in the family Bible. Folded into the relevant pages was a later will than the first one, dividing the property equally between all four sons."

The case of the factory worker saved by the apparent intervention of a person 20 years dead is another piece of evidence in favor of the survival theory. The possibility that in the moment of his own tragic death the first man left a psychic impression of himself in that place does not explain how this lingering psychic impression could act physically when circumstances demanded it. If we suppose that the endangered man happened to pick up the latent image of the dead man, and that at the same time he subliminally became -aware of some danger to himself, without realizing what it was, and that he then converted his subliminal fear into a purely subjective hallucination of an arm pushing him out of the way, we afe constructing a rather cumbersome and unlikely explanation. Some people would consider it a more unlikely explanation than the idea of the dead man's spirit manifesting itself in the form of an image and a psychokinetic force. The possibility remains, of course, that both the image and the force were transmitted by a living worker. Here, as so often, the case is not airtight.

37. The World of Astrology

On February 24, 1975, members of royal families and leading statesmen from all over the world gathered in Nepal to attend the coronation of the country's new king. It was an elaborate and glittering ceremony, filmed for millions of television viewers across the globe. In accordance with Eastern custom, the date of the coronation had been chosen by Nepal's astrologers. King, government, and country had awaited their choice of a favorable date.

The leaders of Nepal are by no means the only Asian rulers of modern times to adhere to traditional oriental astrology. In both Burma and Sri Lanka, formerly Ceylon, new governments take office at the exact times worked out as propitious by official astrologers. In Sikkim, a province of northern India, the then Crown Prince married his American bride in March 1963 after waiting a year for astrologers to choose their wedding day. Pandit Jawaharlal Nehru, one of the founders of modern India and his country's prime minister for 14 years, was a firm believer in astrology. When his first grandson was born in 1944, he at once suggested to the child's mother that a horoscope be made for the baby. In Malaysia too, high-ranking members of the administration take careful note of the times of their children's birth so that an accurate horoscope may be drawn up for them.

No one could regard these eminent believers in astrology as ignorant people who happen to have attained high office. They are men and women of intellectual sophistication, capable of meeting other world leaders on a basis of perfect equality. Interestingly enough, their belief in "the celestial science" is sometimes in contradiction to their political ideology. Thus the government of Sri Lanka, a coalition of Marxist groups that officially regard astrology as an outmoded superstition, have followed the advice of their country's Buddhist astrologers just as devoutly as their more conservative predecessors.

Many Western countries have also come under the influence of astrology at various times in their history, and astrology today claims many followers among the educated and the sophisticated in the West as in the East. Astrological forecasts appear in almost every popular magazine and newspaper in the Western world, and are eagerly read by millions. Whether they believe in astrology or not, most people would probably admit to sneaking at least an occasional glance at articles on astrology. The signs of the zodiac have become household words, and almost everyone knows whether he or she is a Piscean or Leo or Virgo.

Astrology—the subject that was once regarded as "the Queen of the Sciences"—has never been more popular. In both the United States and Europe every community of any size has dozens, sometimes hundred, of professional astrologers, and thousands of amateur ones. Millions of horoscopes are cast every year in the United States alone. There are numerous magazines devoted exclusively to astrology, and other popular occult magazines are crammed with astrological advertisements. Although a good deal of criticism can be—and is—leveled at astrology, most people would probably like to believe that there could be something in it. But something in what exactly? What is the strange body of beliefs we call astrology?

Astrology is based on the belief that there is a relationship between the heavenly bodies and human beings, and that this relationship can be interpreted. More specifically, astrologers claim that the position of the Sun, Moon, and planets at the time and over the place of a person's birth has an important bearing on the kind of individual that person is and on the future course of his or her life. Astrologers believe that the planets are somehow bound up with the rhythms of human life, and that everyone and everything on Earth is affected by the cosmic conditions that prevailed at the time of a person's birth. Thus the planetary patterns at that moment are thought to indicate the pattern of a newborn's personality and destiny throughout the rest of life.

Astrologers study these patterns by means of a horoscope or natal chart. This is a map of the zodiac—the band of sky within which the Sun, Moon, and planets appear to move—showing the exact positions of all the planets at the time a person was born. Astrologers divide the zodiac into 12 zones represented by 12 different signs. The planets are thought to influence a person's life according to the signs they were in at the moment of birth, their distance from each other, and their exact location in the natal chart.

When astrologers began to write forecasts for magazines and newspapers they obviously could not publish a separate horoscope for each of their readers. They therefore devised a system of "Sun Signs" based simply on the date, rather than the precise time, of birth. So today when someone says "I'm a Leo," he means that he was born sometime between July 23 and August 23 when the Sun is located in the zone of the zodiac known as Leo. It was this use of Sun Signs that made astrology accessible to millions of ordinary people, and marked a new era in the long and sometimes star-crossed history of astrology.

Origins of Astrology

The origins of astrology probably go back almost as far as humankind itself. Archeologists have recently unearthed a bone over 30,000 years old bearing marks that appear to refer to the phases of the Moon. Monuments like the great stone circle at Stonehenge in Britain are believed to have been sophisticated astronomical observatories, and to testify to prehistoric peoples' interest in the heavens. In the early cultures of Asia, Europe, and America, people constructed giant watchtowers and observatories so that their priests could search the night sky for the key to human destiny.

It was in the dry and cloudless climate of Mesopotamia, however, that astrology first emerged in something resembling its modern form. Five thousand years ago the priest-magicians of Babylon were already studying and naming the stars. By about 700 B.C. they had discovered the extent of the zodiac and had invented the 12 signs of the zodiac that we now know so well. They had attributed good and bad qualities to the planets and had begun to interpret *aspects* — the supposedly significant angles between one planet and another.

Astrology spread from Babylonia to Egypt and Greece. Some of the Egyptian pharaohs decorated their tombs with astrological symbols, but Egypt does not appear to have become enthusiastic about astrology until long after the golden age of the pharaohs and it was in Greece that astrology as we know it developed.

The Greeks identified the Sun, Moon, and planets with their own gods and goddesses. The planet Venus, for example, was identified with Aphrodite, goddess of love, and Jupiter with Zeus, the king of the gods. The Babylonians had judged the effect of a planet according to its appearance, believing that Jupiter had a favorable influence if it shone white and an unfavorable influence if it were red. The Greeks gave no importance to appearance. Instead they regarded planets as consistently favorable, a "benefic" or unfavorable, a "malefic." Zeus' planet Jupiter was a benefic while Mars, identified with Ares, the bloody god of war, was a malefic. The Greeks also turned the planets into personalities, and combined the practical techniques of the Babylonian astrologers with the philosophies of their own great thinkers to add a moral significance to astrology.

The Greeks made personal horoscopes fashionable. They enabled a Babylonian astrologer to set up a school of astrology on the Greek island of Cos in 280 B.C., and from about 200 B.C. onward a number of widely circulated manuals were published on the subject. The most important of these was the *Tetrabiblos*, written in the second century A.D. by the Alexandrian Claudius Ptolemy, the greatest astronomer of ancient times.

Ptolemy's catalogs and atlases of the stars and planets were unmatched for accuracy until the 17th century, and his was probably the most influential book on astrology ever written. Ptolemy gathered together most of the astrological teachings of his own and preceding centuries in his book, which contained all the essentials that have gone to make up modern astrology, and included full details of how to calculate an individual horoscope.

By the time of Ptolemy, astrology had already captured the imagination of the Roman Empire. Rich man and poor, freeman and slave acknowledged its importance and accepted its doctrines. The great Augustus, first of the Roman Emperors, believed in it fully, perhaps partly because at the time of his birth the astrologer Nigidius had prophesied that he would become "master of the world." Augustus even stamped the sign of Capricorn—his birth sign—on some of the coinage he issued.

The main opponents of astrology in the ancient world were the early Christians. They saw astrology as being basically pagan and fatalistic, teaching that man has a fixed and unalterable future instead of being able to change and redeem himself through baptism and the other sacraments of the Church. At first such opposition had little effect, for the early Church was a small and despised sect whose members were themselves the subject of harsh attack. In fact, many of the Christian denouncements of astrology were replies to those who condemned Christ as a magician, and accused his followers of crimes such as cannibalism and incest. However, with the growth of Christianity and its acceptance in the 4th century A.D. as the official religion of the Roman Empire, astrology gradually fell into disrepute, and its practitioners were regarded as little better than demon worshippers. By the time Rome fell to the barbarians in A.D. 410 there were few, if any, practicing astrologers left in the western half of the Empire, and within a few more decades the art had been largely forgotten.

In the Byzantine Empire of the East, however, astrological writings and techniques survived, and were passed on to the Arabs. Arab scholars made a serious study of astrology side by side with astronomy. They added to the work of their Greek predecessors, particularly in attaching importance to the motion and positions of the Moon in the calculation of horoscopes.

It was through Latin translations of Arabic astrological texts that 12th-century European scholars rediscovered astrology. By the 16th century astrology had again become an acknowledged part of the cultural outlook of all men of learning. The great astronomers of the 16th and early 17th centuries, such as Johannes Kepler, were also practicing astrologers and regularly cast horoscopes as part of their work. Every king and prince had his Court Astrologer to advise him on matters of state. Astrology had by then become the true Queen of the Sciences.

Dr Dee
One of the best known of the 16th-century astrologers who acted as advisers to royalty was Dr. John Dee. This man was no mere stargazer, but a key figure in the intellectual life of his time. Born in 1527 of Welsh parents who had settled in London, Dee was a precocious child. He entered Cambridge University when he was only 15 years old, and throughout his time there he spent

436

no less than 18 hours a day studying subjects that ranged from Greek to mechanics.

Dee continued his studies in the city of Louvain, now in Belgium, where he met and favorably impressed some of the greatest scientists of his age. All this time Dee was perfecting his knowledge of astrology and astronomy, and becoming adept at astrological calculation and interpretation.

Like many other scientists of his day, Dee was more attracted to the new Protestant interpretations of Christianity than to traditional Catholicism. He returned to England in the 1550s when the Catholic Queen Mary was persecuting the Protestants, and his religious views put his life at risk. At this time, Queen Mary's young half-sister, the future Queen Elizabeth I, who was known to have Protestant sympathies, was being kept a prisoner at Woodstock near Oxford. Queen Mary was under pressure from some of her Catholic advisers to get rid of her half-sister by whatever means possible, so Elizabeth was in fear of assassination throughout her imprisonment. She knew she was in danger of being executed on a trumped-up charge of treason, or even of being killed by poison—a standby of 16th-century monarchs who wanted to dispose of dangerous rivals.

It is hardly surprising that Elizabeth was anxious to know what the future held in store for her, and she decided to consult an astrologer. It so happened that Blanche Parry, Elizabeth's confidential maid-in-waiting, was a cousin of John Dee, and on her recommendation Elizabeth turned to Dee for advice. Dee prepared an astrological forecast for Elizabeth, and also showed her horoscopes he had calculated for Queen Mary and her husband Philip of Spain. Elizabeth's horoscope survives in the British Museum, and Dee's interpretation of it appears to have been accurate as well as optimistic. In letters secretly delivered to Elizabeth at Woodstock, Dee is thought to have told her that, although her situation was perilous, her life was in no danger. She was destined to rise to an outstanding position—perhaps to the throne itself—and would probably live to a ripe old age.

Dee's prophecies no doubt pleased and comforted Elizabeth, but the relationship between the two was soon discovered by Mary's secret agents. Dee was thrown into prison, accused not only of having unorthodox religious opinions, but also of showing a confidential document—Mary's horoscope—to Elizabeth and of practicing black magic. He was suspected of attempting to kill Queen Mary by sorcery so that Elizabeth could inherit the throne. Dee was eventually acquitted on all the charges for lack of evidence, but he spent some months languishing in jail. Even after his release he was forced to live in seclusion until Elizabeth came to the throne on Mary's death in 1558.

The new queen remembered Dee's services and regularly consulted him on astrological matters. Dee even decided the date of her coronation using a technique known as *electional astrology*—a method like that still used in many Eastern countries to determine the most favorable time for undertaking some new and important enterprise.

In spite of Queen Elizabeth's friendly regard for Dee she did not display favor too openly. Probably she felt that she could not afford to be publicly associated with a man who had twice been accused of sorcery and might be so again. However, she employed Dee as a secret agent in Europe, where he was believed to be one of her most trusted spies. Dee seems to have gathered some of his intelligence by conventional means—16th century equivalents of the techniques used today by the CIA and the Soviet Union's KGB—but most of the time he used astrology and other occult methods to predict the plans of England's enemies. He also made maps for the Queen and helped to draw up plans for naval defense.

Psychological Warfare
Dee died in 1608 at the age of 81. Forty years after his death the science of the stars was still an influence in politics, and astrologers were playing an important role in the English Civil War—the struggle between Roundheads and Cavaliers to decide whether Parliament or King should rule the country. These astrologers were the psychological warfare experts of the time, producing predictions designed to keep up the morale of the partisans of each side. In London the astrologer William Lilly produced almanacs at more or less regular intervals. In them he prophesied the success of Parliament and the downfall of the Royalists. From Oxford, the headquarters of King Charles, Royalist astrologers published almanacs asserting exactly the opposite.

Not surprisingly these distortions of astrology for political ends tended to bring the art into disrepute. Thinking people concluded that if astrologers could produce diametrically opposite findings from identical sets of data—the positions of the Sun, Moon, and planets in the zodiac—their subject could hardly be considered a science. The same conclusions were reached in Europe where astrology was used as a psychological weapon during the Thirty Years' War fought in central Europe from 1618 to 1648.

When their political opinions were not involved, however, certain 17th-century astrologers seem to have made some amazingly accurate predictions. Thus William Lilly, the astrologer who foresaw the Parliamentary victory, prophesied the 1665 outbreak of plague in London and the Great Fire of 1666 that followed it more than 10 years before these events took place. He expressed these predictions in the form of symbolic drawings, published as woodcuts in the early 1650s. Their meaning was so plain that Lilly was suspected of being involved in a plot to start the Great Fire deliberately, and he was called before a parliamentary committee to explain how he had known about the fire in advance. Fortunately for the astrologer, he was able to convince the Members of Parliament who interrogated him that his predictions had been made on a purely astrological basis.

Successes such as those of Lilly kept the belief in astrology alive, but could not stop its decline. With few exceptions only the most old-fashioned scholars still regarded astrology as a science or discipline by the turn of the century. One exception was Sir Isaac Newton, the great philosopher and mathematician who defined the law of gravitation in the 1680s. He originally took up mathematics in order to practice astrology. Another was John Flamsteed, England's first Astronomer Royal. He took the subject so seriously that he used electional astrology to choose August 10, 1675 as the date for laying the foundation stone of the Royal Observatory at Greenwich.

As the 18th century wore on the practice of astrology almost completely died out in mainland Europe, and in England it was largely confined to the producers of yearly almanacs. These books were published shortly before the beginning of each new year. They included some astrological and astronomical information as well as lists of public holidays, farming hints, and other practical information. Their readers were mostly small farmers, and few of them probably had much faith in astrology to judge from the contents of some almanacs. The publisher of *Poor Robin's Almanac*, for instance, poked fun at astrology with jokes like, "Mars inclining to Venus ensureth that maids who walk out with soldiers on May morning will have big bellies by Christmas."

In the years 1780 to 1830, however, astrology enjoyed a small but significant revival in England. Perhaps because of an interest in the past that marked this period, old textbooks on the subject were reprinted. Some new texts were also written, and two astrological magazines were published. Once again it was possible to find professional as well as amateur astrologers.

These astrologers were a new breed—no longer men of learning, but occultists. These men and women combined their astrology with subjects such as alchemy—the supposed art of turning lead and other base metals into gold—fortune telling by the use of playing cards, and even the manufacture of talismans and other good luck charms.

The astrologers of this period also showed an excessive and gloomy preoccupation with the prediction of death. One of them, John Worsdale, published his analysis of 30 horoscopes in which he sought the dates of his clients' deaths, and he appears to have gained great satisfaction from telling these people of their impending doom. When a young girl named Mary Dickson approached him in August 1822 and asked him to predict the date of her marriage, Worsdale told her with apparent relish that "something of an awful nature would occur, before the Month of March, then next ensuing, which would destroy Life." Mary "laughed immoderately," but was sufficiently interested to ask Worsdale what would be the exact cause of her death. "I told her," reported the astute astrologer, "that it appeared to me that Drowning would be the cause of her Dissolution."

On the following January 7 Worsdale's prediction was fulfilled to the letter when Mary Dickson, who was traveling in a river boat, fell overboard and "when taken out life was found to be extinct."

The English astrological revival never completely receded. Throughout the 19th century astrology continued to attract people in Britain and the United States who were interested in the occult. After 1890 American and British astrology received a considerable boost from the occult revival launched by Madame H. P. Blavatsky and her Theosophical Society—founded in 1875 but not really important until the 1890s—and a host of lesser known occult societies that derived their astrological knowledge from India. These groups saw astrology as part of "the Ancient Wisdom"—traditional lore which, they believed, had been wrongly rejected by modern science—and they placed added emphasis on the occult aspects of the art.

Some Influential Modern Astrologers

Thus in the early 20th century Alan Leo, a British member of the Theosophical Society, wrote a whole series of influential astrological textbooks from the occult point of view. Leo was a highly successful astrologer who claimed that "every human being belongs to a Father Star in Heaven or a Star Angel as did Jesus Christ according to our scripture." (Even some of the early Christians who had clung to a belief in astrology saw the Star of Bethlehem as evidence of astrological truth, but most astrologers before Leo had denied that Christ was actually influenced by the Star of the Nativity.)

Leo's books were often written in obscure and confusing occult jargon, but he had skill in simplifying the techniques. He believed that "the problem of the inequalities of the human race can only be successfully solved by a knowledge of astrology," and much of his writing outlined astrological techniques in a clear way so that the ordinary reader could apply them for himself. With another astrologer, Leo also edited *The Astrologer's Magazine*—later renamed *Modern Astrologer*—whose first issue included the horoscopes of Jesus Christ, of Britain's Prince of Wales (later to become King Edward VII), and of the explorer Henry Morton Stanley.

Leo's magazine was aimed at the general public, and his do-it-yourself books helped to transform 20th-century astrology. Until his writings simplified the subject, astrology required years of painstaking study and the mastery of comparatively advanced mathematics. With his books it became possible for anybody of reasonable intelligence to become a fairly competent astrologer after only a year or two of part-time study.

The result was explosive. As Leo's books were reprinted in

the United States and published in German translation, and as others imitated his approach, a host of new astrologers—some amateur and some professional—joined the ranks of the old guard. By 1930 most Americans, Britons, and Germans who were at all interested in the world of the occult knew at least one person capable of casting and interpreting a horoscope.

Probably the most famous of the astrologers who learned their art from Leo's books was Evangeline Adams. Born in 1865, she was a descendant of John Quincy Adams, sixth president of the United States, and she seems to have inherited his determination and sense of purpose. Believing in her own reading of her stars, she made a move to New York City from her hometown of Boston in 1899. She created an immediate sensation. On her first night in the hotel she had booked into, she read the horoscope of the proprietor and warned him of a dreadful disaster. The next day the hotel burned down—and the proprietor's report of her warning to the newspapers put her name in the headlines. Evangeline Adams so gained the kind of publicity that more than offset the loss of much of her belongings in the fire. She set up a business as a reader of horoscopes, and was soon on the way to becoming America's most popular astrologer.

In spite of—or perhaps because of—her success, Evangeline Adams was arrested for fortune telling in 1914. Although she could have elected to pay a fine and go free, she decided to stand trial and argue her own defense. Armed with a pile of reference books, she told the court precisely how she made her analyses and predictions. To prove her point, she offered to make a reading from the birth date of someone she had never met, without even knowing who that person was. The person chosen was the judge's son, and this judge was so impressed with her reading that he concluded, "The defendant raises astrology to the dignity of an exact science." Evangeline Adams was acquitted, and in New York at least astrology was no longer regarded as fortune telling.

Evangeline Adams' triumph had struck an important blow for the respectability of astrology. She proceeded to open a studio in Carnegie Hall in New York City, where she was consulted by politicians, Hollywood stars, royalty, and Wall Street tycoons. Her clients included the Duke of Windsor, Mary Pickford, Caruso, and the financier J. P. Morgan for whom she provided regular

442

forecasts concerning politics and the stock market. There is evidence that many of her clients took her advice seriously, using it as the basis for major decisions regarding their careers, investments, and political activities. Certainly they paid her substantial fees, and by the 1920s she was a wealthy woman.

In 1930 Evangeline Adams began a series of regular radio broadcasts on astrology, and within a year she was receiving 4000 requests a day from listeners who wanted her to cast their horoscope. Her book *Astrology: Your Place Among the Stars* became a best seller, and a number of present-day astrologers first became acquainted with the subject through it. Nevertheless, Evangeline Adams did not escape attacks on her character. It was said that she was not the true author of most of her book. Aleister Crowley, the notorious British magician and a keen amateur astrologer, claimed that he had written the book for Evangeline Adams in return for a fee—a fee that Crowley maintained he had never received. Many of the horoscopes analyzed in the book were for people whom Crowley particularly admired, such as the 19th-century explorer Sir Richard Burton.

Such attacks did nothing to cloud Evangeline Adams' reputation, however. Throughout 1931 her radio show continued to bring her masses of mail from fans who regarded her as a kindly adviser and friend. In that year, Evangeline Adams prophesied that the United States would be at war in 1942, and the following year she is said to have forecast her own death. She explained that she would be unable to undertake a lecture tour for late 1932, and in November of that year she died.

Such was Evangeline Adams' popularity that the public flocked to the Carnegie Hall studio where her body lay in state. Crowds of fans attended her funeral, and there were thousands of telegrams of condolence. No one before Evangeline Adams had done so much to bring astrology to the attention of the general public. By the time of her death, she had become the most popular and successful astrologer of our century—and possibly of all time.

By comparison, the career of another well-known woman astrologer was played out in a more muted key. Elsbeth Ebertin was an honest, competent, and totally unaffected German astrologer, who was born in 1880 and commenced her professional life as a *graphologist*—an interpreter of character from

443

the study of a person's handwriting.

In 1910 Elsbeth Ebertin met a woman who also claimed to be a graphologist, and who was able to give accurate delineations of character. Yet in talking to her, Elsbeth Ebertin discovered that this woman did not even know the basic principles of graphology. It turned out that she was really an astrologer, but preferred not to admit this to her clients because few of them had even heard of astrology.

Impressed by this woman's ability, Elsbeth Ebertin decided to become a professional astrologer herself. She started to study textbooks issued by a small publishing house called the Astrological Library. These included German translations of Alan Leo's writings and books by Karl Brandler-Pracht, an occultist who was busily engaged in reviving German astrology. By 1918 Elsbeth Ebertin had become a competent astrological practitioner, publicist, and writer. She had a sizeable private clientele, gave lectures on astrology, and published at regular intervals an almanac called *A Glimpse Into the Future*, containing predictions of the future of Germany and the world.

Ebertin's 'Führer' Prophecy

The first issue of *A Glimpse Into the Future* was published in 1917, and the almanac then and later was often impressively accurate in its forecasts. One of Elsbeth Ebertin's most famous predictions was contained in the July 1923 edition. It read: "A man of action born on April 20, 1889, with Sun in the 29th degree of Aries at the time of his birth, can expose himself to personal danger by excessively rash action and could very likely trigger off an uncontrollable crisis. His constellations show that this man is to be taken very seriously indeed. He is destined to play a 'Führer-role' in future battles . . . The man I have in mind, with this strong Aries influence, is destined to sacrifice himself for the German nation, and also to face up to all circumstances with audacity and courage, even when it is a matter of *life and death*, and to give an impulse, which will burst forth quite suddenly . . . But I will not anticipate destiny. Time will show . . ."

In fact Elsbeth Ebertin's forecast anticipated destiny rather well. The "man of action born on April 20, 1889" was none other than Adolf Hitler. In November 1923, four months after Elsbeth Ebertin's prediction, he launched an "excessively rash action"—the unsuccessful Munich *Putsch*. This was the attempt by Hitler, then a relatively obscure political adventurer, to overthrow the legally constituted German government by force. It resulted in the killing of a number of his followers—members of the infant Nazi party. Hitler himself dislocated his shoulder during the fighting and served a term of imprisonment for treason.

As for the rest of Elsbeth Ebertin's prediction, that too was fulfilled. Hitler did indeed play a "'Führer-role' in future battles." In spite of his destructive nature it could be said that he "faced up to all circumstances with audacity and courage," and at the end of his life, in the burning ruins of Berlin, he committed suicide—or, as he himself expressed it to his intimates in the very words of the famous astrologer, "sacrificed himself for the German people."

Elsbeth Ebertin continued publishing her almanac until 1937, when she was apparently forced to close it down as a result of pressure from the Gestapo. Possibly some of her past prophecies came too close to the truth for comfort, and the outspoken nature of her predictions may have made the Nazis fear that publications like hers could exert a political influence not to their taste.

Nevertheless, Elsbeth Ebertin kept up her private practice until her death in an air raid in November 1944. According to her son Reinhold, a distinguished German astrologer of the present day, his mother foresaw the bomb that killed her, but felt she should not move to possible safety out of regard for her neighbors. They took comfort from her continued presence among them, saying "As long as Frau Ebertin is here nothing very much can happen to us."

The Boom since the War

Since the end of World War II astrology has had a boom. All over the world institutes now exist for the serious study of astrology, and in 1960 Harvard University accepted a thesis on astrology for the B.A. degree. The American Federation of Astrologers and the British Faculty of Astrological Studies have thousands of members who pass examinations for a diploma in their subject, and subscribe to a code of ethics. Interest in astrology has never been greater. But can we really believe in horoscopes today?

The successful career of Carroll Righter might indicate that many people still do. At the age of 75 years, Righter is the dean of American astrologers—not just in age, but also in status. He might be said to have taken the mantle from Evangeline Adams, whom he met when he was only 14 years old. As a friend of the family she cast his horoscope and found him likely to be a skillful interpreter of the stars. She urged him to become an astrologer. Some 25 years went by before he finally followed her advice, but when he did, he fast became a leader in the field. Based in Hollywood, he has counted among his clients such past and present stellar names as Tyrone Power, Susan Hayward, Marlene Dietrich, and Ronald Colman. It is thought that he might be a millionaire with earnings from numerous newspaper and magazine columns, day-by-day astrological forecasts, and books on how astrology can help in business and finance, and in marriage and family relationships.

Before he became a professional astrologer in 1939, Righter had been in law practice and had also worked on civic projects. During the Depression he began to use astrology to help the unemployed. He found that he could help direct people to jobs by showing them what their horoscopes said they were best suited for. This made many of them look for work that they might never have considered otherwise.

Another astrologer whose career seems to show that there is a place for astrology in modern life is Katina Theodossiou. This well-known British practitioner is one of the world's foremost business astrologers. She is consultant to more than 50 companies in the United States and Europe, giving advice on such matters as mergers, takeovers, staffing, and investment. Many a company has even been born at the time and on the date that she has suggested by the guidance of the stars.

Katina Theodossiou has also helped bring astrology into the computer age. In one assignment for a New York firm, she programmed a computer in order to produce computerized horoscopes for sale. It was a notable success. She worked on the project for 15 months during which time she fed 40,000 separate items of astrological information into the machine.

Astrologers themselves are divided on the subject of computer horoscopes, but few if any would call Katina Theodossiou to account for insincerity or incompetence.

Astrology has never lacked its critics, however, and there are many people today who would not hesitate to dismiss the subject as a ridiculous and outmoded set of doctrines appealing only to the naive and superstitious. Serious astrologers are the first to admit that their art contains a number of inconsistencies and vague assumptions that are difficult to verify. Still they are convinced that astrology is based on truth, and that it can play a valuable role in helping human beings understand more about themselves and their place in the Universe. Today some orthodox scientists are coming to share their point of view. The very people who have long been most skeptical of astrology are now providing evidence to suggest that the ancient art of astrology may be founded on fact.

38. The Scientific Basis of Astrology

In March 1951 John H. Nelson, an American electronic and radio engineer, published a sensational article. There was nothing sensation about the journal in which the article appeared, however. That was the straightforward *RCA Review*, a technical journal published by the Radio Corporation of America and devoted to all aspects of radio, television, and electronics. Nelson's article was an equally serious account of his research into factors affecting radio reception. But his report was to shatter orthodox views about humans and the Universe, for his findings appeared to confirm the basic belief of astrology—that the planets can and do influence our lives. The story behind Nelson's article began when RCA scientists noticed an apparent connection between the difficulty or ease of shortwave radio communication and the varying positions of the Earth's planetary neighbors. Was this link pure coincidence, RCA wanted to know, or was it the result of some hitherto unknown cosmic influence?

The first step in answering this question was to set up a basic statistical investigation of the phenomenon. RCA asked several astronomers to undertake this task, but all refused. In their opinion the idea that planetary positions could affect radio waves was so ridiculous that it was not worth investigating. However, RCA was unwilling to abandon the inquiry, and assigned Nelson, an experienced radio engineer, to investigate.

As Nelson checked records of radio disturbance dating back to the 1920s he made a series of exciting discoveries. He found that magnetic storms—the cause of radio disturbance—occur when two or more planets, viewed from the Earth, are very close together at right angles to one another or 180° apart. The position of the planets did appear to influence radio reception, and in a way that came as no surprise to the astrologers. These particular relationships—the aspects—between the planets have been important in astrology since ancient times, and none of them is regarded as favorable. The *conjunction*—when the planets are very close together on the same side of the Sun—is considered neutral, being good or bad according to certain factors modifying it. When the planets are in *square*—at right angles to one another—it is seen as disharmonious, difficult, and even evil. The same applies when planets are in *opposition*—180° apart on opposite sides of the Sun.

Nelson's subsequent discoveries also tied in with traditional astrological beliefs. He discovered that magnetic disturbances were notably absent, and that shortwave reception was therefore good, when two or more planets were 60° or 120° apart. These are precisely the aspects that astrology regards as harmonious, easy, and good. Further, Nelson found that aspects of 150° and 135° also had an effect on radio reception—a discovery of particular interest since these aspects were not used by astrologers of the ancient world, but are used by many present-day ones.

The test of a scientific theory is whether it enables the accurate prediction of future events. While Nelson had discovered a number of fascinating correlations between planetary positions and radio reception, they just might have been the result of chance. The real question was whether Nelson could use his findings to predict future magnetic disturbances.

He tried—and his predictions were 80 percent accurate. Later, by refining his methods to include details of all the planets, he increased his success rate to an amazing 93 percent. Nelson had provided the first piece of scientific evidence to show that life on Earth could be influenced by the planets, and the claims of the astrologers—for long regarded as totally irrational—were seen to have some justification.

Nelson's discovery was not an isolated one. Other work carried out by scientists in recent years had also tended to back up astrology's basic beliefs about the influence of the Sun, Moon, and planets on earthly events and on people themselves.

For example, the late Dr. Rudolf Tomaschek, an academic physicist and chairman of the World Geophysical Council, made a statistical analysis of 134 large earthquakes. He found that planetary positions in relationship to the place and time these earthquakes occurred were highly significant. The "earthquake aspects" almost always included one or more of the planets Jupiter, Uranus, and Neptune, and the stronger the earthquake the more likely these planets were to be involved—usually in traditionally sinister aspects such as the square.

Dr. Tomaschek believed in astrology so that, in spite of his academic qualifications, some people were skeptical of his findings. The same criticism could not be leveled at the work of Dr. A. K. Podshibyakin, a Soviet physician who discovered a remarkable connection between physical events on the Sun and the incidence of road accidents in the Soviet Union.

Dr. Podshibyakin's findings, published in 1967, were based on statistics compiled over a number of years at Tomsk Medical College. These studies showed that the day after a solar flare—a magnetic storm on the surface of the Sun—there was a marked increase in road accidents, sometimes to as much as four times the daily average. Dr. Podshibyakin pointed out that this link between solar flares and road accidents was not confined to the Soviet Union, but had also been observed by researchers in West Germany. He gave a possible explanation of the phenomenon, based on the known fact that a solar flare produces a tremendous amount of ultraviolet radiation, which causes changes in the Earth's atmosphere. Dr. Podshibyakin suggested that this radiation affects the human body, slowing it down.

No such explanation can be provided for even stranger influences produced by the Sun and Moon on earthly life—influences that have astonished and puzzled the scientists who have observed them. One such scientist is Dr. Frank A. Brown, Professor of Biology at Northwestern University.

'Biological Clocks'

For the last 25 years Brown and his team have been conducting research into "biological clocks"—the natural rhythms shown by all life on Earth. These clocks manifest themselves in many ways, from the regular sleeping and waking patterns of human beings to the small movements made by certain plants during the night. There have been many efforts to explain the nature of these life rhythms, varying from the idea that they are the response of living beings to air ionization, to the suggestion that

450

each separate organism possesses its own internal timing mechanism—a biological clock in the strict meaning of the term.

None of these explanations satisfied Dr. Brown. He found it impossible, for example, to trace any mechanism by which air ionization could trigger off the purposeful and meaningful activities of life rhythms. Equally, he was unable to find any physical organ in living beings that could serve as a mechanical clock.

Over a 10-year period Brown and his associates ran experiments on a variety of phenomena. These included the movement of bean plants in the night, the amount of running performed by caged rats during successive days, the sleep pattern of flies, the opening and closing of oyster shells, and changes in the color of fiddler crabs.

What emerged was astonishing. All these phenomena followed rhythmical cycles, and those cycles were triggered not by some internal clock, but by cosmic influences—notably those connected with the Sun and the Moon. Thus, for example, rats living under controlled conditions in darkened cages were found to be twice as active when the Moon was above the horizon as when it was below it. They seemed to know instinctively when the Moon was up and responded to it, although they had no way of seeing it.

Equally surprising was the behavior of oysters. When they are in their natural habitat, oysters open and close their shells according to the rhythm of the tides. At high tide they open their shells to feed, and at low tide they close them as a protection against drying out. While the tides are, of course, produced by the gravitational pull of the Moon and Sun, it had always been assumed that the movement of the tides alone caused the opening and closing of the oysters' shells. No one had ever been bold enough to suggest that the oysters were responding directly to the Moon and Sun. Yet Brown discovered that they were apparently doing just that.

What Dr. Brown had done was to remove some oysters from the Atlantic seaboard of the United States, and place them in darkened containers so that no sunlight or moonlight could reach them. He had then taken them to his laboratory in Evanston, Illinois, a thousand miles from the sea. Within a fortnight the oysters had lost the pattern of opening and closing that they had displayed in their old home in the Atlantic, and were following the rhythm of what the tides would have been in Evanston had that town been on the sea. In other words, the oysters were not directly influenced by the tides, but by some other signals apparently related to the Moon and Sun.

The Moon and Madness

What about people? Do the Sun, Moon, and planets really affect us, as astrologers claim? A study published in 1960 by another American scientist, Dr. Leonard Ravitz of Duke University, has shown a direct link between the behavior of human beings and the Moon. His findings coincide with the age-old belief that there is a connection between the Moon and madness.

Over a long period Ravitz plotted the variations in the small electric charges that are continually given off by the human body. He worked with both the mentally ill and a control group of healthy people. He found that the body's electrical potential underwent regular changes in all the people tested, and that these changes coincided with the phases of the Moon. The most marked changes occurred when the Moon was full, and the more disturbed the patient, the greater was the extent of the change.

Dr. Ravitz was therefore able to predict emotional changes in his mental patients, and to confirm that the full Moon does tend to provoke crises in people whose mental balance is already disturbed. "Whatever else we may be we are all electric machines," says Ravitz. "Thus energy reserves may be mobilized by periodic universal factors, such as the forces behind the Moon, which tend to aggravate maladjustments and conflicts already present."

The rhythms of the Moon may also have some effect on the patterns of human birth. Not enough research has been done on this subject to come to any definite conclusions, but it is interesting to note that in 1938 a Japanese scientist made a study of the cosmic factors in 33,000 live births. He found that high numbers of births occurred at the full and New Moons and low numbers one or two days before the Moon's first and last quarters. According to a report published in 1967 an American gynecologist has confirmed these findings from a study of no less than half a million births. This evidence at least supports the theory.

The date of a person's birth depends of course on the time of conception, and this in turn depends on the time of ovulation— the release of an egg from the ovary. Psychiatrist Eugen Jonas of Czechoslovakia has discovered a clear connection between the time of ovulation and the Moon. His studies have shown that a woman tends to ovulate during the particular phase of the Moon that prevailed when she was born. Jonas has even used his findings to provide women in Eastern Europe with a new and entirely natural method of contraception. His charts, drawn up to show the days on which a woman can conceive, have proved 98 percent effective—as efficient as the contraceptive pill.

It has long been believed that a woman's menstrual cycle, with its average of 28 days or the length of time between two full Moon is in some way connected with the rhythms of the Moon, and there is some scientific evidence to support this view. At the beginning of this century, Swiss chemist Dr. Svante Arrhenius made a study of 11,000 women. He found that the onset of menstruation reached a peak at the new Moon. In the 1960s two German researchers, who had kept records of the onset of menstruation in 10,000 women over a period of 14 years, came to a similar conclusion.

There is certainly evidence of a connection between bleeding in general and the phases of the Moon. The American physician Dr. Edson Andrews found, for example, that in 1000 cases of unusually heavy bleeding following tonsillectomies, 82 percent of the bleeding crises occurred between the Moon's first and third quarters. "These data have been so conclusive," said Dr. Andrews, ". . . that I threaten to become a witch doctor and operate on dark nights only."

These are only a fraction of the discoveries scientists have made concerning the influence of cosmic events on life on Earth. Many other experiments also make it clear that the Sun, Moon, and planets seem to exert a profound effect on us and our environment, and that the basic belief of the astrologers is in no way unscientific. Has this led any scientists to a belief in astrology?

Astrology and Jung

Some—but not very many. Nevertheless, the scientists who have come to accept the fundamental claims of astrology have often been outstanding in their fields. The late Carl G. Jung, whom many consider to have been the greatest psychologist of the 20th century, was outspoken in his admiration for this traditional art. He claimed that astrology would eventually have to be recognized as a science. "The cultural philistines," he said, "believed until recently that astrology had been disposed of long since and today could safely be laughed at, but today, arising out of the social deeps, it knocks at the doors of the universities from which it was banished some 300 years ago."

Jung believed so profoundly in astrology that in later life he insisted on having a horoscope for each of his patients. He maintained that the horoscope provided an excellent guide to character and psychological disposition. He also carried out some elementary observations to test the ancient astrological belief that there are significant interactions between the planetary positions in the horoscopes of married couples.

Jung's experimental work was by no means complete, but he did find significant Sun-Moon interrelationships in the horoscopes of the 483 married couples he studied. In pairing off the horoscopes of husband and wife Jung found, for example, that the woman's Moon was frequently in conjunction with the man's Sun—the aspect that astrologers claim most favors marriage.

In recent years Jung's approach to astrological research has found favor with a number of investigators, among them the British philosopher John M. Addey, a dedicated astrologer who is also a competent statistician. Surprisingly enough, Addey's work sprang originally from a feeling that there was a good deal wrong with astrology in its traditional form. "So far as the practical rules . . . are concerned there are a host of uncertainties," he said, ". . . intractable problems which can only be solved by careful, persistent work; . . . our records are scattered and contain many errors . . . The chief obstacle is the opposition of the scientific fraternity, and to silence or check their criticism would seem to be the first step in presenting our case to a wider public . . ."

Addey's first attempt to "silence or check" continuing scientific objections to astrology involved 970 people over 90 years of age whose names appeared in the British *Who's Who*—a biographical directory of the eminent in all walks of life. A horoscope was prepared for each of these long-lived people, and all the horoscopes were compared to see if they had any factors in common.

Addey first checked to see if there was any truth in the ancient astrological tradition that people born under certain Sun Signs

454

are more likely to be long lived than others. No such connection was found. The traditionally long-lived Capricornians, for instance, were no better represented among the 90-year-olds than the traditionally short-lived Pisceans. Addey did, however, discover one remarkable link in the horoscopes of his long-lived subjects. This concerned aspects—the relationships between two or more planets standing at significant angles to one another. Astrologers have always divided aspects into two types: *applying*—when a fast-moving planet is moving *into* a significant angle with a slow-moving planet; and *separating*—when a fast-moving planet is moving *away* from such a position. Addey found that the horoscopes of his 90-year-olds showed a preponderance of separating aspects.

This is precisely what one would expect if there is any truth in astrology, for astrologers have always held that separating aspects indicate the conservation of physical and mental energy, relaxation, and passivity—just the characteristics likely to be found in people who manage to live into their nineties.

Was this result merely a fluke? Addey decided to investigate another group of people with characteristics as opposite those of the 90-year-olds as possible—people who would be likely to expend their energies, be tense, nervous, and active. If the preponderance of separating aspects in the horoscopes of the 90-year-olds was more than a coincidence, then the opposite group should show an equivalent preponderance of applying aspects.

The group that Addey selected for his investigation was one to which he himself belonged—people who had been physically handicapped to some extent following an attack of polio. He chose this group because it is generally accepted by physicians that most polio victims who suffer long-term damage from the disease are of a particular physical and mental type. They tend to be athletically active rather than sedentary, alert rather than sluggish and plodding, and outgoing rather than introspective. When the horoscopes of the polio group were analyzed they completely fulfilled Addey's expectations. Their case was exactly the opposite of the long-lived sample—it showed a significant preponderance of applying aspects.

Addey was, of course, predisposed to a belief in astrology. Other statistical investigations have been carried out by researchers with a far more skeptical approach to the subject. The most outstanding work of this kind has been produced by the French scientist and statistician Michel Gauquelin, who began his research in 1950 with the object of *disproving* astrology.

Gauquelin's Statistical Survey

Gauquelin's first step was to examine the sets of supposed statistical evidence in favor of astrology which had been produced earlier in the century by the astrological writers Paul Choisnard, Karl Krafft, and Leon Lasson. Using advanced statistical techniques Gauquelin had no difficulty in showing that all the evidence produced by Choisnard and Krafft rested on too small test groups or faulty mathematical methods. There remained the work of Lasson, who had investigated planetary positions in relation to people's professions, and had produced some surprising results. Lasson had found that, in an exceptionally high number of cases, Mars figures prominently in the horoscopes of medical men, Venus in the horoscopes of artists, and Mercury in those of actors and writers.

Gauquelin concluded that Lasson's test groups had probably been too small and decided to run an analysis of his own, using the horoscopes of 576 medical academics. To his amazement, he found that an unusually high percentage of these men had been born when Mars or Saturn was either coming over the horizon or passing its highest point in the sky. Gauquelin then checked his findings with a new test group of 508 eminent physicians. Mars and Saturn were prominent in exactly the same way. Taking the two test groups together, the odds against these planetary positions being due to chance were ten million to one.

Gauquelin's results received widespread and favorable coverage in the French press. Their reception by Gauquelin's fellow statisticians and scientists was less favorable. Some claimed that Gauquelin's test groups must have been insufficient; others said that he had merely discovered a national peculiarity, since all his subjects were French. "Your conclusions are nothing but pulp romances . . ." the Belgian scientist Marcell Boll told Gauquelin. "If you undertook the same enquiry in Great Britain, Germany, the United States and Russia you would come out with nothing but other national idiosyncracies."

Undaunted by his critics, Gauquelin tested 25,000 Dutch,

German, Italian, and Belgian horoscopes. The results backed up the French ones, and experiments with new professional groups produced further confirmation. In the horoscopes of 3142 military men either Mars or Jupiter was in a significant position. Politicians and athletes were also linked with Mars, scientists with Saturn, and actors with Jupiter. The odds against these links occurring simply by chance ranged from between one million and 50 million to one. From doctors to artists, every one of the test groups showed that planetary positions were related to profession—and in just the way astrology had always claimed. Statisticians were finally forced to take Gauquelin's results seriously.

Counter-experiments were performed in which Gauquelin's methods were applied to random groups of men and women who did not have a profession in common. In every case these random groups produced results in accordance with the laws of chance. This so impressed a number of Gauquelin's opponents that they withdrew their criticism of his work.

Gauquelin has carried out more than 20 years of statistical research in astrology, but his results should not be overestimated. He has neither proved the truth of every astrological doctrine, nor found that astrological predictions can be completely trusted. What he has shown is that there is a definite relationship between the positions of planets at the moment of birth and the profession a person chooses to follow. This is, of course, in complete accord with traditional astrological beliefs.

What about all the other details that an experienced astrologer claims to be able to detect from a person's horoscope? Has any serious research been carried out on the accuracy of horoscopes as a whole? Not enough, by any means, but sufficient to provide a strong case for further investigation.

Experiments in 'Blind Diagnosis'

Hans Bender, Professor of Psychology at the German University of Freiburg, has been one of the few academics to carry out scientific research in this field. As early as 1937 Professor Bender began to make experiments in "blind diagnosis," in which an astrologer is given an anonymous horoscope with no other information about the person to whom it belongs. The professor then compared the astrologer's findings with known facts about the life and character of the individual concerned. The results of these early tests were inconclusive, and in 1944-45 Bender made more extensive experiments with the astrologer and psychologist Thomas Ring. Their findings were promising and, when World War II had ended, Bender decided to continue the tests on an even larger scale.

Bender tested more than 100 astrologers, using blind diagnosis and another procedure known as "matching." For the matching tests each astrologer was given detailed notes on the lives, personalities, and appearance of up to half a dozen unidentified individuals and an equal number of horoscopes. Their task was to match up the horoscopes with the right individuals.

Results from the matching tests were confusing and unsatisfactory. The findings from blind diagnosis were more rewarding. A large number of the astrologers made statements about the individuals whose horoscopes they had examined which were true, but would be true of almost anybody. A smaller number, however, produced specific statements that were impressively and minutely accurate. Interestingly enough, these astrologers were able to justify each of their statements in terms of the astrological tradition. This made it less likely that their success was due to clairvoyance or to some other psychic gift rather than skill in their art.

Bender continued his investigations with this smaller group. He found that one particular astrologer, Walter Boer, excelled in one type of matching test as well as blind diagnosis. The particular matching test involved written records about two groups of people—one psychologically maladjusted and one normal. The records were locked in a safe to which Boer had no access, and he was given no details about the people concerned except the dates, times, and places of their birth. In a high number of cases he was able to match the psychological conclusions about these people with their horoscopes.

In 1960 American psychologist Vernon Clark carried out even more rigorous tests of this kind. Clark first selected the horoscopes of 10 people, five men and five women, each of them of a different profession. They were a musician, an accountant, a herpetologist (an expert on snakes), a veterinary surgeon, a teacher, an art critic, a puppeteer, a pediatrician, a librarian, and a prostitute. Clark then gave the horoscopes and a separate list of the professions to 20 astrologers and asked them to match up the two. As a control, he gave the same information to a group of 20 psychologists and social workers. The control group came out with the number of correct answers that could be expected to be obtained by chance. The astrologers produced far better results—a hundred to one against them being the result of chance.

Clark remembered, however, that 100 to one shots sometimes romp home, as anyone who plays the horses knows. He also realized that he had to make sure that the results were not due to the astrologers being psychics, unconsciously practicing some form of ESP.

The next series of tests was therefore designed to reduce the possibility of ESP to a minimum. Each of 23 astrologers was given 20 horoscopes divided into 10 pairs. With these were 10 sets of biographical data, one for each of the 10 pairs. The astrologers were told that *one* of each pair of horoscopes corresponded to the biographical data given for that pair. The other horoscope of each pair, they were assured, pertained to someone of the same sex and approximate age, but with a different personal history. In fact these second horoscopes were fakes, prepared for imaginary people. This was the course taken to diminish as much as possible the chances of ESP being involved.

The task of the astrologers was to fit each set of biographical data to the correct one of each of the pairs of horoscopes. Once again the results were good—100 to one against them being the result of chance. This result seemed to prove the possibility of astrological prediction. For if Clark's test astrologers could successfully decide on the basis of a horoscope which person had suffered, say, a broken leg, they could in theory have predicted that broken leg by looking at the same horoscope before the accident happened.

Clark undertook a third test, which again involved the astrologers being given pairs of horoscopes. This time one of each pair pertained to someone who had cerebral palsy. The other, a similar chart, referred to a highly gifted individual. The astrologers had to decide which of these horoscopes belonged to which of the two individuals.

Once more the results were impressive, and the odds were

again 100 to one against them being the result of chance. The odds against the figures for the three experiments together being the result of chance were over a million to one. Clark's experimental findings were examined by statisticians, who found his mathematical techniques to be faultless.

What was Clark's own conclusion? "Never again," he said, "will it be possible to dismiss the astrological technique as a vague, spooky, and mystical business—or as the plaything of undisciplined psychics—or as merely the profitable device of unscrupulous quacks. Those who, out of prejudice, wish to do so will have to remain silent or repeat these experiments for themselves."

So there is evidence that astrology works. But if so, how? There have been many attempts to give a scientific answer to this question. The best known of these is the theory suggestèd by the psychologist Carl G. Jung.

Jung's Theory of Synchronicity

Jung believed in what he called "synchronicity," or the meaningful coincidence. Synchronicity, said Jung, is the other side of cause and effect. In other words, if two events happen at the same time, or shortly after one another, they may be related because one event caused the other. Alternatively neither event may have caused the other, yet the two may still be linked in a meaningful way.

In the case of astrology this would mean that the Sun, Moon, and other cosmic influences do not cause particular events, but they synchronize, or coincide meaningfully with those events. According to Jung's theory, it is not the particular planetary aspects at birth that *cause* an individual to be, say, short-lived. It is merely that these aspects *coincide* with the birth of short-lived people.

An imaginary example may help to make this concept clearer. A man feels hungry and eats a meal at the same time every evening. Each evening as he begins to feel hungry the hands of the electric clock in his apartment always indicate that the time is 7 p.m. But it is not the position of the clock hands that produces the hunger, nor the hunger that affects the clock hands. There is no causal relationship between the two. But there is a synchronistic relationship—both the hunger and the clock time

460

reflect the 24-hour period of the Earth's rotation.

Applying this example to astrology, the planetary positions are the "hands of the clock," and the inborn characteristics and destiny of a person born under those positions are the "feelings of hunger." Neither is the cause of the other, but both reflect some vast cosmic cycle of which we know nothing.

Curiously enough, the theory of synchronicity is almost as ancient as astrology itself, although Jung thought he had invented it. Sophisticated astrologers have adhered to it for centuries, although they have expressed it differently. The way they put it is that "the planets and the signs of the zodiac are symbols of cosmic forces, and the patterns they form synchronize with events on Earth."

Totally different theories have, however, been put forward by some modern scientists to explain the results they have obtained when studying cosmic influences. Dr. Frank A. Brown, famous for his experiments on biological clocks, has suggested that a "trigger mechanism" may account for the rhythms found in the opening of oyster shells and the activity of rats. The Moon and the Sun, Brown suggests, supply an extremely minute amount of some unknown energy to each living organism. In spite of its smallness, this energy is enough to pull a biological trigger within the organism, setting off a chain reaction that ultimately leads to the organism expending a large amount of energy.

Brown's theory is, of course, thoroughly scientific, being expressed in terms of cause and effect. However, there is no more evidence for the existence of either the trigger or the energy that supposedly sets it off than there is for the existence of the "internal clocks" that Brown had previously rejected.

Another explanation of planetary influences has been put forward by Michel Gauquelin, who worked on the relationship between horoscopes and professions. His latest theory arose from a five-year study of 30,000 parents and children during which he discovered that children tend to be born under the same, or similar, planetary positions as their parents were. We inherit our horoscopes, Gauquelin suggests, in the same way that we inherit other genetic factors. Some element in our genetic makeup is sensitive to a certain set of cosmic influences, helping to determine when we are born and affecting the future course of our lives, including our probable choice of the profession we will follow.

Of the prevailing theories, synchronicity—the idea that the positions of the planets do not cause things to happen but merely coincide with those happenings—is still the most popular explanation of how astrology works, and the one to which most astrologers adhere.

In a sense all such theories take second place to two important facts. Cosmic influences have been shown to exist, and astrology—the art of interpreting those influences—can be made to work. This even extends to predicting future events.

39. Nostradamus and After

It is midnight and the astrologer mounts the spiral staircase to his secret study at the top of the house. He knows that he will not be disturbed there, and that his wife will keep any unwelcome visitors away from him. He sits before a three-legged brass stool, lays down his laurel wand between its legs, and proceeds to sprinkle the hem of his robe and his feet with water. For a moment he feels frightened before the power he is about to evoke. Then his courage returns, he places a bowl of water on the stool, and peers silently into the liquid. After a while the power "speaks" to him, and he is "divinely possessed." The water becomes cloudy, and he sees therein visions of the future—pictures of war, famine, earthquake, fire, and disaster. Lighting a taper, he then goes into a trance, in which his travel into future time increases in range and detail. All the while, as the voices from space go on, and the images appear in the water, he writes down his visions in a thick vellum book. His activity lasts until dawn. Then, with the first light, he hears and sees no more. He leans back in his chair, exhausted. Downstairs, his wife will soon be preparing breakfast. In a little while he will join her, eat with her, tell her of the revelations he has seen, and rest until it is time for his labors of divination to start again the following midnight.

All this sounds somewhat like an old-fashioned melodrama, but it was serious business to the man involved in it—the French physician and astrologer Michel de Notredame, known as Nostradamus. To him, there was nothing absurd in what he did and what he saw and heard. To him, it was the natural way —the only way—in which he could, as he put it, "leave a memorial of me after my death, to the common benefit of

463

mankind, concerning the things which the Divine Essence has revealed to me by astronomical revelations."

Nostradamus wrote these words in a dedication to his son in the first edition of his famous *Centuries*, published in Lyons in March 1555. In his work, *centuries* do not refer to periods of a hundred years, but to a series of prophecies numbering 100 to a section. Although the prophecies came to Nostradamus with complete clarity, he did not present them clearly to his readers. Both in order not to offend the Church and to reduce the possibility of mass alarm among the general populace, he wrote his prophecies in four-line rhymes of obscure and symbolic language.

A noted scholar, Nostradamus wrote his verses in a mixture of puns, anagrams (Paris, for example, was written *Ripas*), French, Latin, and a language of his own making. "If I came to refer to that which will be in the future," he explained, "those of the realm, sect, religion, and faith would find it so poorly in accord with their petty fancies that they would come to condemn that which future ages shall know and understand to be true." In a letter to his patron, King Henry II of France—whose death, incidentally, he correctly predicted—Nostradamus added: "Some may answer that the rhyme is as easy to understand as to blow one's nose, but the sense is more difficult to grasp."

Astrology was then at one of its peaks, not to enjoy so much popularity again until the 1930s. In spite of this, Nostradamus was suspected of being in league with the Devil. A virtuous God-fearing man who had been known to burn occult books that went against the canons of the Church, the astrologer quoted the Bible in his defense, from Matthew vii. 6: "Such alone as are inspired by the divine power can predict particular events in a spirit of prophecy." His own "divine virtue and inspiration," he claimed, came directly from God the Creator, who used him as a spokesman for His own plans and intentions for the future.

Employing a blend of learning and intuition, Nostradamus concentrated mainly on *facts* about the future, rather than *dates*. He even got the date of his own death wrong, dying in July 1566 instead of November 1567, as he had predicted. However, it did not affect the success of the *Centuries*, which went from edition to edition, and which has been in print from

Michel de Notredame, known as Nostradamus, whose famous book of
prophecies entitled *Centuries* was published in Lyons in 1555. Nostradamus
followed an ancient ritual, involving robes, a laurel wand, and a three-legged
brass stool in order to receive his visions of the future. Staring into a bowl of
water between midnight and dawn he saw more than 1,000 visions over the
years, including, according to some interpreters, the French Revolution, the
birth and defeat of Napoleon, the rise of Hitler, the assassinations of John F.
and Robert Kennedy, and the destruction of New York. (*Nostradamus and After*)

his day to this—about 400 years running.

His nocturnal methods of divination were based largely on an ancient book called *De Mysteriis Egyptorum*, an edition of which was published in Lyons in 1547. Its author, the 4th-century Greek philosopher Iamblichus, stressed the importance of dressing in robes and using a wand and a three-legged stool. To later disciples of Nostradamus, such trappings heightened the impact of his predictions.

Predictions of Nostradamus

Here is a translation of the third verse of Nostradamus' *Century One*:

> *When the litters are overturned by the whirlwind and faces are covered by cloaks, the new republic will be troubled by its people. At this time the reds and the whites will rule wrongly.*

This has been interpreted as a forecast of the French Revolution of 1789, and the coming of what Nostradamus called the Common Advent, or the assumption of power by the ordinary man. The "reds" and the "whites" was taken to refer to the era of Robespierre and the Terror, white being the color of the Bourbon rulers who were overthrown, and red the color of the Revolutionaries. One of his few predictions with a definite date also anticipates the French Revolution. In a letter to King Henry II on June 27, 1558, Nostradamus foretold an uprising against the Church, stating: "It shall be in the year 1792, at which time everyone will think it a renovation of the age." As it happened, the Republic of France—born and bred out of anticlerical thinking—came into being in September 1792. The year before that saw the flight of King Louis XVI and Queen Marie-Antoinette when, as the astrologer prophesied, they traveled by a "circuitous route" at night before being captured by the mob and beheaded.

It seemed only natural that, as a Frenchman, some of Nostradamus' most successful prophecies should concern his own country. In verse seven of *Century One*, he speaks of "letters intercepted on their way," a prediction that could apply to the celebrated case of Captain Alfred Dreyfus 339 years later. In this case of anti-Semitism that divided the country, the innocent Dreyfus was unjustly convicted on the basis of intercepted letters said to have been sent by him to the Germans. Before getting a public pardon, Dreyfus had a review of his case by an official named Rousseau, as Nostradamus foretold. This minister was so bitterly anti-Dreyfus that he found the officer guilty a second time, even though Dreyfus was soon after fully exonerated.

These predictions were followed by a vision of the atrocities in the City of Nantes in 1793, when 1000 citizens opposed to the Revolutionaries were either guillotined or drowned naked in the river Loire—"Cries, groans at Nantes pitiful to see," were the words of Nostradamus. Napoleon comes in for a number of prophecies, including his birth ("an emperor will be born near Italy who will cost the empire dear"), his retreat from fire-torn Moscow in the winter of 1812–13 ("A mass of men will draw near . . . the Destroyer will ruin the old city"), and his defeat at Waterloo in 1815 when the Leopard (England) and the Boar (Prussia) crushed the Eagle (Napoleon).

As he said himself, however, Nostradamus had foreknowledge of more than just one country or one continent. Some of his most fascinating forecasts concern the United States, its inabitants, and its political leaders. Three times in the ten books of the *Centuries* are mentions such as "the great man . . . struck down in the day by a thunderbolt"; "the great one will fall"; "the world put into trouble by three brothers; their enemies will seize the marine city, hunger, fire, blood, plague, and all evils doubled." These references are generally taken as a warning of the assassination of President John F. Kennedy, a presentiment of the gunning down of his brother, Robert, and a hint that the troubles of Senator Edward Kennedy would be ongoing. The destruction of New York appears to be foreseen by the astrologer in three references stating the "earthshaking fire [which] will cause tremors around the New City"; "the sky will burn at 45 degrees, fire approaches the Great New City"; and the "King will want to enter the New City."

Apart from the devastation and/or invasion of New York, Nostradamus predicted that the whole of the USA would be involved in a cataclysmic third world war. This would be started by China, and would end with a sky filled with "weapons and rockets" with tremendous damage "inflicted on the left" (in this case, the Western Hemisphere). What makes this particular prophecy more chilling than most is how his verse six of *Century Two* apparently describes the atom bomb attacks on Nagasaki and Hiroshima in 1945:

> *Near the harbor and in two cities will be two scourges, the like of which have never been seen. Hunger, plague within, people thrown out by the sword will cry for help from the great immortal God.*

Predating this in time—although not in the *Centuries* themselves, which are not chronological—is his line about "fire in the ruined ships of the West." This has been interpreted as the blazing American vessels and battleships during the Japanese attack on Pearl Harbor in December 1941. As for England, in *Century Ten* the astrologer anticipated the abdication of King Edward VIII, who gave up his throne to marry the twice-divorced American woman, Wallis Simpson. "The young born to the realm of Britain, which his dying father had commended to him . . . London will dispute with him, and the kingdom will be demanded back from the son."

By the time of his death, Nostradamus had predicted such unrelated and varied events as the victory of General Charles de Gaulle to gain the leadership of France, the Hungarian Revolution of 1956, the death of Hitler in his Berlin bunker, the collapse of the French Maginot Line in World War II, and the influenza epidemic that swept through the world in 1918-19—"the pestilence" following the "dreadful war."

The Prophecy of Cazotte

The work of Nostradamus was not formally condemned by a Papal Court until 1781, when it was put on the Index of prohibited books. By then, the visionary's influence and example had built up a following among both the clerical and the secular. One of the most remarkable of the prophets who came after Nostradamus was the 18th-century poet Jacques Cazotte, whose pleasant manners and modest talents were enough to gain him a place in French high society of the day. His most famous recorded prophecy took place on a summer's evening in 1788, toward the end of a garden party given by the Duchess de Gramont. As a protégé of his hostess, Cazotte's principal purpose at such gatherings was to read his latest sonnets or odes. This he usually did in mild, gentle tones. On this particular occasion, however, the poet showed the sharp side of his nature and talent. It came when Guillaume des Malesherbes, one of Louis XVI's ministers, proposed a toast to "the day when reason shall triumph in the affairs of men—even though I shall not live to see that day."

Cazotte swung round on him, and his party mask dropped. "On the contrary, sir," he exclaimed. "You *will* live to see the day— to your cost! It shall come in five years time with a great French Revolution!"

While the guests stood open-mouthed around him, Cazotte turned to several other highly placed politicians and courtiers, and told them what their fates would be. The King's favorite, Chamfort, would join his friend Malesherbes on the guillotine, he predicted; the Marquis de Condorcet would "cheat the executioner" by taking poison; as for the Duchess herself, she would "ride to the scaffold in a woodcutter's cart." As the shock gradually wore off, the aristocrats began to snigger self-defensively among themselves. Then one of the company—an atheist named Jean La Harpe, who later wrote an account of the evening—stepped forward.

"What of me, Monsieur Cazotte?" he asked mockingly. "Don't tell me that I, of all people, am not destined for the guillotine!"

Cazotte smiled at him. "You are not, sir," he replied, "but only so that you can undergo an even more horrible fate. For you, Monsieur Atheist, are to become a devout and happy Christian!"

The laughter at this was even louder. But Cazotte had the final, I-told-you-so laugh. Everything came about as he had said it would, and La Harpe—whose conversion to Christianity was one of the sensations of the day—bequeathed his manuscript about Cazotte and his "ridiculous predictions" to the monastery in which he had become a man of God.

The Visions of Fatima

The prediction of the violent end of Louis XVI remained the outstanding example of predictive powers in the world until the morning of May 13, 1917. On that day, three small children were quietly herding sheep in the hills near the village of Fatima in central Portugal. Ten-year-old Lucia dos Santos and her

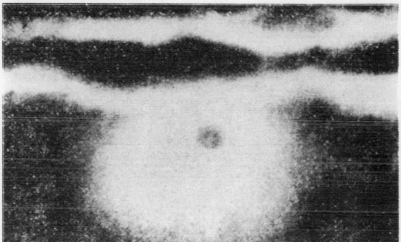

(Top) The three children who saw visions of the Virgin Mary on 13 May, 13 July and 13 October at the village of Fatima, Portugal in 1917. Left to right they are Jacinta, aged seven, Francisco, aged nine, and Lucia dos Santos, aged ten. *(Nostradamus and After)*

(Bottom) Newspaper photograph of the sun on 13 October 1917, when a huge crowd converged on Fatima to see the Virgin appear to the children. As she spoke (to the children alone), the sky was streaked and spattered with colour, and the sun dived towards the earth and then rose again. *(Nostradamus and After)*

Part of the huge crowd, estimated at 80,000, witnessing the movement of the sun at Fatima, Portugal on 13 October 1917. *(Nostradamus and After)*

cousins Jacinta, aged seven, and Francisco, nine, suddenly saw two dazzling flashes of light. The illumination came from a stubby oak tree nearby. Suspended in the center of the "ball of light" was the figure of a beautiful woman. As the youngsters stiffened and gazed at her, she told them not to be afraid. "I will not harm you," she said as she became indistinct and gradually faded away.

Her last words were to ask the children to return to the spot on the 13th of each month until October, at which time a great and dreadful secret would be revealed to them. Despite a beating they received from their parents for "telling lies," Lucia and her cousins—together with some 50 inquisitive villagers—were back on the hill at noon on June 13. The children knelt and said their rosaries, and the beautiful lady radiated into view from the east, like a "glowing messenger from God." This time her message was not so encouraging. She asserted that Jacinto and Francisco would soon be "called to Heaven," and that Lucia would live only in order to spread the Madonna's message. At this, the belief grew that the luminous visitor was the Virgin Mary.

The Virgin Mary's next appearance was on July 13. Before an audience of more than 5000 people—of whom only Lucia, Jacinta, and Francisco could actually see her—she warned of a coming catastrophe that would be even greater than World War I, and that would destroy the world. The first sign of the disaster would be seen in the heavens "a bright, unknown light which will be God's sign that he is about to punish the people of the world for their crimes." Once again the three children were beaten—and even imprisoned. The charge was taking God's name in vain—as well as scaring the souls out of the adults in the village.

However, the children's persistence impressed everyone. In addition, the story of a similar vision that had appeared to two little shepherdesses in La Salette, France in 1846, created more interest and a tendency to belief. Therefore, some 80,000 spectators converged on Fatima on October 13 to watch Lucia receive her briefing on humanity's fate. Like the Madonna of La Salette, the Fatima Virgin spoke of "vast destruction by disease and fire . . . Nature will protest at the evil done by men and earthquakes will occur in protest." As she spoke—again only to Lucia and her companions—the sky was streaked and spattered with color like a giant palette. The sun nose-dived toward earth, then flattened out and rose again. Vivid shadows flitted over the ground. The onlookers prostrated themselves in terror, crying out to God to spare them. But the children remained calm and in command of themselves.

Not long afterward, Jacinta and Francisco died in the post-World War I flu epidemic said to have been forecast by Nostradamus. As a result of her experiences—and to escape from the publicity that was turning her into a sideshow freak—Lucia decided to become a nun. She entered a convent school and became a novice in the fall of 1926. Adopting the name of Sister Marie das Dores, (Sister Mary of the Sorrows), she prepared to receive future warnings from on high. In 1927, she claimed that Christ himself had visited her, and that he had asked her to be ready for "the Lady's" final and most momentous message of all—which would be imparted to her some time in the year 1960.

Before that date arrived, something happened that seemed to be a fulfillment of Lucia's earlier visions. On the night of January 25, 1938, the Aurora Borealis, or Northern Lights, was visible throughout western Europe. The bright streams of green, violet, yellow, and flaming red that forked like lightning in the sky made many people think of the words of the Madonna 21 years earlier, when she spoke to Lucia of the "bright light by night." In 1960—the year Lucia said she would get the Virgin's final message—she was cloistered in the Portuguese convent of Coimbra. Thousands of Catholics throughout the world demanded to know what the Madonna had said to her. But Lucia now aged 53, was not talking. She did not reveal her secret until 1967, and then only to Pope Paul VI.

It is still not known what she said to the Pope—whether she confessed that her story had been a fake all along, or whether he felt that her prophecy was too frightening, too extreme to be made known to mankind. Whatever it was that she whispered to the Pope, it was said that he turned white and swung away from her.

Had the message concerned the inevitability of World War III—which is a possibility—it coincided not only with the major predictions of Nostradamus, but also with those of the renowned American clairvoyant Edgar Cayce (pronounced Casey). Called the "sleeping prophet," Cayce was best-known as a faith healer. Born on a Kentucky farm in March 1877, he was also a visionary, much in the manner of William Blake or the Swedish theologian Emanuel Swedenborg. Cayce first spoke to his "vision visitors" at the age of six. By his death in 1945, he had predicted such things as laser beams, the discovery of the Dead Sea Scrolls, the Wall Street crash of 1929, and the earthquakes, hurricanes, and tidal waves that struck California, Japan, and the Philippines respectively in 1926.

Like Nostradamus, Cayce was deeply religious. A daily reader of the Bible, he believed that he was merely an instrument through which the Almighty channeled his cosmic information. Of the 8000 trancelike readings that he gave over a period of 43 years, none had more influence or significance than his prophecies about a third world war, due to start around 1999, and the end of civilization as we know it shortly after A.D. 2000. He saw the end of the world in a dream in which he was reborn in 2100 in Nebraska, and flew over a desolated United States in an odd-shaped metal aircraft. He also foresaw the total destruction of Los Angeles and San Francisco along with much of the western part of the country.

His vision of the future—as gloomy as any in the doom-laden history of divination—took place in 1936. It dealt with more than just the usual devastation coming out of the sky—the "darts in the sky" that Nostradamus wrote of when prophesying the final war between East and West. To Cayce, there was also danger from below. It came from the submerged and mythical continent of Atlantis, which is allegedly been lying beneath the waters of the Atlantic as a lost civilization for some 12,000 years.

According to Cayce, Atlantis was the original Eden, the first place on Earth in which "man changed his spiritual for his physical form." Because of man's self-destructive inhumanity, went Cayce's prediction, he has been sentenced to extinction by the reemergence of Atlantis, whose inhabitants were the first possessors of death rays, atomic bombs, and machine-minds. Before this comes about, however, Communism will have been destroyed. Again like Nostradamus, Cayce feared the growth and increasing power of Marxism. (In *Century*

Nine, Nostradamus warns that "the anti-Czar will exterminate everyone.") Cayce, however, believed that the attempt to "level not only the economic life but also the mental and spiritual welfare as well, will not last very long." He adds: "When one forgets to love one's neighbor, the Lord cannot have clemency, and such a situation cannot continue."

While time sped toward the day of reckoning set by Cayce for 2000, a simple old Italian woman, Mamma Rosa, was being honored by the latest visitations from the Virgin. In the two years between 1965 and 1967, Mamma Rosa had been informed that "the world is in mud . . . the world is being lost little by little . . . the world is on the threshold of terrible tribulations." In June 1967, she was asked by her vision to "do everything to console the minds as the hour of terrible punishment has struck . . . the warning has sounded. . . . We are already 130 years after La Salette and 50 years after Fatima . . . carry only love and peace in the heart. Then when the terrible moments of darkness come you will have Jesus . . . and you will be strong." In December 1967, Mamma Rose was told by the Madonna that she had been chosen as Christ's messenger because "of all people you are the most ignorant."

The Future according to Nostradamus

Do the seers never foresee a rosy future? There does not seem to be much hope and light in most of the prophets' visions. However, gloomy as he was for the most part, Nostradamus had a sincere and often-stated belief in a Golden Age that was to succeed the holocaust.

This gleam of optimism in the *Centuries* was seized upon by the Nazis during World War II (another event foreseen by the astrologer), and was perverted to their own use. This came about when Goebbels, the Minister of Propaganda, was introduced to Nostradamus' work by his wife, who chose the rhymes nightly as bedtime reading. Goebbels found the verses to his occult taste, and, together with the Gestapo chief, twisted their meanings to announce predictions of a total German victory. In May 1940, the Germans dropped copies of the altered *Centuries* by air over France to demoralize the populace. The Allies later retaliated by scattering their own version of the rhymes for propaganda purposes over the towns and cities of Germany.

Because Nostradamus deliberately obscured his meanings, his verses lend themselves to greatly different interpretations. His disciples have been accused of something worse than differing interpretations, however. They have been indicted for fitting prophecies to known facts. Many also regard the prophecies themselves as falling within the Theory of Probabilities, which states that if forecasts are sufficient in range and number, some of them must inevitably come true. Whether or not this theory is accepted, Nostradamus' account of the third world war tells of the appearance of Lucifer in the shape of a man, the collapse of the papacy, and the dominance of Communism.

With the razing of Rome, Paris, New York, and London, there will be 27 years of pain and bloodshed while the "King of Horror" deploys his aerial forces to eliminate his "enemies," according to details of the prediction. The red flag will flutter over the ruins of the Vatican, and the hemisphere-to-hemisphere firing of atomic warheads and weapons will ensure that "the universal conflagration shall be preceded by many great inundations, so that there shall scarce be any land that shall not be covered with water. . . . Before and after these inundations in many countries there shall be such scarcity of rain, and such a great deal of fire, and burning stones shall fall from Heaven, that nothing unconsumed shall be left. All this shall happen before the great conflagration."

However, there is a silver lining in the cloud: all the death, anguish, and havoc is for the ultimate good of mankind. Nostradamus stresses that the diasters and tribulations at the end of the 20th century are necessary in order to prepare the ground for building the ideal world—rather in the way that filthy and decaying slums are demolished to make way for sound new housing. Nostradamus dedicated *Centures* to his young son, whose "years are too few and months incapable to receive into thy weak understanding what I am forced to define of futurity." In this dedication, the astrologer closes on a note of cheer and optimism with a prediction that the best of all possible worlds will follow the worst.

"After this [the man-made and natural disasters] has lasted a certain time, there will be renewed another reign of Saturn, a truly great and golden age."

40. The I Ching

Confucius—the Chinese wise man and philosopher whose teachings helped shape his country's entire civilization—was almost 70 when, in 481 B.C. he stated, "if some years were added to my life, I would give 50 to the study of the *I Ching*, and might then escape falling into great errors." At the time, Confucius had already worn out three pairs of leather thongs that bound the tablets on which his copy of the world's "most revered system of fortune telling" was inscribed. As it turned out, he had only two more years to live instead of 50, but he spent them in deep and exhaustive study of the meanings and mystery of the *I Ching*, known as the *Book of Change*. This book, he said, had "as many layers as the earth itself." Hundreds of years later, when the Samurai warrior class ruled Japan, it was said that Samurai planned military strategy by consulting *I Ching*— and that they continued to do so right up to the 19th century.

No one can be sure of how old the *I Ching* (pronounced EE Jing) is, but it is believed to date from 2852 B.C. as the work of the legendary Emperor Fu-hsi. The contents of the book were systemized by King Wen in 1143 B.C., and his work was further clarified by his son, the Duke of Chou. Still later, Confucius edited and added explanatory notes to the *I Ching*. For all of this, the *Book of Change* remains full of symbolism with hidden and puzzling meanings.

Each hexagram symbolizes a specific human characteristic or condition of life, which is reflected in the symbolic name it bears. For example, hexagram 1 is "creative"; 11 is "peace"; 20 is "contemplation"; 37 is "the family"; 46 is "ascending"; 55 is "prosperity"; and 64 is "before completion." These hexagrams are formed by two sets of three lines, called trigrams, each of

474

which also have their own name. The trigrams affect the reading of the *I Ching* by their own special qualities, images, and position —whether at the top or bottom of the hexagram.

It was King Wen who formulated the 64 hexagrams, gave them their names, and put the text message with them from the original work of Fu-hsi. After King Wen's death, his son Chou added notes to help explain the meanings of individual lines of the hexagrams, and the overall symbolism of them. The West owes its knowledge of *I Ching* to James Legge, a 19th-century specialist in Chinese studies. He translated the *Book of Change* into English in 1854, and his is the only thorough, scholarly translation of the entire book in English.

A Whole System of Philosophy

One of the most important things to remember about *I Ching* is that it is a whole system of philosophy. It is based on a code that embodies the traditional moral and mystical beliefs of the Chinese. Therefore, a querant cannot go frivolously to the *Book of Change*. Nor will he or she get an easy, direct "yes" or "no" answer. Questioners are thrown back on themselves for the interpretation of the answers, which are intended only as a guideline. As Raymond Van Over says in his edited version of *I Ching*: "It directs the questioner's attention to alternatives and the probable consequences of our actions if we choose one path instead of another. If the oracle wishes to direct our action in a specific direction or through a particular channel, it will tell us how a Superior Man would conduct himself. In this subtle way, our actions are directed toward a positive goal while still allowing us the free will to choose our own ultimate destiny. We can, of course, decide not to act as the Superior Man, and take any course we choose."

With the question in mind, there are two ways of consulting the *I Ching*: one by tossing three coins of any kind, and the other by throwing 50 yarrow stalks in a given sequence. The second method is long and complicated, and, since there is no proof that it gets any different results, can be left to the strict traditional or purist. Therefore, let us see how using the coins works.

The tossing of the coins reveals which hexagram the querant should consult as applicable in his case. A toss turning up two

tails and one head is written as a solid line, —————. A toss
of two heads and one tail is written as a broken line, ——— ———.
Three tails are written ———x——— and three heads, ———o———
There are six tosses, and the first toss becomes the *bottom* line
of the first trigram. Each succeeding toss is written as a line
above the other until all six lines are drawn. Then, the questioner
refers to a chart that gives him the name of the hexagram so
indicated. Complications come in with what are called "moving
lines"—three heads or three tails—which can refer the
questioner to more than one hexagram. However, these do not
always come up. In some cases, one or more individual lines of
the hexagram are read as well as the text, commentary, and
additional notes. In other cases, only the text is read. The coin
toss says what to do in the way it forms the hexagram. In no
case will the advice be immediately clear, for each hexagram
has layer upon layer of meaning.

It has been said of the *I Ching* that, over the centuries, some
3000 scholars have tried to unravel its mysteries. This indicates
that the book can hardly be regarded as just a fortune-telling
system—more complicated and venerable than the horoscopes
in our daily newspapers, perhaps, but no more important or
valid than they are. When the book is studied for its ideas and
ideals more than its prophetic properties, it can open the way to
an understanding and finer appreciation of the universe's
unceasing evolution and movement.

The more intuition used by the questioner of *I Ching*, the
greater will be the range of choice open to him—for the book
aims not to tell the future as such, but to determine whether or
not the questioner is acting in accordance with his best interests.
More than that, it can relate the individual's best interest to the
wider world—even the universe. In fact, to become the Superior
Man—which is one of the book's ideals—the questioner must
necessarily follow the Right Path. He can only do this when he
considers the fate and fortune of his fellow human beings.

Those who consult the *Book of Change*, either for themselves
or as an interpreter for others, should look after their copy of
the book with veneration and care—even if it is merely a
paperback. When not in use, it should be wrapped in a piece of
good clean cloth and placed on a shelf high enough that no one
can look down on it. Just before using it, a person should wash

his hands thoroughly in respect for the book. That done, he should place the *I Ching* facing south on a table in the center of the room and burn incense on another table that's lower. The seeker should prostrate himself three times on the floor while facing north. Only then, according to the strictest rules, is he ready to ask his question.

Yin and Yang

In the hexagram answers, the lines are based on opposites— starting with solid and broken for the drawing of the lines themselves. The solid lines stand for what is positive, light, active—all embodied in the Yang. The broken lines stand for the opposite of these: negative, dark, passive—the Yin. In Chinese philosophy, Yang stands for the hard, outgoing approach to life; Yin for the soft, shaded outlook. These two primary cosmic forces are like the two sides of a coin—one cannot exist without the other. Further, though they are in opposition to each other, they are also interdependent.

Anyone whose coin tosses refer him to this hexagram will discover that he is in need of a "proper direction." He is told that his immaturity and folly is the result of "uncultivated growth" and that he has rushed to the "foot of a mountain" where lies a "dangerous abyss." However, the *I Ching* goes on to say: "Yet such rashness may bring good fortune—fortune to be utilized when the moment comes . . . It is our sacred duty to correct the follies of youth through education." This can be interpreted to mean that the questioner has reached a given stage in his life, which is bound up with the universal situation. What the seeker must do is to decide whether he will advance or retreat, whether he will continue just as before, or alter his actions so that his course is not so rapid, so dramatic, so impulsive.

Whatever the questioner does, the decision—and the responsibility for that decision—are totally his. From this it might seem that the *Book of Change* is as remote and unfeeling as a recorded message on the other end of the telephone. However, this point of view is both an oversimplification and a misreading. The *I Ching* offers the advice of a wiser and older friend who looks at the problem broadly rather than from one person's narrow self-interest. In his updated version of the *Book of Change*, John Blofeld stresses the fact that the *I Ching* is unique because, in place of "rigid prophecies" it makes suggestions "based on an analysis of the interplay of universal forces, not about what *will* happen but what *should* be done to accord with or to avoid a given happening."

The *Book of Change* indicates that a man must not fight against the whirlpool when he is cast into it, but must *move with it* to survive. By continuing in what the *I Ching* calls the "course of righteous persistence"—one that harms no one and is in the public good—a person will eventually find his reward in this life rather than the next.

41. The Nature of Time

On a cold April night in 1898 the *S.S. Titan*—the largest, most luxurious, and above all, the safest ocean liner in the world—set out on her maiden voyage. She was plowing the Atlantic between the English port of Southampton and New York when the unthinkable happened: she struck an iceberg, foundered, and sank. Most of her 2500 passengers were lost. This was not too surprising when it was realized that the 70,000-ton ship had only 24 lifeboats, capable of holding less than half those aboard. Even so, this tragedy of giant proportions went unnoticed by the public in 1898. Why? Because the sinking occurred in a novel entitled *The Wreck of the Titan*, a story made up by a struggling and little-known English writer named Morgan Robertson. The book caused only a ripple at the time it was published.

Fourteen years later, however, Robertson's novel was belatedly hailed as a sensation, and described as "the most astounding instance of prophecy" of the 19th or 20th century. For, on the chilly night of April 14, 1912, the real 66,000-ton liner *Titanic* hit an iceberg and sank, with a calamitous loss of life. Like the fictional ship with such a similar name, the *Titanic* was on her maiden voyage across the Atlantic. Also like her fictional predecessor, she was a triple-screw vessel capable of a top speed of 25 knots. Both ships had a large number of passengers and crew, and far too few lifeboats for them—only 20 on the real one. Finally, both vessels were said to be unsinkable. One of the *Titan* deck hands in the book told a passenger that "God Himself could not sink the ship." With her 16 watertight compartments, the real ship *Titanic* was considered by her owners to take "first place among the big steamers of the world," and to be absolutely safe.

Almost as the *Titanic* went down, her survivors were already starting to talk of how the ship had been "doomed," and how they had felt all along that "something terrible" was going to happen. No one had forecast the catastrophe of the *Titanic* as accurately and vividly as the author Robertson had done in 1898, but there were some who later provided evidence of foretelling the tragic fate of the ship. Two seers who had been consulted by one of the passengers—the British journalist W. T. Stead—both said they had warned him against traveling on water in advance of his fatal journey. One of the fortune tellers had told Stead he would sail to America within a year or two from the time of the consultation. "I see more than a thousand people—yourself among them— struggling desperately in the water," he told Stead. "They are screaming for help, and fighting for their lives. But it does none of them any good—yourself included."

Stead himself had forewarnings of the ship's—and his own—unhappy end. Some years earlier, while editor of a London newspaper, he had published a fictitious account of the sinking of a huge ocean liner, supposedly written by a survivor. Stead added a prophetic editor's note to the story saying: "This is exactly what might take place, and what will take place, if liners are sent to sea short of boats." A few years after this, Stead wrote a magazine article in which he described the catastrophe of a liner colliding with an iceberg. Only one passenger in Stead's fictional article escaped with his life. Incredible as it seems, Stead also had a dream in which he saw himself standing on the deck of the sinking *Titanic*—without a life belt, and with the last lifeboat pulling away into the night.

Stead ignored all signs and omens of things to come, and lost his life on the *Titanic*. The case was different for a countryman of his, J. Connon Middleton. In a letter published in the journal of the Society of Psychical Research in London, Middleton recounted an "uncomfortable" dream which made him "most depressed and even despondent." He had booked passage on the *Titanic* to attend a business conference in New York, he said. Ten days before the sailing date, he dreamed of the vessel "floating on the sea, keel upward, and her passengers and crew swimming around her." He had the same dream the following night, but this time, he told his wife, he seemed to be "floating in the air just above the wreck." Two days afterward, he received a cable that the conference had been postponed, and lost no time in canceling his booking. It was a lucky cancellation.

Colin Macdonald, a 34-year-old marine engineer, might also have died on the *Titanic*. However, he had a strong feeling of bad things to come for the big new ship. Three times he refused to sign on as the *Titanic*'s second engineer. In 1964 Macdonald's daughter was interviewed by a leading American psychical researcher and psychiatrist. She told him that her father had a "strong impression" that something was "going to happen" to the *Titanic*, and that there were also other times when he foresaw the future. The second engineer who took the *Titanic* job Macdonald turned down was drowned.

A Change of Attitude

At the time of the *Titanic* disaster, 20th-century man was just beginning to question the prevailing materialistic philosophy that denied the unexplained. Precognition—that is, knowledge of future events by means outside the five senses—was viewed as freakishness or trickery. This was so whether the foreknowledge came through dreams, palmistry, astrology, or simply a feeling that something—usually threatening—was about to happen. One scholar, cited by James Laver in his book *Nostradamus*, put it like this: "As the 19th century drew to its close, the rationalist and the materialist seemed to have established a permanent empire over thought.... [But] in times when the air is heavy with the sense of impending disaster ... men find their rationalism shaken, and turn once more to the old superstitions which perhaps, after all, are not quite so completely superstitious as 'advanced' people used to think."

The big debate was on the question of time. Ordinarily we use it as a measurement. In the simplest physical sense of the concept of time, we use it exactly like length, width, or volume. In this sense time does not exist independently. It is linear and ongoing, just as clocks and calendars are linear. But this concept of time does not take into account our intimate psychic relations with time past and time future, and ignores another time that we all experience—dream time. Taking these into account, it is possible to conceive of time as an entity in its own right—a psychic entity perhaps, but none-theless real. If this was so, what was time's nature? Did time exist outwardly, or was it only in people's minds? Was it stationary or mobile? Was it strictly contained in separate capsules of past, present, and future, or did all three exist side by side at the same moment? This last notion was most passionately argued. There were those who believe that the future already exists, and that we approach coming events the same way as passengers on a train arrive at stations lying ahead of them along the line. Short of suicide, there was no way of intentionally avoiding these stations—and, it was argued, suicide itself could be the name of one of the stops ahead. In his book *What is Time?*, G. J. Whitrow relates how a Cambridge University philosopher used the death of the British queen in 1714 to give an example of the view that the future exists now. "At the last moment of time—if time has a last moment—it will still be the death of a Queen," the university professor stated. "And in every respect but one, it is equally devoid of change. But in one respect it does change. It was once an event in the far future. It became every moment an event in the nearer future. At last it was present. Then it became past, and will always remain past." This view agrees with what the American psychologist and philosopher William James called the "block universe," in which the future is like a strip of film whose pictures are revealed to us as the film unfolds.

A contrary view holds that people can affect their future by acting on warnings of things to come. This belief that man is not just a pawn to be maneuvered about and then finally sacrificed on the chessboard of the future, was restated in the late 1950s by the American novelist Jack Kerouac. He had one of his characters say: "Mankind will someday realize that we are actually in contact with the dead and with the other world—right now we could predict, if we only exerted enough mental will, what is going to happen within the next hundred years, and be able to take steps to avoid all kinds of catastrophes."

Strangely enough, it was neither philosopher or scientist who did most to analyze dreams, time, and visions of the future, and put them into a system. It was an aircraft designer, John William Dunne. His system was complicated and controversial, but not implausible. Dunne, who designed and built the first

British military airplane, first became fascinated by "nighttime revelations of the future" in 1889 when he had an otherwise ordinary dream that foresaw the success of a Cape Town-to-Cairo expedition. From then on, he made a habit of writing down his dreams immediately on waking—or at whatever time of day he recalled them—and then waiting for some element in the dreams to come true. His dreams were not at all unusual until 1916, when he had a "night vision" of an explosion in a London bomb factory. Such an explosion occurred in January 1917, with 73 workers killed, and more than a thousand injured.

An Experiment with Time

By then, Dunne had come to the conclusion that he was "suffering, seemingly, from some extraordinary fault in my relation to reality, something so uniquely wrong that it compelled me to perceive . . . large blocks of . . . experience displaced from their proper position in Time." That realization, and the persistence of other clairvoyant dreams, led him to write his best-selling book, *An Experiment with Time*. He described the book as "the first scientific argument for human immortality." On its publication, he was flooded with letters from readers claiming to have had similar extrasensory experiences. This led him to note in the book's second edition: "It has been rather surprising to discover how many persons there are who, while willing to concede that we habitually observe events before they occur, suppose that such prevision may be treated as a minor logical difficulty, to be met by some trifling readjustment in one or another of our sciences or by the addition of a dash of transcendentalism to our metaphysics. It may well be emphasized that no tinkering or doctoring of that kind could avail in the smallest degree. If prevision be a fact, it is a fact which destroys absolutely the entire basis of all our past opinions of the universe."

In his book *Man and Time* J. B. Priestley devotes a whole chapter to Dunne. Although Priestley himself is best known as a novelist and playwright, he is also recognized as one of Dunne's chief interpreters. "Those of us who are Time-haunted owe him [Dunne] an enormous debt . . ." Priestley starts out.

It is to Dunne's work on dreams that Priestley gives greatest importance. Dunne, he said, established that ordinary dreams contain "a definite element of prevision of precognition." Following from this, Dunne effectively showed that the dreaming self cannot be entirely contained within time as we usually think of it. According to Dunne's time theory, we live in the flow of time as Observer 1 in Time 1. To the side of us is another self, Observer 2 in Time 2. From this, Priestley explains how Dunne's theory applies to seeing the future in dreams.

"What [Observer 2] observes are what Dunne calls 'the brain states' of Observer 1 (his experience in Time 1)—'the sensory phenomena, memory phenomena, and trains of associative thinking' belonging to ordinary waking life. Now when Observer 1 is awake, 2 is attending to what Observer 1 is discovering in Time 1, using the three-dimensional focus with which we are all familiar." [By this is meant the concept of ordinary time as flowing from the past through the present into the future.] Priestley goes on:

"But Observer 2 in Time 2 has a four-dimensional outlook. This means that the 'future' brain states of Observer 1 may be as open to Observer 2's inspection as 1's past brain states. But it also means that when Observer 1 is asleep, his three-dimensional focus can no longer act as guide or 'traveling concentration mark' for Observer 2. The latter is now left with his four-dimensional focus, which has a wide Time 1 range—much of it 'future' to Observer 1.

"But Observer 2 cannot attend and concentrate properly. Now and then he may succeed, as he must do in a clear precognitive dream. Usually, however, unguided by the inactive sleeping Observer 1, Observer 2 with his four-dimensional focus is all at sea. . . .

"This relation between Time 1 and Time 2, between Observer 1 and Observer 2, enables Dunne to explain why we find most of our dreams so bewildering."

Priestley gives some examples of dreams that support Dunne's ideas of prevision. One of the most interesting is that of Dr. Louisa E. Rhine, who wrote about it herself in the American *Journal of Parapsychology*. She felt that the dream had helped her save the life of her one-year-old son. In her article she wrote: ". . . I had a dream early one morning. I thought the children and I had gone camping with some friends. We were camped

484

in such a pretty little glade on the shores of the sound between two hills. It was wooded, and our tents were under the trees; I looked around and thought what a lovely spot it was." In the dream she decided to wash the baby's clothes and carried him with her down to the stream. She put him on the ground, went back to the tent to get the soap she had forgotten, and returned to find her son—who had been throwing pebbles into the water —lying face down in the stream, drowned.

She woke up "sobbing and crying," worried over the dream for a few days, and then forgot about it. It did not return to her until later that summer, when she and a group of friends went camping in a spot just like the one in her dream. She went to the stream to wash the baby's clothes, settled her son on the bank, and walked back for the missing soap. As she did so the infant picked up a handful of pebbles and began to toss them into the water. "Instantly," she stated, "my dream flashed into my mind. It was like a moving picture. He stood just as he had in my dream—white dress, yellow curls, shining sun. For a moment I almost collapsed. Then I caught him up and went back to the beach with my friends. When I composed myself, I told them about it. They just laughed and said I had imagined it. That is such a simple answer when one cannot give a good explanation. I am not given to imagining wild things." Such "displacement of time" can happen to anyone any night during sleep, and its frequent occurrence reinforced Priestley's faith in Dunne.

Dunne's Belief in our Immortality

In the last part of his *Man and Time* chapter on Dunne, Priestley cites Dunne's strong belief that we are immortal. He interprets this part of Dunne's theory as follows:

"It is true that we 'die' in Time 1 when our Observer 1 reaches the end of his journey along the fourth dimension. And then all possibility of intervention and action in Time 1 comes to an end. This limits Observer 2's experience (through Observer 1's brain states) of Time 1, but it does not involve the death of Observer 2, who exists in Time 2. No longer having any Time 1 experience to attend to . . . Observer 2 now experiences Time 2 as Observer 1 did Time 1: that is, it is for him ordinary successive time as we know it. He has to begin learning all over again as his four-dimensional focus moves along the fifth dimension of Time 3. People and things will be the same and yet not the same. We catch glimpses, though confused and distorted, of this afterdeath mode of existence in our dreams.

"He [Dunne] suggests that in our Time 2 'afterlife,' once we have understood how to live it, we shall be able to blend, combine, build, with all the elements of our Time 1 existence, using them more or less as a composer does his notes, an artist his paints."

Priestley himself collected many stories about premonitions and other unusual time experiences. Among them was one reported to him by Sir Stephen King-Hall, a writer who was a naval officer for many years. Sir Stephen's story was as follows:

While on duty as officer of the watch on the *Southampton* in the war years of 1916, Sir Stephen had an overriding premonition that a man would fall overboard when the ship got to a small island off the coast of Scotland. His feeling grew stronger the nearer the convoy his ship led came to the island. With only his premonition to go on, Sir Stephen gave orders to the crew to get ready to save a man overboard. Of course, his orders were challenged by his superior officer.

". . . The Commodore said, 'What the hell do you think you are doing?'" Sir Stephen recounted. "We were abreast the island. I had no answer. We were steaming at 20 knots and we passed the little island in a few seconds. Nothing happened!

"As I was struggling to say something, the cry went up 'man overboard' from the *Nottingham* (the next ship in the line, 100 yards behind us) then level with the island. Thirty seconds later 'man overboard' from the *Birmingham* (the third ship in the line, and then abreast the island). We went full speed astern; our sea boat was in the water almost at once and we picked up both men. I was then able to explain to a startled bridge why I had behaved as I had done."

In the 1930s, Air Marshal Sir Victor Goddard had a precognitive experience that seemed made to order for time theorists such as Dunne and Priestley.

While flying over Scotland during a storm, Sir Victor decided to descend in the area of the abandoned Drem airfield to get his bearings. He flew lower. When he was about a quarter of a mile away from Drem, something extraordinary happened: he found himself in both the present and the future.

"Suddenly the area was bathed in an ethereal light as though the sun were shining on a midsummer day," he said. The field was astir with activity as mechanics worked on biplanes in newly repaired hangars. Although Sir Victor was only 50 feet above the hangars, his plane went entirely unnoticed. He flew back into the storm and continued on his way.

What Sir Victor had seen came to pass four years later when Drem was rebuilt and reopened as a flying training school. "And then I knew that I had to sort out my ideas about free will and fate and determinism," Sir Victor declared.

In deciding this, Sir Victor was only one of the many divination converts who had gone before, and of the many more who were to come.

INDEX